Bureaucracy, Politics, and Decision Making in Post-Mao China

This volume and the conference from which it resulted
were sponsored by the Joint Committee on Chinese Studies
of the American Council of Learned Societies
and the Social Science Research Council,
with funds provided by the Andrew W. Mellon Foundation.

Bureaucracy, Politics, and Decision Making in Post-Mao China

EDITED BY

Kenneth G. Lieberthal
David M. Lampton

UNIVERSITY OF CALIFORNIA PRESS
Berkeley   Los Angeles   Oxford

University of California Press
Berkeley and Los Angeles, California
University of California Press, Ltd.
Oxford, England
© 1992 by
The Regents of the University of California

Library of Congress Cataloging-in-Publication Data

Bureaucracy, politics, and decision making in post-Mao China / edited
   by Kenneth G. Lieberthal and David M. Lampton.
       p.   cm.—(Studies on China ; 14)
   Includes bibliographical references and index.

   1. Bureaucracy—China.   2. China—Politics and government—1976– —
Decision making.   I. Lieberthal, Kenneth.   II. Lampton, David M.
III. Series.
JQ1509.5.D4B87   1992
354.5107'25—dc20   91-9476
                                                                      CIP

ISBN 978-0-520-30149-8 (pbk. : alk. paper)

STUDIES ON CHINA

A series of conference volumes sponsored by the Joint Committee
on Chinese Studies of the American Council of Learned Societies and
the Social Science Research Council.

To Jack W. and Mary Jane Lampton
and to the memory of
Milton M. Lieberthal,
with love and gratitude

CONTENTS

ACKNOWLEDGMENTS

The chapters in this volume were written as papers for the conference on the "Structure of Authority and Bureaucratic Behavior in China" held in Tucson, Arizona, from June 19 to 23, 1988. We wish to thank the American Council of Learned Societies (ACLS) and the Social Science Research Council (SSRC), and more particularly the Joint Committee on Contemporary China, for providing the financial wherewithal to make that conference possible and for the intellectual guidance and support as this volume moved toward publication. Throughout the period of developing the conference and then producing this volume, Dr. Jason Parker at ACLS was of enormous assistance; we express our gratitude to him.

In 1987 and 1988, as we began to plan for the conference, we drew upon the advice of Professors A. Doak Barnett, Thomas Bernstein, and Susan Shirk. They steered us between the danger of trying to focus the conference and papers so tightly that we would create an analytic strait-jacket and the danger of opening up the analytic aperture so widely that there would be no focus to the meeting and resulting volume. We hope that the conference, and this work that resulted from it, have achieved that desired balance.

We wish to thank our editors at the University of California Press: Sheila Levine, for shepherding the manuscript through the review, editorial, and publication processes, and Amy Klatzkin and Gladys Castor for their many editorial contributions.

We want to thank also those who attended and contributed to the conference, in addition to the authors of the chapters in this volume: Dr. Christopher Clarke, United States Department of State; Professor Kenneth Jowitt, University of California, Berkeley; Professor Michel Oksenberg, University of Michigan; Professor Ivan Szelenyi, University of California, Los Angeles; and Professor Ezra Vogel, Harvard University. Bruce Dickson of the University of Michigan provided excellent assistance as rapporteur for the conference.

Finally, we want to thank our families for giving up time we would otherwise have spent with them, that we might bring this project to fruition.

Kenneth G. Lieberthal
David M. Lampton

ONE

Introduction: The "Fragmented Authoritarianism" Model and Its Limitations

Kenneth G. Lieberthal

The reforms that began at the end of the 1970s created opportunities for unprecedented scholarly access to government agencies in the People's Republic of China (PRC), thus vastly increasing our potential for understanding bureaucratic relationships and policy processes there. The resulting research quickly began to yield a small harvest of publications,[1] which moved our understanding beyond the limitations of the documentary sources and refugee interviewing on which scholars had relied for the most part until then.[2] It became increasingly possible to probe perceptions, to trace in detail specific policy decisions, to become familiar with the recommendations made by various staff organs, to match formal bureaucratic relationships against actual behavior of officials, and so forth. This volume demonstrates some of the returns from this unprecedented access.[3]

1. For example, Michel Oksenberg, "Economic Policy Making In China: Summer 1981," *China Quarterly*, no. 90 (June 1982): 165–95; several chapters in Elizabeth J. Perry and Christine Wong, eds., *The Political Economy of Reform in Post-Mao China* (Cambridge: Council on East Asian Studies/Harvard University, 1985); Dorothy Solinger, "China's New Economic Policies and the Local Industrial Political Process: The Case of Wuhan," *Comparative Politics* (July 1986), 379–99.

2. Expatriate interviewing in Hong Kong had long been used by scholars of China to enrich their understanding of the country's operations and dynamics; but until the early 1980s no in-depth interviewing of current officeholders was possible. The types of analyses that effectively employed expatriate interviewing include A. Doak Barnett, *Cadres, Bureaucracy, and Political Power in Communist China* (New York: Columbia University Press, 1967); and Gordon Bennett and Ronald Montaperto, *Red Guard* (Garden City, N.Y.: Doubleday, 1971).

3. The chapters in this volume originated as papers written for a 1988 conference on China's bureaucratic practice. This conference, sponsored by the Joint Committee on Chinese Studies of the American Council of Learned Societies and the Social Science

A mapping of China's major bureaucratic sectors shows, however, that scholarly penetration of China's far-flung bureaucratic leviathan proved highly uneven. The decision by leaders in Beijing to intensify the country's *economic* relations with the outside world afforded particularly extensive contact with economic organs. Scholars could interview pertinent Chinese officials, staff in the country's enterprises, and numerous foreigners who conducted business with the Chinese. Beijing's dealings with the World Bank provided additional information to those concerned with economic decision making.[4] From this access, a burgeoning literature began to flesh out a model for understanding economic decision making in the Chinese polity that is reviewed below.[5] This model might be called "fragmented authoritarianism." Its key features are discussed below.

China, of course, consists of more than a set of economic bureaucracies. In broad terms, the country's national political organizations are perhaps best grouped into six functionally defined clusters.[6] Each cluster has a number of different bureaucratic units in it, and each is also assigned a distinctive set of tasks. These clusters and their core tasks are:

Economic Bureaucracies. These seek to make the economy grow in order to satisfy the material needs of the country. A wide array of specific bureaucratic hierarchies fall within this cluster, and there are many horizontal and vertical cleavages in it. But priority commitment to economic growth generally enhances the resources and prestige of the organs in this cluster, albeit *specific* strategies of growth inevitably favor some units (e.g., the banking system) over others (e.g., the planning system).

Propaganda and Education Bureaucracies. These have responsibility for shaping the values and knowledge of China's citizens. They encompass the formal propaganda organs (including the mass media), the educational system, and most research units.

Research Council, convened in Tucson, Arizona, on June 19–23, 1988. Only Barry Naughton's chapter was commissioned after the conference. All chapters have been revised since the conference.

4. Harold Jacobson and Michel Oksenberg, *China's Participation in the IMF, the World Bank, and GATT: Toward A World Economic Order* (Ann Arbor: University of Michigan Press, 1990).

5. See, inter alia, David M. Lampton, ed., *Policy Implementation in Post-Mao China* (Berkeley and Los Angeles: University of California Press, 1987); Perry and Wong, *Political Economy;* Kenneth Lieberthal and Michel Oksenberg, *Policy Making In China* (Princeton: Princeton University Press, 1988).

6. This grouping is more amalgamated than that in A. Doak Barnett, *Cadres, Bureaucracy, and Political Power,* 456. The grouping presented here reflects numerous discussions with Chinese officials and various studies on the policy-making process in China.

Organization and Personnel Bureaucracies. These run the system of personal dossiers and provide critical staff work for individual career assignments. While these bureaucracies do not themselves actually make personnel decisions, they can strongly influence those decisions through their power to collect and utilize data on individuals.

Civilian Coercive Bureaucracies. These provide the civilian fist that is used as necessary to protect the communist system and to implement policies. They include the public security system, the judicial system, the prison and forced labor administration, and intelligence/counterintelligence units. As with the economic bureaucracies, there have been sharp internal tensions within and among these bureaucracies, but, in general, periods of high coercion provide bureaucratic benefits to many of the units in this group.

Military System. The People's Liberation Army (PLA) is virtually a separate state within the Chinese system.[7] It is directly subordinate to the Party leadership, and its leading body, the Military Affairs Committee of the Party, is coequal in rank with the government State Council. In addition to providing security for the country against external threats, the military has in the past been assigned extensive domestic political roles. This bureaucratic cluster also includes the military-related science and technology system and the extensive production, transport, and service facilities run by the General Logistics Department (*houqin bu*) of the PLA.

Communist Party Territorial Committees. There is, in addition to the above, a core political function that is exercised on a territorial basis by Communist Party secretaries. Each of these individuals attempts to coordinate and prioritize activities within his or her geographical domain and to represent the interests of that domain in dealings with both higher and lower levels.

China has other important bureaucratic systems, such as foreign affairs, united-front work, and mass-organization work, that are not included in the above listing. But the above six clusters of bureaucracies identify the core organs that have nationwide hierarchies and that exercise strong executive power. This "cluster" approach downplays the distinction between Communist Party and government organs—a distinction that, as Susan Shirk explains in chapter 3 in this volume, can be politically very important. But this "cluster" approach has the virtue of grouping bureaucratic systems in much the same way that the Chinese leaders organize themselves to run their system.[8] It has the additional

7. The PLA includes the army, the navy, and the air force.
8. See chapter 4 in this volume.

virtue of enabling us to identify reasonably clearly the contours of the access foreign scholars have gained to China's bureaucratic labyrinth.

Other than the economic bureaucracies—for which foreigners have enjoyed extensive contacts at all levels of the national hierarchy and in many regions of the country—foreign access has been limited and selective. Of the remaining five areas, perhaps the greatest access has been to the propaganda and education cluster. The education portion of this cluster became quite open to foreign contacts during the 1980s.[9] Within the propaganda portion, access to Chinese writers and to people in the mass media proved particularly extensive.[10] The core propaganda apparatus in the Communist Party itself (that is, the propaganda departments under various Party committees) remained more opaque.

Very few scholars gained extensive access to the personnel, civilian or military security, and Party territorial clusters for intensive interviewing. Only two authors have published work based on direct interviewing of personnel officials,[11] and no one has published a book-length study based on direct access to either the security apparatuses or the territorial Party leaders. Even in the most open periods of reform, moreover, Chinese officials have considered direct questions about either the security clusters or the core Party bureaucratic operations to be inappropriate and overly intrusive.[12]

A second bias in the interviewing done to date involves the *bureaucratic levels* that have been accessible to foreign scholars. Some scholars have been able to undertake systematic interviewing up to the vice-ministerial level, with occasional meetings with individuals above that rank. But no scholars have enjoyed systematic access to individuals with the active rank of minister or higher.[13] The functional "cluster" unevenness in

9. See, e.g., Suzanne Pepper, *China's Universities* (Ann Arbor: University of Michigan Center for Chinese Studies, 1984); and Ruth Hayhoe, *China's Universities and the Open Door* (Armonk, N.Y.: M. E. Sharpe, 1989).

10. See, e.g., Perry Link, ed., *People or Monsters?* (Bloomington: Indiana University Press, 1983); and Yitsi Mei Feuerwerker, *Ding Ling's Fiction* (Cambridge: Harvard University Press, 1982).

11. Melanie Manion, "The Cadre Management System, Post-Mao," *China Quarterly*, no. 102 (June 1985): 203–33; and John Burns, "China's Nomenklatura System," *Problems of Communism* (Sept.–Oct. 1987): 36–51.

12. To my knowledge, one American scholar was able to interview at some length during 1988 a county-level Party leader about Party matters, but the results of this interview have not been published. While some other foreign scholars have gained access to territorial Party secretaries, the topics of discussion have almost invariably focused on non-Party issues.

13. A. Doak Barnett is the only foreign scholar who has been able to interview an active member of the Politburo concerning bureaucratic dimensions of the decision-making process: A. Doak Barnett, *The Making of Foreign Policy In China* (Boulder: Westview Press, 1985).

interviewing is thus further complicated by incompleteness in the hierarchical levels of China's political system to which foreigners have gained access.

The result is that the "fragmented authoritarianism" model contained in the literature is based overwhelmingly on intensive research on only one of the six "clusters" and on access only to certain parts of the multitiered Chinese bureaucratic hierarchy. The editors of this volume have contributed to the slim literature that has explicated a "fragmented authoritarianism" model for China's policy process, and we convened the 1988 conference, whose papers make up this book, as a vehicle for both elaborating upon and testing the limits of the validity of our findings as they apply to other clusters and bureaucratic levels. In organizing this conference we sought to include scholars who had gained direct access to each of the "clusters" noted above, as well as individuals who had focused on every major level of the national bureaucratic hierarchy.

As the chapters in this volume indicate, we succeeded in obtaining contributions from scholars who had interviewed in four of our six "clusters." (No scholar, to our knowledge, has enjoyed sufficient access to the civilian security cluster or to territorial Party secretaries to provide major insights into these bureaucratic clusters.) In addition, while we have included chapters that focus on each national bureaucratic level of power (Center, province, major municipality, county, and township) and on urban and rural localities, we have left a number of empty "boxes" in a hypothetical matrix of clusters and bureaucratic levels. This volume does not, to put it differently, treat every cluster on each level of the national bureaucratic hierarchy.

Nevertheless, this volume does, for the first time, focus the attention of scholars who have gained direct, sustained access to Chinese officialdom in various clusters on the task of explaining the characteristics of the policy-making process in these different clusters. Special chapters by Carol Lee Hamrin and Nina Halpern focus on the Center above the level of ministries and commissions to understand better the interplay of personal and organizational elements in leading China's vast bureaucratic apparatus at the very top. The result of this array of rich presentations is a more textured, contoured understanding of the structures, processes, and types of relationships characteristic of various Chinese clusters and bureaucratic levels than has previously been available. The result enables us to identify both similarities and differences among the various parts of the Chinese system.

To appreciate the distinctive, broad-gauged contributions these chapters make to our understanding of the Chinese bureaucratic system, a brief review of the "fragmented authoritarianism" model provides a helpful starting point. This model has been embodied in several works that the editors authored or coauthored,[14] as well as in other works.[15] The chapters in this volume add new richness to our understanding of "fragmented authoritarianism," provide an understanding of the limitations to which this model is subject, and explain the reasons for those limitations. They also provide a basis for anticipating the systemic consequences of various changes in China's political priorities and the degree of malleability in the Chinese bureaucratic system. But first, the essentials of the "fragmented authoritarianism" model can be described as follows.

THE STARTING POINT: THE "FRAGMENTED AUTHORITARIANISM" MODEL

Just as the reform era itself created opportunities for intensive research on Chinese bureaucratic practice, the content of the reforms influenced the specific research agenda in important ways. Decentralization of decision-making authority was a key reform initiative, and much research sought to understand better the dynamics of a system in which Beijing seeks to work with lower levels rather than to dictate to them.

There are, in broad terms, three dimensions to the study of decentralization and centralization: value integration; structural distribution of resources and authority; and processes of decision making and policy implementation.[16] These three dimensions are not mutually exclusive, but they do highlight different aspects of the system under scrutiny. The "fragmented authoritarianism," explained below, focuses especially on the latter two dimensions.

Values can provide a strong basis for integration of policy making and implementation. In China under Mao, for example, the top leaders used massive doses of ideological indoctrination as a vehicle for achieving greater fidelity to the goals of the leaders even in the absence of informational and other resources adequate to assure the desired level of compliance. In contemporary Japan there is often sharp conflict in policy before a consensus has been reached, but the various parties to the decision

14. David M. Lampton, "Chinese Politics: The Bargaining Treadmill," *Issues and Studies* 23, no. 3 (1987): 11–41; David M. Lampton, ed., *Policy Implementation;* Lampton's chapter in this volume; Kenneth Lieberthal and Michel Oksenberg, *Policy Making;* Kenneth Lieberthal et al., *Paths To Sino-US Automotive Cooperation* (Washington: U.S. Trade Development Program, 1989); Kenneth Lieberthal and C. K. Prahalad, "Multinational Corporate Investment in China," *China Business Review* (March–April 1989): 47–51; Kenneth Lieberthal and Michel Oksenberg, "Understanding China's Bureaucracy: The First Step to a Better Corporate Strategy," *China Business Review* (November–December 1986): 24–31.

15. See especially Lester Ross, *Environmental Policy in China* (Bloomington: Indiana University Press, 1988).

16. I am indebted to Jae Ho Chung for sensitizing me to this framework of analysis.

can then act with confidence in the knowledge that all concerned will obey the "consensus" decision once it has been made.[17] Shared values, in short, can substantially affect the operations of a political system. Value consensus can basically reduce the need of the political leadership to develop additional resources to assure fidelity to their priorities and compliance with their policies.

Political structure, by contrast, examines the formal allocation of decision-making authority. Various political systems have, of course, adopted a very wide array of allocations of power, and significant structural variations may appear even in one political system over time. In China, for example, the government ministries exercised considerable power over the economy during the First Five-Year Plan of the mid 1950s, the Communist Party expanded its relative influence over the economy during the Great Leap Forward of 1958–61, and the military became a key decision-maker regarding the economy during the late 1960s. The reforms of the 1980s brought a significant devolution of budget-making authority (a process that had actually begun in earnest in 1971), with Party and government officials in major municipalities gaining greatly increased influence over economic decision making. These variations amounted to structural changes in the distribution of basic decision-making power in China's economic sphere.

In general, the structure of centralization and decentralization is highly complex. These terms encompass, for example, considerations about the span of control of various organs, the levels at which particular decisions are nested, the bases of resources of various players in the system, the degree of specificity that characterizes decisions, the amount of flexibility formally allowed in policy implementation, and so forth.[18] The clarity with which organizational boundaries and decision-making procedures are specified affects structural centralization.

Structural dimensions of centralization and decentralization by themselves, of course, provide at best an inexact guide to the real operations of a political system. The focus of much scholarly analysis is the actual policy process that characterizes decision making and implementation. Forces that influence that process and help to shape it include, inter alia, the values held by participants in this process, the structural distribution of authority and resources, and the structure of rewards.

The "fragmented authoritarianism" literature touches on all three

17. I am indebted to Ezra Vogel for this insight.

18. Frederic Pryor introduces a number of different dimensions of centralization and decentralization in his *Property and Industrial Organization in Communist and Capitalist Nations* (Bloomington: Indiana University Press, 1973), chap. 8; H. Franz Schurmann applies a few of these distinctions to China in his *Ideology and Organization in Communist China* (Berkeley and Los Angeles: University of California Press, 1968).

dimensions of analysis: value integration, structural elements, and policy process. To a significant degree, however, the literature has emphasized the latter two. This fact probably reflects three problems. First, the study of values is inherently very difficult, and this is especially true in a society like China that does not permit the types of survey research and participant observation that are best suited to reaching well-grounded conclusions about value integration. Second, the huge changes in value hierarchies that the reforms demanded as compared with the late Maoist era produced a generally unstated consensus among Western scholars of China that the level of value integration among PRC officials during the late 1980s was low. And third, as was noted above, foreign scholars have gained the greatest access to the economic bureaucracies;[19] the relative ease of observing bargaining over control of tangible resources in this sphere quite naturally focused the attention of researchers on the material (instead of the value) dimension of the Chinese policy process. Because of these factors, the fragmented authoritarianism model has devoted most of its attention to the structural allocation of authority and the behavior of officials related to policy process, especially those behaviors that have characterized the reforms.

The fragmented authoritarianism model argues that authority below the very peak of the Chinese political system is fragmented and disjointed. The fragmentation is structurally based and has been enhanced by reform policies regarding procedures. The fragmentation, moreover, grew increasingly pronounced under the reforms beginning in the late 1970s, as the following brief examples illustrate.[20]

Structurally, China's bureaucratic ranking system combines with the functional division of authority among various bureaucracies to produce a situation in which it is often necessary to achieve agreement among an array of bodies, where no single body has authority over the others. In addition, the reforms' decentralization of budgetary authority enabled many locales and bureaucratic units to acquire funds outside of those allocated through the central budget, which they could use to pursue their own policy preferences. This cushion of "extrabudgetary" funds in turn permitted many locales to become less sensitive to the policy demands from higher levels.

19. The published work on the "fragmented authoritarianism" model draws primarily from only a portion of the activity in the economic sector. While some work on economic *management* decision making tends to validate key assertions in the "fragmented authoritarianism" paradigm (see, e.g., Lieberthal and Prahalad, "Multinational Corporate Investment"), the paradigm has been developed primarily around the dynamics of decision making concerning major economic *investment* projects.

20. The following paragraphs draw heavily from Lieberthal and Oksenberg, *Policy Making*, chaps. 2 and 4, and from the chapters in Lampton, *Policy Implementation*.

Procedurally, several major changes designed to produce more effective information and incentive systems had the additional effect, according to the fragmented authoritarianism model, of contributing to the fragmentation of authority of China's economic decision making. The leaders reduced the use of coercion—purges, labeling, demotions—against those who propose ideas that eventually are rejected, thus emboldening participants to argue forcefully for their proposals. The stress laid on serious feasibility studies during the 1980s also, de facto, encouraged various units to marshal information to support their own project preferences, often in competition with others. The encouragement given to many organs to become increasingly self-supporting through bureaucratic entrepreneurship also strengthened the tendency of bureaucratic units to work vigorously to promote and protect their own interests in the policy-making process. The general decline in the use of ideology as an instrument of control increased the "looseness" of the system, and decentralization in personnel management permitted many bureaucratic units additional initiative. All of these changes thus combined to reduce the extent to which organs respond in disciplined fashion to instructions from higher levels.

The resulting situation proved to be quite complex, and no simple characterization captures even its essential features. To an extent, the above developments seem to have produced increased bargaining in the Chinese bureaucratic system. "Bargaining" involves negotiations over resources among units that effectively have mutual veto power. Fragmentation of authority encouraged a search for consensus among various organs in order to initiate and develop major projects. This consensus, in turn, required extensive and often elaborate deals to be struck through various types of bargaining stratagems. Perhaps the fact that the issues under study generally concerned the allocation of real resources made it more likely that visible bargaining would characterize much of the decision making in the economic cluster. In any case, the fragmented authoritarianism model focused attention on the importance of bureaucratic bargaining, and one major concern of this volume is to determine the conditions under which such bargaining does and does not occur.[21]

This system still retained some important elements of coherence. Research found that bureaucracies retained a real sense of mission and purpose. It also revealed striking instances of "policy communities" that formed around particular projects and issues and that cut across formal bureaucratic lines. This research, moreover, did not conclude that the leaders at the top of the system are helpless. Rather, it portrayed a system

21. Chapter 2 in this volume provides the fullest analysis of considerations concerning the phenomenon of bureaucratic bargaining in China.

in which the information available to the leaders, the strategies of the leaders themselves, and the actual policy implementation are affected in significant fashion by the structural and procedural aspects of the bureaucracies, at least in the economic cluster.

The fragmented authoritarianism model thus did not present the Center as helpless, the bureaucracies as unable to cooperate, or the locales as all-powerful. But it did seek to identify the causes of fragmentation of authority among various bureaucratic units, the types of resources and strategies that provide leverage in the bargaining that evidently characterizes much decision making, and the incentives of key individuals in various units,[22] in order to gain a better grasp on the ways in which bureaucratic structure and process affect Chinese policy formulation, decision making, and policy implementation. On balance, as was noted above, this model lays considerable stress on bargaining relationships.

The fragmented authoritarianism model echoes some of the literature on bureaucratic politics, such as Graham Allison's *Essence of Decision*.[23] Allison argues that organizational processes (what he terms "standard operating procedures") and bureaucratically shaped politics influence decisions, and thus that rational-actor assumptions about decision making (in his case, regarding national security) do not fully capture the forces that shape policy-making and implementation. Similarly, the fragmented authoritarianism model regarding China under the reforms does not argue that rational problem solving at the top does not occur. It rather details other dimensions of the system that are not adequately captured in a straightforward application of a rationality model.

The fragmented authoritarianism model thus seeks to put into better perspective two well-developed groups of literature concerning policy-making in post-1949 China.[24] The first group posits essentially a rationality model for understanding Chinese political outcomes. This literature implicitly assumes both that top-level leaders can exercise enormous leverage over the political system as a whole and that these same leaders make decisions by identifying problems and then adopting responses to those issues that derive logically from their own value preferences[25]—or power needs in intraelite struggles.[26] Books in this literature, whether

22. This was modeled on the notion of "bounded rationality" as originally developed by Herbert Simon. See Herbert Simon, *Administrative Behavior*, 2nd ed. (New York: MacMillan, 1957).

23. Graham Allison, *Essence of Decision* (Boston: Little, Brown, 1971).

24. The following few paragraphs draw heavily from Lieberthal and Oksenberg, *Policy Making*, chap. 1.

25. See, e.g., Harry Harding, *Organizing China* (Stanford: Stanford University Press, 1981).

26. See, for example, Lucian Pye, *The Dynamics of Chinese Politics* (Cambridge, Mass.: Oelgeschlager, Gunn & Hain, 1981).

they focus on elite politics per se,[27] or on the politics of various functional areas, such as public health,[28] agriculture,[29] or education,[30] explain policy decisions almost exclusively in terms of leadership perceptions and preferences.

The second group stresses the extent to which China is what has been termed a "cellular" society. This literature focuses on the consequences of various policies over the years that have decentralized decisions and produced bureaucratic devices that permit localities effectively to block upward flows of information and to blunt higher-level initiatives that cascade down on local leaders. While this literature initially focused primarily on economic linkages,[31] in more recent versions it has been extended to the political system, too.[32] The experiences of businessmen who dealt with China during the 1980s added much anecdotal evidence to support the cellular model of the Chinese system, as localities repeatedly demonstrated an ability to frustrate the policies of the upper-level authorities.[33]

To repeat, the fragmented authoritarianism model acknowledges the great insights offered from elite-oriented rational-actor approaches and from a cellular conception of the system. However, it adds a third necessary ingredient to the equations: the structure of bureaucratic authority and the realities of bureaucratic practice that affect both the elite and the basic building blocks of the system.

27. Such as Roderick MacFarquhar, *The Origins of the Cultural Revolution*, vol. 1, *Contradictions Among the People 1956–1957;* vol. 2, *The Great Leap Forward 1956–1960* (New York: Columbia University Press, 1974 and 1983).

28. David M. Lampton, *Health, Conflict, and the Chinese Political System* (Ann Arbor: University of Michigan's Center for Chinese Studies, 1974).

29. Kang Chao, *Agricultural Production in Communist China, 1949–1965* (Madison: University of Wisconsin Press, 1970).

30. Joel Glassman, "Change and Continuity in Chinese Communist Education Policy," *Contemporary China* 2 (September 1978): 847–90.

31. Audrey Donnithorne, "China's Cellular Economy: Some Economic Trends since the Cultural Revolution," *China Quarterly*, no. 52 (October–December 1972): 10–16.

32. Shue argues that in fact this cellular structure characterized rural China in the late Maoist era but has been eroded by the marketizing elements in the 1980s reforms and their political repercussions: Vivienne Shue, *The Reach of the State* (Stanford: Stanford University Press, 1988). Potter argues that this cellular notion continues to have great power as an analytical framework for understanding rural China under the reforms: Sulamith Heins Potter, "The Position of Peasants in Modern China's Social Order," *Modern China* (October 1983): 465–99; and Sulamith Potter, *China's Peasants: The Anthropology of a Revolution* (New York: Cambridge University Press, 1990). The cellular model in both urban and rural areas has proven controversial from the time Audrey Donnithorne first proposed it. See, for example, the linked articles by Donnithorne, "Cellular Economy," and Nicholas Lardy, "Reply," *China Quarterly*, no. 66 (June 1976): 340–54.

33. By the late 1980s a well-known assertion by local officials in China was that "they (the Center) have their policies, and we have our countermeasures" (*tamen you zhengce, women you duice*).

The structures that link the top and the bottom of the system—in order to function—require negotiations, bargaining, exchange, and consensus building. Fragmented authoritarianism finds wanting both strictly "top down" and "bottom up" views of Chinese politics. This model, rather, focuses attention on the effects of the interactive processes among the constituent elements of the Chinese polity. In so doing, it finds that the system is somewhat but not totally fragmented. The fragmentation has not reached the point where its constituent parts have the legitimate autonomy characteristic of a pluralist system.

FRAGMENTED AUTHORITARIANISM IN BROADER PERSPECTIVE

The authors of the major works that have contributed to the fragmented authoritarianism model recognize that this model reflects research primarily on economic decision making. An important contribution of this volume is its exploration of the extent to which this model adequately conveys the dynamics of decision making beyond the economic cluster of bureaucracies (and within that cluster, beyond decision making on major new investment projects). Every chapter makes a substantial contribution to this effort. The following discussion culls out some of the important factors that emerge from this study and that modify to a greater or lesser extent the fragmented authoritarianism model as an adequate description of the entire Chinese bureaucratic system.

Like most of the literature on bureaucratic bargaining in China, Barry Naughton's contribution in chapter 9 focuses on decision making concerning major investment projects. Naughton notes the irony that Chinese leaders intended the reforms to *reduce* the amount of bargaining in the management of the economy by substituting market forces for bureaucratic management of the decision-making process. Instead, the reforms *increased* the role of bargaining in this sector, and they changed the types of resources that the various parties brought into the bargaining arena.

The two key resources that structure bargaining positions regarding proposed major investment projects, according to Naughton, are control over information and skills and control over resources. The bureaucratic bargaining literature to date has emphasized the latter almost to the exclusion of the former. As is often noted elsewhere, the reforms have, on balance, shifted control over resources—especially over budgetary resources—to lower bureaucratic levels in the system. But this same reform effort has effectively created greater central-level control over economic information and skills.

Enhanced availability of information for the Center commenced with the rehabilitation and expansion of the State Statistical Bureau, which had been devastated during the Cultural Revolution. It then proceeded further via two channels: considerable relaxation of the rules governing release of economic data;[34] and the establishment of various new policy-research organs at the central level to enhance directly and indirectly the ability of the leaders to produce more highly coordinated economic policy based on greater availability of information. In chapter 5 Nina Halpern analyzes the important influence on policy process that the new policy-research institutes exerted. As a result of these measures, the Center could undertake more sophisticated economic projections and planning.[35]

This shift in several types of resource did not reduce bargaining in the system. The Center no longer retained the direct economic levers necessary to obtain its wishes by simple command. Nevertheless, it did command information, expertise, and some critical resources that the localities would need in order to pursue economic development effectively, especially in terms of infrastructure development. As a consequence, the Center used its superior information and skills to bargain with the localities to obtain cooperation in the pursuit of the Center's priorities.

As the Center's priorities became better informed, therefore, its bargaining position vis-à-vis the localities was correspondingly enhanced. In contrast, the greater transparency of the Chinese system under the reforms created the impression that the prereform planned economy was characterized by an extremely strong Center. In reality, lack of information and skills at the Center kept this level of the system considerably weaker than outward appearances suggested.

As Naughton's focus on information and skills highlights, the reforms produced very complex changes in the distribution of pertinent resources in the Chinese political system. Focusing on decision making in the economic cluster, Naughton finds, not surprisingly, that the net result is an enriched and highly complex set of bargaining relationships. Other chapters in this volume provide information both on the sectors of the system in which bargaining plays less of a role and on the conditions under which bargaining flourishes in the Chinese polity.

Carol Lee Hamrin, in chapter 4, focuses on a key layer of bodies—comprising "leading groups"—that links the top few leaders with the country's far-flung bureaucratic network. This arrangement groups most of the major bureaucracies into broad functional clusters and assigns a small group, typically led by a member of the Politburo or its

34. World Bank demands encouraged this process. See Jacobson and Oksenberg, *China's Participation.*

35. Carol Hamrin provides the most extensive analysis available of the process of economic projection and planning, in *China and the Challenge of the Future* (Boulder: Westview Press, 1990).

Standing Committee, to manage that policy cluster and to act as liaison between it and the top decision-makers. These "leading groups" do not appear on organizational charts, and their membership is not announced. But they serve vital functions in the Chinese system: they work up materials for the consideration of the top leaders, initiate pertinent policy research, resolve some issues that cannot be handled at a lower level, and coordinate activities among the various bureaucracies in each bureaucratic cluster.

Hamrin provides far more detail on the origins, development, functions, and politics of these leading groups than has ever been presented before. Noting that these groups grew out of a clustering of the bureaucracies that originally took place in order to facilitate personnel assignments, Hamrin stresses that these bodies have become an extraordinarily concentrated expression of centralized power in China. At this level, the system is highly personal. The heads of these various "leading groups" typically have known each other for many decades, and their relationships cannot fruitfully be analyzed in terms of a fragmented authoritarianism model. There is, rather, a great deal of informal contact and maneuvering, with control over the various "leading groups" an important prize in the political jockeying in the capital.

In chapter 5 Nina Halpern focuses the analysis just one step below the "leading groups." She deals with the research institutes that were established—primarily at Zhao Ziyang's initiative—to develop policy options for the top leaders. While he was premier of the State Council, Zhao devoted considerable attention to creating an extensive "in-house" policy-research capability. The research institutes he established lacked line functions, but as staff organs they nevertheless influenced in important ways the information flows within the government and enhanced the ability of the leaders to develop and implement coordinated policies.

The institutes greatly increased the leadership's information on policy externalities, which effectively enhanced the leaders' ability to formulate coordinated policies. These institutes also gave the top leaders greater leverage vis-à-vis their own line organs by reducing their dependence on the line organs for vital information. And the research institutes forced many of the line bureaucracies to consider more fully the externalities of their policy proposals during the drafting process, as the bureaucrats knew that their proposals would have to compete with those of the pertinent research institutes. The Maoist system did not encourage this broader vision.

Nina Halpern's analysis emphasizes that at this level of the system bargaining (which, again, focuses on exchange and mutual veto power) does not capture the essence of the relationship between the research institutes and the top decision-makers. The institutes, after all, did not seek to trade off resources as much as they sought to influence policy thinking. A command relationship, in which the institutes faithfully provided the top leaders with the information they sought, would have drastically reduced the real benefits of the institute structure for the leaders. Halpern characterizes the resulting relationship as one of "competitive persuasion."

This relationship mixed both formal bureaucratic and highly personal elements. In essence, the institutes competed with line bureaucratic units (and with each other) to persuade Zhao Ziyang and other top officials of the wisdom of the institutes' policy proposals. Their effectiveness depended in part on the personal ties between the institute leaders and the top political leaders, as is shown by the changes (generally, for the worse) in the stature and effectiveness of various institutes since Zhao Ziyang's ouster in mid-1989. But the fact that the institutes demonstrably had the ear of powerful officials also made line bureaucratic units take the institutes seriously and try to adjust their own policy advocacy to a system in which these institutes provided the top leaders with serious information and analytical work. The net result contributed to the enhanced availability of information to the top leaders that is noted in chapter 9.

Below the level of the top leaders and the research institutes, the system is dominated by bureaucratic bodies, most with line functions. Key issues about these bodies concern their responsiveness to political leaders, the extent to which their actions are governed by formal rules and regulations, and the ways in which they deal with each other. This is an extremely complex system, but the various chapters in this volume permit some important generalizations to be made.

As Melanie Manion illustrates in chapter 8, on the cadre retirement policy in the personnel system, the ability of the top leaders to reach clear and detailed decisions seriously affects the functioning of the system as a whole. Bureaucratic middlemen tend to regard policies that are flexible and ambivalent as the equivalent of having no policies at all. They are more likely to implement policies to the extent that the policymakers reduce the middlemen's risks, constrain their actions, and coordinate the various demands made on them. But these suggest that the crucial elements are matters of policy content and coordination, not of bureaucratic structure and rules. Where policies lack the necessary specificity, clarity, and "fit" with other related activities, the middlemen studied by Manion would simply fail to implement them. This was thus not a bargaining situation so much as it was a matter of policy compliance. And policy compliance depended crucially on the ability of top leaders to produce well-coordinated sets of clear, detailed policies.

Indeed, the importance of policy content versus bureaucratic institutionalization of the Chinese system is evident time and again in these chapters. For example, even in the mid and late 1980s, nobody seems to have seriously questioned the right of the top leaders to reach any decisions (and enforce any redistribution of power) that they saw fit. This ability of higher-level leaders throughout the system to impose their will on lower levels without serious institutional (versus self-imposed policy) constraints shows through repeatedly, as in Paul Schroeder's treatment of the relations between Wuhan and Hubei and in David Zweig's analysis of the approach taken by county governments to subordinate administrative towns and townships. Bureaucratic behavior inevitably limits the information available to the top leaders and may produce various distortions in policy implementation. But no institutional regulations in themselves seriously constrain the options available to the top leaders as a group.

This is a system, then, where the balance between policy and institutional integrity tips very heavily in favor of the former, even under the reforms. In chapter 3 Susan Shirk stresses, in this regard, that the reform agenda required that the top political leaders adopt reform as the official political line. Only within this context could government officials at lower levels implement the reforms. The government alone, Shirk argues, could not have generated the reform policies against the wishes of the Party apparatus. The fact that the top leaders adopted "reform" as the political line, however, enabled lower-level government officials to implement many reform policies even in the face of obstructionism by the Party bureaucrats who wished to slow down this process. Shirk does not argue that the adoption of a political strategy by the top leaders is by itself adequate to produce results in China. She asserts, rather, that the adopted political strategy creates the framework within which subsequent bargaining generally occurs. The bargaining, in turn, reflected several facets of the reform effort: its focus on economic issues; disagreements among the leadership about specific reform policies; and lack of consistency and specificity that characterized reform decisions.

In sum, the picture above suggests that the top leadership in China remains very powerful, despite the reforms. At the top, bureaucratic boundaries fade even as leaders compete for control over bureaucratic resources. Personalities and personal relationships assume tremendous importance at the pinnacle, and then through "leading groups" and other devices the small coterie of very top officials ties into the huge bureaucratic clusters through which they govern China. While the reforms have decentralized administrative control over many resources, they have also in various ways (especially through the enhancement of the availability of information) increased the potential leverage of top leaders vis-à-vis their own bureaucracies. While no changes have occurred that effectively limit the right of the highest leaders to change the rules of the system itself, the leaders' ability to elicit lower-level compliance is reduced when there is evidence of leadership tentativeness or disunity.

Several chapters in this volume deal specifically with bureaucratic clusters that do not concern the economy. In these other clusters, there appears to be far less evidence of bargaining relationships than has generally been found in decision making and policy implementation in the economic cluster. This may, of course, in part reflect the possibility that it is simply more difficult to identify bargaining behavior in bureaucratic sectors that deal more with intangibles such as propaganda and education, but the pertinent chapters suggest that the differences are real and are important.

Lynn Paine's examination of the educational system casts light on a bureaucratic cluster that produces, in her words, a "mushy" product—that is, it is very difficult in the short term to determine the payoff of specific investments of resources in education. Overall, moreover, the educational system is bureaucratically weak at every level. It consumes, rather than generates, resources, and it has repeatedly been associated with producing values and behaviors that the top leaders have regarded as anathema. Paine finds that this mushy, resource-poor bureaucratic system is not characterized by extensive bargaining among its various units. Paine reveals, not bargaining to protect and enhance resources, but a process of "groping," where the Center sets vague standards, the locales implement the policies quite flexibly, and then there are iterations of interactive adjustment as units with very limited organizational resources seek to find ways to accomplish their tasks. In the process, these units adopt what Paine describes as "loosely jointed coping mechanisms" to get things done. The Chinese Communist Party remains extremely powerful in defining the boundaries of the acceptable in the educational sphere, but the policy dynamics within this sphere bear little relationship to those regarding major economic decision making.

Jonathan Pollack's examination of the military system intrudes into an area where very little was known previously about policy process. Pollack portrays the People's Liberation Army as a virtual internal empire within the PRC, and he sees it as having early on reached a compact with the Party in which the military would remain loyal so long as it could protect its vast and varied domain. Within this system, Pollack argues, personal ties rather than institutional positions determine the power of people at and near the top of the system. The closer to the apex of the military system, in short, the less command derives from specific rules and norms and the more it is personalistic.

Pollack examines Deng Xiaoping's far-reaching reforms in the military in terms of their stress on budgetary restraint, effectiveness in producing new technology, and progress in creating more resilient institutions. While Pollack suggests that Deng made very substantial progress along all of these lines, he argues that during the 1989 crisis the military system reverted very much to its more personalistic, prereform character.

Although Pollack is not able to address directly the issue of bargaining relationships in the military, the thrust of his analysis suggests that the overall effect of the reforms had been to strengthen the role of central organs within the military. Greater need for technological improvements to prepare for modern warfare effectively enhanced central coordination in all phases of the weapons research, development, testing, and evaluation system. He does not present evidence that would suggest that the reforms in the military, like those in the civilian economic sphere, led to policy processes in which bargaining became increasingly important to policy outcomes. Possibly the pertinent policies—stress on high technology, on professionalism, on institutionalization, and on budgetary restraint—created an environment less conducive to wide-ranging bargaining. Because there remain sharp limitations on our information about this sphere—despite the fact that Jonathan Pollack breaks considerable new ground in chapter 6—the answers to many questions about policy process in the military must at this point remain tentative. This is especially true since, in the wake of June 4, 1989, many of Deng's efforts to professionalize the military have yielded to renewed emphasis on politicization of the armed forces.

The chapters that focus, therefore, on personnel (Manion), education (Paine), and coercion (Pollack) find that the reforms of the past decade do not appear to have nurtured the pervasive bargaining relationships that researchers have found in the economic sphere. To be sure, some bargaining characterizes the dynamics of every functional system, but the differences of degree suggested here are substantial and important. Bargaining behavior evidently requires at least that tangible resources be at stake and that substantive policies permit leeway in implementation. These conditions are not met in significant measure for much of China's bureaucratic behavior.

Three chapters focus specifically on distinctive subnational bureaucratic levels in China: Paul Schroeder examines the provincial level (relations between Hubei and Wuhan when the latter was granted provincial budgetary status); Andrew Walder analyzes fiscal and budgetary dynamics at the municipal level; and David Zweig illuminates the political dynamics of rural urbanization at the subcounty level. All three focus substantial attention on *economic* decision making at these three levels.

Schroeder, in chapter 10, stresses the failure of the Chinese system, even under the reforms, to develop political or legal formulas that would permit the development of stable definitions of authority. The result,

which he details in his examination of the changing formal status of
Wuhan municipality vis-à-vis Hubei province, is fluidity, competition,
incessant bargaining, and a resulting muddle. Where jurisdictional issues
arise (as they do constantly, given the many changes initiated by the
reformers), the legal system is not mature enough to settle the issues and
to provide case-law precedents to guide the behavior of others. Vague
policies from the Center essentially produce bargaining among lower-
level units, where the parameters of the situation remain uncertain. This
chapter illustrates well the interconnections among the formal administrative system, the legal system, the economic system, and substantive
policy decisions in shaping the results of reform initiatives. Schroeder
finds that the actual relationships among these various elements are fluid
and that the system as a whole, therefore, lacks the institutional regularity necessary to permit reform decisions to have their desired effect.

Andrew Walder, in his analysis in chapter 11 of the processes that
determine the financial flows between city budgets and enterprises, argues that bargaining activity does not necessarily stem from fragmentation of authority, as the fragmented authoritarianism model has stressed.
Walder notes, indeed, that the key characteristic of the municipal fiscal
environment is that of *concentration* of power rather than of its fragmentation. But this concentration of budgetary power and resources occurs in
a larger environment of unreformed prices, unequal capital endowments, and unclear rules and regulations. He finds plenty of bargaining
behavior in the process of determining financial flows between the city
budgets and enterprises he examines, but these negotiations are intended to reduce individual responsibilities, avoid risks, and assure
broad equity (or "fairness") in the distribution of and accounting for
financial resources. Walder concludes that it is more important to understand the characteristics of the environment that structure bargaining
than to concentrate attention on the dynamics of the resulting bargaining itself.[36]

Looking at rural urbanization, David Zweig examines the sphere
where the reforms since the late 1970s reportedly had gone the farthest
toward reducing bureaucratic authority in favor of having decisions
driven by market forces. Small-scale rural enterprises have flourished
with the dissolution of the communes and the policy decision to permit
peasants to leave farming in favor of working in small towns. These

36. Barry Naughton in chapter 9 also seeks to explain bargaining between enterprises
and local municipal bureaus. Naughton utilizes the concept of "bilateral monopoly"—
where both the bureau and the enterprise are too important to each other for either to deal
with the other in cavalier fashion. While Naughton's specific analytical construct differs
from Walder's, his approach is in line with Walder's admonition to look at the structural
relationships that contour bargaining activity.

changes suggest that rural towns are relatively freewheeling places, but
Zweig's research paints a distinctly different picture. While the production and marketing of agricultural produce are no longer monopolized
by local officials, the county's control over development assistance and
investment for expanding urban infrastructure has assured a continuing—and in many cases an expanding—role for the county government
in county-towns and townships. Bureaucratic administrative control over
rural town development, as a consequence, remains very powerful, and
the characteristics of that control—such as lack of institutional constraints on the authority of upper levels—will sound very familiar to
those who have read the other chapters.

The Schroeder, Walder, and Zweig contributions draw remarkably
similar pictures in their examination of various subnational levels in
China. They all agree that the reforms significantly decentralized control
over economic resources, that subnational bureaucracies became more
important in decision making on economic issues, that the system lacks
clear rules and a stable distribution of authority, and that these circumstances have combined with vague or inconsistent policies from above to
produce and contour widespread bargaining behavior. Very considerable budgetary power, moreover, now appears to be concentrated at the
level of the municipality and of the rural county (at least, in the latter
case, vis-à-vis the rural townships). This concentration of power has not
reduced bargaining—it has, rather, reshaped it.

These explorations into four bureaucratic clusters and of the top and
bottom of the system challenge and modify the fragmented authoritarian model in several important ways. They may be briefly summarized as
follows:

> The reforms have not produced straightforward decentralization of
> China's bureaucratic system. Rather, they have had complex ef-
> fects. Reform policies have consciously decentralized decision mak-
> ing in the economic sphere and have given lower bureaucratic lev-
> els more control over fiscal resources. The reduced role of ideology
> has reinforced fragmentation of the system. But countervailing
> trends, such as enhancement of the Center's authority to acquire
> and analyze information, have also been nurtured by the reforms.
> The resulting system structures new bargaining relationships and
> dynamics of decision making, but the Center continues to hold
> serious cards in this economic game.
>
> Fragmentation of the bureaucratic system is most severe in the do-
> main from the ministries through the provinces. Above the minis-
> tries and below the provinces, this is a political system characterized
> by extraordinary concentrations of power. The key to whether bar-

gaining occurs at the bottom of the system is not simply the extent to which power is fragmented.

The reforms since the late 1970s have produced only very limited progress toward institutionalizing the political system. While top leaders no longer launched disruptive political campaigns to shake up the bureaucratic institutions, the system as a whole failed to develop institutional ways of allocating authority on a stable basis. The legal system does not function in a fashion that enables it to adjudicate key issues and establish stable precedents. Law and regulation combined do not pose effective bars to the adoption of policies that redistribute power and violate past commitments.

While formal rules do not constrain the top leaders in reshaping the system, three other factors do limit considerably the effective leverage of those leaders. First, officials at lower levels tend to ignore or circumvent top-level decisions that are vague or inconsistent. Second, substantive policy goals, especially those of the reformers, demand that top leaders allow their subordinates considerable leeway, as any other approach chokes off information, reduces enthusiasm and creativity, and precludes China's developing the dynamic society envisioned by the reformers. Third, top leaders generally recognize that policy implementation, especially regarding major economic projects, can be slowed down and made more difficult by unenthusiastic provincial and lower-level officials, and thus they often seek to bring those officials on board rather than to coerce them into compliance.

For many parts of the political system, processes other than bargaining tend to play very important roles in determining how bureaucratic units deal with each other. These may include, inter alia, the personal maneuvering at the apex suggested by Carol Hamrin, the competitive persuasion noted by Nina Halpern, or the coping mechanisms detailed by Lynn Paine. Bargaining is more likely to occur where tangible resources are at stake, both parties need each other, and the rules that govern decisions are not fixed and clear. Quite often, one or both of the first two of these conditions is not present.

Another way to put the findings in this volume into perspective is to look at the Chinese political system as being in transition from a traditional hierarchical system toward a more modern, market-oriented system. In the former, activities are guided primarily by traditional vertical relationships within the bureaucratic apparatus, while in the latter a wider range of activities is shaped by pure rule-guided and especially market relationships. This is a basic set of changes sought by the post-1978 reforms. Figures 1.1 and 1.2, which build upon, modify, and am-

Pattern of Relationship

		Vertical	Horizontal[a]
Bureaucratic Location of Parties	Both in	**1** Pleading[b] Command Patron-client	**2** Bargaining *Guanxi*[c]
	One in, one out	**3** Corruption Rent seeking[e] Patron-client Bargaining[f]	**4** Persuasion[d] Corruption[d] Rent seeking[de] *Guanxi* Bargaining
	Both out	**5** Patron-client	**6** *Guanxi* Bargaining[f] Market[g]

Fig. 1.1. Traditional Polity

[a]Includes relations between ministries and provinces, which are of the same bureaucratic rank in China.

[b]Behavior by the lower-ranking of the parties.

[c]Use of personal ties to obtain favors.

[d]Relations between officials and foreigners, retired cadres, village elders, or others whose prestige or resources give them a position of rough equality with the officials with whom they are dealing.

[e]"Rent seeking" refers to a type of corrupt behavior where officials essentially charge a form of "rent" to gain access to those things that are under their control, such as permission to operate in a particular locale, authorization to produce a particular item, access to goods under official control (such as steel produced on the mandatory plan), and so forth.

[f]In situations of bilateral monopoly (discussed in chapter 9 in this volume).

[g]*Unlike* those in the "modern" polity, "market" relations in the traditional polity refer only to some transactions in the economic sphere.

plify a presentation David Zweig made at the Tucson conference, provide a framework for an understanding of the resulting situation.

In the traditional system, relations are shaped primarily by informal criteria, such as personal connections and actual control over resources. The more modern variant posits a greater role for formal institutional boundaries, accepted rules, and laws. In short, in the more modern polity, the role of personal elements is reduced and that of more formal criteria is enhanced.

As is indicated in these charts, for each of these two types of polity there are three basic structural relationships: those where both parties

Pattern of Relationship

		Vertical	Horizontal[a]
	Both in	**1** Persuasion[b] Command Rule-guided behavior	**2** Market[c] Rule-guided behavior
Bureaucratic Location of Parties	One in, one out	**3** Service according to regulations	**4** Persuasion[d] Market[c] Rule-guided behavior
	Both out	**5** Merit-based assistance	**6** Market[c]

Fig. 1.2. Modern Polity

[a]Includes relations between ministries and provinces, which are of the same bureaucratic rank in China.
[b]Behavior by the lower-ranking of the parties.
[c]"Market" discipline is not limited to economic relations.
[d]Relations between officials and foreigners, retired cadres, village elders, or others whose prestige or resources give them a position of rough equality with the officials with whom they are dealing.

are inside the bureaucracy, those where one is in and one is out, and those where both parties are outside the bureaucracy. Within each of these, moreover, the charts distinguish relationships among unequal parties (vertical/asymmetrical relationships) from relationships among basically equal parties (horizontal/symmetrical relationships). The resulting ranges of types of behavior for each structure of relationship in the traditional and modern polities are indicated.

In the more modern version of vertical/asymmetrical relationships, pleading is replaced by persuasion and patron-client ties are replaced by rule-guided behavior (box 1), corruption (including rent-seeking) is supplanted by service according to regulations (boxes 3 and 4), and assistance is rendered on the basis of merit (box 5). The modern analogue of horizontal/symmetrical relationships substitutes rule-guided behavior for bargaining and corruption/rent-seeking and has pure market relationships replace *guanxi* (boxes 2, 4, and 6).

To repeat, an objective of the 1980s reforms in China was to shift *from* a situation where activities are guided primarily by traditional vertical relations within the bureaucratic apparatus *to* one where a wider range of activities is shaped by pure rule-guided and especially market relationships.[37] Thus, the reformers sought to move the polity from a bureaucratic leviathan that operates in traditional fashion toward a polity that acts in more modern fashion and in which the bureaucratic apparatus plays a narrower role.

As the chapters in this volume confirm, the reality of the reforms fell far short of the ultimate goals of shifting to more modern forms of behavior and of sharply curtailing the scope of bureaucratic activity. Rather, the major changes in the 1980s moved an increasing array of decisions from the "Both In" vertical cell (box 1) in the Traditional Polity chart to the "Both In" horizontal cell (box 2) and the "One In, One Out" vertical and horizontal cells (boxes 3 and 4) in that same chart. The actual scope of bureaucratic activity remains surprisingly pervasive,[38] and these changes reflect the fact that the reforms in many ways flattened China's bureaucratic hierarchy and increased the importance of nonbureaucratic sectors without changing the nature of relationships to those of a more modern polity. Only within the decision-making apparatus developed directly under Zhao Ziyang's aegis in the *Zhongnanhai*, as is detailed by Nina Halpern, did behavior move in very substantial measure toward the appropriate box (box 1) in the chart Modern Polity.

One important result of these shifts that is not highlighted in this volume is that they have nurtured corruption and rent-seeking behavior both within the bureaucracies and between officials and the population. These behaviors reflect in part the combination of the rapid development of nongovernmental efforts, the commercialization of many governmental activities, continued bureaucratic power to intervene in the market, and confusion over norms. Note that these forms of behavior predominate even as the unofficial party acquires resources that create a relatively symmetrical relationship with the official party. Thus, the very process of reform itself has created conditions that nurture corruption by relaxing former rules and habitual practices, diffusing authority and resources, and creating confusion over guiding norms.

The charts and the discussion of the fragmented authoritarianism model reflect a preliminary way of looking at the trends in the kinds of

---

37. The thrust of Chinese national policy is no longer fully in this direction, at the time of this writing in 1990.

38. This is not to argue that there has been no diminution in the scope of bureaucratic activity since Mao. Clearly, many aspects of personal life that formerly were considered part of the responsibility of the propaganda and public security apparatuses now fall outside of the operational concerns of these bureaucracies, although the boundaries remain vague and shifting. Similarly, much petty production and trade takes place without active bureaucratic interference.

relationships—and in the resulting behavior—that are occurring under the reforms in the PRC. The particular data in the various chapters flesh out this framework in some detail. No polity operates in a purely "modern" fashion (nor should it), but the differences between low levels of institutionalization combined with expansion of the role of the market to produce widespread rent-seeking behavior and corruption, versus far greater use of law and regulation to achieve market-driven outcomes, is serious and important.

THE VOLUME IN PERSPECTIVE

The chapters in this volume are far richer than the above comments can convey. Each provides analytical insights, a "feel" for the bureaucratic arena being addressed, and, typically, illustrative material that conveys a nuanced appreciation of the forces that shape political and bureaucratic outcomes in China. Overall, however, they do not provide substantial comment on the extent to which the system has changed over time, on the role of the Chinese Communist Party in the polity, on the impact of culture on policy process, and on relations between state and society. These are all important issues for putting into perspective the content and coverage of chapters that follow, and this "Introduction" thus concludes with a few comments on each of these matters.

How Constant Has China's Bureaucratic Practice Remained?
The 1980s reform era created the impression of major change in the way China was governed. In part, those perceived changes were substantive and important. As was noted above, for example, the reforms significantly redistributed flows of information in the system and greatly reduced the role of ideology as a factor in structuring policy formation and implementation. But there is a danger of exaggerating the changes that the reforms produced in China's bureaucratic practice. As figures 1.1 and 1.2 highlight, the system has moved only very partially in the directions sought by the reformers.

Clearly, there have been important continuities as well as changes. The fundamental structure of the Chinese bureaucratic system that was established in the 1950s, for example, remains in place to the present and continues to exert tremendous influence on policy process. Mao Zedong himself altered the scope of authority of the various bureaucratic clusters over time in his quest to keep the political system responsive to his desires. Deng Xiaoping and his reform-minded colleagues continued this practice by considerably enhancing the resources and authority of the economic cluster at considerable cost to the organization/personnel, propaganda/education, coercive, and Party territorial clusters. At the beginning of the

1990s it appears that hard-liners may attempt to increase the resources of the five "losing" clusters of the reform era as part of their strategy for building support for turning back some reform initiatives. While all of these efforts have redistributed authority and resources, none has fundamentally changed the nature of the system. The "losing" clusters during each period remain in the wings as potential resources for political contenders who seek a change of course.

A number of additional factors make it difficult to judge the extent to which bureaucratic practice under Mao differed from the findings presented in this volume. For the Maoist era, we obviously lack the kind of detailed studies based on direct access that are contained here. In addition, the Chinese media were far less informative about this earlier period than they became during the 1980s. And many Chinese interviewees, acting in the best of faith, nevertheless tend to recall past situations in conformity with the current official views concerning those previous periods. Thus, the 1980s demonology concerning the Maoist era has affected recapitulations of decision making during that era.

Even the extent of pressures for change effected by the 1980s reformers is not unprecedented in the PRC. The Chinese reforms beginning in the late 1970s sought changes in important areas: bureaucratic organization, the scope of responsibility and definition of tasks of key bureaucracies, the distribution of bureaucratic resources, and the nature of the process by which decisions are made. In broad terms, the reform leadership of the country tried to make the system less personalized, less ideological, less centralized, and more sensitive to economic rewards for greater efficiency and dynamism.[39]

But the bureaucracies under Mao also had to adapt to very different environments in terms of the intensity of ideological pressure,[40] the openness to the outside world (i.e., to the USSR and Eastern Europe during the 1950s),[41] the decision-making models they should follow,[42] fiscal and budgetary environments,[43] and so forth. In short, pressures for change of this magnitude have been a recurrent feature of China's

39. See, e.g., Harry Harding, *China's Second Revolution* (Washington, D.C.: The Brookings Institution, 1987).

40. See Schurmann, *Ideology and Organization*.

41. See, e.g., O. B. Borisov and B. T. Koloskov, *Sino-Soviet Relations, 1945–1973* (Moscow: Progress Publishers, 1975), on the extent of Soviet contact with Chinese governing bureaucracies.

42. See Schurmann, *Ideology and Organization*, and Roy Grow, "The Politics of Industrial Development in China and the Soviet Union" (Ph.D. dissertation, University of Michigan, 1973).

43. Xu Yi and Chen Baosen, eds., *Zhongguo de caizheng* (China's Finance) (Beijing: People's Press, n.d.); and Audrey Donnithorne, *China's Economic System* (New York: Praeger, 1967).

bureaucratic world.[44] As is detailed in this volume, moreover, the 1980s reforms achieved only part of their ambitious agenda for change.

The question concerning the extent to which the bureaucratic world detailed in this volume also characterized the Maoist period must, therefore, remain unanswered. Significant changes have undoubtedly occurred in some aspects of policy process, especially since the role of ideology in the system has diminished greatly and the reforms appear to have significantly flattened bureaucratic hierarchies. But there may be more continuity than we assume, and researchers should keep this possibility in mind as they undertake further studies on the Maoist era.

The system as described and analyzed in this volume probably will remain more constant in the future than changes in elite-level political rhetoric might suggest. It is made clear, for example, that, while there is no constitutional or even normative bar to the central leadership's radically altering the distribution of authority crafted by its predecessors, this would require either that one leader emerge as a new strongman or that strong agreement be reached among all the top leaders that the system should move in this new direction. Without such agreement, policy decisions will lack the clarity, consistency, and detail that are necessary to bring a high probability of lower-level compliance. Without such agreement at the very top, to put it differently, there is apt to be widespread sabotage of national directives by officials at each subnational level. If the top-level initiatives move the system toward a more centralized system producing less information, moreover, then lower levels will be in a position quietly to achieve greater degrees of freedom through manipulation of information that goes to the leadership. In short, by focusing on fundamental structure and process, we examine here factors that indicate that the Chinese system is not nearly as malleable as are the dynamics of political contention at the apex of the system.

At the time of this writing there is a possibility that China will experience dramatic political change in the coming years. The factors under scrutiny here are of such a fundamental nature, however, that to some extent any successor system is likely to embody many of the features and dynamics that are discussed in these pages. Major changes would, of course, be evident, but the issues explored would very likely retain significant salience even if leaders who reject communism were to govern China.

What About the Communist Party?

The Chinese constitution recognizes the Chinese Communist Party as the "sole leader" of the Chinese system. Even the major reform docu-

44. See, e.g., Harry Harding, *Organizing China.*

ments, such as Zhao Ziyang's speech to the Thirteenth Party Congress,[45] reserve for the Party the responsibility of making all key decisions, of checking on their implementation, and of retaining the power of appointment of individuals to every important post. Yet the actual state of the Party—its organization, work methods, and to some extent even its bureaucratic identity—remain matters on which there is little information and much confusion among foreign scholars.

Discussion of the Party is bedeviled, of course, by the difficulty of gaining access to information. The Chinese press during the 1980s became relatively frank about problems in the government, but it treated the Party gingerly. Broad comments about difficulties in the Party tended to be supported only with flimsy anecdotal data. Solid research— if any has been done—remains unavailable to foreign analysts. Foreigners themselves understandably have felt that probing the details of Party organization and functioning would stretch too far the hospitality they have been accorded by their Chinese hosts. Yet, as Susan Shirk indicates in chapter 3, it is terribly important to clarify the role and dynamics of the Party in the Chinese political system.

More attention must be paid to career mobility within the Party, personal characteristics of Party members, personal ranks in the Party, and other factors that affect relative authority and that therefore contour behavior of Party officials. In addition, much more effort must then be made to understand the procedures by which issues are considered within the Party and the views of various Party bodies. It is, of course, quite possible that the extent of the Party's role varies considerably by sector—probably being more important in propaganda, organization, public security, and rural work, and less important in the urban economy and the military (although even this may vary considerably over time). Only empirical research can determine this. Until this research is considerably more advanced than at present, however, all comments about the functioning and evolution of the Chinese system—indeed, about the structure of authority within that system—must be made with some caution.

In sum, the fact that even a volume such as this, which investigates in detail the decision-making process in various bureaucratic arenas, basically is forced to give little consideration to the Chinese Communist Party is a cause of some concern. Work on the Chinese Communist Party should be put high on the agenda of research in the China field, although it is difficult to be optimistic about how much can be learned about the Party in the environment of the early 1990s. Given the fact that in most government units the top Party officials are also the top govern-

45. Text in *Beijing Review* 30, no. 45 (9–15 November 1987): 1–27.

ment officeholders, it may be that lack of direct consideration of the Party itself does not seriously distort our understanding of policy process. But future research should seek to provide the empirical base for determining whether (or to what extent) this is the case. This volume does not satisfactorily accomplish this task.

How About Chinese Culture and Society?

The analyses provided in these chapters typically make little or no reference to Chinese cultural characteristics. It has been argued that Chinese culture is crucial for understanding political and bureaucratic behavior in the PRC, as cultural approaches explain the nature of political alliances, expectations of political behavior, attitudes toward authority relations, and even the fundamental strength of political organizations.[46] These authors probably would not argue against the idea that cultural factors affect the style and some other aspects of political and bureaucratic behavior. For example, the weakness of formal legal authority, the legitimacy of virtually unbridled concentration of power, and a proclivity toward negotiation may all be in part attributable to cultural influences. The authors nevertheless find that they do not have to utilize cultural variables to explain the major behavior patterns they identify.

There is also little consideration of the relations of state and society. The various chapters include careful analysis of the relationships among top leaders, key staff organs, and various bureaucratic units. The chapters by Naughton, Walder, and Zweig also address the issue of the relations between local government units and various enterprises. The focus here is explicitly on the political system and its internal dynamics, however, not on the relations between this system and the larger Chinese population.

ORGANIZATION OF THE VOLUME

The volume begins with analyses that are national in scope. David M. Lampton considers systematically the conditions that structure bargaining behavior, and Susan Shirk analyzes overall reform strategy and implementation. In their focus on the Center, Carol Lee Hamrin examines the evolution, structure, and politics of the "leading groups" headed by the top leaders, and Nina Halpern explicates the impact on policy process of the development of think tanks at the Center.

Four authors then take up various bureaucratic functional clusters:

46. The most forceful and thorough proponent of this approach is Lucian Pye. See, inter alia, *The Dynamics of Chinese Politics* (n. 26 above); *The Spirit of Chinese Politics* (Cambridge: MIT Press, 1968); and *The Mandarin and the Cadre* (Ann Arbor: University of Michigan Center for Chinese Studies, 1988).

Jonathan Pollack on the military; Lynn Paine on the educational system; Melanie Manion on the personnel system; and Barry Naughton on the economic system. Finally, three authors focus specifically on subnational levels of the system: Paul Schroeder on the provincial level; Andrew Walder on the municipal level; and David Zweig on county level and below in the countryside.

Many of the "functional" chapters in fact deal with both national and local levels, and each of the last three examines the politics and policy process of localities in their relationship to other levels of the political system. Thus, although the chapters are arranged to march "down" the national governing hierarchy, the actual relationships among these chapters are more complex than may appear on the surface. In this tension between orderly appearance and complex reality, this volume imitates the bureaucratic system about which it is written.

PART ONE

National Issues

TWO

A Plum for a Peach:
Bargaining, Interest, and Bureaucratic
Politics in China

David M. Lampton

*China is a centrally planned society without central planning. China is a
centralized polity without centralized authority. These aspects are in dialectical
relationship to each other.*
—INTERVIEW WITH CHINESE CITIZEN, FEBRUARY 1988, IN NEW YORK

*In Article 16 of the constitution adopted by the Thirteenth Party Congress
we find the following: "In case of controversy over major issues in which
supporters of the two opposing views are nearly equal in number, except in
emergencies where action must be taken in accordance with the majority view,
the decision should be put off to allow for further investigation, study and
exchange of opinions followed by another vote." In the previous constitution, the
section was the same except that the last word was "discussion."*

*Within connection networks, the law of exchange generally works. . . . I will
give you a plum in return for a peach. . . . The practice of exchanging power
for goods, exchanging goods for power, and exchanging power for power and
goods for goods is extensively pursued and injures the public interest to profit
the private interest, and lines one's pockets with public funds.*
—*PEOPLE'S DAILY*, 10 DECEMBER 1986, P. 1

*China's economic reforms have changed the monopoly of public ownership
and the pattern of equal distribution. As a result different interest groups are
emerging in the society. These groups, representing various economic forces,
make different demands on the reforms. Conflicts arise as they evaluate the
social changes from their own perspectives. . . . Not only do interest gaps exist
between different groups, but views of people within groups are divergent.*
—*CHINA DAILY*, 4 APRIL 1988, P. 4

Some preliminary elements of this chapter appeared as "Chinese Politics: The Bargaining
Treadmill," *Issues and Studies* 23, no. 3 (March 1987): 11–41. In making subsequent revisions, the suggestions of James Reardon-Anderson, A. Doak Barnett, Thomas P. Bernstein,
and Harry Harding were most helpful. Finally, I thank Kenneth Lieberthal and all the
participants in the conference on "The Structure of Authority and Bureaucracy in China"
for their trenchant comments.

How are we to understand the structure of authority and the political process in China, particularly in the era of reform? How substantially have these structures and processes changed in the course of reform and how are they evolving?

Are the quotations with which this chapter opened simply the rhetorical fig leaves covering the knuckles of an iron-fisted and highly capable centralized regime? The violence of Tiananmen Square in mid-1989 superficially supports such a conclusion. Or, on the contrary, is there sown within these disjointed vignettes a serious understanding of the Chinese system of authority and the bureaucratic apparatus?

In this chapter I argue that bargaining is *one of several forms of authority relationship in China,* that it has been of central importance in the Chinese policy process throughout the Communist era, and that it became increasingly important in the first decade of reform in the post-Mao era. Even in the wake of the violence of Tiananmen, cooked up by an aging cabal of Party elders holding few (or no) formal positions of authority, bargaining remains a key feature of the system. By "bargaining" I mean an authority relationship of "reciprocal control . . . among representatives of hierarchies."[1] Bargaining has been conspicuous in technical and economic decisions, though it is by no means limited to this domain. Other forms of authority relationships are documented elsewhere in this volume: hierarchy and command, market relations, patron-client ties, pleading, and rent-seeking or corruption.

One of the principal conceptual contributions of this entire volume is to point out that there are many forms of political and authority relationships in China and that the kind of authority relationship depends on where in the social and bureaucratic hierarchies the respective parties are located, who the various parties to the authority relationship are, and what resources they possess. Bargaining occurs among proximate leaders, persons of equal rank, or among immediate superiors and subordinates. Bargaining is most in evidence when one is dealing with two or more bureaucracies of approximately equal resources, none of which can carry out an undertaking without the cooperation of the other(s), but which cannot compel the cooperation of the other(s) and cannot persuade a senior authoritative leader or institution to compel the other(s) to cooperate. Senior authoritative leaders may not intervene, because they lack the knowledge to decide, they do not care, their resources are insufficient to enforce a decree, or the leadership is itself divided.

To be more specific, the circumstances that favor a bargaining process are situations in which there is collective leadership, disagreement

1. Robert A. Dahl and Charles E. Lindblom, *Politics, Economics, and Welfare* (New York: Harper Torchbooks), 324, 326, 472–73, 498, and 501.

among authoritative elites, parties of about equal bureaucratic rank, decisions of high complexity with multiple trade-offs, and decisions in which interdependencies are complex and extensive. Issues that must be resolved in such circumstances frequently are addressed through an intensive process of consensus building in which leadership, at all levels, is hesitant to act until there is a consensus among subordinates and among competing bureaucracies.

The Chinese system is distinctive, not because bargaining occurs (which is a generic feature of politics, per se), but because frequently so many individuals and organizations must agree or acquiesce before one gets action. Americans sometimes see themselves as uniquely hamstrung by a "checks and balances system"; the Chinese decision system often is hamstrung by a complex bargaining process and the need to build a consensus.

There are several reasons that bargaining became more prevalent in the decade of reform (1978–1988) following Mao Zedong's death: leadership became more collective, and political agendas were dominated by complex economic and development issues that reflected great interdependencies, many trade-offs, and high complexity. Perhaps even more important, the very notion of partial social interests articulating their needs was legitimized in the wake of the Chairman's death, and extreme collectivist ideology was delegitimized. Finally, the unrelenting growth in the size of both state and Party bureaucracies, combined with the decentralization of economic power, proliferated the number of organizational bases with clout.

Nonetheless, even under Mao there was extensive bargaining among localities and functional bureaucracies, reflecting the need to resolve conflicts among interdependent localities and bureaucracies when the rigidities of the vertical command system obstructed timely and appropriate decisions. The potential of the marketplace to make decisions was almost entirely untapped.

If one examines the literature on Chinese foreign and domestic politics, there is a curious and conspicuous disjuncture. Analysts have long realized that bargaining and negotiating processes are central to interactions with foreigners; the Chinese, we have been told, are master bargainers.[2] However, when we look at domestic political processes, we see that

2. Richard Solomon, *Chinese Political Negotiating Behavior*, RAND Corporation, December 1985 (R-3295); Jaw-ling Joanne Chang, "Peking's Negotiating Style: A Case Study of U.S.–PRC Normalization," Occasional Papers, School of Law, University of Maryland, no. 5 (1985); Lucian Pye, *Chinese Commercial Negotiating Style*, RAND Corporation, January 1982 (R-2837); Kenneth T. Young, *Negotiating with the Chinese Communists* (New York: McGraw-Hill, 1968); Paul E. Schroeder, "The Ohio-Hubei Agreement: Clues to Chinese Negotiating Practices," *China Quarterly*, no. 91 (1982): 486–91.

there has been insufficient appreciation of the role that bargaining and negotiation play in the consensus-building and decision-making process. Richard Solomon's observation about negotiations with foreigners applies with nearly equal force to internal politics. "Chinese officials sometimes give the impression that agreements are never quite final. They will seek modifications of understandings when it serves their purposes, and the conclusion of one agreement is only the occasion for pressing an interlocutor for new concessions."[3]

This chapter will address these questions: What role does bargaining play in the repertoire of authority relations? What resources provide the greatest leverage in what types of bargaining situations? In what policy domains is bargaining most pronounced, in what areas is it least in evidence, and why? What do political participants bargain over, and who is entitled to enter the process? What tactics do participants employ to enhance their positions? What factors account for the behavior of particular bargainers? What consequences does bargaining have for the political system and its policy outputs and outcomes?

A COMPARATIVE FRAMEWORK FOR VIEWING BARGAINING

Political leadership in any society has two inescapable tasks: the *calculative* function (to identify problems, to assess the options for solution, and to make choices) and the *control* or *coordination* function (to assure that multiple actors comply with policy and coordinate their actions when necessary). As Robert Dahl and Charles Lindblom explained long ago, in discharging these tasks, leaders must choose from a limited number of basic means: hierarchy or "command" structures, markets (or price mechanisms), voting and preference counting systems, and bargaining.[4] Each tool provides *both* a means by which leaders and followers gain information and make choices ("calculation") *and* a means by which leaders control (or coordinate) subsequent behavior. *Every* society employs a combination of each tool, and every polity is therefore a "mixed" system; what distinguishes one polity from another is the *mix*, the issues with respect to which various tools are employed, the levels of the society at which various mixes prevail, and the stability of the mix.[5]

Looking at the PRC developmentally, in the first decade of reform in the post-Mao era we see that there was a relative *decline* in the use of hierarchical command (and within many, but not all, hierarchies there was a delegation of authority downward). Within the elite there was more

3. Solomon, *Negotiating Behavior*, viii.
4. Dahl and Lindblom, *Politics, Economics, and Welfare*.
5. Ibid., 93.

collective leadership. There was an *increase* in the use of market mechanisms, but it proceeded only far enough to create opportunities for corruption and other rent-seeking behavior by those in the hierarchy who were
best positioned to reap benefits from manipulations of the disjunctures
between the administrative hierarchy and the marketplace. There was a
limited *increase* in the use of voting and preference counting systems
(particularly in county and below governance and in the use of public
opinion surveys). There was a significant *increase* in the use of bargaining,
because the agenda was dominated by complex economic and technical
issues, with multiple trade-offs, in the context of a collective leadership
and bureaucracies of growing size and technical complexity.

What do we mean by "bargaining" and what are its practical and
theoretical consequences? Dahl and Lindblom provide a departure
point. "Bargaining is a form of reciprocal control *among leaders.* . . . Leaders bargain because they disagree and expect that further agreement is
possible and will be profitable. . . . *Bargaining commonly means reciprocity
among representatives of hierarchies*" (emphasis added).[6] Bargaining, therefore, is a process of reciprocal accommodation among the leaders of
territorial and functional hierarchies. Bargaining occurs because these
leaders believe that the gains to be made by mutual accommodation
exceed those to be made by unilateral action (if that were possible) or by
forgoing agreement altogether.

A bargaining perspective does *not* mean that China is on the road to
free enterprise—indeed, bargaining can be one means by which established hierarchies endeavor to prevent the further erosion of their
power, a way to avoid the increased use of market forces. Moreover,
bargaining does not mean that established hierarchies are being dismantled; on the contrary, bargaining is one reflection of the fact that there
are large, competitive bureaucracies and territorial administrations that
are absolutely central to the functioning of both the society and the
polity. Bargaining does not necessarily result in more coherent policies
or more efficient governance. Bargaining is more akin to protracted
guerrilla warfare within and between large-scale organizations.

Consequently, bargaining has sown within itself a number of patholo-
gies among which are blocked leadership, minority veto, control by the
organized (which in China generally means powerful bureaucracies, to
include localities), and an inability to assure that the policy to emerge
from one bargaining process is consistent with another, for coherence
among policies is difficult to assure. Bargaining is a process characteristic
of what Jerry Hough calls bureaucratic (and I would add localist) plural-

6. Ibid., 324, 326, 472–73, 498, and 501.

ism, though its cultural roots in China run much deeper than just the post-1949 bureaucratic structure.[7]

THE SYSTEMATIC CAUSES OF BARGAINING ACTIVITY

Bargaining results from several structural factors, many of which existed prior to the demise of Mao Zedong, and several of which made bargaining substantially more pronounced in the era of reform after his death. The enduring factors are several. First is the existence of massive, parallel, and interdependent (but inadequately coordinated) bureaucracies and territorial administrations, which must coordinate policy but which lack established mechanisms to do so without negotiations and protracted consensus-building efforts.

Second, divergent societal interests become embedded in the various state and Party bureaucracies, experts and technocrats come to play an increasingly potent role, and bureaucracies develop their own distinctive ideologies and cultures. Central, territorial, and bureaucratic leaders cope with the resulting complexity and conflict through accommodation and arduous consensus-building efforts.

Third, though the scope of state planning underwent important changes between 1978 and 1988 (with guidance planning assuming a more prominent role and mandatory planning playing a declining role), the process of moving resources in society was still a political and bureaucratic decision in considerable measure. Without a market to match supply and demand, and voting and preference counting systems practically nonexistent, elaborate bargaining mechanisms developed to fill the void.

Fourth, work by Vivienne Shue goes some distance in further explaining why bargaining activity has been an enduring feature of the Chinese polity under communism.[8] To simplify Shue's rich argument: the Chinese polity is a "honeycomb" structure in which localist and familial values are dominant. The "Center's" capacity to impose its objectives and norms generally is quite limited; the alternative to compulsion has generally been negotiation. This honeycomb structure is the origin of what Naughton called "the implementation bias," that is, the situation in which *every* central initiative will be distorted in favor of the organization or locality responsible for implementation.[9]

7. Jerry F. Hough, *The Soviet Union and Social Science Theory* (Cambridge: Harvard University Press, 1977).

8. Vivienne Shue, *The Reach of the State: Sketches of the Chinese Body Politic* (Stanford: Stanford University Press, 1988).

9. Barry Naughton, "The Decline of Central Control over Investment in Post-Mao China," in *Policy Implementation in Post-Mao China*, ed. David M. Lampton, 51–79 (Berkeley and Los Angeles: University of California Press, 1987).

Fifth, territorial administrations and vertical functional organizations (the *kuai* and the *tiao*) embody a variety of interests,[10] and the minister (*buzhang*) of a ministry has the same rank in the system as a provincial governor (*shengzhang*). With respect to any given issue, specific ministries find that their interests and policy preferences correspond with, or diverge from, those of a complex array of other ministries and territorial units. Local leaders not only are advocates for their own territory's interests, they also are mediators of disputes among the autonomous, but interdependent, vertical hierarchies that intersect in their localities. Local leadership engages in this mediation with its *own* agenda. Central leaders at the commission, vice-premier, and Politburo levels become arbiters among provinces and ministries. One can view the Chinese hierarchy as a top-down command system or, sometimes more accurately, as an inverted sieve in which issues that cannot be resolved at lower levels are kicked up to the next higher level able to negotiate a resolution. As Susan Shirk recounts in chapter 3, there is a desire to resolve conflicts at the lowest possible level. The problem is, however, that deadlocks among entities at lower levels assure that higher levels remain overwhelmed by squabbling subordinates.

Finally, another enduring aspect of the Chinese political milieu is the deeply shared value among both superiors and subordinates that "fairness" exists when there has been "consultation" and when the outcome of "consultation" is not to leave an individual, family, locality, or organization without adequate wherewithal to subsist and accomplish its assigned duties, unless there is a self-evident and overriding social interest that can be demonstrated. Even then, fairness requires that there be "just" compensation. What constitutes "just compensation" can become the subject of protracted negotiation.

In addition to those factors that have accounted for bargaining relationships throughout the Communist era, the first decade of reform created circumstances that favored even more bargaining behavior. Most notably, during the period 1978–88 China was in the awkward transition stage of reform. A small, growing, and dynamic market sector uneasily coexisted with the rigidities of the still dominant administered economy. The scarcities and rigidities of the dominant system provided opportunities (and problems) for the decontrolled sector, and vice versa; bargaining behavior (legal, illegal, and quasi-legal) of all sorts was the result.

Moreover, the pursuit of individual, local, and organizational interest was legitimate in a way in which it never was under Mao. And, the

10. Paul E. Schroeder, "Regional Power in China: Tiao-Tiao Kuai-Kuai Authority in the Chinese Political System" (Ph.D. diss., Ohio State University, 1987).

pursuit of interest became absolutely essential in China's greatly expanded intercourse with the outside world after Mao's death.

Further, the very nature of the post-Mao agenda—modernization and economic growth—lent itself to bargaining, for a number of reasons. The agenda was dominated by economic and technical choices in which the trade-offs among issues were complex, and powerful domestic bureaucracies frequently found themselves at loggerheads without the benefit of market, voting, or command systems adequate to resolve issues.

And finally, structurally, prior to June 1989, there was a carefully balanced Politburo Standing Committee of Zhao Ziyang, Hu Qili, Li Peng, Yao Yilin, and Qiao Shi. The cleavages evident among the bureaucracies and localities were mirrored in the leadership. An elite that could not agree among itself found it difficult to enforce its will on recalcitrant and deadlocked subordinates.

WHAT DO LEADERS BARGAIN OVER?

I shall first indicate the breadth of issues over which bargaining occurs and then examine two specific cases that reveal the process more clearly. While the issues and arenas recounted below emphasize national organizations and national issues, these processes are mirrored throughout the bureaucracy and units at all levels. *The range of policy issues* that generate bargaining is broad. One bargains over what is scarce: in the PRC, financial resources, power and position in the hierarchy, high-quality goods and services, and access to the international system and to highly skilled personnel are among those things most sought.

Bargaining is intense in the budgetary process. Budgetary resources are allocated among the various functional "systems" (*xitong*).[11] Each "system's" prior share of the budget, particularly the "operating" portion of the budget, is the base from which marginal changes are negotiated for the next year—"the fixed sum system."[12] Within "systems" and individual bureaucracies, resources (particularly "operating" resources) are treated as a "lump" (*kuai*) to be "carved up" (*qie*) among subordinate entities according to the percentages previously applicable.[13]

Bargaining, therefore, occurs around the edges of the budget. Which units will suffer marginal cuts and reap modest gains, and which units will have their budgets charged for investments that benefit other systems or organizations, all become important questions.[14] One of the recurring

11. David M. Lampton, Interview File (hereafter I.F.), no. 25 (1982), China, 6.

12. *Foreign Broadcast Information Service: Daily Report, China (FBIS)*, 29 October 1985, K3, from *Renmin Ribao* (People's Daily), 11 October 1985, 5.

13. I.F., no. 25 (1982), China, 2–3.

14. I.F., no. 9 (1982), China, 6.

budgetary issues in building the Gezhouba Dam, for instance, was how much of the budget of the then Ministry of Water Conservancy and Electric Power (MWCEP) should be spent on increasing the lock capacity of the dam to meet the needs of the Ministry of Communications, the agency responsible for inland shipping. The Ministry of Communications could make demands, knowing that the cost of meeting its desires would not come from its budget, because *all* project expenditures are charged against the budget of the lead agency, in this case the MWCEP.[15]

In speaking of how investment allocation decisions are made, Barry Naughton explains, "We can speculate that . . . actual allocation decisions are determined largely by the influence that different Beijing-based bureaucracies can bring to bear, and by various ad hoc sharing arrangements. . . . Ministries struggle to protect their power bases and keep subordinates busy; in order to succeed in this struggle, they must insure that at least their share of the total investment is not too drastically reduced."[16]

Revenue raising also involves negotiation. In the early 1980s, when Beijing was experimenting with a system in which enterprises were being permitted to keep a portion of profits ("profit retention")—which effectively reduced central revenues in the short run—"enterprises negotiated long and hard for the best possible retention rates."[17] As was explained in a 1982 interview in a Beijing ministry, many factories'

> retention rates are decided by the local bureau and province. The State Planning Commission has a "general principle" that the profit retention rate should not be higher than 12–13 percent, though he [the interviewee] noted it has changed every year and the situation has been "chaotic" [*hen luan*]. The average is about 10 percent, though in some cases it is as low as 5–6 percent and in some cases it is higher. [Critical to determining where in the permitted range the allowed profit retention will fall is an assessment of the degree to which the enterprise is disadvantaged by the price system.] . . . For example, the price for agricultural machinery is low and in favor of the peasants. So, they [the agricultural machinery enterprises] cannot change the sales price, but they can try to get to retain a higher percentage of the profit.[18]

Similarly, with the experimental implementation of a tax system in the 1980s that created the prospect of enterprises keeping more money and

15. I.F., no. 7 (1982), China, 9–10. The same process was evident at the Danjiangkou Dam Project.

16. Barry Naughton, "The Decline of Central Control Over Investment in Post-Mao China," in Lampton, ed., *Policy Implementation*, 68.

17. David Bachman, "Implementing Chinese Tax Policy," in Lampton, ed., *Policy Implementation*, 133.

18. I.F., no. 23 (1982), China, 9–10.

then remitting taxes *directly* to the Ministry of Finance (thereby bypassing counties that had previously taken a slice of the financial pie), some counties began to discriminate against enterprises in which the new revenue system was first being introduced, "and may have demanded kickbacks in exchange for supplying the trial enterprises with the desired commodities."[19] In summarizing the politics of the process of moving from a profit remission to a tax-based revenue system, Bachman says:

> In an effort to win approval for *ligaishui* [the substitution of taxes for profit remission], central leaders apparently compromised on contentious issues. The Center made two fateful agreements that have checked the more revolutionary implications [of change]. . . . Beijing stated that enterprises would retain about the same amount of money under [the new system] . . . as they had retained under profit retention. It also announced that there would be no change in the distribution of central-local finances. In other words, to overcome the (potential) resistance of key local interests (factory managers and local officials), the Center agreed that the redistributive dimensions of the *ligaishui* would be minimal.[20]

Lieberthal and Oksenberg note the complex revenue-sharing deals that were worked out in Shanxi province. In speaking of fourteen large coal mines, they observe:

> In the past, these large mines transferred all their profit to the *provincial government*. Under the new revenue system [*ligaishui*], the mines no longer remitted all profits to the province. Instead, they [the mines] retained their profits and paid a tax [to the Center]. . . . The Center then devised a way to compensate Shanxi for this loss in revenue, namely, to reduce the amount which the Center collected in revenue from Shanxi (emphasis added).[21]

Localities and bureaucratic organizations also bargain over new revenue sources and subsidy levels. Authorities in one county explained to me how the Center and localities had negotiated an arrangement whereby localities would build small-scale hydroelectric plants (which the Center wanted) in exchange for the localities' being able to dispose of the resulting revenue as they wished (*yusuanwai*). Moreover, any excess electrical power beyond local needs would be purchased by the centrally managed power grids, at a high price, even if the grid did *not need* (and could not use) the energy at the time the locality wished to sell it.[22]

19. Bachman, "Implementing Tax Policy," 138.

20. Ibid., 141. See also 144.

21. Kenneth Lieberthal and Michel Oksenberg, *Bureaucratic Politics and Chinese Energy Development,* 1987 (prepared for the Department of Commerce, Contract No. 50-SATA-4-16230), 345.

22. I.F., no. 18 (1982), China, 4–5.

In one Beijing interview, the rationale for electrical price subsidies was explained. "I then asked why they subsidize small electrical power plants with higher purchase prices and why they sell power in the Gansu highlands at a way lower price than elsewhere? He said in explaining subsidies, 'political factors are key.' 'Sometimes cost benefit analysis counts for nothing.' . . . [He said] that provinces are important political powers and you can't ignore them."[23] Provinces are potent bargainers because they often are represented in the Central Committee and have complex interpersonal and other ties with those in the elite; because they have the principal power to appoint (with central approval) those occupying key positions in both territorial and functional units within the province; because they often are major sources of central revenue; and, in the end, because it is they who must implement policy.

In late 1987 a group of economic officials was in the United States. On the West Coast they became involved in a discussion about how the government in Washington, D.C., decides where to build various construction projects. They were told by the American respondent that political connections played a decisive role, to which one member of the Chinese group responded, "Why, that's not very different from the way we do things in China."[24]

In the more consumer- and profit-oriented environment of 1978–88, the desire of firms to enter new, growing, and more lucrative markets, and the desire of ministries and enterprises previously in those markets to protect their shares, gave rise to competition and an intense bargaining process. Take washing machines, for instance. They are comparatively simple to make, previously they were manufactured by the light-industry ministry, and they are in high demand, with good profit margins. Predictably, the Ministry of Light Industry did not want the Ministry of Machine Building to begin making washing machines. But, the State Planning Commission (SPC) approved this, and many conferences were held as a result.[25]

Indeed, conferences to bargain over market shares and product lines appear to be a way of life. For example, in 1981 there was a conference on machines for civil use, attended by the SPC, the Ministry of Machine Building, and other related ministries and localities. The conference covered bikes, radios, fans, TVs, watches, clocks, electric meters, refrigerators, sewing machines, and washing machines; it fixed production levels and determined which factories would make what. The conference

23. I.F., no. 25 (1982), China, 4–5.
24. National Committee on U.S.–China Relations, *Notes from the National Committee*, vol. 17, no. 1 (1988): 6.
25. I.F., no. 23 (1982), China, 7–9.

lasted ten days, and the meeting was preceded by discussions that occurred over a year.[26]

Ministries (and other units) also clash continually over their respective
jurisdictions. Oksenberg recounts the difficulties that Bo Yibo encountered in efforts to reduce the overlapping and duplicative organizational
structure in the shipbuilding industry:

> The solution which Bo and other top leaders embraced . . . was to group
> factories in a single industry into a single, independent corporation operat-
> ing directly under the Machine Building Commission. A pilot project in the
> shipbuilding industry was to group the major shipyards in Shanghai into a
> single corporation. Previously, the shipyards were under several jurisdic-
> tions: the Sixth Ministry of Machine Building, the Ministry of Communica-
> tions, and several municipal departments. However, neither the Sixth Minis-
> try nor Communications wished to lose their shipyards. . . . Bo Yibo, with
> the staff of the Machine Building Commission behind him, nevertheless had
> to conduct the extensive negotiations for the formation of the new corpora-
> tion personally. Several trips to Shanghai were necessary. Even then, with all
> of his prestige, the result was a hybrid organization. The ministries con-
> curred only when it was decided the head of the new corporation would be
> one of the vice-ministers of the Sixth Ministry and the head of its board of
> directors would be a vice-minister of communications.[27]

Concisely, therefore, bargains are struck over revenue sources, budgets, personnel, organizational jurisdictions, market shares, production
rights, subsidy levels, investment allocations, and jobs. Anything that is
scarce and is sought by organizations can provide the raison d'être for
bargaining.

WATER PROJECTS: THE BARGAINING PROCESS UP CLOSE

Because water is a scarce resource with multiple uses (with one use
frequently precluding another), and because water traverses administrative boundaries (with upstream users affecting the interests of those
downstream), analyzing how decisions are made in this field clearly reveals the bargaining dimensions of Chinese politics. The controversies
swirling around the planning, construction, and management of the
Danjiangkou and Three Gorges dam projects reveal both the complex
constellation of interests that must be accommodated and the broader
character of the political system, at least with respect to economic, organizational, and technical decisions. Further, both of these projects involve
ongoing decision processes that straddle the Maoist and post-Mao eras;

26. Ibid.
27. Michel Oksenberg, "Economic Policy-Making in China: Summer 1981," *China Quarterly*, no. 90 (1982): 176–77.

they thereby reveal the continual role of bargaining in the Chinese polity, as well as its even more prominent role in the era following the Chairman's death.

The Danjiangkou Dam

The middle and lower reaches of the Han River in Hubei province flood often; it is a constant menace to the major metropolis of Wuhan at the confluence of the Han and Yangtze rivers. In 1955 China's government began a flood-diversion project along the Han (Dujiatai), which was part of a more comprehensive development plan for the entire Han River Basin. In 1958 the State Council approved construction of the Danjiangkou Dam as stage two of that development effort.

During its construction a number of problems slowed the project, as is detailed elsewhere.[28] Here the focus is on several issues that became the foci of protracted bargaining during the planning, construction, and management phases: the dam's height; the priorities to be assigned irrigation, flood control, and electrical power generation; the problem of relocating displaced persons; and the issue of local opposition.

When construction started on Danjiangkou, the dam's *initially planned* height was 175 meters, with the water level to be maintained at 170 meters (above sea level).[29] However, throughout the entire construction phase (which ended in 1974), there was intense controversy over what the dam's height should, in fact, be. During construction, the bargaining process produced agreed-upon dam heights of 140 meters, 152 meters, and 162 meters, as well as the initial height of 175. Throughout much of the construction period, no one knew how high the dam would be; the foundation that was built could support a much higher dam. Further, even in 1989, debate was still going on about whether to heighten the dam—sixteen years after construction was "finished."

In 1965 the planners (who wished to minimize construction and displaced-person costs) accepted a dam height of 152 meters, but Hubei and Henan provinces (the two provinces that shared the resulting reservoir) wanted a higher dam (so they would get more electrical power and irrigation water). In 1966 the dam was approved for 162 meters (which Hubei and Henan wanted), but the water level was to stay at the 145-meter level (as in the 152-meter dam) until the problem of what to do with displaced persons could be solved. The negotiating process produced a perfectly predictable outcome. The difference between the two sides was split down the middle, with one side getting an acceptable dam height and the other avoiding the immediate problem of displaced per-

28. David M. Lampton, "Water: Challenge to a Fragmented Political System," in Lampton, ed., *Policy Implementation*, 157–89.
29. I.F., no. 5 (1982), China, 7.

sons and attendant costs.[30] One interviewee explained: "In 1965 . . . the
Center approved a revised dam height of 152 meters with a water level
of 145 meters. Because Hubei and Henan were unhappy with this . . .
the Center agreed in 1966 to a 162-meter dam, with an initial water level
of 145 meters to gradually be raised to 157 meters as the relocation
problem was solved."[31]

The essence of the problem was that as the dam's height rose the
opposition of counties and special districts that would be inundated became more intense; the number of persons who would be displaced
would grow, and the number of cadres who would lose jobs would esca-
late, and all of this would greatly magnify political conflict and increase
expenditures. The kernel of the bargaining outcome was that nobody
got all of what they wanted, when they wanted it; few persons, organizations, or localities lost everything (at least immediately); and the number
of dislocated persons and financial expenditures rose more gradually
than would have been the case had they proceeded with the initial plan.

Though we cannot see the entire bargaining process, aspects of it are
clear. One of the most contentious issues concerned the fact that Hubei
province would get most of the flood control and electric power benefits
and Henan province would get excessive numbers of refugees (in proportion to its benefits). Intense negotiations between the two provinces were
conducted to redress this imbalance.

> The leadership of the two provinces got together and Hubei agreed to take
> 80,000 of Henan's displaced persons (*yimin*). According to *central* figures,
> there were a total of 356,000 refugees, with 130,000 in Henan and 226,000
> in Hubei province. . . . They said the *local* figures put the total number of
> displaced persons at 390,000 [obviously higher than the central estimate]. I
> asked why Hubei agreed to assume the burden and was told plainly that
> Henan was poor, their displaced persons' plight was worse, and "Henan's
> benefits from the reservoir were not as great."[32]

Perhaps because the Center pays local authorities for each displaced
person, the central authorities had an estimate for displaced persons well
below that of the local authorities, whose receipts went up with the
number of refugees. In this kind of bargaining situation, proponents
tend to minimize costs imposed on others and puff up the benefits to
localities; the localities whine about the damage and *mafan* ("bother")
and deprecate their benefits.

These negotiations resulted in a written agreement between Hubei
and Henan, an agreement that specified the distribution of electric

30. I.F., no. 9 (1982), China, 3–4.
31. I.F., no. 11 (1982), China, 4.
32. Ibid., 4–5.

power, water, and displaced persons.[33] Henan, though poorer and weaker than Hubei along many dimensions, did quite well in the bargaining process. Why? First, desperation can be a valuable political resource. Henan's provincial leaders could continually argue that if the refugee problem was not adequately solved, they would be unable to effectively remove people from areas to be inundated. In all political systems, people who are highly motivated to resist can exact large tolls. Second, the delays that Henan could impose on "closing" a deal were, in themselves, very expensive for Hubei. Every year that Wuhan's industries were starved for power and floods caused destruction all along the Han River proved enormously costly to Hubei. Just by being able to slow progress, Henan could inflict costs on Hubei higher than the concessions Hubei would have to provide Henan to close a deal. In short, the weak can be strong!

A second ongoing issue has been whether the principal use of Danjiangkou should be electrical-power generation, flood control, or irrigation. To manage the dam to maximize one objective is to diminish the extent to which the other purposes can be fully realized. To use water for irrigation means that less water flows through the turbines to generate power. "The contradiction is sharp," I was told in one interview.[34] To maximize power output, the water level needs to be kept high; to provide insurance against flood, the water level should be kept low. To irrigate fields, the water level should be high, but water should not run through turbines and thereafter "uselessly" (from the vantage point of the local farmer) flow downstream.

Each of these purposes is not only of more importance to some mass constituencies than others (e.g., electrical power for industry and water for peasants, to greatly oversimplify), each purpose is also organizationally embodied in a particular ministry or set of bureaus within ministries. Agricultural concerns are the responsibility of the Ministry of Agriculture, Forestry, and Animal Husbandry. Electrical power has its bureaucratic proponents in the Electrical Power Ministry (or in the Electrical Power Bureau when there is a consolidated Ministry of Water Resources and Electrical Power), heavy industrial organizations, and big urban areas with great concentrations of population and industry. As for flood control, the Ministry of Water Conservancy historically has seen itself as the defender of the peasantry against flood. Territorial actors also have different interests. For instance, with respect to Danjiangkou, Henan province (upstream) was concerned primarily about irrigation water (although Zhengzhou did want more electrical power), and Hubei's provin-

33. I.F., no. 26 (1983), U.S., 2.
34. I.F., no. 10 (1982), China, 3.

cial government (downstream) was more concerned with flood control and Wuhan's electrically starved industry (e.g., Wuhan Iron and Steel). One sees, therefore, a Byzantine process of negotiation within provinces (between the province and "its" special districts and municipalities and the many vertical functional organizations that intersect in its domain) and between and among provinces.

In the case of Danjiangkou, complex and literally never-ending discussions among ministries and localities occurred over the dam's utilization priorities. Initially, flood prevention was the first priority, followed by electrical power, irrigation, navigation, and aquaculture, in that order.[35] Since then each ministry keeps raising the issue of the priority of "its" use, continually trying to reopen the case in order to better its position.[36] Issues frequently are never resolved; they just ebb and flow over time.

Another contentious issue that resulted in the dam's not being built to its designed height, an issue that still weighed against raising it in the late 1980s, is the opposition of localities along the reservoir's edge. My interview notes recount:

> Another reason the 175-meter dam was not built as planned . . . was because of the displaced persons problem. The fact is, I was told, that Henan province, even though it had no particular need for the flood control aspects of this dam, would agree to the higher dam, but it was Henan's Nanyang Special District which adamantly opposed it then, and does today, for the obvious reason that it would be one of the areas to be inundated heavily.[37]

> In Hubei province, it is Jun Xian [county], with a long and illustrious history dating from the Tang, and Yun Xian. In Henan province it is Zhechuan Xian. These three old county towns would go under water and Xiangyang Special District in Hubei province and Nanyang Special District in Henan opposed it. According to . . . [my interviewee], the provincial government in Henan would go along with this [raising the dam] because of the benefits to Zhengzhou [the provincial capital] and irrigation, but they can't persuade the affected localities.[38]

The Three Gorges Project

The Three Gorges, which sits astride the Hubei and Sichuan border, is a strategic choke-point at which floods that originate in Sichuan province (and devastate Hubei, Hunan, and other localities downstream) could theoretically be contained. Moreover, the reservoir that would be formed by a dam in the Three Gorges could drive turbines that would energize

35. I.F., no. 9 (1982), China, 1.
36. I.F., no. 21 (1982), China, 5.
37. I.F., no. 9 (1982), China, 5.
38. Ibid., 7.

much of central and eastern China's energy-starved industry. Finally, raising the water level in the gorges could improve navigation and increase the size of ships able to reach Chongqing, now China's largest city. So strategic is the Three Gorges that leaders from Sun Yatsen, through Mao Zedong, to Deng Xiaoping, Zhao Ziyang, and Li Peng have considered the project.

The undertaking has been approved at least twice "in principle" in the post-1949 era (once in 1958 at the Chengdu Conference and again in April 1984),[39] only to have the start of construction aborted because approval to commence actual building had been made contingent upon the resolution of myriad, presumably minor, technical, financial, and political details, such as, How high should the dam be? What is to be done with the displaced persons, inundated factories, cadres out of work, grain production and tax revenues that would evaporate, and administrative centers? Who pays, how much, for all this relocation, and where do you put the people? What would be the effect of such a huge project on upstream fisheries and estuaries and harbors above and below the dam? What would be the useful life of the dam, given siltation? How will shipping across the dam be affected, and how much shipping growth is it prudent to plan for? Is flood control best achieved by one gigantic project, or several smaller ones? Who will receive the resulting electrical power? Can it be efficiently transmitted to distant locations where it is most urgently needed, and at what cost? Is a dam of this scale safe? Or would it be, as Mao and the Ministry of National Defense at times feared, a huge "bowl of water on our heads"?

Each of these questions has no obvious answer, and the various possibilities all have their popular and bureaucratic constituencies, which are not averse to making their case in protracted consultations. I shall not recount here the more than three decades of the project's tribulations; these have been well documented elsewhere.[40] But I can advance a generalization that I believe will accurately predict both bureaucratic and local behavior most of the time—an "iron law of bargaining." The locality or bureaucracy will almost always exaggerate the costs that another unit's proposal will inflict, minimize the benefits received, exaggerate the *mafan* (bother) to itself, exaggerate the benefits others receive, understate its own resources, overstate the resources of others, and generate one-sided data supportive of its case.

As a result of such processes, in the case of the Three Gorges Project, promoters of the project face a bargaining dilemma: to weld a coalition big enough to win support for the dam, they must provide benefits to a

39. I.F., no. 26 (1983), U.S., 1; also, Lieberthal and Oksenberg, *Bureaucratic Politics,* chap. 6.
40. Lieberthal and Oksenberg, chap. 6.

vast constellation of groups. But this requires a dam so enormous that the resulting costs and negative outcomes create intense opposition, high financial expenditures, and other risks that top decision-makers are loath to ignore.

The system has been unable to reach closure on this issue after almost three decades of wrangling. In May 1983 the State Planning Commission (SPC), then headed by Yao Yilin, convened a meeting to assess the Three Gorges feasibility study, which had been submitted to it by the MWCEP and the Yangtze River Valley Planning Office (YRVPO). This study assumed a water level of 150 meters, which was comparatively low and thereby would reduce both negative outcomes (displaced persons and inundated urban and rural land) and simultaneously reduce benefits (to shipping, flood control, and electrical-power generation). Yao declared:

> For more than twenty years the debate over the Three Gorges water resources project has concentrated principally on the problem of the dam's height. That a high dam generates more electricity and that the flood control results are better is easy to see. However, the inundation is too much, the investment is too big, the masses upstream are unable to agree, the burdens on the state finance also cannot be borne. However, the relevant ministries and localities have not been reconciled to the low dam and, because of this we have debated for many years and still are unable to decide. If we continue to debate, I think this generation of ours will be unable to accomplish anything on this.[41]

The battle continues without respite. In December 1988 the cover on *Beijing Review* proclaimed, "Three Gorges Project Given the Go-Ahead." Scarcely a month later Vice-Premier Yao told the fourth meeting of the Standing Committee of the Seventh Chinese People's Political Consultative Conference, "In the next five years, it is absolutely impossible to start the Sanxia Project, so people do not need to spend too much energy debating the issue for the time being."[42]

WHO BARGAINS, IN WHAT ARENAS, AND WHAT STRATEGIES ARE EMPLOYED?

Who Bargains?

Generally, only *proximate leaders* bargain—that is, equals in the hierarchy, and entities (persons, organizations, factions, localities) one step above and one step below that level. These are the actors that can legitimately make demands. For instance, provinces bargain with one another and

41. Li Rui, *Lun San Xia Gongcheng* (Hunan: Hunan Kexue jishu chubanshe, 1985), 135–36. This quote is cited in Lieberthal and Oksenberg, 304.

42. *Zhongguo Tongxun She* (China Bulletin), Hong Kong, 23 January 1989, in *FBIS*, no. 16 (1989), 33.

with ministries as equals, with prefectures and counties immediately below, and with the primary central commissions (e.g., the SPC, the State
Economic Commission, etc.) immediately above.

One's capacity to affect policy content (as distinct from implementation) diminishes greatly as one moves downward *from the point of decision.*
In policy formulation, bargaining goes on between the principal bureaucracies and territorial administrations, except at the lower reaches of the
hierarchy, where low-level territorial and bureaucratic actors must take
account of the very real, albeit more diffuse, social forces that they seek
to manage. Nonetheless, there is a representative quality to the process,
inasmuch as each bureaucratic or territorial actor sees part of its job as
being to reflect at least the minimal interests of subordinates, not so
much out of democratic considerations as out of the realization that
effective implementation requires the cooperation of subordinates and
the realization that one's own interests are inextricably linked to one's
organization or locality.

Depending on the policy issue, the *implementation* process not only
involves intense bargaining among the territorial and functional bureaucracies, it also frequently involves officials dealing with a broad range of
individuals and small social groups that have no formal standing or
political role, yet who must be reckoned with if policy is to be effectively
implemented, at least without coercion. As the modernization of China
proceeds, the fragmentation of Chinese society proceeds apace, and as it
does, the array of social forces affecting implementation will multiply. As
this occurs traditional Chinese fears of chaos and immobilization are not
unwarranted.

How to meet urgent problems, of a vast scale in a timely manner, in a
bargaining system that seeks consensus amidst increasing pluralization is
a genuine problem for the system. Obviously, there are alternative tools
at hand, such as command and hierarchy or greater use of the market.
Each of these also has liabilities; more command and hierarchy reduces
flexibility and innovation; increased use of the market increases inequali-
ties and accelerates pluralization.

In What Arenas Does Bargaining Occur?

There are several arenas (or types of arenas) that play central and recurrent roles: the SPC, other commissions, the Standing Committee of the
State Council,[43] the Politburo, state councillors, ad hoc interprovincial
and interministerial committees, the National People's Congress, the national finance and planning conferences, materials-allocation confer-

43. Michel Oksenberg, "Economic Policy-Making In China," 174–80, provides an excellent description of the roles of commissions, vice-premiers, the SPC, and the Standing
Committee of the State Council.

ences, central work conferences, and specific policy-issue committees. *These forums are replicated at all system levels.* At this, we see only the tip of the iceberg of conflict-resolving arenas. Below I concentrate simply on national arenas.

The SPC (in 1989 consisting of the pre–April 1988 State Planning Commission and the old State Economic Commission) is one of the most important bargaining arenas. As a commission, the SPC stands as a buffer between individual ministries and the State Council. In an interview I was told that the way in which allocations among ministries are determined is "complicated" and that there is "lots of discussion." The interviewee went on to say that every province and municipality wants allocations that they consider small but that become a huge sum when aggregated. The SPC is the organ charged with mediating these conflicting claims and avoiding deficits and material bottlenecks.[44] Because the SPC is divided into functional bureaus, conflict patterns within the organization tend to reflect those in the wider bureaucratic environment.[45]

Another, and indeed higher, arena for bargaining among territorial and functional interests is the State Council, meaning either its Standing Committee (with a large permanent bureaucracy of its own, which needs a great deal more study) or the entire State Council. Conflicts that cannot be resolved by individual commissions or ministries are referred upward to this next higher level. For instance, to paraphrase one interviewee, "Say there is a high value investment to be made . . . and say four provinces or municipalities all want it . . . obviously this is a difficult task. . . . The SPC can reach agreement with mayors, but if that is not possible, it then goes to the Standing Committee of the State Council."[46]

It appears from my interviews, as well as from the work of Oksenberg, that one of the key systemic problems is that an excessive number of issues cannot be resolved by the ministries and localities themselves, even though, as Susan Shirk says in chapter 3, there is a desire to resolve issues at the lowest possible level. This can overwhelm the top echelons of the State Council (and Politburo) in a Niagara Falls of issues, a torrent whose volume is greatly increased by the fact that market mechanisms are not in place that elsewhere greatly reduce the number of items requiring conscious bureaucratic (political) decision in the first place.

In an effort to reduce the number of issues kicked to the next higher level, the Chinese have repeatedly tried to merge organizations that habitually conflict (and yet need to coordinate policy). The Water Conservancy and Electric Power ministries are just one of several such cases. In 1982, for instance, the Water Conservancy and Electric Power

44. I.F., no. 24 (1982), China, 7 and 4.
45. I.F., no. 27 (1983), U.S., 1.
46. I.F., no. 24 (1982), China, 5.

ministries were merged. As one interviewee expressed the logic of the move, discussions would now be "in the family" rather than "between families."[47] This union ended in divorce in April 1988, once again, with the re-creation of the Ministry of Water Resources and the merger of the Electric Power Ministry and other units into a new Ministry of Energy Resources.[48] What is fascinating is that even when the water-conservancy people had been joined in a "shotgun union" with the electric-power people, individuals from each of the old ministries still referred to their new organization as the Ministry of Water Conservancy and Ministry of Electric Power, respectively.

Not only are conflicts resolved in the SPC and the State Council, there also is a rich repertoire of regularized and ad hoc procedures, conferences, and committees to resolve disputes in both the *formulation and the implementation* phases of the policy process at all system levels. Among the most important are the National Finance Conference and the National Planning Conference. One informant described the National Planning Conference as a Chinese market in which delegations from various provinces and ministries worked out deals. Lieberthal and Oksenberg explain that in the planning process the Ministry of Finance (MOF)

> must go over the draft plan from the SPC with a view to its financial feasibility and implications. Not surprisingly, the perspectives of the three major participants in this process (the line ministries and provinces; the SPC; and the Ministry of Finance) often differ as to both the revenue and expenditure implications of their proposals. . . . The key forums for resolving the differences among these various groups in the annual planning cycle were generally the National Planning Conference and the National Finance Conference. . . . Since not all problems could be solved at these meetings, a central work conference that brought together provincial Party first secretaries as well as Politburo members and other key officials usually met to reach final decision on particularly contentious issues. The Politburo itself met separately to determine its position, where necessary.[49]

When the Politburo finds itself deadlocked, the supreme leader, in this case Deng Xiaoping, and before him Mao Zedong, becomes the court of last resort. From a system-development perspective, the critical questions for the future are these: Will the system be able to reduce the number of issues bumped up to this level for resolution? And will individual leaders assume less importance as institutions achieve greater legitimacy?

Finally, one of the most interesting developments of the first decade of reform in the post-Mao era was the rise of the National, and local,

47. I.F., no. 25 (1982), China, 1.
48. *Beijing Review* 31, no. 7 (1988): 10–11.
49. Lieberthal and Oksenberg, *Bureaucratic Politics*, 61.

People's Congress (NPC) as an arena for bargaining. For instance, during the March 1989 session of the NPC, *Xinhua* carried the following report, quoting one NPC deputy named Yang Lieyu: "However, he noted, as most provincial governors and mayors of major cities are NPC deputies, who usually spoke a lot, asking for everything ranging from favorable policies to energy and raw materials, from cabinet members and ministers, deputies' group discussions sometimes became bargaining sessions between the central government and local authorities."[50]

Strategies for Bargaining and the Necessary Resources

Strategies are contingent upon the actor under consideration, the policy issue in question, whether one is trying to promote, or frustrate, a specific initiative, the bundle of interrelated issues on the agenda at the same time, one's resources and position in the hierarchy, and the wider social-political-economic contexts. A few examples may serve to illustrate the rich and sophisticated diversity of strategies employed.

Foot-in-the-door and "fishing projects." In this gambit, the bargainer tries to secure a commitment that will permit work on a project to start. The idea is to obtain an initial commitment that is nonthreatening to potential or actual adversaries but that will not preclude the possibility of enlarging the project at some later date, thereby creating a situation in which each stage's sunk costs (combined with the presumed benefits of the next phase) become justification for taking the next step toward the initiator's ultimate objective.

At the Fourth Session of the Sixth National Chinese People's Political Consultative Conference, a speech by Qian Jiaju concisely explains the strategy: "In the past 30-odd years . . . we had a fondness for big projects but ignored actual effects, and thus paid an enormous price . . . from those "fishing projects" (which were said to need limited investment at the beginning according to the planners but later involved more and more additional funds after they were started). We should not follow this stupid practice any more."[51]

For this strategy to work, several conditions must be met and several resources must be in the bargainer's possession. First, and most important, the decision under consideration must be separable into stages, and each stage must generate sufficient benefits to be defensible in its own terms. For instance, dams can be raised, and each level of dam can, at least possibly, provide benefits that justify each step in its own terms. Obviously, some decisions are all or nothing, and any benefits are contin-

50. *Xinhua*, in English, 28 March 1989, in *FBIS*, no. 59 (1989), 20.
51. *FBIS*, no. 99 (1986), W4.

gent on completion of the whole process. Such issues make this strategy difficult to employ.

The bargainer seeking to use this strategy must have the capacity to disguise "his" ultimate objective, or at least convince potential opponents that the first step will not offend their interests and that subsequent steps are not preordained. Some decisions cannot credibly meet this condition, and some bargainers simply are too identified with the ultimate objective to disassociate themselves from it. For instance, because the YRVPO has worked for a *high* Three Gorges Dam for decades, any attempt by it to promote a more modest project would be seen as the entering wedge for its more expansive ambitions.

Whipping Up Support and Faits Accomplis.   In this strategy, local or ministerial leaders use the media to fan support for a project, begin work on it, and then point to their responsiveness to "public opinion" as the rationale for, in effect, having presented superiors with a fait accompli. "And, if one whips up opinion through newspapers and broadcasting stations and starts the so-called preliminary work before the feasibility study of a project is completed, so as to make the project an accomplished fact and force the central authorities to agree with the plan, one's practice, I think, is definitely a violation of the basic procedure."[52]

For this strategy to be feasible, the bargainer must have resources that he or she can independently deploy without central approval. As Naughton points out in his study of the loss of central control over investment resources, the "localization" of control over capital was one of the most profound changes of the first decade of post-Mao reform.[53] The combination of decentralized resources *and* decentralized decision authority have created a situation in which the Center has been presented with faits accomplis on an enormous scale in the capital construction area.

Another precondition for this strategy to be effective is that the sanctions for presenting higher authorities with faits accomplis cannot be too severe. The fact that so many local leaders have felt free to proceed in defiance of central preferences is one indication of the Center's diminished reach in the wake of 1980s reform.

Painting a Rosy or a Black Picture—Cooking the Books.   In the same way that supporters of an initiative try to minimize perceived costs and uncertainties, opponents frequently exaggerate them. For instance, in one interview I asked about the price tag for the Three Gorges Project,

52. Ibid.
53. Naughton, "Decline of Central Control," 51–79.

noting that I had seen cost estimates that varied by a factor of five. My respondent, who was an ardent supporter of the project, bluntly replied that those who advance extremely high estimates "oppose the Three Gorges Project."[54]

For this strategy to be effective, the bargainer must possess seemingly credible information. It is no accident that each ministry and locality has its own statistical units that tend to produce data supportive of local or organizational goals. I noted above, for instance, that central and local estimates concerning the number of refugees that would be generated by the Danjiangkou Dam diverged in a predictable fashion, with each side of the dispute promoting data most consistent with its interests. Similarly, respondents at one ministry at which I interviewed assumed that the figures I quoted from another ministry had been distorted in a way consistent with that other ministry's interests. One implication of this process is, of course, that more information will not necessarily speed up the decision process, unless the data are collected using agreed-upon methodologies in the first place.

A Little Something for Everyone.   This is a coalition-building process in which the scale of an undertaking is enlarged to provide benefits to all of the strategic groups that could obstruct agreement. In cases such as the Three Gorges Project, there may exist a situation in which any enlargement of the scale of the project not only attracts some wavering elements, it also scares away others by virtue of the project's very size. The costs of building a big enough coalition may simply be prohibitive, both economically and politically.

Getting to Key Decision-Makers, "Old Friends," and Relatives.   The utilization of political networks cannot be overlooked.[55] In the bargaining process, one's success may hinge on the "connections" (*guanxi*) one possesses and the IOUs that can be collected. Personal networks, though not limited to organizations, are built into them. A leader, such as Yu Qiuli, who has extensive personal networks throughout the planning, energy, and military bureaucracies has great power and influence, not only because he directly controls powerful organizations, but also because he has been able to place loyal friends into a broad range of other organizations.[56]

When asked how political actors promote their interests, one inter-

54. I.F., no. 7 (1982), China, 11.

55. John W. Lewis, "Political Networks and the Chinese Policy Process," an occasional paper of the Northeast Asia–United States Forum on International Policy (Stanford University, 1986).

56. David M. Lampton, *Paths to Power: Elite Mobility in Contemporary China* (Ann Arbor: Center for Chinese Studies, 1986), chap. 5.

viewee placed particular emphasis on face-to-face meetings with decision-makers and contacts with old friends. Close personal ties with decision-makers, he asserted, could be decisive.[57] Also not to be overlooked, in the "new China" as in the "old," marriage patterns establish lines of influence and obligation that can be decisive in certain bargaining settings (we need to know a great deal more about this).

THE IMPLICATIONS OF A BARGAINING SYSTEM VIEW

What are some of the practical consequences of bargaining for both the process of making policy and the outputs and outcomes of that process? I believe that five consequences are of particular importance:

Decisions generally are slow in coming; the process of consensus building and negotiation is protracted. The more geographic areas and functional systems that must be involved in the process the more laborious will be the process of negotiation.

It is difficult to definitively say when a decision really has been made. Frequently, decisions are made "in principle," with nettlesome details left for future resolution. The requisite resolution of these details may never occur. Decisions concerning the building of nuclear power plants and the Three Gorges Project are excellent examples of this phenomenon.[58] There is an indeterminacy to outcomes. Issues seem to rise like Lazarus on the agenda; they never stay buried. This process is the political equivalent of protracted guerrilla warfare.

Even once a policy is formulated and adopted, the implementation process is characterized by negotiation among and between levels of the hierarchy, sometimes all the way down to the grass roots. Each level slightly deflects policy in a direction favorable to its interests; by the time one has moved through six, seven, or more layers of the system, the cumulative distortion (not to mention bureaucratic constipation) can be great. Almost invariably, unanticipated and unwelcome consequences are part of the implementation process from the Center's perspective.

One of the biggest mistakes that the Center can make is to set too many high-priority goals simultaneously. For both formulation and implementation to be effective, the elite must be united on the objective and willing to expend considerable political and economic resources as a seemingly endless bargaining process unfolds. There

---

57. I.F., no. 27 (1983), U.S., 2.

58. James Reardon-Anderson, "China's Decision to Go Nuclear," paper presented at the 15th Sino-American Conference, Taipei, Taiwan, June 8–14, 1986.

is no substitute for elite attention *and* the focused use of resources in the bargaining process. However, the ability to focus elite attention and resources is often diluted by divergent priorities among elite members, their different support bases, and the shared desire of the entire leadership to produce rapid change. This shared desire to produce rapid change almost assures that the elite will bite off more than it can chew.

Because bargaining is extensive, the legal framework is poorly developed, and social norms and system legitimacy suffered egregious harm in the Cultural Revolution era, it is exceedingly difficult to separate legitimate and necessary bargaining activity from corruption. It is essential that the system create a legal framework and affirm widely shared values, procedures, and norms to govern this activity. The race is between the process of establishing these norms and the loss of system legitimacy. This may be the most important race in which Beijing's leaders are running.

THREE

The Chinese Political System and the Political Strategy of Economic Reform

Susan L. Shirk

The greatest challenge of China's economic reform is the political one. The national leaders who seek to improve the functioning of the economy by introducing market reforms must formulate and implement these reforms through the Communist political system. Their political strategy of economic reform, if it is to succeed, must reflect the actual power relationships operating in the political realm. The political system is not static, however; economic reforms in communist states usually are accompanied by some reform of the communist political system. Changes in the political institutions and rules of the game modify the context in which bargaining over economic reform policies occurs. From the standpoint of communist political elites, political reforms, such as modification of the relationship between the Communist Party and the government, are instruments for furthering economic reforms, important elements of their political strategy of economic reform.

Political bargaining over policy proposals for economic reform is very intense. A transformation of the economic structure involves redistributing authority and rewards among sectors, bureaucratic agencies, and regions. Those who benefit from market reforms naturally support them and strive to get the best possible deal under the new rules. The groups who were favored and protected by the old command economy and who feel threatened by changes in the economic system resist the reforms or fight to retain as much of their original privileges as they can. As Vice-Premier Tian Jiyun observed in a 1986 speech: "The overall reform of the economic structure is, in a sense, a readjustment of power and interest, in which a large amount of contradictions exist. Among them, there are contradictions between the central authorities and the localities; between the state, the collective, and the individual; between

59

one department and another; between one locality and another; between departments and localities; and so on and so forth" (Tian 1986).

Theoretically, these changes in the economic system, by increasing efficiency, should benefit everyone. But as economic theorists have observed, the redistributive effects of changes in the rules of the economic game are bound to create group conflict (Pratt and Zeckhauser 1985). Only if there is an institutional framework for resolving these conflicts through bargaining will economic restructuring occur.

In this chapter I examine the formal institutional relationships and rules of the game governing national economic policy-making as they have evolved during the 1980s in China. I argue that the political strategy of economic reform devised by Deng Xiaoping and Zhao Ziyang has used effectively the institutions of the Chinese political system to bargain with various groups and build support for reforms; but by compromising and postponing the most contentious issues, the strategy created new economic problems, which put political obstacles in the path of reform.

THE RELATIONSHIP BETWEEN THE COMMUNIST PARTY AND THE GOVERNMENT: PRINCIPAL AND AGENT

The relationship between the Communist Party and the government is at the core of any Leninist political system. The Party is "the organized expression of the will of society" (Schurmann 1968, 110). It leads the work of the government (usually called by Chinese the "state," *guojia*), but remains distinct from the government.

Although the Chinese Communist Party (CCP) is intertwined with the state and with the society, it is a distinct political institution.[1] The CCP is an elite membership organization with 47.75 million members, less than 5 percent of China's total population (*Xinhua*, 17 June 1988). Most Party members are employed as workers, farmers, professionals, and so forth and only participate in Party activities part-time. Yet they are required to obey the direction of Party committees within their work unit and at higher levels. When I talk about the "Party" I am referring to it as a formal bureaucratic institution with over 1 million professional, full-time staff called Party cadres and a permanent structure at all levels of the political system. At the apex of the CCP is the national Party organization headed by the Standing Committee of the Politburo, the Politburo, and

---

1. This view of the Communist Party as an institution distinct from the government challenges Lieberthal and Oksenberg's perspective of a merged institutional structure (1988). While I agree with Lieberthal and Oksenberg that there is a unified chain of command at the apex of the Chinese political system, I see this authority structure as a manifestation of the delegation relationship between Party and government, not as evidence of the lack of boundaries between Party and government.

the Central Committee, which are served by a Secretariat and other departments. At provincial, municipal, and county levels there are similar leadership bodies (CCP committees) and staff offices. Every agency of the national, provincial, and county governments has within it a Party committee and, until recently, a Party leading group. Although some members of these Party oversight bodies play two roles, as both government and Party officials, these bodies are clearly defined as part of the Communist Party.

The language of Western institutional economics is useful for conceptualizing the formal authority relationship between Communist Party and government: It is an "agency relationship" in which the Communist Party is the "principal" and the government is the "agent." The Party has formal political authority over the government, which does the actual work of administering the country. The Party's authority over the government is based primarily on its authority to appoint and promote government officials (*nomenklatura*) (Burns 1987).[2] The Party also sets the general policy line (*luxian*), which the government implements, and oversees the work of the government. Finally, it is responsible for the ideological remolding of government cadres and of all other members of society.[3]

The relationship is analogous to the relationship between the ruling party and the government bureaucracy in a democratic system. (In a parliamentary democracy, the majority party in Parliament appoints the cabinet and directs the work of the bureaucracy. In a presidential democracy, two principals, the president and Congress, lead the bureaucracy.)[4] The Party politicians oversee the work of the government bureaucracy. The bureaucrats may appear to work autonomously, because the politicians intervene infrequently. But the bureaucrats know that they cannot stray too far from the preferences of their principals. If they do, they will be publicly criticized and fired by their political masters, a lesson that Ann Burford (head of the U.S. Environmental Protection Agency) and Yang Zhong (PRC Minister of Forests) learned the hard way.

The crucial difference between communist and democratic systems is

2. According to the Constitution, top positions in the state bureaucracy are filled by the National People's Congress, but, as Yan Jiaqi says, "the political reality is that the candidates nominated or recommended by the CCP are always elected" (Yan Jiaqi 1988).

3. "In authoritarian systems without active legislatures, the principal form of control over the bureaucracy has been the mass party, particularly its Leninist variant. The Leninist party exercises control over the bureaucracy by managing appointments and promotions, monopolizing leading posts, supervising the indoctrination of state officials, disciplining Party members who hold government positions, and setting the bureaucracy's principal policy guidelines" (Harding 1981).

4. For an interesting comparison of Party-government relations in democratic and socialist systems, see Yan Jiaqi (1988).

the political accountability of the principals. In communist systems the Communist Party is not formally accountable to the citizenry; it claims to reflect the will of the people by leading them toward a communist future, but there is no institutional mechanism making them accountable to citizens' present preferences. In a democracy, the politicans are elected and therefore are the agents of their constituents. If they enact policies or allow their bureaucratic agents to take actions that violate their constituents' perceived interests, they will be voted out at the next election.

Although the Communist Party has the ultimate authority in a communist polity, it cannot administer the country on its own. Like any principal in a large organization, it has limited information. The only way for a principal to solve this problem of limited information is to delegate authority to agents. The Communist Party allows the government bureaucracy to make and implement policies because the bureaucrats have better information than Party leaders can possibly have. The bureaucrats have specialized information, while the Party leaders must know about everything; the bureaucrats are close to the problem, whereas the Party leaders are remote.

Once a principal has delegated authority to its agents, the problem of control arises. How does the Communist Party know whether government bureaucrats are carrying out policies that conform with the Party's preferences? Bureaucratic agents naturally distort the information they pass up to their political masters, in order to place themselves in a good light. In democracies, elected politicians manage the agency problems of "hidden action" and "hidden information" through various mechanisms (Arrow 1985). They require regular submission of reports, hold public hearings, or enfranchise interest groups to scrutinize administrative actions. By empowering concerned groups to oversee bureaucratic agencies, they reduce the costs of constant monitoring while guaranteeing that their influential constituents are satisfied. As elected politicians, they do not need to know about all actions of appointed officials, only those actions that might displease their constituents. As Mathew McCubbins and Tom Schwartz put it, democratic politicians prefer a "fire alarm" approach to the control of bureaucratic agents to the much more costly "police patrol" approach (McCubbins and Schwartz 1984). In communist political systems, however, the Communist Party is reluctant to enfranchise constituent groups to oversee government operations; the Party's political monopoly depends on the political demobilization of the population. Without the help of citizen groups, Party leaders have a particularly difficult time acquiring information about government actions. Despite their two-thousand-year tradition of bureaucratic authoritarianism, the

Chinese are no better than any other communist regime at monitoring bureaucratic behavior.[5]

Faced with this structural problem (and the immediate practical problem of controlling bureaucrats who had served the pre-Communist regime), Soviet Communist Party leaders in 1919 developed a method that we now call "parallel rule." The Chinese system of Party control over the government is essentially identical to the Soviet system on which it was modeled. Communist Party members are appointed to the top positions in government agencies, and in each agency all Party members are organized under a Party committee (subordinate to the Party committee at the next level). The hierarchy of government organs is overlaid by a parallel hierarchy of Party committees that enables Party leaders to supervise Party members in the government and lead the work of the government.

The Communist parties in both the Soviet Union and China established specialized functional departments at central and provincial levels to oversee the work of government economic agencies. Staffed by specialists, these Party organs for agriculture, industry, finance, and so forth gradually took over the policy-making functions from the government, especially at the provincial level.[6] The state administrative apparatus became redundant, a "duplicate administrative structure," as Lin Biao described it in 1969 (Harding 1981, 284). The Communist Party became the locus of bargaining over economic policies. A 1953 regulation, "The Decision on the Central Authorities' Leadership Over the Work of the Government," formalized this fact: "All the major and important general and specific government policies, and all major questions concerning the government's work, must first be submitted to the central authorities for examination and approval. And only after the relevant discussions are carried out by the central authorities, and the relevant decisions or approval given by the central authorities, can major and important general and specific government policies begin to be implemented" (Zhou 1987).

5. This problem is not remedied by letters to the editor, denunciations to higher-level officials, open meetings with government officials, or any of the other practices vaunted by the Chinese press as signs of the new "democracy" in China. Public opinion polls are a partial remedy to the Party's information problem (and from the perspective of an authoritarian elite are preferable to elections because they provide information without imposing accountability), but they do not provide sufficiently specific information on the actions of particular agencies.

6. "In the past all levels in the localities set up certain organs as counterparts to the government, and also assigned some industrial secretaries, agricultural secretaries, standing committee members in charge of finance and trade or culture and education, and so on. They monopolized government work to a greater extent than at the central level, hence the amount of work involved in separating party from government there is greater than at the central level" (Zhao 1987b).

The Chinese Communist Party leaders, for reasons not yet entirely clear, took the method of parallel rule even further than the Soviets. As former Premier Zhao Ziyang said, "China is one of the socialist countries most seriously afflicted by lack of separation of party and government" (Zhao 1987c).[7] The Chinese established in all government agencies Party "leading groups" or "fractions" (*dang zu*) responsible for actually administering the work of the agency. Although these institutions originated in the Soviet Union, they came to play a more significant role in China.[8] The Party leading group within a government agency is much more powerful than the Party committee (author's interviews). The Party committee only supervises the lives and thoughts of the Party members within that agency. But the Party leading group has authority over the non-Party bureaucrats as well as those who are Party members. The Party leading group plays a decision-making role, setting policy for the entire sector (*xitong*), not just for the agency.[9] For example, the Party leading group in the Ministry of Metallurgy leads the work, not only of the ministry, but also of subordinate provincial and municipal bureaus and even of steel mills run by the ministry and bureaus. It has the authority of appointment, removal, and transfer of officials for the entire sector (Burns 1987). The Party leading group is much smaller than a Party committee, consisting only of three to five people (usually the Party secretary, the minister, and several vice-ministers). The Party leading group essentially appropriated the authority of the official heads of the government agency, creating a confusing system of dual administrative leadership.[10]

At the enterprise level, the Chinese Communist Party also went beyond the Soviet Party in playing an administrative role (Ma 1987; Zhao 1987c). Soviet Party committees have always limited their role to supervision of Party members in the enterprise while allowing the manager full responsibility for production. The Chinese, since the Eighth Party Congress (1956), have put the manager under the leadership of the Party

7. Franz Schurmann (1968) made the same observation twenty years ago.

8. Schurmann (1968) described the function of the Party fraction as more limited than that of the Party committee. Basing his analysis only on Party rules and handbooks, he said that the fraction only supervised Party members within the agency, while the committee had decision-making powers within the agency (160). Barnett (1967), whose findings were based on interview data, described the Party fraction as "the real center of power and authority in the ministry, more important even than the Party committee" (24).

9. The Guangdong Party handbook quoted in Schurmann (1968, 160) implied the broader authority of the leading group when it stated, "Party fractions, in cases where it is necessary to carry out their tasks, may direct the work of the basic-level Party organizations in the unit concerned."

10. "In the government setup, the CCP bypasses the government executives at all levels by leading all government departments directly through the 'leading party groups' in government institutions" (Yan 1988).

committee. As Zhao Ziyang himself said in 1987, the issue of Party control over factory management became a "yardstick for supporting or opposing party leadership. . . . Every time we undertook a campaign, this setup was strengthened, to the extent that the Party committees monopolized many administrative matters" (Zhao 1987c).

Under this system the Chinese Communist Party not only controlled the government with a tight, constant "police patrol," it actually substituted itself for the government. The organizational lines between the Party and government blurred, and the delegation relationship disappeared almost entirely. For example, the head of the CCP committee overseeing all the Party leading groups and committees within the agencies of the central government sat (and still sits) in the government's State Council (author's interview). The Finance and Economics Leadership Small Group, five to seven top leaders who make most of the important economic policy decisions, although formally a Party unit, was located in the government section (Northern) of Zhongnanhai when Zhao Ziyang, as premier, was in charge of economic policy; when Zhao was transferred to Party secretary, the Finance and Economics Leading Group moved to the Party section (Southern) of Zhongnanhai (author's interview).[11] Carol Hamrin in chapter 4 in this volume describes the extent to which Party and government functions merged in all of the leadership groups that make decisions in specialized policy domains.

Such tight control could only be achieved at a tremendous price. The informational advantages of bureaucratic delegation, that is, expertise and specialization, were lost. Poorly educated veteran Party officials made policy decisions on the basis of political instincts rather than technical knowledge. Party members serving in government agencies were promoted more for political loyalty than for professional accomplishment (Harding 1981).

No longer willing to pay the price of poor-quality decisions and inefficiency, the Party leaders moved to transform the relationship of Party and government in the 1980s. The Party delegated more responsibility to the government bureaucracy, especially in economic policy-making. The Standing Committee of the State Council, meeting twice a week, took charge of the economy (although it still received recommendations from the Finance and Economics Leadership Small Group). The Politburo, having earlier abolished its specialized economic units, limited itself to setting the overall political line of economic reform and ratifying

11. Lieberthal and Oksenberg (1988) cite as evidence of organizational integration the fact that top Party and government organs are both housed in the Zhongnanhai compound. I cite as evidence of organizational boundaries the fact that within Zhongnanhai, Party organs are grouped together at the southern end and government organs are clustered at the northern.

important economic policies made by the government. At the provincial level, specialized Party departments overlapping their counterpart government departments were abolished (Zhao 1987b). In enterprises, the Party's role was reduced, and administrative responsibility was restored to managers. The CCP Constitution was revised to gradually eliminate the Party leading groups within government agencies (*Renmin Ribao*, 2 November 1987).[12] Civil service reforms were proposed to establish a dual structure within the bureaucracy, a cadre of professional civil servants, selected by meritocratic examination and promoted on professional criteria, alongside the administrative officials appointed and promoted by the Party organization departments (Zhao 1987b; Yan 1988; *Xinhua*, 18 November 1987; Burns 1988).

The expanded discretion of the government bureaucracy is illustrated by a recent example of conflict over agenda setting in the State Council. (Agenda setting is a prerogative of the bureaucracy typical of most political systems.) In February 1988, Bo Yibo, vice-chairman of the CCP Central Advisory Commission, came to a regular State Council meeting with a commission proposal on transportation safety, probably designed to embarrass the government bureaucracy for recent accidents. Wan Li, the vice-premier chairing the State Council meeting (the premier, Li Peng, had left to participate in a Politburo Standing Committee meeting) refused to alter the agenda to allow discussion of the issue. According to the unofficial report of the incident, the State Council leaders had learned in advance about Bo's intention and had obtained Deng Xiaoping's support for sticking to the original agenda. Bureaucratic authority has widened, but at this stage it still is fragile and dependent on the support of the preeminent leader, Deng Xiaoping (Lo 1988).

The widening of government's discretionary authority did not destroy the principal-agent relationship between Party and government. Zhao Ziyang emphasized that the CCP Central Committee should retain its leadership over the government "in political principles and orientation and in major policy decisions," and continue to appoint leading cadres for central state organs; and that the provincial Party committees also should retain political leadership and personnel appointment powers.

12. Zhao Ziyang in his work report to the Thirteenth CCP Congress said, "Party leading groups in government departments should gradually be abolished, since the practice of making these groups responsible to the Party committees of the next higher level which have approved their establishment is not conducive to unity and efficiency in government work" (Zhao 1987b). At a Party meeting on Party work in central state organs in March 1988, Politburo Standing Committee member and premier, Li Peng, explained that while Party leading groups in government ministries and commissions would be abolished "step by step," Party committees would be retained and become "even more important" (Li 1988).

The 1984 reform of the *nomenklatura* system decentralized the authority to appoint, remove, and promote government personnel to lower-level Party organizations but still left it in Party hands. Chinese leaders promise that in the future the Party will supervise the work of the government but not substitute itself for the government. Separation of Party and government will actually strengthen Party leadership of the government. "Leaders must keep very cool; they must stand high and see far, consider things carefully, and avoid getting entangled in a pile of routine affairs. They cannot truly play a leading role if they are entangled in trivia all day long" (Zhao 1987c). Another commentator pointed out that while state organs "can choose either to accept or not accept the Party's policies," if a state organ refuses to follow the Party's policies, which are "absolutely correct," "then Party organizations and Party members within the state organs should supervise and ensure the correct implementation of the Party lines and the general and specific policies, by giving play to the exemplary role of the Party members within the state organs" (Zhou 1987). In other words, if the government does not agree with the preferences of the Party, then the Party should use its authority over Party members in the bureaucracy to impose these preferences on the government.

The Party's control over the government has made the economic reform drive possible. Party leaders have the power to propose new directions for reform and prod the bureaucracy to action. The government bureaucracy would never have taken such bold initiatives on its own. Deng Xiaoping and Zhao Ziyang were able to dominate a conservative minority within the CCP to promulgate a Party line of economic reform. By making support for economic reform the current political-ideological line, the Party has made it impossible for anyone, inside or outside the government, to publicly oppose the reform drive (although people's definitions of reform vary widely). And by replacing thousands of incompetent or conservative government officials at central and local levels, the Party has empowered a new cohort of officials, eager and able to promote economic reforms.

The delegation of greater discretion to the government bureaucracy also offered substantial advantages to a Party leadership intent on economic reform. Enhancing the independence of the bureaucracy gives government officials a greater incentive to be efficient and to take actions that are economically rational but politically risky. As Tang Tsou has observed, modernization requires that the Party grant all professionals, including government bureaucrats, greater autonomy (Tsou 1983). By shifting the locus of economic policy-making from the Party to the government, reformers made it more difficult for Party conservatives (who until recently retained their power in the Politburo) to sabotage the reform drive.[13] And by delegating policy-making to government commissions and ministries, they devised a reform package acceptable to key economic groups.

On the other hand, Party conservatives were obviously unhappy with moves to restrict the Party's powers. Party resistance to limiting its role was even stronger at the provincial and local levels, where Party officials continued to meddle in economic affairs. Some of the formal organizational reforms, such as eliminating Party leading groups within ministries or closing down specialized Party departments in provinces, were implemented only halfheartedly and were reversed by the conservatives after 1989. Nonetheless, the locus of bargaining over national economic-reform policies was moved over to the government side, where it remained even after 1989.

THE POLICY-MAKING PROCESS: MANAGEMENT BY EXCEPTION

Under the revised delegation relationship between the Chinese Communist Party and the government, the locus of bargaining over economic policy has shifted to the government arena. The Communist Party sets the general line for the economic reforms, but it delegates to government the formulation and implementation of specific policies. The Standing Committee of the State Council has become the main policy-making arena, while the Standing Committee of the Communist Party Politburo is much less active.[14] The State Council is advised by a network of recently established policy research centers, described by Nina Halpern in chapter 5.

The Chinese government bureaucracy makes policy according to the decision rules characteristic of "management by exception" (Lawler 1976). At each level of the organizational hierarchy, agency representatives make decisions by a rule of consensus. If they all agree, the decision is automatically ratified by the higher level. If the bureaucrats cannot reach consensus, then the decision is referred to the higher levels, and if the higher levels cannot agree, then either nothing happens or the ultimate principal, the Communist Party, intervenes to impose a solution.

The advantages of management-by-exception, from the standpoint of the principals (the leaders of the government and the Communist Party) are that (1) it exploits the superior information of subordinates; (2) it

13. Ironically, it was China's proto-legislature, the National People's Congress, under the leadership of Party conservative Peng Zhen, that was responsible for sabotaging some of the government's reform proposals, such as the bankruptcy law.

14. According to Barnett (1985), the same shift from Party to government can be observed in the making of foreign policy.

relieves the principals of the costs of constant intervention in the policy process; (3) it gives all the agents who will implement a policy a voice in the formulation of that policy; and (4) it gives agents an incentive to resolve their differences and come to agreement.

Most corporations and many political systems delegate policy-making to subordinate agencies and use management-by-exception as the most efficient way to manage this delegation relationship. Parliamentary systems like Japan or France may appear to be dominated by their bureaucracies, but they are actually ruled by parliamentary party majorities who have effectively used management-by-exception to allow their bureaucratic agents to work out policy packages. If the politician principals seem invisible and rarely intervene to overrule a bureaucratic decision, it is because they have structured the bargaining game to produce outcomes satisfactory to them (and to their most influential constituencies).[15]

The structure of the government bureaucracy reflects the Communist Party's notion of which groups should be represented in policy deliberations. Establishing a particular set of bureaucratic agencies, and organizing collective choice so that individuals represent the preferences of their agencies, enfranchises certain groups but not others (it is striking, for example, that the national labor organization is represented in key economic meetings in Hungary but not in China [Comisso, personal communication, 1984]). Just as a ruling party in a democracy structures decision-making processes so that its most important constituents are satisfied, the leaders of the Chinese Communist Party structure decision-making processes so that their most important constituents are satisfied.

The Chinese bureaucracy is organized by function (education, culture, public security) and by economic sector (agriculture, coal, machinery). Ministries are expected to articulate the interests of their particular sector. When ministers or vice-ministers are called together to discuss a policy proposal, they are expected to represent the perspective of their

15. Management-by-exception is not the prevailing mode of decision making in the American political system. Bureaucratic agencies make their recommendations directly to the president or Congress, and the locus of bargaining is the congressional committee, not the bureaucracy. One possible reason for this difference between presidential and parliamentary systems is the separation of powers characteristic of presidential systems. Congress and the president, as dual principals, share authority over the bureaucracy; Congress is reluctant to shift the decision-making process to the bureaucracy for fear that the president might strengthen its influence over that process. In parliamentary systems, and in the Chinese communist system at the present time, the ruling party has no rivals for control of the bureaucracy and therefore can delegate to it decision making using management-by-exception. We may speculate that if the National People's Congress becomes a genuine legislature and exercises its authority over the bureaucracy, the Party might retract its generous grant of decision-making authority from the bureaucracy (unless the Party is able to completely dominate the NPC like a ruling parliamentary party in a democracy). These speculations are based on my conversations with Mathew McCubbins.

particular ministries. Press articles criticizing "selfish departmentalism" (e.g., *Renmin Ribao*, 21 January 1983) seem futile and naive when we recognize that Chinese government institutions are structured to encourage expressions of departmental points of view.[16]

At higher levels, the commissions (State Planning Commission, State Economic Commission, State Science and Technology Commission) and the State Council promote the aggregation of departmental interests, but they also reinforce the articulation of sectorial interests. Within the State Economic Commission and the State Planning Commission bureaus are divided by economic sector, so that the head of the energy bureau, for example, argues for resource allocations to the coal, petroleum, electricity, and nuclear power industries. Within the State Council the degree of aggregation is greater. Each vice-premier and state councillor is assigned responsibility for a sector or a function, such as agriculture, industry, or finance. While such divisions of responsibility encourage specialized expertise in policy-making, they also guarantee that sector-based bargaining continues right up to the top of the government hierarchy (Chen 1987).[17] The comprehensive agencies have their own organizational viewpoints as well: The State Planning Commission represents the macroeconomy, the State Economic Commission represents the enterprises, and the Ministry of Finance represents the central state (author's interviews).

When the Chinese CCP leaders set up their national economic bureaucracy in 1953, they gave industry a stronger voice than agriculture. There was only one ministry representing agriculture, but over ten ministries representing various industries. Because the fiscal system was set up to obtain revenue almost entirely from the earnings of state factories, central-government officials had a financial interest in keeping agricultural prices low and industrial profits high. This bias toward industry reflected the policy of Soviet-style industrialization, which prevailed at the time. Once institutionalized in the government structure, the bias

---

16. Ellen Comisso (1986) argues that in communist regimes, the control of the Communist Party over bureaucratic careers makes it impossible for managers and government bureaucrats to articulate the particularistic interests of their units. Comisso has identified the key principal-agent relationship in communist regimes, but fails to recognize the advantages to the principal of delegation and management-by-exception. The Communist Party expects officials from subordinate government agencies and enterprises to articulate particularistic interests, and benefits from the bargaining among these interests.

17. Vice-heads of provinces, cities, and counties are also assigned sectorial jurisdictions and are expected to bargain to get more benefits for their sector. One county cited as an example in the press had one head and thirteen deputy heads: "At the official work meetings they attended the deputy county heads asked the county head for power, material resources, and manpower in the interest of the parts they represented, thus bothering the county head instead of helping him carry out his work. For this reason, it is not good to have too many deputies" (*Xinhua*, 5 July 1987).

was perpetuated, as the continuing underinvestment in agriculture illustrates (Lardy 1983).

The bureaucratic reorganizations that have been a frequent occurrence since the 1950s are efforts to change the structure of interest articulation and aggregation, as well as to improve efficiency. Whenever ministries are merged or divided, raised to commission level or demoted to bureau level, the voices of various sectors are strengthened or weakened. The elevation of education from ministry to commission status in 1987, for example, was designed to give education more clout in the contest for government resources, in addition to enhancing coordination of educational activities under different ministries. Lynn Paine, in chapter 7 in this volume, describes the disadvantages the education sector suffers because of its organizational weakness.

Management-by-exception requires a bureaucratic hierarchy with formal equality among the units at any one level. If one ministry could impose its preferences on the entire group, then the advantages of management-by-exception would be lost. The Chinese government, by putting all ministers (as well as all bureau heads, all vice-ministers, etc.) at equal rank, satisfies this requirement. (An important exception is the Ministry of Finance, which by virtue of its revenue function, which is critically important to the survival of the state, ranks at the commission level [Lieberthal and Oksenberg 1988]). Although each ministry's actual influence varies with the prestige of its minister (and State Council overseer), its function, its control over subordinate enterprises, its financial contribution, and so forth (Oksenberg 1982; Lieberthal and Oksenberg 1988), the formal status of each ministry is the same. It is also crucial that the ministries are subordinate to organizations at the next level of the hierarchy. The State Planning Commission and the State Economic Commission (and to a lesser extent the State Science and Technology Commission) have formal leadership relations (Lieberthal and Oksenberg 1988) over the ministries and can resolve issues that ministries have been unable to agree on. At the apex of the government sits the State Council, which has leadership authority over all its subordinate agencies and can impose a solution when neither the ministries nor the commissions can find one.

The obvious fact that bureaucracies are organized by sector and function, not by geographic region as legislatures are, is worth emphasizing. Regional concerns are brought into government policy-making in a number of ways. The State Economic Commission and the State Planning Commission have regional as well as sectorial bureaus that voice the demands of the Northeast, the Southwest, and so forth. And whenever economic policy proposals are being debated, the heads of the relevant provincial (and some municipal) bureaus are invited to participate; provincial governors or vice-governors attend the most important policy work conferences. Each province sends a delegation to the annual national planning and budgeting meetings to lobby in its own behalf. Provinces are equal in rank to ministries, and disputes between provinces and ministries often filter up to the commission or State Council level. Yet, provinces do not have permanent formal representation in the bureaucratic arena where most economic policy-making now occurs.

The lack of formal regional representation in government policy-making is an institutional anomaly if we consider that since 1957, and especially since 1980, the provinces have received an increasingly large share of resources and authority. Moreover, the two most important constituencies for top Communist Party leaders currently are the central-government bureaucracy and the provincial officials. The institutional "payoffs" to the first group are quite clear, that is, extending bureaucratic autonomy and expanding the size of the bureaucracy. Yet the resources and authority of the provinces have not been recognized by institutional changes. (Provincial demands for an institutionalized voice at the Center could result in a strengthening of the national legislature, the National People's Congress. Or provincial officials might advocate shifting economic policy-making from the State Council, where they are not represented, back to the Politburo, where they currently are the largest bloc of votes.)

The Chinese government has been making economic policies according to management-by-exception at least since the early 1980s.[18] Research by Lieberthal and Oksenberg (1988) and by Lampton (1987) found that consensus was the rule governing economic decision making in the central government, and that any participant could veto proposals.[19] In contrast to a legislative setting in which majorities rule, minorities have the power

18. A serious deficiency in our understanding of Chinese politics is the lack of a "base line" with which to compare current political practices. The analysis here, as well as previous studies of Chinese policy-making based on documents (e.g., Teiwes 1979, 1984; MacFarquhar 1974, 1983; Oksenberg 1971), suggests that during Mao Zedong's reign the locus of economic policy-making was the Communist Party instead of the government. Little discretion was delegated to government institutions. It would be valuable to confirm this conclusion with information from retrospective interviewing in China.

19. A consensus-decision rule does not necessarily require unanimity. A bureaucrat from a weak agency may not have an effective veto. If eveyone knows that an agency is weak and that its position will not be sustained by the higher level, it may be unable to block a measure or force a compromise, whereas a bureaucrat from a strong agency could succeed in doing so. The writings of Lampton (1987), Oksenberg (1982), Lieberthal and Oksenberg (1988), and Shirk (1989) have suggested that agencies that generate revenues, have control over a large number of enterprises, and have ties to top Party leaders have more clout than agencies without these resources, but more case studies of policy-making are needed before we can speak with any certainty about the differential ability of agencies to veto measures under management-by-exception in China.

to obstruct action in bureaucracies run by management-by-exception. Whenever an agency refuses to compromise and consensus cannot be reached, the issue is "tabled" or is referred to a higher level for resolution. As the secretary-general of the State Council complained, "many problems remain unsolved for a long time simply because of the objection from a minority. . . . Too many people exercise veto in our public organs" (Chen 1987).

Much of the time of the government bodies above the ministries is taken up by what the Chinese call "coordination" (*xietiao*) work, which means resolving conflicts among subordinate units. The State Economic Commission (SEC) and (to a lesser extent) the State Planning Commission are supposed to provide final resolution to interagency (as well as interregional and agency-region) disputes.[20] But because the internal organization of these bodies reinforces sectorial and regional divisions, disputes often are passed up for resolution at an even higher level. The Standing Committee of the State Council spends much of its twice-weekly meetings resolving interministerial (or interprovincial or ministerial-provincial) differences over relatively minor issues (author's interviews). A temporary institution called the "Adjustment Office" (*tiaojie bangongshi*) was established under the premier during the mid-1980s (Lieberthal and Oksenberg 1988) to settle conflicts that were obstructing the progress of reforms and take some of the load off the Standing Committee of the State Council.

Bargaining among bureaucratic agencies is structured by management-by-exception. Every agency representative must decide whether to sign on to a lower-level decision that does not entirely satisfy its preferences, or hold out and force the intervention of the higher levels. To make this decision the agency representative must seek information about the preferences of the higher-level bureaucrats to anticipate what their decision would be. Unless the agency representative has reason to believe that the higher levels would make a decision more favorable to their agency's interests than the lower-level decision, the representative will compromise to reach agreement at the lower level. After all, a bureaucrat or an agency that consistently refuses to compromise will certainly not be popular with upper-level leaders. Agency officials are the

20. The Economic Reform Bureau of the SEC spent most of its time resolving disputes among subordinate units sparked by changes in the economic structure, such as disputes between ministries and Wuhan over control of factories after Wuhan became an independent planning entity (author's interview). After the SEC and the SPC were merged in June 1988, the State Council was so overloaded with disputes to resolve that in 1990 they set up a new commission responsible for *xietiao* work, the Production Commission, consisting of the former SEC Production Dispatch Bureau (*shengchan diaodu zu*) and Enterprise Management Bureau (*qiye guanli zu*), to relieve their burden (author's interviews).

employees of the State Council and are appointed by the Communist Party. A reputation for rigidity may be punished by demotion or other measures.[21] Therefore, in most circumstances an agency will settle for a less-than-optimal decision at the lower level instead of gambling on a better decision at a higher level. From the standpoint of the principal, management-by-exception works well when it allows key groups to articulate their interests but creates incentives for them to compromise their differences without forcing the principal to intervene.

By this standard, Chinese management-by-exception has not worked well during the late 1980s. From the perspective of the top leaders of the government (articulated by Chen Junsheng, then secretary-general of the State Council), the work of the government has been impeded by constant arguing and "the escalation of coordination." Problems that once were solved at lower levels are now being pushed up to the State Council (Chen 1987). There are several reasons why the management-by-exception system is working poorly. First, divisions within the Party leadership encourage intransigence among subordinates. Conflicts among principals increase uncertainty for agents and lead them to gamble on the higher-level resolution of the conflict. Even without specific information (usually acquired through factional relationships) that someone at the top will support their position, subordinates expect more favorable treatment when there is leadership conflict. Central and provincial officials currently are the two major constituencies within the CCP Central Committee.[22] Top Party leaders compete for power by building up support among these two key groups. They welcome opportunities to appeal to particular officials by pressing their interests when policies are decided. Yet even while top leaders are glad to have opportunities to build support by helping ministers or provincial officials, they complain that incessant bureaucratic wrangling has overloaded the system.

A second reason for the growing burden of coordination work is that participation in policy deliberations has been expanded to include representatives of more groups. Each policy is debated in a series of meetings to which a large number of affected units, both local and central, as well

21. There is no evidence that uncooperative behavior is punished by cutting an agency's budget, which often is the case in democracies run by management-by-exception.

22. In this sense the relationship between Party and government in China is not a pure agency relationship. There is reciprocity between principal and agents in all agency relationships; the principal generally believes that the organization will run more smoothly if the agents are kept satisfied. But Party leaders in China are politically dependent on government officials to an even greater degree because these officials belong to the CCP and participate in choosing the leaders of the CCP. Top provincial and ministry officials are constituents as well as agents of the Party leaders. This fact may help explain why Communist parties, even when they use tight "police patrol" control of the government, seem to do such a poor job of oversight.

as technical experts, are invited. The composition of these meetings is not set by any rules (in contrast to policy deliberations in Congress or other democratic legislatures), allowing the top government leaders who are orchestrating the process a high degree of flexibility. The widening of consultation is designed to prevent overconcentration of power in the hands of a few individuals in the Party. Deng Xiaoping, in his important 1980 speech "On the Reform of the System of Party and State Leadership," argued that it was this overconcentration of power that had produced the Cultural Revolution and other excesses of Mao Zedong's rule (Deng 1980). By expanding participation in the policy process, Deng and other top Party leaders hope to improve the quality of decisions and build support for them among key constituent groups. But inviting more groups to sit at the bargaining table also complicates the process of building consensus. Instead of a small, stable group of participants who are willing to trade votes on one issue because they trust others to pay them back on the next issue, there is a larger, ad hoc group that finds agreement much more problematical.

Finally, economic reform, by creating new financial interests among bureaucratic and regional agencies, has made bargaining among them more intense. Policies designed to improve economic incentives by allowing ministries, provinces, local industrial bureaus, and so forth to retain a share of their *renminbi* (Chinese currency) and hard-currency earnings have made bureaucratic agencies more profit-conscious. They fight more fiercely to obtain preferred policies because the stakes are higher. For example, the dispute about which ministry would take charge of the production of refrigerators and washing machines, which took five years to resolve in the era of economic reform (*Renmin Ribao*, 17 July 1984), would have been settled more quickly and easily under the old system. The creation of new financial incentives sometimes makes it easier to work out a compromise by giving all affected parties a share in the deal. There are many examples, especially at the local level, of potentially profitable joint ventures and other projects that were approved only because every agency with approval authority was given a percentage of the profits (Lieberthal and Oksenberg 1988). But, on the other hand, this new mode of resolving differences by dividing the profits encourages agencies to press their demands in the bargaining process. They recognize that assertiveness can pay off in several percentage points of a profitable venture. As the secretary-general of the State Council notes, "A profitable undertaking invariably draws the intervention of many departments, with every department demanding a slice of the cake, and none will make any concession. Sometimes this ends in a confrontation" (Chen 1987).

Management-by-exception tends to bog down in the Chinese government bureaucracy because the bureaucracy is so poorly institutionalized. There are few rules about who participates in which decisions. The sequence of decision gates is ambiguous in all policies except those related to the planning and budgeting cycles. Policy decisions are not permanent, because a leader who does not like the outcome of one work meeting can call for another with a different set of participants.[23] When Chinese officials talk, they often differentiate between "hard" and "soft" decisions (author's interviews). Moreover, all the conflicts among agencies, among provinces, and between agencies and provinces, must be resolved by higher-level bureaucratic organs. There is no administrative law or independent judiciary to settle jurisdictional disputes among them. The absence of judicial institutions puts the entire load of conflict resolution on the central government and the Party.

POLICY OUTCOMES UNDER MANAGEMENT-BY-EXCEPTION

The policy outcomes produced by the Chinese system reflect the structure of the government bureaucracy and the process of management-by-exception. Scholars of communist political systems have noted that policies in such systems tend to be incremental (Hough 1977; Bunce 1981). Drastic changes in policy direction or massive shifts in the allocation of resources are inhibited by the requirement that every agency must agree to them. The consensus rule produces policies under which everyone benefits, or at least no one loses too much. As one high-level policy adviser in China put it, "We must use all our policies to 'coordinate' interests among agencies and localities" (author's interview). Radical change is rejected, delayed, or watered down in the process of building consensus. Party principals occasionally can impose policies on their bureaucratic agents if the issue is of overwhelming urgency. But such instances are rare because the cost of dictating policy to a reluctant agency usually is failure of implementation.

An example of a major policy change delayed by lack of consensus is the restoration of ranks in the Chinese military, first proposed in 1980 but not implemented until 1988. (The military-ranks issue is discussed by Jonathan Pollack in chapter 6 in this volume). In 1984 the People's Liberation Army received new uniforms with epaulets in preparation for

---

23. Governments with a higher degree of institutionalization solve the problem of instability in institutional choice by implicit contracts agreeing not to reconsider issues already decided by the group (Schwartz 1988). China has not yet established this institutional rule. Therefore, as Chen Junsheng writes, "A decision is formally made, a correct one at that, but just because it involves the interests of a certain department, unit, or locality, some people will refuse to put it into effect under all kinds of pretexts, and the result is a lot of arguing back and forth" (Chen 1987).

the restoration of ranks. The final decision to restore ranks was delayed until October 1988 because of conflict between retired officers and active officers over whether the retired officers should receive formal ranks. As a Hong Kong newspaper account described the situation, "These two opinions were locked in stalemate for a long time, and a consensus of opinion could not be achieved. This slowed down the process of restoring military ranks." The stalemate was broken by a compromise that restricts formal ranks to active officers but "soothes" the retired officers with special medals and an affirmation of their previous ranks (Fu Meihua 1988).

In China the normative reflection of consensus decision making in economic policy-making is an ideology one might call "balancism" (*pinghengzhuyi*). According to this ideology, the function of the state is to balance out inequities among units created by arbitrary policies, particularly administratively set prices. Fairness (*gongping*) requires that no unit lose too much because administrative prices make them less profitable than other units or because past decisions (such as investments in fixed assets) work against them under current formulas. All government bodies are supposed to adjust their policies to prevent large disparities in benefits among units. The expression "*ku le bu zhun*," meaning "disparity between sadness and happiness," is frequently used by government bureaucrats to explain that a particular policy modification was necessary to guarantee equity. Representatives of ministries, localities, or enterprises who are in a strong competitive position to benefit from economic reforms (i.e., their products are in demand in the market, the irrationalities of the price system work for them, and they are more efficient and productive in their operations) often complain that government organs worry too much about taking care (*zhaogu*) of the weak and not enough about promoting the strong (author's interviews). (In chapter 11 in this volume Andrew Walder analyzes this redistributive tendency in economic policy-making at the municipal level.)

The conservative bias of management-by-exception makes the political challenge of economic reform formidable. Introducing a market through a bureaucracy, especially one operating under management-by-exception, is extremely difficult. Under the consensus rule even a minority of ministries or provinces who prefer the status quo to the proposed changes could obstruct progress in reform. The Party principals retain the authority to take significant policy initiatives—the reform drive has been sustained despite short-term economic problems and group conflicts because Deng continues to promote reform ideas—but they must obtain the agreement of at least most of the bureaucratic institutions that will implement the policies.

Zhao Ziyang's political strategy of economic reform was designed to meet this challenge. First of all, it was a strategy of gradualism. Rather than rushing ahead with a comprehensive, radical transformation of the entire system, which would threaten the vested interests of many, Zhao was extremely cautious. Zhao recognized that there were many political risks inherent in economic reform and that therefore they were "required to act carefully in reforms, like wading across a river by holding on to the rocks in it" (*Gongren Ribao*, 13 March 1985). He understood that "the reform of the economic structure is actually a process in which various interests and relations are readjusted and redistributed" and that if the interests of a particular department or locality were harmed by a particular reform, it would oppose the reform (*Hongqi*, March 1987). Gradual reform might be a long-term process, requiring as long as several generations, but no other strategy had a chance of success in the context of China's political system.

To minimize the threat to central economic agencies, Zhao Ziyang made the crucial decision to create a dual-track system, gradually expanding the market sector while maintaining the plan sector, instead of replacing plan with market at one shot. The policy allowing enterprises to sell their above-quota output on their own at market prices created an economic incentive for managers to press for more market opportunities and allowed central planners to save their functions and their face. Stimulated by the new incentives, the economy grew rapidly, especially in the market sector. This strategy of "letting the economy outgrow the plan" (Barry Naughton, personal communication, 1984) created a transitional dual economy, with numerous accompanying economic problems, but it was politically very successful.[24]

The sequencing of reforms also reflects the political realities of the policy-making process. Zhao Ziyang decided to postpone the most redistributive policies, which would create the most intense conflict within the bureaucracy, namely, the "hard budget constraint" (i.e., bankruptcy) and price reform. Forcing enterprises to take sole responsibility for their own profits and losses (*zi fu yingkuei*) is an essential component of market rationality, but it is politically infeasible under current conditions. From the perspective of "balancism" it would be unfair to punish enterprises that cannot make profits because of external, "objective" (*keguan*) causes (i.e., prices, demands of planners, fixed assets, etc.). The burden would fall mainly on a few sectors (coal, steel, heavy machinery) and the inland provinces where these sectors are concentrated (author's interviews).

Zhao Ziyang began talking about price reform in 1984. He set up a

---

24. I have no evidence that this policy was produced by bargaining within the government bureaucracy, but it was clearly designed to satisfy the interests of the bureaucracy.

group to prepare price reform policies and announced in early 1985 that the State Council would soon take action on price readjustment in industry as well as agriculture (*Xinhua*, 1 January 1985). The fact that a thorough adjustment of industrial prices (i.e., raising the prices of raw materials such as coal, iron, and steel) was continually postponed and has yet to be introduced,[25] whereas food prices have been liberalized, suggests that it is the potential for intense bureaucratic conflict, as well as the public reaction to inflation, that stopped Zhao from pushing ahead with urban price reform.

Participants in economic policy-making often explain the delay in these two key dimensions of reform as a reflection of Zhao Ziyang's caution on tackling issues that would be opposed by the most powerful agencies within the government bureaucracy, namely, the State Planning Commission, the Ministry of Finance, and the heavy-industry ministries. Zhao pushed up against the stone wall of the state bureaucracy, they say, and he went through only where he found loose stones; he did not waste time pushing against stones that would not move (author's interviews).

The policies that have emerged from the bureaucracy since 1980 suggest that the progress of economic reform was sustained by appeasing the powerful heavy-industry ministries. When reform proposals were first introduced, heavy-industry interests expressed open opposition to them (Solinger 1982). As the prime beneficiaries of the Soviet-style command economy, they viewed economic reform as a direct threat. By replacing some ministers and making reform the ideological line, the Party discouraged outright opposition from the heavy-industry ministries. And over time, the bureaucrats in these ministries came to recognize that they could do better by demanding a larger share of the benefits of reform than by opposing all reforms (author's interviews).

In exchange for their support of various reform policies, the heavy-industry ministries received valuable side-payments. The clearest example of such a side-payment is the "departmental contracts" (*bumen chengbao*). The ministries in charge of fuels, raw materials, and transportation perceived that they were falling further and further behind under the dual economic system. Sectors with many enterprises operating under low (or no) plan quotas could sell on the market and reap high profits from the higher market prices, while their sectors had to continue to produce almost entirely for the plan. The petroleum, coal, metallurgy, railroads, and communication ministries, and the airline, petrochemical, and nonferrous metals corporations demanded and received special "departmental

25. The prices of specific materials were adjusted during this period, but a comprehensive industrial price reform was not undertaken. The issue of price reform was raised once again during the summer of 1988 but abandoned in the fall when inflation rose to an alarmingly high rate.

contracts." The ministries contracted with the State Planning Commission to receive a certain amount of investment and inexpensive plan inputs in exchange for delivering a certain amount of output to the plan for the next five years. Any production above this amount the ministries and their subordinate enterprises were free to sell on the market at higher prices (*Xinhua*, 10 February 1985; *Shijie Jingji Daobao*, 25 May 1987). The contracts guaranteed access to the market and higher profits to these particular agencies, which allocated the plan burdens and market opportunities to the enterprises under them. The departmental contracts were very popular with the State Planning Commission, because they helped guarantee plan procurement (the lure of the market sector had made this task increasingly difficult), and naturally with the ministries, which benefited from them (author's interviews). The departmental contracts violated the reform principle of increasing enterprise autonomy from administrative control, but they were politically expedient.

The need to obtain the support of the influential heavy-industry ministries for the package of economic reforms probably also explains the striking stability of the shares of central budgetary investment allocated to economic sectors during the period of economic reform. Heavy industry, which claimed the lion's share of state investment under the old system, found its investment allocation cut drastically in 1979–80 when top leaders sought to improve proportional balance by shifting resources to light industry (Solinger 1988). The blow to heavy industry was so severe, and its representatives complained so persuasively, that heavy industry's share of investment was increased again after 1982 (State Statistical Bureau 1985). Since that time heavy industry has continued to receive favored treatment by the Center, and light industry has increased its share of *total* investment only because most investment is now controlled at the local, not the central, level. Meanwhile, agriculture, which is weakly represented in the central government, has seen its share of central investment reduced despite a 1979 promise that it would be increased (*Xinhua*, 5 October 1979).

Many reform policies bear the mark of consensus decision making. One example is the decision to create a new tax system for industrial enterprises with a policy called "substituting tax for profits" (*li gai shui*). The goal of this policy was to place the financial relations between enterprises and the central government on a stable, institutionalized basis. Instead of each enterprise bargaining for a particular rate of profit retention, all enterprises producing the same product would have to pay at a uniform tax rate. When this policy was originally proposed in 1983 the Ministry of Finance recommended a moderately high tax rate. At a series of meetings called to discuss the proposal, representatives of

THE CHINESE POLITICAL SYSTEM

heavy-industry ministries and inland provinces complained that under such a heavy tax burden their many unprofitable enterprises would be forced to close. To achieve consensus it was necessary to revise the policy. The tax rate was reduced, but then the Ministry of Finance came in with simulations predicting that the policy would reduce state revenues. The revenue gap was filled by tacking on a so-called adjustment tax (*tiaojie shui*), which was applied only to the most profitable medium-sized and large state enterprises (most of them in coastal cities like Shanghai). The adjustment tax was set on an individual-enterprise basis, thereby violating a fundamental principle of reform but creating the compromise necessary to win approval of the policy (author's interviews).

The constraint of consensus building also requires that every policy change leave no one substantially worse off than before. The *li gai shui* tax regulations guaranteed enterprises that they would pay in taxes no more than the profit they remitted the year before. Whenever the *li gai shui* policy resulted in a loss of revenues to a particular province, the central government made compensation by reducing the share of total revenue the province was required to remit to the Center (Lieberthal and Oksenberg 1988). Officials agree that the only politically feasible approach to price reform is to compensate those who are hurt by it, with wage subsidies to urban consumers in the case of food prices, and with tax exemptions for manufacturing enterprises in the case of raw-materials prices. One reason that industrial price readjustment has become more elusive over the course of reform is that as the central treasury becomes increasingly strained (because local governments and enterprises are allowed to retain a larger share of financial revenues), it is more difficult for the Center to come up with the financial side-payments necessary to make the package broadly acceptable (author's interview).

Gradualism, postponement of the most divisive issues, side-payments, and compromise—all are the marks of a market reform filtered through a political system characterized by management-by-exception. Zhao Ziyang's strategy recognized the necessity of building consensus of support for economic reform. As he himself put it, "When adopting a reform measure, we must do our best to benefit all quarters concerned so that our reform will always have the support of the broad masses of the people and its success will be guaranteed" (Zhao 1987a).[26]

26. A more critical view of Zhao's reform strategy, expressed recently in a *People's Daily* article advocating price reform, is that the strategy involved the implementation of only those reforms that were "shallow and easy" and "of immediate benefit to the masses" without altering the fundamental character of economic relations. "Reform Involves Risks and Difficulties, Pass the Barrier Through Arduous Efforts," *Renmin Ribao*, 9 June 1988, *FBIS*, 9 June 1988, 37.

CENTER AND LOCALITY: FEDERALISM IN A UNITARY STATE

The People's Republic of China is a unitary state, with formal authority constitutionally held by the central government. Yet in reality, China, even before the introduction of economic reforms, was much more decentralized than the Soviet Union (Schurmann 1968). Beginning in 1957, the Center shared with the provinces the authority to approve projects, control industrial enterprises, plan production, allocate materials, and collect fiscal revenues. Despite periodic attempts at recentralization, the trend since 1957 has been progressive decentralization to the provincial level (Naughton 1985, 1987; Wong 1985, 1986).

Why China took the path of administrative decentralization is a highly significant but as yet unanswered question. Schurmann suggests that decentralization was made possible by the strength of the Communist Party at the provincial level; in contrast, the Stalinist purges decimated the Soviet party at the regional level (Schurmann 1968). Building on Schurmann's point, we might speculate that because of the strong Party base in the provinces, the CCP leaders created a Central Committee in which provincial representatives played a major role. The leadership enfranchised three major blocs within the Central Committee, officials from the (government and Party) Center, officials from the provinces, and People's Liberation Army officers.[27] Leaders competed for power by building support among these key constituencies. Whenever a Party leader perceived that rival leaders were blocking his policy initiatives by their control over the central bureaucracy, he attempted to build support for his initiatives by "playing to the provinces." According to this analysis, Mao Zedong stressed administrative decentralization to win provincial support for policies promoting revolutionary transformation in 1957, 1964, and 1967–70, and Deng Xiaoping used the same strategy to win provincial support for economic reform policies in 1980.

Administrative decentralization offers economic as well as political advantages to the central leadership. Provincial officials are the agents of the central Party and government. Delegation of authority, whether to government ministries or to provincial departments, improves efficiency by exploiting the superior information of agents. And in a state-run economy, a profit-sharing rule, like the one included in the fiscal decentralization policies promulgated in 1980, improves the incentives for agents to be more efficient.

The prior decentralization of the Chinese system has had profound consequences for the course of the post–1978 economic reforms. The

27. Although this analysis concentrates on only two blocs within the Party, the central bureaucracy and the provinces, the third bloc, the military, played a very important role during certain periods, such as the 1970s.

cumulative effect of the progressive devolution of authority and resources from 1957 through the Cultural Revolution was to create a political system in which a substantial share of the planning decisions, management of factories, control of raw materials, and receipt of fiscal revenues
was in the hands of local officials. Provincial Party secretaries also had an
important voice within the CCP Central Committee. When Deng Xiaoping looked around for a group that could become the core of a reform
coalition and that could counter the vested interests of the central economic bureaucracy in the command economy, he soon identified provincial officials. These local officials would play a key role in the implementation of reform policies because they controlled most of the enterprises in
the country. And as the largest bloc within the Central Committee (36.8
percent in the twelfth and 39.4 percent in the thirteenth [*South China
Morning Post* 1987]) they could provide critical political support within the
Party if and when conservative leaders tried to challenge the reforms.

To win the support of provincial officials for the reform drive, Deng
Xiaoping introduced a radical fiscal decentralization in 1980. This policy,
officially called "apportioning revenues and expenditures between the
central and local authorities, while holding the latter responsible for
their own profit and loss" (*Caizheng* 1980) allowed provinces to fix for
five years the amount of revenues they must remit to the Center and
keep a proportion or all of the revenues over that amount. Provinces
were assigned to five different categories of treatment, ranging from
Guangdong and Fujian, who retained 100 percent of their above-quota
revenues, to the three municipalities of Beijing, Shanghai, and Tianjin,
who retained none of their above-quota revenues. In addition, provinces
and the lower levels were permitted to keep all the profits from the
enterprises controlled by them (Donnithorne 1981; Fujimoto 1980; Han
1982). The main advantage of this policy, colloquially called "eating from
separate kitchens" (*fen zhao chifan*), was the strong incentive for local
authorities to expand their revenue base by developing their local economies. True, the growth motivated by new fiscal incentives produced
some undesirable consequences: uncontrollable local investment, most
of it going into profitable but reduplicative and wasteful processing
plants, leading to supply shortages, inflation, and budget deficits; local
protectionism; and excessive local imports, causing national imbalances
in foreign exchange.[28] The results of fiscal decentralization were dis-

28. "In recent years, the power of the localities to act autonomously has been expanded,
and the system of 'eating in one's own kitchen' has been practiced in finance: in order to
increase their own financial revenues, the various places have neglected the question
whether it is in conformity with the needs of the whole nation, and blindly developed the
processing industry which reaps the greatest profits, resulting in duplicative construction;
they even go so far as to refuse the sales of high quality productions from other places in

torted by the irrational price structure and the lack of hard budget constraints, rather than by the fiscal policies themselves. The entrepreneurial energy sparked by fiscal decentralization was impressive nonetheless. And as a political strategy to win provincial support for economic reform, it was extremely successful.

Many of the other reform policies introduced in the 1980s also reflect the strategy of "playing to the provinces." Under the leadership of Zhao Ziyang, whose entire career was based in the provinces, administrative decentralization became a key element in the political strategy of economic reform. Central ministries were told to send down (*xiafang*) control of their enterprises to provincial or municipal authorities. Local authorities were authorized to retain enterprise depreciation funds and expand other sources of extrabudgetary revenues. The financial freedom of provincial officials was further enhanced by transforming capital-construction funds into bank loans and by granting more autonomy to provincial bank branches. In the realm of foreign trade, provinces were permitted to set up their own trade corporations and delegated authority to approve imports and joint ventures. And after the implementation of the 1988 foreign trade responsibility system, provinces contracted with the Center to share the foreign exchange revenues from trade (as well as the local currency profits and losses from trade), much as they do local fiscal revenues (Yao 1988). The one reform policy that harmed the interests of provincial authorities, the 1983 *li gai shui* tax system, which took the financial profits of local enterprises away from provinces, was scrapped after four years; in 1987 it was replaced with profit-sharing contracts (*chengbao*), which restored the provinces' claim to local-enterprise profits (author's interview). Policies granting special financial and planning authority (called *jihua danlie*) to eleven cities (fourteen, as of February 1989), special foreign trade and investment authority to four special economic zones and fourteen coastal cities, and full provincial status to one region (Hainan Island) enhanced the economic power of China's most flourishing cities and brought these cities into the reform coalition along with the provinces.

The result of all these reform policies has been to shift the center of gravity in economic administration from central agencies (*tiao*) to local government (*kuai*).[29] This shift is more valuable for provincial and munici-

---

local commercial departments, with a view to guaranteeing a market for their own productions, with the effect of carving up the regions" (Xue 1983). One fact that vividly illustrates the phenomenon of local expansion is that as of 1988, Zhejiang, a province with only 70 counties and cities, had 115 beer breweries (Gu and Li 1988).

29. Although the national reformist leaders have bent over backward to appeal to provincial interests, the provinces still are under the sway of the Center. True, the Center lost some of its leverage when it dispersed control over revenues, material resources, and rents. Provincial officials bent on making profits often evade central regulations (Shirk

pal authorities than previous decentralizations because it occurs in the context of an increasingly marketized economy. With the market offering everyone new opportunities for making money, whoever controls access to the market has the opportunity to collect "rents" (Krueger 1974). Reform policies have both expanded market exchange and decentralized from Center to locality the rents collected by administrative regulation of the market. Having been delegated the authority to approve construction projects and imports, and to set license fees and other local commercial taxes, provincial and municipal authorities can, in effect, sell tickets to the market (*Xinhua*, 5 May 1988). If they charge money and use it to develop local infrastructure, as the Tianjin mayor, Li Ruihuan, was famous for doing (author's interviews), they are called statesmen. If they charge money and put it in their own pockets, they are called corrupt criminals. And if they take their payment in the currency of political support, they are called political bosses. The rent-decentralizing implications of many reform policies explain why provincial and municipal authorities are such enthusiastic supporters of economic reform.

   At least some of these local rents were spent on expanding the size of local government. Top Party leaders, eager to win the support of local officials (and appease central ones), have tolerated a dramatic buildup of the national administrative apparatus. The average annual increase in the number of government cadres reached 330,000 per year; before 1980 the average increase was 110,000 per year. By the end of 1986 the total staff of government offices and organizations was 7.34 million, 78.2 percent higher than 1978 (Tang 1987). The increase in administrative expenditures that accompanied this growth in the size of government (a 250 percent increase over 1978) can be seen as a side-payment to keep local- and central-government officials satisfied during the period of reform.

1988). Yet the Center remains the principal. It retains formal authority over the provinces by virtue of its power to appoint provincial governors and Party secretaries and to set the contracts (fiscal, production plan, and foreign trade) for each province. The formal authority of the Center over the provinces fundamentally constrains the bargaining between provincial and central officials. If a provincial Party secretary or governor steps out of line, the central Party leaders can punish him or her by demotion or transfer. The competition among provinces for the best revenue-sharing contract with the Center gives the Center another way to reward or punish the behavior of provincial officials. The provincial agents may have been delegated more authority than before, but they are still agents. If central officials do not punish provincial officials for failing to implement central directives, it is because the central officials choose not to—because they need the support of provincial officials in the Central Committee—not because they are unable to. This principal-agent perspective emphasizes the dependence of the provinces on the Center, in contrast to Lieberthal and Oksenberg's depiction of central-provincial relations as an interdependent relationship with the balance generally in favor of the Center (Lieberthal and Oksenberg 1988).

The prior dispersal of resources and authority not only laid the foundation for Chinese leaders to make local officials the core of its reform coalition, it also had the surprising effect of motivating central economic bodies like the State Planning Commission and the Ministry of Finance to support important reform policies. These central organs were frustrated after years of trying to sustain central management of the economy in an environment characterized by dispersed material inputs and revenues. Planning and financial officials saw their actual control over the economy slipping away over the years. From their perspective, a formal sharing rule, dividing the functions, resources, and revenues between Center and province, was preferable to a continuing erosion of de facto control. At least the sharing rule would prevent further deterioration of their position and permit them to retain their current degree of economic control. This perspective of central comprehensive agencies explains why the Ministry of Finance proposed the 1980 fiscal decentralization, the State Planning Commission proposed the 1984 planning reform, and the Ministry of Foreign Economic Relations and Trade proposed the 1988 reform in foreign trade contracting (author's interviews).

China's form of decentralized communism has helped the Party leadership build political support for economic reform. Not only did it make provincial and municipal officials a natural constituency for reform, it also gave central economic officials a reason to support reforms that would preserve the sharing of control between Center and locality. One hypothesis that stems from this analysis is that the Soviet Union, which begins reform as a much more centralized system, will find the political challenge of economic reform even more difficult than China's.

CONCLUSION: EVALUATING THE POLITICAL RECORD OF ECONOMIC REFORM

The political challenge of economic reform in communist states is to devise policies that build a coalition of support for the reform drive while also improving economic efficiency. The reformist leaders at the top of the Communist Party, Deng Xiaoping and Zhao Ziyang, appeared to have done a masterful job at designing a political strategy of reform that suited the Chinese political institutions. While maintaining the CCP's leadership over the government, they delegated to the government bureaucracy increased discretion. This modification of the principal-agent relationship between Party and government seemed to dilute the influence of conservative Party leaders who might have sabotaged the reform drive, at the same time that it improved the quality of policy decisions. Yet, as the ultimate principals, the top Party leaders retained the power to take policy initiatives, set the ideological line, and replace government cadres. The management-by-exception method of decision making employed under this revised delegation relationship between Party and government provided the framework for bargaining out reform policies that could be supported by key bureaucratic agencies. Although the widening of consultation within the government bureaucracy made the task of building consensus more difficult, it meant that the policies that emerged would be satisfactory (or at least tolerable) to all groups. Zhao Ziyang's strategy of gradual reform, playing to the provinces while postponing the most redistributive measures and working out compromises by giving side-payments, was effective at sustaining the momentum of reform until 1988.

The political choices made during 1980–88 built a coalition of support for economic reform but made the political challenge of future reforms much more difficult. The path of reform reflected more a political logic than an economic logic. By postponing industrial price reform and the introduction of a hard budget constraint, the reformist leaders stimulated rapid economic growth accompanied by material shortages, budget and foreign exchange deficits, inflation, and corruption. These new economic problems backfired on the reform drive at both the elite and the mass level. They provided ammunition for Party conservatives who opposed radical reforms and made a play to reclaim dominance within the Party. At the mass level, the social mobilizational effects of market reforms and public dissatisfaction with inflation and corruption sparked social protest, beginning in late 1986 and building to the massive demonstrations in eighty-four cities during spring 1989. The conservatives pointed to protests as evidence that reform was leading to social chaos (*luan*) and that new Party leadership was needed to restore stability. Despite the achievements of Deng and Zhao at brokering reform policies through the Chinese bureaucratic system, the combination of elite power struggles and social unrest destroyed the momentum of reform in 1988–89. As the principal-agent framework would predict, once the conservatives strengthened their hold on the Communist Party leadership organs (with the firing from the Party secretary position of Hu Yaobang in 1987 and Zhao Ziyang in 1989), the policies emerging from the government changed from reform to retrenchment. Whether the reform drive will recover its momentum in the future depends on the outcome of the competition for Party leadership after Deng Xiaoping's death.

REFERENCES

Arrow, Kenneth J. 1985. "The Economics of Agency." In *Principals and Agents: The Structure of Business,* edited by John W. Pratt and Richard J. Zeckhauser. Boston: Harvard Business School Press.

Barnett, A. Doak. 1967. *Cadres, Bureaucracy, and Political Power in Communist China.* New York: Columbia University Press.

———. 1985. *The Making of Foreign Policy in China: Structure and Process.* Boulder: Westview Press.

Bunce, Valerie. 1981. *Do New Leaders Make a Difference? Executive Succession and Public Policy Under Capitalism and Socialism.* Princeton: Princeton University Press.

Burns, John P. 1987. "China's Nomenklatura System." *Problems of Communism* 36 (September–October): 36–51.

———. 1988. "Reform of Contemporary China's Civil Service System: Proposals of the 13th Party Congress." Paper presented to the Annual Meeting of the Association for Asian Studies, March 1988.

Caizheng. 1980. "The Temporary Provisions for Carrying Out a Financial Management System of 'Apportioning Revenues and Expenditures Between the Central and Local Authorities, While Holding the Latter Responsible for Their Own Profit and Loss.' " *Caizheng,* no. 12 (December); *Joint Publications Research Service (JPRS),* no. 77592, 16 March 1981, 35–39.

Chen Junsheng. 1987. "Increase the Work Efficiency of Public Organs." *Renmin Ribao,* 19 March, *Foreign Broadcast Information Service (FBIS),* 1 April, K33–39.

Comisso, Ellen. 1986. "Introduction: State Structures, Political Processes, and Collective Choice in CMEA States." In *Power, Purpose, and Collective Choice, Economic Strategy in Socialist States,* edited by Ellen Comisso and Laura D'Andrea Tyson. Ithaca: Cornell University Press.

Deng Xiaoping. 1980. "On the Reform of the System of Party and State Leadership," 18 August. *Selected Works of Deng Xiaoping, 1975–1982.* Beijing: Foreign Language Press, 1984.

Donnithorne, Audrey. 1981. *Centre-Provincial Economic Relations in China.* Canberra: Australian National University, Contemporary China Papers, no. 16.

Fu Meihua. 1988. "Inside Story on the Restoration of Military Ranks in China." *Kuang Chiao Ching* (Hong Kong), 16 May, *FBIS,* 20 May, 20–24.

Fujimoto, Akira. 1980. "The Reform of China's Financial Administration System." Japan External Trade Research Organization, *China Newsletter,* March, 2–9.

Gongren Ribao. 1985. "Reforms Must be Carried Out Step by Step." *Gongren Ribao,* 13 March, *FBIS,* 25 March, K26–27.

Gu Wanming and Li Li. 1988. "Expanded Use of Extra-Budgetary Funds." *Xinhua,* 17 January, *FBIS,* 28 January, 13–14.

Han Guochun. 1982. "A Brief Introduction to the System of 'Appportioning Revenues and Expenses Between the Central and Local Authorities, While Holding the Latter Responsible for Their Own Profit and Loss in Financial Management.' " *Caizheng,* no. 7 (5 July), *JPRS,* no. 82018, 19 October, 16–19.

Harding, Harry. 1981. *Organizing China: The Problem of Bureaucracy, 1949–1976.* Stanford: Stanford University Press.

Hongqi. 1987. "Fully Understand the Long-Term Character and Difficulty of the Reform." *Hongqi,* March, *FBIS,* 16 March, K13–15.

Hough, Jerry. 1977. *The Soviet Union and Social Science Theory.* Cambridge: Harvard University Press.

Krueger, Anne. 1974. "The Political Economy of the Rent-Seeking Society." *American Economic Review* 64: 291–302.

Lampton, David M. 1987. "Water: Challenge to a Fragmented Political System." In *Policy Implementation in Post-Mao China,* edited by David M. Lampton. Berkeley and Los Angeles: University of California Press.

Lardy, Nicholas. 1983. *Agriculture in China's Modern Economic Development.* Cambridge: Cambridge University Press.

Lawler, Edward E. III. 1976. "Control Systems in Organizations." In *Handbook of Industrial and Organizational Psychology,* edited by Marvin Dunnette. Chicago: Rand McNally.

Li Peng. 1988. "Li Peng Addresses Party Work Meeting." *Xinhua,* 22 March, *FBIS,* 23 March, 15–16.

Lieberthal, Kenneth, and Michel Oksenberg. 1988. *Policy Making in China: Leaders, Structures, and Processes.* Princeton: Princeton University Press.

Lo Ping. 1988. "Notes on the Northern Journey." *Cheng Ming* (Hong Kong), 1 April, *FBIS,* 1 April, 42–46.

McCubbins, Mathew, and Thomas Schwartz. 1984. "Congressional Oversight Overlooked: Police Patrols vs. Fire Alarms." *American Journal of Political Science.*

MacFarquhar, Roderick. 1974. *The Origins of the Cultural Revolution.* Vol. 1, *Contradictions among the People, 1956–57.* New York: Columbia University Press.

———. 1983. *The Origins of the Cultural Revolution.* Vol. 2, *The Great Leap Forward, 1958–1960.* New York: Columbia University Press.

Ma Hong. 1987. "Ma Hong, General Director of State Council Economic and Social Development Research Center, Answers Reporter's Questions." *Guangming Ribao,* 29 October, *FBIS,* 13 November, 37–38.

Naughton, Barry. 1985. "False Starts and Second Winds: Financial Reforms in China's Industrial System." In *The Political Economy of Reform in Post-Mao China,* edited by Elizabeth J. Perry and Christine P. W. Wong. Cambridge: Harvard University Press.

———. 1987. "The Decline of Central Control over Investment in Post-Mao China." In *Policy Implementation in Post-Mao China,* edited by David M. Lampton. Berkeley and Los Angeles: University of California Press.

Oksenberg, Michel. 1971. "Policy Making Under Mao, 1949–68: An Overview." In *China: Management of a Revolutionary Society,* edited by John M. H. Lindbeck. Seattle: University of Washington Press.

———. 1982. "Economic Policy-Making in China: Summer 1981." *China Quarterly,* no. 90 (1982): 165–94.

Pratt, John W., and Richard J. Zeckhauser, eds. 1985. *Principals and Agents: The Structure of Business.* Boston: Harvard Business School Press.

Renmin Ribao. 1983. "Resolutely Stop Acts of Wrangling Detrimental to the Overall Interests," 21 January, *FBIS,* 24 January, K5–6.

———. 1984. "Breaking with Departmental Bias, On the Importance of Strengthening Sectoral Management during Industrial Reform," 17 July, 1.

———. 1987. "Draft Revision of Some Articles of the Constitution of the Chinese Communist Party," 2 November.

———. 1988. "Reform Involves Risks and Difficulties, Pass the Barrier Through Arduous Efforts," 9 June, *FBIS,* 9 June, 37–38.

Schurmann, Franz. 1968. *Ideology and Organization in Communist China.* 2d ed. Berkeley and Los Angeles: University of California Press.

Schwartz, Thomas. 1988. "The Meaning of Instability." Paper presented to the Department of Political Science, University of California, San Diego, June.

Shijie Jingji Daobao. 1987. "Different Types of Contracted Managerial Responsibility Systems Used by Enterprises," 25 May, 7.

Shirk, Susan L. 1988. "The Acquisition of Foreign Technology in China: The Bargaining Game." Paper presented to the 17th Pacific Trade and Development Conference, Bali, Indonesia, July.

———. 1989. "The Political Economy of Chinese Industrial Reform." In *Remaking the Economic Institutions of Socialism: China and Eastern Europe,* edited by Victor Nee and David Stark. Stanford: Stanford University Press.

Solinger, Dorothy J. 1982. "The Fifth National People's Congress and the Process of Policymaking: Reform, Readjustment, and the Opposition." *Issues and Studies* 18, no. 8 (August 1982): 63–106.

———. 1988. "Disinvestment and the Politics of Pleading." Paper presented to the Annual Meeting of the Association for Asian Studies.

South China Morning Post. 1987. "Paper Analyzes New Central Committee." *Saturday Review,* 7 November, *FBIS,* 9 November, 18–19.

State Statistical Bureau. 1985. *China: A Statistical Survey in 1985.* Beijing: New World Press.

Tang Tian. 1987. "The Readjustment of the Cadre Distribution Structure Is Imperative." *Liaowang,* no. 36, 7 September, *FBIS,* 18 September, 18–19.

Teiwes, Frederick C. 1979. *Politics and Purges in China: Rectification and the Decline of Party Norms, 1950–1965.* White Plains, N.Y.: M.E. Sharpe.

———. 1984. *Leadership, Legitimacy, and Conflict in China.* Armonk, N.Y.: M. E. Sharpe.

Tian Jiyun. 1986. "Speech at a Conference of Central Organs." 6 January. *Xinhua,* 11 January, *FBIS,* 13 January, K21.

Tsou, Tang. 1983. "Back from the Brink of Revolutionary-'Feudal' Totalitarianism." In *State and Society in Contemporary China,* edited by David Mozingo and Victor Nee. Ithaca: Cornell University Press.

Wong, Christine P. W. 1985. "Material Allocation and Decentralization: Impact of the Local Sector on Industrial Reform." In *The Political Economy of Reform in Post-Mao China,* edited by Elizabeth J. Perry and Christine P. W. Wong. Cambridge: Harvard University Press.

———. 1986. "Ownership and Control in Chinese Industry: The Maoist Legacy and Prospects for the 1980's." In U.S. Congress, Joint Economic Committee, *China's Economy Looks Toward the Year 2000,* vol. 1. Washington, D.C.: U.S. Government Printing Office.

Xinhua. 1979. "Decisions on Some Questions Concerning the Acceleration of Agricultural Development," 5 October. In *The People's Republic of China, 1979–1984: A Documentary Survey,* edited by Harold C. Hinton, vol. 2. Wilmington: Scholarly Resources, Inc.

———. 1985. "Zhao Comments," 1 January, *FBIS,* 2 January, K9–11. "Metallurgical Conference's New System Approved," 10 February, *FBIS,* 12 February, K16–17.

————. 1987. "Forum Discusses Deng's Speech," 5 July, *FBIS*, 6 July, K5–8. "New Management Systems to Categorize Cadres," 18 November, *FBIS*, 18 November, 17–18.

————. 1988. "Provisional Regulations Banning Unjustifiable Impositions on Enterprises" (promulgated by the State Council on 28 April 1988), 5 May, *FBIS*, 9 May, 31–33. "Central Committee Reports on CPC Membership," 17 June, *FBIS*, 17 June, 17.

Xue Muqiao. 1983. "China's Current Economic Situation, Analysis and Prospects." *Renmin Ribao*, 3 June, *FBIS*, 13 June, K34–41.

Yan Jiaqi. 1988. " 'Separation of Party and Government Work' in China as Viewed From a Comparative Angle." *Wen Wei Po* (Hong Kong), 23 March, *FBIS*, 14 April, 42–45.

Yao Yilin. 1988. "Report on the Draft National Economic and Social Development Plan for 1988." Paper presented to the First Session of the Seventh National People's Congress, 26 March. *Renmin Ribao*, 17 April, *FBIS*, 20 April, 18–27.

Zhao Ziyang. 1987a. "Report on the Work of the Government." Paper presented to the Fifth Session of the Sixth National People's Congress. Beijing Domestic Service, 25 March, *FBIS*, 26 March, K1–25.

————. 1987b. "Advance Along the Road of Socialism with Chinese Characteristics." Work Report to Thirteenth National CCP Congress. *Xinhua*, 25 October, *FBIS*, 26 October, 10–34.

————. 1987c. "On the Separation of Party and Government." Speech to the Preparatory Meeting for the Seventh Plenary Session of the Twelfth Central Committee on 14 October 1987. *Xinhua*, 26 November, *FBIS*, 27 November, 13–16.

Zhou Yi. 1987. "The Question of Party Leadership During Political Structure Reform." *Lilun Yuekan*, no. 7 (25 July), *FBIS*, 1 September, 18–23.

PART TWO

The Center

FOUR

The Party Leadership System

Carol Lee Hamrin

Changes in the Chinese Party and state political system during the 1980s were important efforts after Mao's death to redress serious flaws in a governing structure that has inhibited economic development, exacerbated social conflict, and suppressed personal freedoms. Discussions of political reform by Chinese researchers over the past decade indicated, however, that they have had much difficulty in understanding the exact nature of the leadership system and in identifying necessary and possible changes. The tragic events of 1989 showed clearly that reforms of the Party leadership system over the decade were far from sufficient to prevent the recurrence of economic instability and large-scale social disaster.

In any effort to understand the purposes and flaws of the system, a large part of the analytical problem is that the formal institutions and flow-charts discussed in the public domain do not capture the essence of the actual functioning system, which includes organizations and relationships not discussed in public. In part, this opaqueness seems intended to obscure the extent and means of Party control over Chinese society; it originated in the underground mentality of the 1930s and 1940s when secret Party control of ostensibly independent organizations was a central element of united-front policies. Many Chinese themselves are only vaguely aware of the "shadow" structure and process that links the Party with the more visible formal bureaucratic organs and that guide, coordinate, and interact with the latter.

This study presents the personal views of the author, not those of the U.S. Government. Because of the continued sensitivity of this topic in China despite some recent public mention of previously secret leadership arrangements, I use information obtained from formal interviews and informal conversations with Chinese citizens without any details. No classified information is used. My special thanks go to Doak Barnett, Christopher Clarke, and Kenneth Lieberthal for their suggestions on revising this chapter.

Lack of clarity in part also reflects the many changes over time in China's relatively unstable governing structure. To say there are gaps in knowledge is thus an understatement. Information restrictions make us feel like the unfortunates gazing at the shadows on the wall in Plato's proverbial cave. Recent information has allowed us to discern the basic shapes of the shadows, and their movement. For now, we still "see through a glass darkly."

In this chapter I attempt to generalize about the hidden part of the system at its apex, where a handful of senior leaders are the nerve center for three gigantic bureaucracies with at least 5 million cadre (600,000 Party, 4.4 million government, and an unknown number military), assigned to scores of central units and subordinate clone structures in the localities. This elite in turn supervises 10.8 million cadre in state enterprises and 13 million in state education, science, and health units.[1] How do the top leaders organize themselves to use this structure to understand and direct developments in China?

Not surprisingly, there is constant fluidity here, and there has been much evolution over time. Problems change; political considerations and socioeconomic crises intervene; powerful leaders with quite different personalities shape the system to suit their preferences. Nevertheless, a rough outline sketch of the structure and process of the Chinese leadership system can be drawn.

In this sketch, a little-understood level of Party organization emerges as particularly important in defining leaders' duties, shaping their relationships, and linking them with the bureaucracies—the powerful central commissions (*weiyuanhui*) and central leading small groups (*lingdao xiaozu;* hereafter this type of organization will be referred to in a generic sense as leading groups or LGs). These organs, each led by a member of the Politburo or its standing committee, include in their membership the senior Party, state, and military officials with expertise and responsibility in a given specialized functional sector or system (*xitong*). Their primary task is the formation of major policy goals and guidelines. Lower-level organs, including State Council leading groups, work out concrete policies and oversee policy coordination and administration.

The following description and analysis of the leadership system leads to the conclusion that control of leading groups is a key aim of actors in China's perennial power struggles, which implies that the groups have considerable effectiveness in centrally coordinating and directing complex policy programs. But direct evidence is still insufficient to resolve the issue of how, and how effectively, leading groups actually function to

1. These figures came from a high-level official, in an interview with Doak Barnett in the summer of 1988. I am grateful to Professor Barnett for sharing this and other information below.

shape the vast and fragmented Chinese bureaucratic system. No doubt this has varied over time and under different leaderships.

EVOLUTION OF THE LEADERSHIP SYSTEM

In late 1987 two researchers in the Party History Research Institute provided new insight into how the central leadership structure had evolved prior to 1978, as follows.[2] Beginning in 1942, with a reorganization of the wartime base areas to overcome lack of coordination among Party, government, military, and mass organizations, the fundamental principle of highly centralized Party leadership was established. Policy directives by Party committees at the various levels were to be implemented unconditionally by the Party groups (*dangtuan*) of the military-political commissions (*junzheng weiyuanhui*) set up within each military, government, and mass organization. Party committee members divided functional responsibilities among themselves.

A variation of this structure, modified according to the Soviet system, emerged after 1949. Party committees were set up in each non-Party organization and given responsibility for supervising (not actually engaging in) administrative work. This was done through subdivisions corresponding to the propaganda, organization, and united-front departments of the Central Committee. But at the same time, Party core groups (*dangzu*) in each organization were responsible directly to the next higher level (whether Party committee or core group is unclear) for actual implementation of policy. This central-command system was closely related to the militaristic mass-campaign approach to governance continued into the immediate post-1949 period of reconstruction and reorganization. There were periodic attempts to limit Party involvement in direct administration, but these ceased with the campaign against "decentralism and localism" following the purge of Gao Gang and Rao Shushi.[3]

During the 1950s the leadership structure was modified several times in attempts to suit the increasing complexity of state administration and the proliferation of cadre, but without weakening overall Party control. A small handful of senior leaders (at that time a small Politburo or a small Secretariat, eventually the Politburo standing committee) decided

2. The following history, except for specific items of information taken from the source cited in notes 3 and 4, came from Pang Song and Han Gang, "The Party and State Leadership Structure: Historical Investigation and Prospects for Reform," *Social Science in China* 8, no. 4 (December 1987): 29–56.

3. Reporter, "Major Change in the Form of CCP Leadership," *Liaowang* overseas edition 43 (26 October 1987), 3–4, in Foreign Broadcast Information Service, *China Daily Report* (hereafter FBIS-CHI) 87-209 (29 October 1987), 22, cited two central Party directives dated February 1951 and November 1951, which spelled out a separation of functions between Party and state organs.

macropolicy and supervised governance through bodies responsible for daily administration in three separate bureaucracies: Party and mass work was handled in meetings convened by Deng Xiaoping as secretary-general or after 1956 in the Secretariat led by Deng as general secretary; military affairs were under the military commission; and government matters (economic and foreign affairs) were discussed in State Council plenary session attended by all vice-premiers and ministers. (The source does not discuss legislative, judicial, and police work.)

In October 1955, in addition to the normal central committee departments responsible for Party work, the central committee and each provincial Party committee set up new subordinate departments as functional counterparts to the main government and judicial subsystems. These included industry and transport, finance and trade, culture and education, and judiciary departments.[4] After this time there was little cadre mobility across systems. These new departments originally were intended to manage personnel affairs but not professional, policy matters. There was an effort to separate responsibility for three stages of the policy process: Party organs making general policy decisions; judicial and planning organs fleshing them out as laws and economic plans; followed by government implementation.

Beginning in June 1958 at the height of the Great Leap Forward with a decision to foster recentralization of leadership in the Party, however, the Party exercised more and more direct administrative authority, greatly reducing the autonomy of state, judicial, and social institutions, as well as of the press. The Politburo retained the power of decision over major principles and policies, but transferred authority for concrete policy, legislation, and oversight from state and judicial bodies to the Secretariat. The government became essentially the executive organ of the Party rather than the state, with only minor authority for policy details. In 1959 judicial organs were merged into the public security organs at all levels, and the Ministry of Justice and notary offices were abolished. All state supervisory organs were replaced by Party supervisory committees (*jiancha weiyuanhui*). Meanwhile, the Party's Military Commission strengthened its control over the military bureaucracy as well.

Great Leap Forward slogans, like "The Party exercises overall leadership" and "The Party secretary in command," were institutionalized when Party committees took direct control in economic enterprises and social institutions; Party core groups did the same in state and judicial organs. Policy execution often took the form of mass campaigns.

4. Ibid. This source contradicted that in note 2 by saying that the Party and the government departments performed the same functions. I believe that this latter article, which telescopes the history dealt with at greater length in the former article, was telling us the end result, not the original intent, of setting up the Party departments.

Central to this change in structure was the formation, beginning in 1958, of the Central Committee's leading small groups (*lingdao xiaozu*), duplicated in lower-level Party committees. This introduced dual subordination in professional affairs for each organ—to the relevant LG at the same level, as well as in the next higher level. The original central leading groups were responsible for policy oversight of five sectors: finance and economics; political (legislative and security) and judicial work; foreign affairs; science; and culture and education. It would appear that this reorganization was aimed in part at creating one group to consolidate and coordinate the economic subsectors; using one group to coordinate both Party and government foreign affairs work; and giving science-and-technology higher priority and autonomy by separating it from culture. These leading groups have remained the most important leading groups through the 1980s.

At first, during the Leap, the concentration of power in Party organs accompanied a general decentralization of power. But over time there was a reconcentration of power at higher and higher levels. In the 1960s regional Party committees with no counterpart governments took over much of the authority of lower-level committees. The Maoist personality cult reflected and fortified a structural bias toward personal dictatorship in each Party organ. The Party secretary in charge of any unit, functional system, or leading small group had considerable discretion in his sphere of authority and often ended up making arbitrary, uninformed decisions on major matters of state. Yet not he but the powerless administrators were required to achieve actual policy implementation. Authority and responsibility were increasingly divorced, resulting in ineffective government. The Cultural Revolution was the natural product of the development of the negative aspects of this monolithic (*yiyuanhua*) Party leadership structure, the basic structure that reemerged after the institutional anarchy during that time.

NORMS OF THE LEADERSHIP SYSTEM

Functional Systems and Coordinating Points

Formal organization charts of the Chinese political system showing the three main bureaucracies, as well as academic studies of the functional systems that cross bureaucratic lines, still tend to leave mysterious the actual working relations among bureaucracies, systems, and units. During the 1980s new information about the details of this leadership system revealed attempts to institutionalize horizontal coordination mechanisms to overcome the inherent tendency of the vertical hierarchies to produce uncoordinated or even conflicting demands and policies. There were informal personal ties and professional communications, of course. But at least in the mid-1980s there were also "comprehensive coordination points" (*zong·kou zi*) and subordinate coordination points (*kou*) intended to integrate related functional systems and subsystems so as to create general policies and to effect coordinated policy implementation.[5]

This coordinating system was referred to as *gui kou*, that is, administration according to fixed or specified coordination points (*kou* could be translated more literally as "channels" or "gates"). This *xitong* and *kou* system was replicated further down the line, in the provincial and municipal leadership setups.

There was a pyramidal structure to this coordinating system, such that from bottom to top, there were tiers of organs and groups that had an increasingly broad scope of responsibility and weight of authority. Presumably, as a policy problem was kicked up the pyramid because of either urgency or controversy, it was more apt to be considered in a comprehensive, strategic context. The tiers of coordination points might be envisaged as these:

1. Paramount leader (*zuigao lingxiu*) with ultimate overall authority, who had the strongest (sometimes sole) influence over divisions of responsibility within the Politburo.
2. Politburo standing committee members plus select elders who were responsible for coordinating all major policy decisions. With the leader, they decided who among them would oversee each of the handful of penultimate policy arenas. They had to answer both to each other and to the paramount leader.
3. Party leading small groups or committees that oversaw each of the main policy sectors (related functional systems). Each was headed by one or two Politburo standing committee members, although the actual work might be coordinated by a deputy head or a secretary-general.
4. Administrative offices or departments (in the Central Committee, State Council, and army) that channeled policy information and recommendations upward and decisions downward to appropriate implementing organs. These usually would be headed by members of the Secretariat, the State Council standing committee, or the Military Commission, and might also be Politburo members.

5. Editor(s) of the "Current China's Economic Management" Compilation Group, *Zhonghua renmin gongheguo jingji guanli dashiji* (Chronicle of the Economic Management of the People's Republic of China; hereafter referred to as *Chronicle*) (Beijing, China Economics Publishers, 1986), a major source of information for this chapter, used these terms, as have Chinese officials and scholars, but without precise definition of their meaning and usage. Doak Barnett informed me that in the summer of 1988 he was told by Chinese officials that these terms were no longer in use, at least at the State Council level.

Division of Responsibilities

The central leading groups and commissions and their subordinate bodies typically had sweeping mandates. Detailed descriptions of the work of the Political and Legal Affairs Commission and the Science and Technology LG, for example, revealed similar broad tasks of policy planning, command, and coordination, as well as supervision over personnel and implementation.[6]

The Finance and Economics LG had similar responsibilities, including coordination, investigation, and research, proposing major policies, supervising policy implementation, and sponsoring reform experiments. The Foreign Investment LG was to

(a) draw up policies and plans for using foreign investment and submit these suggestions to the State Council; (b) supervise the work of localities and government departments involved with foreign investment and undertake arbitration and adjustment when major problems arise; (c) and supervise the relevant authorities in their task of drafting investment laws.[7]

Units subordinate to the LGs were responsible for actually carrying out these many varied tasks, since LGs themselves had very small staffs. For example, in 1984 the administrative body for the Foreign Investment LG was upgraded from a "Special Economic Zones (SEZ) work group" in the State Council General Office to an SEZ Office, with a mandate to

(a) research, draft documents for and to *manage* the SEZs, the implementation of Guangdong and Fujian Provinces' "special policies and flexible measures," and the relevant general programs and policies of development and construction of Hainan Island and the opening up of coastal cities; (b) coordinate and resolve contradictions that appear in implementation; (c) examine and study the situations and experiences of all countries concerning the running of economic development zones, export processing zones [etc.]; and (d) to assume the burden of other matters assigned by the Central Committee and State Council pertaining to the work of opening to the outside.[8]

A number of tentative conclusions can be drawn regarding the policy process according to the system of LGs:

Policy-making. "Central authorities," meaning the Politburo, reserved the ultimate right to determine general programs and major policies.

6. See Appendix A for details, which were taken from *Chronicle* (PLC, 376; S & T LG, 487; and the SEZ Office, 543).
7. *China Business Review*, January–February 1987, 10, citing the National Council for U.S.–China Trade files.
8. Ibid.

These high-level decisions probably were made most often at the Polit-buro standing committee level, which met once each week.[9] Decisions were heavily influenced by information and recommendations brought to it by the responsible head of the LG or commission involved. He would be held responsible by peers and elders for developments in his policy arena.

The full memberships of the Politburo and of the State Council met only about once a month, in plenary session, judging from official Chi-nese press reports on their activities that were released regularly for a time after the Thirteenth Congress. Their agendas appeared to include only the most major issues, such as the coastal development strategy or the reorganization of the State Council. Their executive bodies—the standing committees—probably met once or even twice each week, for several hours at a time. Each time, the agenda was likely to be limited to one or two major topics for discussion, perhaps with minor issues pre-sented for pro forma approval. Given the heavy work load, it is quite likely that much of the thorough consideration of policy was done by the LGs, while the drafting and shaping of policy documents was done by their staff offices.[10]

The frequency of LG meetings was unclear. A. Doak Barnett's study of the foreign affairs apparatus indicated that the Foreign Affairs LG had no regular schedule for its meetings, but met "fairly frequently," and at times "as often as once a week."[11] Outside specialists on an LG agenda topic were often invited to provide briefings or even join in the discus-sion. The openness of discussions in LGs may well have differed mark-edly, depending on the personal style of the leader. Barnett was told that Li Xiannian was "fairly permissive," thus creating an atmosphere for genuine discussion in the Foreign Affairs LG. Others have said that Zhao Ziyang often would come to the Foreign Affairs LG meetings with deci-sions already made at higher levels, just informing them and giving directions for implementation. This LG might not be typical, however, given the sensitivity of the issues and the limited distribution of informa-tion. The business of the other LGs might have been more open.

There was a tradition of annual meetings convened by LGs as part of

9. A high-level Party official, in an interview with Doak Barnett, summer 1988.

10. For example, in 1988 the State Council discussed and approved provisional regula-tions on leasing small-scale state enterprises. These regulations (8 chapters and 40 articles) presumably were drafted by the government's staff office for the Finance and Economics LG, following a decision—presumably at the Politburo level—several years earlier to allow the practice.

11. A. Doak Barnett, *The Making of Foreign Policy in China: Structure and Process* (Boulder, Colo.: Westview Press; and the Johns Hopkins University School of Advanced Interna-tional Studies, Foreign Policy Institute: SAIS Papers in International Affairs, 1985).

the annual planning process. These meetings passed on instructions and vetted the opinions of lower-level units in a given functional system. Such sessions were probably used to discuss longer-term plans as well. The Foreign Affairs LG brought ambassadors home each summer for a wide-ranging discussion and briefing session with Beijing-based staff. The national political and legal affairs conference usually was held in March. Some functional national conferences, however, were very irregular. The Science and Technology (S & T) conference met only in 1985 and 1988.

The LG offices were responsible for delegating the task of "fleshing out" general policy guidelines as specific, concrete policy work plans and supervising their implementation. Staff offices did not make formal policy decisions but rather coordinated policy research and experiments, channeled information and draft policy papers, and made the formal assignments for actual implementation by the relevant organs. And of course, as in any bureaucracy, many policy adjustments no doubt were made "on the ground," in the very process of guiding daily operations at lower levels.

Coordination.   The LGs through their staff offices were supposed to perform a wide variety of tasks that would protect burdened (and often elderly) decision-makers. They were troubleshooters, problem-solvers, and arbitrators, particularly for complex, major issues that crossed geographic and bureaucratic lines of responsibility. If the Planning and Economics commissions failed to resolve a policy disagreement, for example, something all too common in fact, it was bucked up to the Finance and Economics LG staff office or higher.

Innovation.   LGs and their offices were clearly much more than coordinating bodies, however, since they were tasked with coming up with new ideas and future plans and with conducting experiments with policy. They were responsible too for recommending organizational changes to improve management.

Supervision.   Major crises would either come to an LG or prompt the creation of a special temporary LG or commission. An example in early 1988 was the investigation group under state councillor and secretary-general of the Finance and Economics LG, Zhang Jingfu, that looked into an air crash and a train accident. The group investigated, assigned blame, and recommended both remedial measures and punishment for those responsible—including the resignation of the new Central Committee alternate and minister of railways, Ding Guangen.

Personnel. In the course of carrying out their duties, LGs touched on many personnel issues: coordinating more rational assignments; checking on the ideological and organizational environment of cadre; and inspecting and chastising irresponsible officials. We know that the Organization Department shared some of its personnel responsibilities with both the United Front Work Department[12] and the Propaganda Department.[13] It seemed probable that the LGs also would have had at least an advisory or veto role in assignments of leading officials in the organs under their supervision. The fact that control over LGs was such a sought-after political prize for senior leaders tended to corroborate their influence over personnel and organization decisions as well as financial and material resources within their arena.

Lines of Authority

The leading groups officially were not line authorities. Documents and requests, as well as research papers, were sent directly to the formal Party, state, or military institutions, not funneled solely through the LGs. Policies shaped within the LGs had to be endorsed by the relevant formal organization, whether the Politburo or the Secretariat, the State Council, or the Military Commission, and then documents were issued by the relevant general office.[14] Nonetheless, the possibility remained that LG leaders and members may have passed orders directly to unit leaders, bypassing official channels.[15]

The exact process of interaction between formal and informal authorities was not known and probably differed considerably by issue and system. Theoretically, the LGs would frame policies, and their staff offices would draft documents for discussion and approval by other bodies. The directors of the LGs presumably had considerable flexibility in determining which issues needed to be brought before the Politburo for

12. John P. Burns, ed., "Contemporary China's Nomenklatura System," *Chinese Law and Government* (Winter 1987–88): 48–49, indicated that beginning in 1980, control over cadre in the political consultative conferences, nationalities and religious affairs organs and associations was shared with the united-front departments.

13. Burns, pp. 38–47, indicated that also beginning in 1980, control over cadre in the propaganda and culture system was shared with the central Propaganda Department, the Party core groups of the relevant ministries, and the lower-level Party culture and education departments.

14. *Chronicle,* p. 376, in discussing the Political and Legal Affairs Commission, for example, insisted that each political and legal department still should send requests and reports directly to the (general offices of the?) Central Committee, State Council, and Military Commission.

15. See Appendix B for ways in which Politburo members may carry out their oversight responsibilities.

decision or just to the Secretariat, State Council, or Military Commission for administrative action; which should be brought to full plenary sessions or just to the smaller executive standing committees; and which warranted full discussion or merely rubber-stamp approval.

CHRONIC PROBLEMS AND POST-MAO REFORMS

The sub-Politburo level of organization, including LGs or committees and staff offices, for the sake of analysis could be likened to the White House staff organizations, such as the National Security Council and the Office of Management and Budget, and the domestic affairs councils, such as the Council of Economic Advisors, in that they provided personal policy support for the president. In both systems, these organizations could operate something like an "inner cabinet" chosen and shaped personally by the top leader. In both systems, short-term domestic political considerations and personal and party loyalties tended to weigh heavily in policy recommendations and decisions within these bodies. These staff organizations were largely immune from outside oversight.

A brief comparison of the two functionally similar setups in the United States and China is helpful in pointing out the vast differences between the Chinese and the American "inner cabinets" in terms of independence and scope of power and influence. In the United States, the many limitations on the independence and influence of the inner cabinet include most importantly the limits on the president's own powers posed by constitutional limits on tenure, the electoral process, the need to obtain rather than command congressional cooperation, and the independence of the courts and the press. Major White House organs also have statutory definitions of their authority and composition. These types of limits on power are either nonexistent or very weak in China.

Moreover, the power of the inner cabinet in the United States is reined in by the stability and strength of the regular executive bureaucracies, with their professional permanent staff, and the direct and independent access to the president by most regular cabinet members, whose experience and stature usually outweigh that of White House staff. In China, by contrast, the inner and outer cabinet members are often the same people wearing two hats, as concurrent Party and government officials; as a result, there are much weaker checks and balances between bureaucracies.

American cabinet members, even though they too are political appointees, are constrained in their work by the congressional approval and review processes, and their limited ability to change and control their own permanent employees, protected by independent personnel systems. The institutions and processes of both Party and state that might have provided checks on the "cabinet" in China, however, have been severely weakened over the decades by constant reorganization, purges, and abrupt changes in policy direction. The informal as well as the formal norms of operation are easily ignored or overridden.

The most obvious difference between the Chinese and the American "inner cabinet" is in the scope of authority. The Politburo's policy groups are ultimately responsible for the direction of all government, economic, and social institutions nationwide. All countries, of course, face the problem of how to link concentrated executive leadership with administrative bureaucracies and nongovernmental groups. But most systems have large social sectors that are autonomous of the government. In China the enormous confluence of leadership over all sectors within one small body, and often in practice one individual at the apex of the system who has wide discretionary authority, greatly magnifies the impact of personality and politics on the system.

Beginning in August 1980, Deng Xiaoping periodically expressed an urgent need for reforming this Party and state leadership system, not merely making changes in personnel. He blamed poor governance on overconcentration of power, arbitrary and patriarchal personal rule, life tenure and special privileges, the holding of concurrent posts, over-staffing, lack of distinction between Party leadership and government administration, as well as a general lack of accountability according to rules. He called for "radical reform," focused on the organs at the highest levels. Deng's stated priorities—in reaction to the disaster of Mao's latter years—were to ensure against personal dictatorship and to create realistic policies.[16]

After the restoration of the Party Secretariat in February 1980 under Hu Yaobang as general secretary, and the reorganization of the State Council in September under Zhao Ziyang as the new premier, Deng, Hu, and Zhao experimented with major changes in the Party and state structure as well as in personnel. In general, the changes were modeled after the Eighth Party Congress setup of 1956–66, with some innovations, such as the creation of the Central Advisory Commission. Procedural, institutional, and legal reforms in this period are best viewed as mechanisms for the Party to delegate authority and responsibility and to create forums for the expression of public opinion, but without giving up its monopoly on power.

By 1986, however, these changes were viewed by many as insufficient

16. Deng Xiaoping, "On the Reform of the System of Party and State Leadership," 18 August 1980, in *Selected Works of Deng Xiaoping (1975–1982)* (Beijing, Foreign Languages Press).

and even superficial. It was openly acknowledged that the bureaucracy had quickly regained and surpassed its former size—like mushrooms after the rain. Corruption was spreading; oligarchy had replaced autocracy. Partial streamlining, rejuvenation of the cadre ranks, and professionalization of policy research and implementation served to regularize procedures and create more realistic policy. But many in the elite became convinced that only the symptoms had been treated, while the disease—labeled "bureaucratism," for short—remained chronic, even potentially fatal to the effectiveness and legitimacy of Party rule. Chen Yizi, a senior adviser to Zhao Ziyang on economic and political reform (who fled China after June 1989), listed some of the continuing flaws resulting from Party monopoly of power: (1) the Party is immersed in routine work and ignores major policy problems; (2) the Party becomes absorbed in addressing conflicts of interest, and social disputes over specific policy decisions by Party and government lead to endless confusion and disputation over trifles; and (3) Party monopoly of all policy decisions means that public grievances over policy failures inevitably create discontent with the Party.[17]

In June 1986 Deng Xiaoping again lent the weight of his authority to a new phase of political restructuring; on Party Day, July 1, his August 1980 speech on leadership reform was republished as the "blueprint" for political reform. Over a dozen cities were allowed to begin experimenting with political reform, and a central Political Reform Study Group was organized in September, with a mandate to draft a reform plan, only some of which was publicly endorsed at the Thirteenth Party Congress.

Continued Political Abuse of the Leadership System

Knowledge of these political-reform preparations in 1986 motivated leading intellectuals to speak out in speeches and articles recommending far-reaching changes in the system, even touching on separation of powers and multiparty elections. This in turn raised expectations and demands of students for democracy when election of candidates to the National People's Congress (NPC) began in the fall. The student demonstrations in turn precipitated the fall of General Secretary Hu Yaobang, but a major cause was his conflict with key Party elders over control of high-level Party leadership organs, where Hu had been forced to share

17. Chen Yizi, "Socialism in the Course of Practice and Exploration," parts one and two of a speech of July 1986 originally titled "The Economic Reform and the Political Reform," *Shijie jingji daobao* (World Economic Herald), 10 August 1987, 3–4, in FBIS-CHI-87-174 (9 September 1987), 20–26; and "Reform of the Political Structure Is a Guarantee of Reform of the Economic Structure," part three, same newspaper, 13 July 1987, 3–14, in Joint Publications Research Service (JPRS) Political, Sociological, and Military Information on China.

power ever since the Twelfth Party Congress.[18] This clash over senior shares of power was a classic example of how the politicization of the system continued to work against stable, effective government.

In 1985–86 Deng and Hu had been trying to turn over some of the functional leadership responsibilities to younger people affiliated with Hu, most notably Hu Qili in Party administration and ideology, Qiao Shi in political-legal and personnel affairs, and Qin Jiwei in military matters. Their plans included reorganizing the leadership units responsible for these arenas to make them more responsive to the needs of the reform program. There were calls for changes in these management systems along lines already pioneered by Zhao in economic and science affairs. But Hu Yaobang's competitors perceived a grab for power wrapped in the mantle of reform.

Much of the actual power struggle was carried out through reorganizing and reassigning membership in Party leading groups or commissions. As a result, institutional reforms became intertwined with—and subverted by—the power struggle. For example, from 1983 to 1986 each ideological campaign had involved a name change and reorganization in the propaganda LG, with the directorship (under supervision of Hu Qiaomu) passing back and forth between Deng Liqun and Hu Qili. Whereas in early 1987 Deng Liqun was in charge of the group set up to "combat bourgeois liberalization," Hu Qili regained influence in the spring when the slogan shifted to include "promote reform and opening up." It is likely that there was a similar shift in control over economic policy in early 1987, when a new campaign to "increase production and practice economy" probably required Zhao Ziyang to share his authority in this sphere with more cautious economic leaders, including Li Peng.

Through 1987, although Zhao nominally became the acting general secretary and supervised the drafting of the Thirteenth Congress work report, most of Hu's responsibilities were assumed by a group of Party elders whom Deng assigned to head new leading groups with responsibilities for the personnel and organizational arrangements to be announced at the congress.[19] In a sense, this group acted as a functioning

18. Bo Yibo and other elders shared control of the Party Rectification Commission; Chen Yun controlled the Discipline Inspection Commission; Hu Qiaomu controlled ideology and propaganda work; Xi Zhongxun was involved in Party administration; Peng Zhen controlled the Political and Legal Affairs Commission, and a number of older generals had a say in military affairs.
19. The Hong Kong *South China Morning Post,* 19 June 1987, 10, in FBIS, 19 June 1987, K6, stated that Bo Yibo and Yang Shangkun were involved in a leading group overseeing preparations for the congress. Bo and Yang took respective responsibilities for civilian and military arrangements, with input from Peng Zhen, Xi Zhongxun, Song Renqiong, Yao Yilin, and Wan Li; the Central Party School president, Gao Yang; and for the military from Wang Zhen, Yu Qiuli, and Wu Xiuquan. *Cheng Ming* 122 (1 December 1987): 6–9, in FBIS

Politburo while reformist leaders like Wan Li, Hu Qili, and Tian Jiyun were under a cloud. By summer 1987, however, a more balanced group was responsible for the congress arrangements: Zhao, Yang, Wan Li, Hu Qili, and Yao Yilin. The changing composition and focus of the special groups set up to look into political reform also reflected the political struggle of 1987.[20]

Trends under Zhao Ziyang

In his report to the Thirteenth Congress, General Secretary Zhao Ziyang proclaimed the intent to continue earlier efforts to create a more efficient and open governing structure by defining—and enforcing—a more limited role for the Party. Because of pressures from conservatives and Zhao's need to strengthen his grip on Party organs, it became clear that political reform would involve dividing functions, not separating powers, among China's governing institutions. That is, the Party would delegate authority to, but not share power with, legislative, executive, and judicial bodies. The logic of the approach was spelled out in a lengthy article from the Party History Research Office published in December 1987: (1) solving problems in leadership structure is the fundamental step required to democratize the state; (2) reform of the leadership structure is the key to political reform and an important component of comprehensive reform; and (3) separating the Party from the government is the key link in changing the leadership structure.[21]

The Party was to limit its direct involvement to the strategic policy-making and personnel functions essential to its continued dominance of the political system. By the late 1980s the Party leadership had delegated a modicum of concrete policy-making and executive power to the government, legislative power to the National People's Congress, and judicial authority to the courts. In addition to further progress on these fronts, in 1988 there seemed to be some incipient movement toward reducing the independence of the military bureaucracy and making it truly a state institution. The legislative "branch" is clearly in transition as a result of the turnover of leadership from Peng Zhen to Wan Li; but little was said about plans for future reform in elections or lawmaking. Greater future

---

87-230 (1 December 1987), 13, mentioned a Thirteenth Congress personnel or nominating group, which was to recommend members of the Central Committee, the Discipline Inspection Commission, and the Advisory Commission. It was headed by Bo and included elders Yang, Wang Zhen, Song Renqiong, and Wu Xiuquan as members. Later, Yao Yilin and Gao Yang joined. Both groups were reported to have subordinate working groups of younger leaders.

20. For details of the personnel and activities of these groups, see Appendix C.

21. Pang Song and Han Gang, "The Party and State Leadership Structure," 49–50.

autonomy was also being promised to nonstate organizations, but again little movement in that direction has occurred.

This strategy of separating functions and delegating authority was limited to the lower and middle reaches of the system and is premised on changes in precisely the opposite direction at the very top. The power of the Politburo standing committee and its leading small groups or commissions, which had macropolicy decision and command authority over all three bureaucracies, was being strengthened. This trend was clear in changes at this level reported in the Hong Kong press in the months following the congress.

The primary motive of reformers in making such changes seemed to be to improve bureaucratic accountability and efficiency as well as policy realism, rather than to introduce democratic checks on the exercise of power. In speeches in 1986, both Vice-Premier Wan Li and the State Council secretary-general, Chen Junsheng, complained of continuing poor work performance in the bureaucracy, as manifested in lack of policy creativity, avoidance of responsibility, persistent wrangling, and nondecision. Chen highlighted both a cultural and an institutional inability to resolve conflicts of interest and coordinate consensus decisions in a positive manner at the lowest possible level. He referred to a chronic "escalation of coordination," such that decisions were constantly being referred up the ladder of authority, and blamed this phenomenon on overcentralization of power, overstaffing, and a too detailed division of labor. As a result, the central leadership was bogged down in details, with no time, energy, or ability to determine strategic programs.[22]

In response to such problems, Zhao Ziyang emphasized the importance of delegating power, clarifying responsibility, and introducing work evaluation and internal supervision systems at every tier. One approach to improving coordination was to expand membership in the central leading groups to include representation from all relevant organizations, with some overlapping membership between groups.

Public supervision was viewed as a necessary but distinctly secondary aim of reform; it still was to be achieved indirectly, through public opinion surveys and appointed or indirectly elected representatives to the legislature and united-front organs. There was only hesitant progress

22. Wan Li, "Making Decision Making More Democratic and Scientific Is an Important Part of Reform of the Political System" (speech given to a national research symposium on soft science in July 1986), *Renmin Ribao*, 15 August 1986, excerpts in Benedict Stavis, ed., "Reform of China's Political System," *Chinese Law and Government* 20, no. 1 (Spring 1987): 21–25, and Chen Junsheng, "Increase the Work Efficiency of Public Organs," excerpts from a speech delivered at a forum for secretary-generals of eight provinces and municipalities, 29 June 1986; originally published in *Mishu Gongzuo* (Secretarial Work) 1987, no. 1; in *Renmin Ribao* (People's Daily), 19 March 1987, 5, in FBIS 1 April 1987, K33–38.

toward achieving "transparency" (*toumingdu*) of the political process through freer press discussion of government structure and actions. Yet this is a prerequisite for any public supervision, given the general public ignorance regarding the purpose, functions, and laws or regulations related to China's governing bureaucracies, not to mention the habitual fear of critiquing government performance.

Another goal of leadership reform—to diminish high-level factionalism—was never mentioned explicitly but seemed implicit in the obvious effort under Zhao to limit the involvement of Party elders in the central leadership organs as well as to make membership largely statutory and thus less open to personal factional appointment and manipulation. The plans to eliminate Party core groups in the government and introduce a civil service system were intended to regularize the functioning of the government, by helping to insulate it from appointment and command according to personal loyalties rather than professional qualities. It also would have helped to clarify duties and lines of authority. But expanding the scope of the civil service and introducing similar mechanisms into other bureaucracies, including Party and security apparatus, would have been critical to the success of civil service reform. So would an expansion of the transparency and supervision of the government from the outside, whether it be in sessions of the National People's Congress and the Chinese People's Political Consultative Congress or the public media.

Events of late 1988 and 1989 were traumatic setbacks for this political-reform process. Succession politics took over the leadership agenda, focusing energies once more on control of elite organs of power. The reemergence of this style of politics at the end of Deng Xiaoping's ten year tenure indicated the enormous difficulty of digging up the roots of flaws in the system. Leadership instability in late 1989 and 1990 was characterized by institutional reorganization and an ongoing purge of personnel throughout the bureaucracy. A hiatus in political reform seemed inevitable until some time after Deng's passing when a post-Deng leadership had taken solid form.

POLITBURO LEADERSHIP ARRANGEMENTS

The work arrangements of the Politburo remained the heart of the leadership system—in terms of both power politics and policy coordination—throughout the 1980s. Despite instability in the system and changes over time, elements of pattern regularity or "norms" for Politburo behavior were discernible that will continue to shape China's future into the post-Deng era. The select group of Politburo standing committee members and elders who oversee broad arenas of specialized responsibilities rely to a great extent on personal leadership of the Politburo commissions and

LGs to do this. The Military Commission and the Discipline Inspection Commission are the only functional groups established by the Party constitution, but they appear to play roles in the leadership arrangement similar to that of the other groups, which are established and defined by policy directives.

These organs thus are a prime focus of the constant maneuvering for power. And the organizational norms shape the unwritten rules of behavior. An important but largely invisible strategic aim of the power game is to "lock up" one or more policy arenas under sole control of yourself and your supporters, while making sure the control of the others is divided among two or more individuals, preferably also including your own supporters. Creating, abolishing, reorganizing, and renaming leading organs is a favorite tactic. Enhancing the authority or scope of a policy arena increases the status of its leader, and vice versa. But all of this politicking must be done without blatantly violating the rules of collective leadership and informal requirements that leaders and members of LGs have some relevant functional experience and expertise. To inhibit monopolies of functional power, the norms require dual or even multiple lines of authority, a practice endemic throughout the political system.

The preeminent power of the senior leader can here be seen in practical institutional terms, for he exercises a great deal of discretion in assigning the functional responsibilities within the Politburo and intervening in any policy arena. But ideological and institutional norms provide a means of checking his power as well, although they are weak. The top leader is constrained to balance appointments at this level among factions based on personal loyalties. The chronic nature of the problem of succession is also easily understood in institutional terms. An aspiring successor seeks to place loyalists in positions of influence in all arenas, as Hu Yaobang sought to do in 1985–86, and Zhao Ziyang in 1987–88. But in doing so, he must avoid either threatening the power of the incumbent leader or galvanizing opposition from rivals claiming the high moral ground of collective leadership—nearly impossible tasks.

The flexibility, ambiguity, fluidity, and personal nature of these lines of authority thus should be underscored, but a general outline sketch of the unwritten norm follows.[23]

1. National security (*guojia anchuan*) affairs. This arena usually is kept in the hands of the top leader as chairman of the Military Affairs Commission (Deng, like Mao before him). Little is known about this powerful arena, but it seems that at times it may have had wide-ranging authority for both military affairs and internal security.

2. Political-legal (*zheng[zhi] fa[lu]*) affairs. Normally, internal security,

23. Personal communication.

along with the legislative and judicial functions, is channeled through a Political and Legal Affairs Commission or LG, which oversees the National People's Congress, the procuratorate and court systems, as well as the police and intelligence forces. Currently, the ministries of state security, justice, public security, and probably civil affairs and supervision are in this arena, judging from official cabinet lists. In the 1960s this arena included the Party's Investigation Department.

3. Party (*dangwu*) affairs. These normally are overseen by the top Party executive—now the general secretary, perhaps with a senior deputy. Intra-Party communication, record keeping, and research is the responsibility of the General Office.

Closely coordinated supervision over propaganda and personnel work—what is often referred to in the Chinese press as "ideological-political work"—is sometimes channeled directly through the Propaganda and Organization Departments and sometimes first through a Propaganda and Ideology (*xuanquan sixiang*) LG and an Organization and Personnel (*zuzhi renshi*) LG. The former group has had a variety of names over the years; the latter group may have been reconstituted only recently or may function only prior to national Party meetings, which confirm high-level appointments. For an unknown length of time after 1969, the two were combined. The Discipline Inspection Commission and various temporary organs, such as the Rectification Commission (1983–87), have served as overlapping (sometimes competing) forums for oversight of cadre.

A United Front (*tong[yi] zhan[xian]*) LG oversees both reunification work (through the Taiwan Work LG and the Hong Kong–Macao Work Committee) and domestic "united front" relations with non-Party groups. The United Front Work Department oversees the People's Political Consultative Conference, the noncommunist parties, policy toward intellectuals, and government and social organs for religious and minority affairs.

Traditionally, Party work includes rural policy—originally conceived of as "peasant organization work" in the broadest sense, and thus covering rural population control, youth-to-the-countryside work, rural education, and so forth.[24] There are specialized youth,

24. At least in the late 1980s, rural policy appeared to be set by a party Rural Affairs Work Department; one of its leaders was Du Runsheng, who supervised related policy-research work as director of both the Party's Rural Policy Research Center and the Rural Development Research Center in the State Council. Tong Li, "Choice of Thoughts on China's Rural Reform—An Introduction to Du Runsheng's Book 'Choice for Rural China,'" *Nongmin Ribao* (Peasant Daily), 25 January 1989, 3, in FBIS-CHI-89-022 (3 February 1989), 31, contained the only reference I have found to the Central Rural Work Department and Du's position in it, but I accept the source as authoritative on this particular issue.

labor, and women's organizations. Political reform, too, appeared
to be a policy arena tightly controlled by party organs.[25]
4. Foreign affairs (*waishi*) work. This arena often has been narrowly
conceived as diplomatic relations and is supervised by the Foreign
Affairs LG. Under both Mao and Deng the senior leader has
retained responsibility for China's overall foreign policy orientation, including relations with the superpowers. This would be a
logical duty for the "commander-in-chief." Geographic or functional responsibilities in foreign affairs are delegated to other
senior leaders, and decisions for foreign military, Party, cultural,
and economic relations are shared with the appropriate functional LGs.[26]
5. Government (*zhengfu*) affairs. Traditionally, these have been conceived of largely as economic affairs and normally are run by the
top economic administrator (premier), often with another leader
(ranking vice-premier).[27] This work is channeled through the Finance and Economics LG and its subordinate specialized leading
groups or work groups, and the Science-and-Technology LG.

This outline of leadership organs strongly suggests that much of the
actual work of the Politburo is done "in committee," with the functional
commissions or LGs serving as forums for policy discussion by the members of the Politburo, supported by advisers and policy research organs.
Recent reports of Politburo plenary meetings reveal what most have
suspected, that the full body meets briefly and infrequently (now once
monthly for a morning) to consider policy options already researched
and discussed in the LGs, approved by members of the Standing Committee and privileged elders, and then packaged for ratification by the
Politburo.

The importance of knowing the unofficial divisions of labor at the top

25. See Appendix C.
26. Barnett, 43 ff., discussed this group. He referred to it as a "small group." The Hong
Kong press and FBIS translation services are inconsistent in using "small group," "leading
group," "work group," etc.; most references seem to be to *lingdao xiaozu*, which *Xinhua*
translates either as "leading group" or as "leading small group."
    Personal communication has indicated that under Deng's overall leadership, shared
secondarily with Li Xiannian since 1977, Hu Yaobang had special responsibilities for relations with Japan as well as Party relations; Zhao Ziyang, for Sino–U.S. relations; and Li
Peng, for Sino-Soviet relations. This picture matched a division of labor evident in leaders'
public appearances and commentary.
27. Personal communication, buttressed by the obvious concentration of leading State
Council officials in economic duties, and Chinese media references to Yao Yilin's nearly
coequal role to Zhao Ziyang in overseeing the economy after 1980. See *Xinhua* (in English),
2 November 1987, FBIS-CHI-87-211 (2 November 1987), 46, which said that Yao at some
unspecified point was "head" of the Finance and Economics LG.

is reflected in comments by economic specialist Ma Hong, while visiting Japan in April 1987: "As Party general secretary, Hu Yaobang was only in charge of Party affairs. He was not involved in the business of economic reform. Comrade Deng Xiaoping and Premier Zhao Ziyang have been leading economic reform. I myself never discussed reform plans with Mr. Hu. It seems that people in Japan were unaware of the parameters of his job. It is wrong to think that he had overall authority."[28]

Hu Yaobang ran into political difficulty by 1986 in part because he sought to expand control beyond Party affairs, thereby encroaching on the turf of key elders. And Zhao Ziyang's irregular practice of retaining control of economic affairs after leaving the premiership was one source of his problems in 1988–89 (along with his efforts to restrict interference from "retired" elders). It was widely assumed that he was forced to share more of his economic authority with Li Peng and Yao Yilin in late 1988. Thus, the norms of functional divisions of power continued to play a critical role in Chinese politics.

The Sub-Politburo Leadership Structure
The normal membership of a central leading group or commission comprises (a) the group head; (b) usually a deputy or even two; (c) statutory members (defined by regulations) who sit on the LG because of formally assigned functional duties in the bureaucracy; and (d) discretionary members such as advisers, who are often outgoing retirees, or a secretary-general chosen personally by the leader. The head and the deputies are most likely appointed by the senior leader or general secretary, no doubt through an arduous process of political balancing and compromise with other factional leaders. An LG typically brings together all the senior officials in China with responsibility for different aspects of a comprehensive functional arena.

An important question for further research is the extent of involvement in LG deliberations—as full or "ex officio" members, advisers, and observers—by elders seemingly "retired" to the Central Advisory Commission or to the NPC standing committee. Deng Xiaoping in 1980 envisaged that both the Discipline Inspection Commission and the Central Advisory Commission would give "guidance, advice, and supervision," and the NPC constitutionally supervises the State Council. The definition and scope of these duties is unclear.[29]

A report by Bo Yibo on the work of the advisory commission in 1983 revealed that a number of its standing committee members had been assigned specific leadership duties much beyond the level of mere ad-

---

28. *Yomiuri Shimbun*, 17 April 1987, 5.
29. Deng Xiaoping, "On the Reform of the System."

vice.[30] This type of involvement may have helped to set the stage for the "comebacks" of the elders in 1987 and 1989, including membership in leading groups responsible for preparing the Thirteenth Party Congress, when they recommended key organizational and personnel changes.[31]

The staff work for an LG may be done either through a section of the relevant General Office or a separate office (*bangongshi*) that has a ministry-level or vice-ministry-level ranking.[32] The staff will be located in the Party, the government, or the military, depending on the post of the leader assigned. For example, when Zhao Ziyang gave up the premiership after the Thirteenth Congress, he retained control of the Finance and Economics LG. However, its office in the State Council was abolished, and a new section opened up in the Party's General Office, with new personnel. The office physically moved from the State Council section to the Party section of the Zhongnanhai compound.[33]

Both LGs and offices are subdivided functionally. For example, in the Finance and Economics LG before the Thirteenth Congress Li Peng was in charge of "such industrial sectors as energy, transportation and raw material supply."[34] The office had three sections: policy investigation and research; daily work (administration); and Party affairs (propaganda and personnel).[35] In the State Council, the deputy secretaries-general each have responsibility for the sectoral LG offices or sections of the General Office.[36]

30. Bo Yibo, in an interview with *Liaowang*, cited in *Xinhua* (in English), 19 October 1983, in FBIS, 20 October 1983, K1, said the Advisory Commission members had made arrangements for appointments of cadre to central organs, taken part in streamlining the government at all levels, and taken part in preparing for designating some new economic-planning regions (such as the Shanxi Coal Base and the Shanghai Economic Region). James L. Huskey, "China: Working Directory of Selected Foreign Policy, Cultural and Media Institutions," USIA Office of Research, November 1987, 9, listed the Huangs and Geng as members of the Foreign Affairs Leading Group.

In personal communication, a foreign expert working with the Computer Leading Group mentioned another example—Party elder Li Da's membership in the Computer Leading Group and the participation of NPC vice-chairmen Huang Hua, Huang Zhen, and Geng Biao in Foreign Affairs LG meetings. Li's group would appear to be the "electronic computer and large-scale integrated circuit LG," different from and perhaps subordinate to the Electronic Vitalization LG.

31. See note 18 above.

32. Personal communication, and *Chronicle.*

33. Personal communication. Regarding the physical move of the office, see chapter 3 in this volume, by Susan Shirk.

34. *Xinhua* (in English), 9 April 1988, FBIS-CHI-88-069 (11 April 1988), 15.

35. Personal communication.

36. Personal communication, buttressed by the widely known functions of the deputies during the 1950s and 1960s.

Politburo members have their own personal sources of policy information and advice, of course. But there is also an extensive system of policy
research offices (*zhengce yanjiushi*) and investigation-and-research small
groups (*diaocha yanjiu xiaozu*), sometimes referred to as "brain trusts"
(*zhinengtuan*), operating at several levels within this leadership system.
These organs and their personnel probably would be comanaged by the
Propaganda LG and the relevant LG's office staffers responsible for
research. For instance, in 1979 four research small groups were organized for the new State Finance and Economics Commission (functioning as an LG) by Party propaganda specialist Deng Liqun under the
supervision of Politburo member Hu Qiaomu, but they were also responsible to the commission's secretary-general, Yao Yilin. At the same time,
all government organs were told to create policy-research offices.[37]

I suspect that a desire to "liberate" policy-research specialists from the
propaganda czars partly explained the proliferation in the 1980s of research centers answering to Zhao Ziyang's office in the State Council and
to the various LGs rather than to the Secretariat. Examples included the
State Council's General Office policy-research office; the Economic,
Technical, and Social Development Research Center under the Finance
and Economics LG; the S & T Development Research Center jointly
under the Science and Technology Commission and the S & T LG; and
the Economic System Reform Institute under the Reform Commission,
which serves the Economic Reform LG.

Following the retirement of Hu Qiaomu and Deng Liqun in late 1987,
as decision-making power had been shifted back from the Secretariat to
the Politburo, the Secretariat's policy-research office was disbanded and
new research organs were set up under the Politburo. There was mention of an investigation and studies room of the Party General Office.[38]
The structure and membership of many such research groups is fluid,
with individuals pulled in from permanent bodies, such as the Academy
of Social Sciences or the research sections of commissions and ministries.
Staffers from the general offices and these research organs together
provide most members for temporary drafting groups (*qicao xiaozu*, or
weiyuanhui, or *tanzi*) set up to draft policy documents.

37. *Chronicle*, 292. The choice of Deng Liqun was logical, given his several "hats" at the
time: deputy director of the Party's General Office, probable deputy director (to Hu
Qiaomu) of the Propaganda LG, director of the Secretariat's Policy Research Office, and
vice-president (with Hu as president) of the Academy of Social Sciences. Both men spent
most of their careers from Yan'an days onward supervising policy-research organs, such as
those at *Hongqi*, *Renmin Ribao*, and the Central Party School, as well as the Academy.

38. Personal communication; see *People's Daily*, 14 August 1988, 1 and 2, in JPRS-CAR-
088-052 (2 September 1988), 14–15, for an article by the research organ of the General
Office.

A Working Model

On March 6, 1958, a joint circular from the Central Committee and the State Council established a Central Foreign Affairs Small Group (*zhonggong zhongyang waishi xiaozu*) and a State Council Foreign Affairs Office. This directive can serve as a simplified basic model of the normative structure and function of LGs.[39] Chen Yi, Politburo member, vice-premier, and foreign minister, became director (*zu zhang*) of both organs, with responsibility for "leading all aspects of foreign affairs work."

Other LG members were the Politburo alternate and vice–foreign minister Zhang Wentian; Secretariat member Wang Jiaxiang; vice–foreign minister (and probably also a leader in the Party's Investigation Department), Li Kenong; head of the State Council's Overseas Chinese Affairs Office and deputy director of its Foreign Affairs Office, Liao Chengzhi; deputy director of the State Council Foreign Trade Office and president of the Chinese People's Institute for Foreign Affairs, Liu Ningyi.

Foreign military and Party relations were represented respectively by Chen Yi as a marshal and member of the Military Commission, and by Wang Jiaxiang, who oversaw the Party's International Liaison Department. In recent years the statutory members of the LG have included the equivalents to those of 1958 but have been expanded to include official representatives from the International Liaison Department, the Ministry of National Defense, and the NPC's Foreign Affairs Committee.[40]

The 1958 circular went on to specify that the State Council Foreign Affairs Office was to be the "working body" (*banshi jigou*) of the LG and the "general coordinating point" (*zong kou zi*) for the State Council's management of foreign affairs work. All the (meager) evidence thus far suggests that staff offices are fairly small, ranging from ten to forty staffers.[41] Actual administrative responsibilities are handled by the organs with formal responsibility. Thus, in 1958 management duties for international activities of the government and mass organizations were assigned to six lower-level coordination points (*kou zi*).[42]

The circular called on the localities to set up corresponding systems to "unify the leadership over foreign affairs work." At the local level, military relations are included, but not Party ties, which are likely handled through parallel Party staffing and administrative organs.

The foreign affairs system probably has changed less than others over time, but there have been permutations. In 1985 there were two foreign

39. *Chronicle*, 106.
40. *Kuang Chiao Ching* 184 (16 January 1988): 10–13, in FBIS-CHI-88-012 (20 January 1988), 9–12.
41. Personal communication, and Barnett, *The Making of Foreign Policy*, 67.
42. See Appendix D for a list of these points.

affairs offices, ranking as "first-level organs directly subordinate to the Central Committee and to the State Council" and, in regard to relevant problems in foreign affairs, they could separately issue documents directly to relevant units.[43]

By the mid-1980s there was a large research apparatus serving the Foreign Affairs LG. This included the small staff of the State Council's International Studies Center, the foreign affairs section of the Secretariat's policy-research office, the Institute of Contemporary International Relations, and the Shanghai Institute of International Studies, for all of which senior adviser and former ambassador Huan Xiang had some responsibility before his death. The Foreign Ministry's Comprehensive Issues Bureau and Institute of International Relations also are used by the LG.

Variations and Conundrums

Variations on the basic LG model have been apparent over time. An obvious one is that some of these functional leading organs are called commissions, and some, LGs. In early 1980 the Political and Legal Affairs Commission replaced the Political and Legal Affairs LG; this was reversed in mid-1988 and was rumored to be changing again in 1990. The use of commission format only for military and for political and legal affairs suggests a throwback to the powerful "political-military commissions" set up in the CCP in the early 1940s, patterned after the Soviet and Comintern system of the 1930s. "Commission" may imply more direct command rather than guidance over subordinate administrative units. This distinction was suggested in a report on the 1988 change in political-legal work, but in fact it has been a distinction without a difference for most of the PRC's history.[44]

At times, leading groups have been established in the name of the State Council rather than the Party. For example, the equivalent of the Finance and Economics LG from 1948 to 1953 and again in 1979 was a state Finance and Economic Commission. The State Council Science and Technology LG, set up in 1982 under Zhao Ziyang's leadership, seemed in every way but name to be a central Party group. I was told by the staff of the *Science and Technology Daily* that the paper was subordinate to the Central Committee, even though it was officially the newspaper of this "State Council" LG. These anomalies may largely reflect the tactical use of reorganization for specific power or policy purposes.

Regarding the ranking of these leadership organs, the Military Commission both constitutionally and in practice ranks higher than the oth-

43. *Chronicle*, 614.
44. See *Wen Wei Po* from Hong Kong, 24 June 1988.

ers; for a time, the Party constitution mandated that its leader must be a member of the Politburo Standing Committee. The other LGs are also perceived by Chinese officials to differ in power and influence, but it seems that this depends largely on the personal status of the group leader.[45] For example, Zhao Ziyang automatically gave extra clout to the Finance and Economics LG by remaining its leader for a time after he was appointed general secretary, just as he effectively upgraded the S & T LG and the Economic System Reform Commission by heading them as premier.

Other, more specialized LGs, headed by lesser-ranked vice-premiers or state councillors, would appear to be subordinate to the more comprehensive LGs, although the exact relationship is not known. Obvious examples are the Foreign Investment LG and the Electronics LG; directors of both were also members of the Finance and Economics LG, responsible, respectively, for foreign economic relations and for industry and communications.

Other variations in the model, which may in part reflect the relative importance of a given arena, include the size, number, and stature of the staff office(s) and the addition of an administrative layer, such as a small group or a working group in between the LG and its office or offices.[46] As an example, in 1986 the Finance and Economics LG set up a State Council economic-reform-plan work group headed by Tian Jiyun, served by an existing economic-reform planning office with its six subgroups for reform in prices, finance and taxation, investment, monetary policy, wages, and foreign trade.[47]

Another point of confusion is the exact relationship of LGs to the Secretariat and the Politburo, and their relationship to each other. In the late 1950s and early 1960s, the Secretariat appeared to operate as a central layer in a vertical line of authority running from the Politburo

45. Dr. Christopher Clarke of the Department of State has discussed with me some indicators that the functional sectors may have had relative ranking at times, perhaps reflecting the ranks of the LGs, but the evidence is inconclusive.

46. To illustrate, according to *Chronicle,* 614, in May 1985 a circular was sent out jointly by the Central Committee and State Council general offices stipulating that "the foreign affairs section of the State Council General Office change its title to the office of the State Council foreign affairs small group (*waishi xiaozu*), to operate in conjunction with the office of the Central Foreign Affairs Work LG (*zhongyang waishi gongzuo lingdao xiaozu*)." (Note the name change of the latter since 1958.) It would appear that the State Council small group is the same organ as the "*waishikou*" mentioned by Doak Barnett in his 1985 study, headed by State Councillor Ji Pengfei. Barnett's group included the state councillor and foreign minister, Wu Xueqian, and minister of foreign economic relations and trade, Chen Muhua, under Ji. Ji also coordinated the State Council small group for Hong Kong Macao affairs as part of a Party Hong Kong Macao Work Committee, and the State Council Hong Kong Macao Office, which served both.

47. Personal communication.

down to the State Council, but in the early 1980s the Secretariat and the State Council appeared more equal in stature. Barnett in 1985 referred to the Foreign Affairs LG as belonging to the Secretariat even though it has always been headed by a member of the Politburo Standing Committee.[48] One possible explanation for this seeming contradiction would be dual leadership; one media article said that LGs answer to "the Secretariat and Politburo." Another possibility is that Barnett's findings reflected a temporary de facto shift of decision making from the (increasingly aging and inactive) Politburo to the Secretariat as of 1984, a trend reversed at the Thirteenth Congress in 1987.

CONCLUSION

Through the decade of the 1980s, despite periodic professions of intent to introduce more democratic and efficient reforms into the Party leadership system, each round of reform was in fact aborted by leadership struggle. In every instance reform leaders perceived and acted on the prior imperative to consolidate control of the central Party apparatus, thereby rendering "reforms" meaningless in terms of the secondary priority of improved governance. In early 1990 the leadership publicized new regulations that strengthened Party control over the "multiparty cooperation" system in a transparent and cynical effort to justify a halt to serious political reform. These setbacks along the way jeopardized the prospects for maintaining the gains of economic reform. But the collapse of similar Leninist political structures in Eastern Europe fueled not only a growing conviction within the bureaucratic elite that only a fundamental change in this system could offer hope for China's future, but also a fearful determination in the leadership never to let that happen.

APPENDIX A: TYPICAL CENTRAL LEADING UNITS

The Political and Legal Affairs Commission was set up in 1980 and "(a) under central guidance, researches and handles the major problems in political and legal work nation-wide and submits proposals to the Center; (b) assists the Center in handling requests from subordinate units for instructions on reports (which are still to be sent directly to the Party, government, and military organs, not to the commission); (c) in coordinating the work of all political and legal organs, fosters a uniform consciousness and uniform action regarding problems common to each, in accordance with the general program and policies of the Center; (d) examines and studies the conditions of thorough execution of the program and policies, and of state laws and decrees; (e) examines and studies the

48. Barnett, *The Making of Foreign Policy*, 43.

organizational and ideological situation of the political and legal cadre; (f) and handles other work as assigned by the Center."

The S & T LG was set up by the Central Committee and the State Council in 1982 (and the S & T Commission reorganized) "for the purpose of strengthening leadership of S & T work and to put each aspect of S & T work of the army and the people nationwide under the unified planning and unified command of an authoritative and efficient elite organ and to advance work in coordination." (This is a nearly exact quotation from Deng Xiaoping, when demanding changes in the irrational assignments of technicians and use of S & T resources by the Planning Commission, in Deng Xiaoping, "Decide on Major Construction Projects, Make Proper Use of the Talents of Scientists and Technicians," 14 October 1982, in *Build Socialism with Chinese Characteristics* [Beijing: Foreign Languages Press, 1985], 8.)

The LG's essential tasks were to "(a) unify, organize and manage the ranks of personnel in S & T nationwide, and transfer, concentrate, and employ them according to need; (b) unify the long-term plan for leading S & T, including the S & T restructuring plan for industries and key-point enterprises, and make each plan able to interpenetrate and to dovetail; (c) study policy decisions on important technological policies; (d) decide on the introduction and absorption of important technology; and (e) coordinate the S & T work of each department."

APPENDIX B: LEADERSHIP MECHANISMS

Politburo members may carry out their oversight responsibilities in a variety of ways, of course, informal as well as formal. Besides family members, personal assistants and bodyguards, each has a staff of aides (secretaries), who may be assigned as liaison for specific arenas (political, military, and so on). In the Chinese system, like the Soviet system, these secretaries tend to be better educated than the leaders and actually do much of the work, making important decisions on their own. According to one foreign expert who worked in the propaganda system through the 1960s, each unit knew to call directly to the secretary assigned it by Lu Dingyi, who headed the Propaganda LG.

Little is known about the workings of the secretarial system at this level, but the fact that former political secretaries of top leaders have regularly become prominent officials in their own right was suggestive of the key roles they play. Examples include Gan Ziyu, science, planning, and propaganda official, once Nie Rongzhen's secretary; Wu Mingyu, former State Science and Technology Commission vice-chairman and later deputy director of the State Council Economic, Technological, and Social Development Research Center, Zhang Jingfu's former secretary; Zhou Taihe, Economic System Reform Commission adviser, Chen Yun's former secretary; and He Guanghui, the Reform Commission's deputy director, former secretary to Li Fuchun and Bo Yibo; Wang Xicheng, former Finance and Economics LG office director and later Propaganda Department deputy director, Li Xiannian's former secretary; and so on. Zhao Ziyang appointed his own political secretary, Bao Tong, as the secretary to the Politburo standing committee. What his role was, or his relationship to staff offices and other secretaries, personal or organizational, is not known.

APPENDIX C: EVOLUTION OF POLITICAL REFORM GROUP

The Central Political Structure Reform Study Group was established in September 1986 under Zhao Ziyang, according to *Ta Kung Po*, 7 April 1988, 2, in FBIS-CHI-88-070, 12 April 1988, 30–31. The group included Hu Qili, Tian Jiyun, Bo Yibo, and Peng Chong. Its staff office was the Political Reform Research Center (*Xinhua*, 27 February 1988) run by Zhao's secretary and Politburo Standing Committee secretary, Bao Tong. Staff members included Zhou Jie, deputy director of the Party's General Office; Yan Jiaqi, director of the Political Science Institute of the Chinese Academy of Social Sciences; and the vice-minister of the Economic System Reform Commission, He Guanghui, former secretary to Li Fuqun and Bo Yibo. At that time, reformers Hu Qili, Tian Jiyun, and Bao Tong seemed to play the leading roles. In November they set up seven special groups to study the separation of Party and government functions, Party organization and inner-Party democracy, delegation of powers and structural reform, the cadre and personnel system, socialist democracy, the socialist legal system, and the basic principles for political structural reform.

One of the seven special study groups, on cadre and personnel-system reform, originated several months earlier as a joint work team of the Organization Department and the Ministry of Labor and Personnel; see *Liaowang* Overseas Edition 20 (16 May 1988), 16–17, in FBIS-CHI-88-101 (25 May 1988), 23–25.

Beginning in September 1986, experimental political reforms were carried out in some localities, and these speeded up after the Thirteenth Congress. Examples include the abolition in the Chengdu Military Region of 109 redundant or "temporary" organizations such as excess cadre offices, self-study university offices, and policy-implementation(!) offices. In June 1987 the Hunan Party and government dissolved 72 of their 141 nonpermanent offices. In December 1987 the Beijing Haidian district Party committee closed down its departments for commerce, education, and rural affairs, as well as its street affairs committee.

After the fall of Hu Yaobang, however, Hu Qiaomu, Deng Liqun, and the Central Party School president, Gao Yang, joined the work of the main political reform groups as "visiting members," and gradually through 1987 leadership shifted to less reform-minded officials. Early in the year a new group was set up under He Guanghui to focus on the practical and immediate issue of restructuring the central organs in the course of the upcoming Party and state congresses. It may have been this group that recommended the return of power to the Politburo and the effective downgrading of the Secretariat to an administrative status similar to that of the State Council.

The central study group was disbanded in September, and a new LG for the Reform of Central Government organs was set up under Li Peng, with the Organization Department director, Song Ping, as deputy director, and as members the General Office director Wen Jiabo; the State Council secretary-general,

Chen Junsheng; the minister of personnel, Zhao Donghuan; and He Guanghui, who headed the LG's office. After the Thirteenth Congress, in mid-December, the Politburo agreed on an overall framework for restructuring the central organs, to be implemented through the Secretariat and the State Council. *Liaowang* Overseas Edition 17 (25 April 1988) [no page numbers given], in FBIS-CHI-88-080 (26 April 1988), 23–26, mentions that the group under Li Peng was responsible for formulating implementation procedures. They substantially revised the plan, which was then approved on 28 November 1987 by the Politburo Standing Committee prior to review by the Second Plenum of the new Politburo.

APPENDIX D: COORDINATION POINTS FOR MANAGEMENT OF INTERNATIONAL ACTIVITIES (1958)

1. Ministry of Foreign Affairs: for the NPC Standing Committee, the Chinese People's Institute of Foreign Affairs, all political and legal affairs departments in state organs, the Red Cross, and General Relief societies. (It is not clear to what extent intelligence and counterintelligence is coordinated with the MFA).
2. Ministry of Foreign Trade: for the Ministries of Finance and Commerce, the People's Bank, the International Trade Advancement Society, and "various units" involved in industry and commerce.
3. Foreign Cultural Liaison Committee: for departments concerned with the arts, education, science, sanitation, sports, news, publishing, broadcasting, and the Chinese People's Association for Friendship with Foreign Countries.
4. National Science Planning and Technical Commissions (later the State Science and Technology Commission): for scientific and technical cooperation activities and exchanges with foreign countries by the Academy of Sciences and each government department.
5. Ministry of National Defense: international activities in military affairs.
6. Overseas Chinese Affairs Commission: overseas Chinese affairs.

FIVE

Information Flows and Policy Coordination in the Chinese Bureaucracy

Nina P. Halpern

Scholars have recently begun to argue that the structure of authority within the Chinese bureaucracy is not the centralized, hierarchical one described earlier, but rather a fragmented one.[1] They suggest that although this fragmentation is not entirely a post-Mao phenomenon, the post-Mao administrative and economic reforms have greatly increased it by promoting the dispersal of resources throughout the bureaucracy. The resources on which these scholars have focused, in addition to formal, legal grants of authority, are basically two: finances and status (including personal relations). They have paid little attention to a third source of informal authority within the bureaucracy: control of information.

This neglect is unfortunate because the dispersal of policy-relevant information among functionally specialized units can be an important cause of fragmented authority. One measure of the centralization of authority is the ability of the central government to adopt and implement coordinated policies. In this chapter I focus on the problem of policy coordination, viewing it primarily as a problem of information flows from lower-level units to the leadership and between those units themselves. Specifically, I examine a new set of institutions created within the post-Mao bureaucracy—several research centers under the State Council—and ask how they affected the flow of information and the leadership's ability to coordinate policy, particularly during the period in which Zhao Ziyang served as premier, from 1981 to 1987.

I suggest three ways in which these new institutions might have promoted policy coordination by changing information flows and the behav-

1. David M. Lampton, "Chinese Politics: The Bargaining Treadmill," *Issues and Studies*, March 1987, 11–41; Kenneth Lieberthal and Michel Oksenberg, *Policy Making in China* (Princeton: Princeton University Press, 1988).

ior of lower-level units. Although the dispersal of other resources contributed to the fragmentation of authority in the post-Mao era, the changes
stemming from changing information flows were more complicated and
probably, on balance, produced greater centralization. But in addition to
directly influencing the flow of information to the leadership and thus its
ability to coordinate policy, these new institutions both reflected and
promoted an ideology of rationalism, which could potentially alter—if
only slowly and indirectly—the basis of authority within the Chinese
bureaucracy. The discussion in this chapter thus provides insights into
the cohesiveness and basis of central authority in post-Mao China.

By examining the relationship between the research centers and top
leaders and bureaucratic agencies, I address the merits of two competing
models of the bureaucratic process: the "command model," emphasizing
the existence of a relatively unified and effective chain of command reaching from the top leadership down to the ministries and local units, and the
"bargaining model," emphasizing the fragmentation of authority and the
exchange nature of interactions between superiors and subordinate units.
I suggest that a third model better captures the bureaucratic process in
which the research centers were engaged: "competitive persuasion." This
model probably has little relevance to decisions that are primarily political
or a response to crisis conditions (such as the June 1989 decision to use
military force against the demonstrators at Tiananmen); it is intended to
apply only to normal bureaucratic decision-making processes where information and expertise are regarded as important.

THE PROBLEM OF POLICY COORDINATION

Policy coordination is a central problem in any bureaucratic system. "Coordination" can be defined in many ways,[2] but here I borrow I. M.
Destler's definition, which focuses on processes of decision making and
implementation:

> Coordination involves above all (1) *the management of policy decision processes*
> so that trade-offs among policy interests and goals are recognized, ana-
> lyzed, and presented to the president and other senior executives before
> they make a decision; and (2) *the oversight of official actions*, especially those
> that follow major high-level decisions, so that these actions reflect the
> balance among policy goals that the president and his responsible officials
> have decided upon.[3]

2. See, for example, Aaron Wildavsky, *Speaking Truth to Power* (Boston: Little, Brown,
1979), 131–33, for four definitions of coordination: as efficiency, reliability, coercion, and
consent.
3. I. M. Destler, *Making Foreign Economic Policy* (Washington, D.C.: The Brookings Institution, 1980), 8.

In the Chinese context, we can substitute for "president and other senior executives" "top leadership," particularly the premier and other members of the State Council and Politburo standing committees. The above definition of coordination is useful as long as one focuses on policy decisions made at the top level. Many less important decisions are of course made at lower levels, and thus "policy coordination" should include processes of mutual adjustment (bargaining, consensus building, markets) by which trade-offs are implicitly or explicitly recognized and resolved without reaching the leadership. As Lindblom argued, coordination can be performed in either a centralized or a decentralized fashion; which type predominates is an empirical question.[4]

Although coordination may be, as Seidman and Gilmour claim, the bureaucratic equivalent of "the philosopher's stone" (i.e., the elusive key to the universe and solution to all human problems),[5] it is still possible to analyze the conditions that produce lesser rather than greater degrees of coordination, and to examine the efficacy of various devices designed to improve coordination.[6] Lack of bureaucratic coordination has two basic sources: (1) ignorance of the relevant trade-offs and complementarities between policy areas, due to functionally divided modes of information collection and communication; and (2) fragmentation of authority among relevant actors (who possess divergent goals).

Centralized ignorance and fragmented authority are interrelated problems. As Weber recognized long ago, expertise and knowledge, growing out of functional specialization, are the sources of bureaucratic power vis-à-vis its "political masters": "[Even] the absolute monarch is powerless opposite the superior knowledge of the bureaucratic expert."[7] Because information is such a valuable resource, each agency has an incentive to attempt to monopolize the information necessary for an understanding of its particular policy sphere, and not to share it fully either with other agencies or with its bureaucratic superiors. Lacking information and expertise necessary to evaluate the recommendations of lower-level units, political leaders will often permit those units to become

4. Charles E. Lindblom, *The Intelligence of Democracy* (New York: Free Press, 1965).

5. Harold Seidman and Robert Gilmour, *Politics, Position, and Power,* 4th ed. (New York: Oxford University Press, 1986), 219.

6. This analysis is hampered by the fact that when lack of information and ignorance of the relevant trade-offs prevent coordination, the problem will often go unrecognized, whereas improved analytical capability may bring greater recognition of the connections between policy areas without a corresponding ability to choose the desired trade-offs or enforce such decisions. One should not count the latter condition as a more "uncoordinated" one than the former. Recognition of the problem may not be the equivalent of solving it, but it moves one a step closer.

7. Max Weber, "Essay on Bureaucracy," in *Bureaucratic Power in National Politics,* ed. Frances E. Rourke, 2nd ed. (Boston: Little, Brown, 1976), 62.

de facto decision-makers in their own policy spheres. The problem of dispersed information is particularly acute when policy decisions must take account of conditions and impact in many sectors. In a horizontally segmented bureaucracy, agencies have little incentive to collect or communicate information about the effect of decisions on other units' jurisdictions. Yet, if policy is to be coordinated, the leadership must somehow acquire such information.

Policy coordination can be improved through one or more of the following: (1) developing mechanisms to generate new *information* on policy externalities or to pool information already being collected within agencies (or some combination); (2) redistributing *authority* among bureaucratic actors; (3) altering the *incentives* of lower-level actors so that their independent actions produce coordinated outcomes. Because bureaucratic structure produces the problem of coordination, these objectives must generally be pursued through the creation of new institutions or the restructuring of existing ones, institutions here meaning formal structures as well as established processes and procedures. Informal patterns may also be altered, in part by changes in formal institutions, so as to enhance coordination.

THE COORDINATION PROBLEM IN THE CHINESE BUREAUCRACY

Chinese media discussions and interviews with Chinese officials make it clear that serious coordination problems exist within the Chinese bureaucracy. These problems stem both from a lack of necessary information and analytical capacity at the top and from a failure of subordinate units to comply with leadership decisions. For example, a 1986 *Liaowang* article stated: "Because of the existing demarcation in the spheres of control of the departments and regions, the macrocontrol of technical imports has in reality become a power structure system with complex and complicated relationships which are reciprocal but not coordinated."[8] The article went on to argue the need to develop genuine, quantitative feasibility analysis that takes account of economic, financial, and social costs and benefits of technical imports. This article pointed to the inadequacy of the information base necessary for the leadership to make decisions on technical imports that take account of relevant trade-offs in terms both of economic efficiency and of alternative social goals.

Other articles pointed to difficulties of implementing coordinated policies and to the failure of bureaucratic agencies to coordinate among them-

8. Cao Jiarui, "China's Technological Imports—Present Status and Problems (Part 3)," *Liaowang*, no. 20 (19 May 1986), 12–13, in *FBIS*, 30 May 1986, K13.

selves. A *Liaowang* article entitled "On Wrangles" complained: "After a formal and correct decision is made, some refuse to carry it out under all kinds of pretexts, simply because the decision involves the interests of a certain department, unit, or locality. Arguing back and forth in so-called special circumstances, they impede the smooth implementation of the decision."[9] The article also criticized the failure of agencies to "promote horizontal ties": "Some offices and departments make arbitrary decisions, issue documents, or map out regulations on matters obviously involving several other departments. Unwilling to reconcile, the latter assume a tit-for-tat attitude. As a result, something approved by one department cannot get through other departments, making those at lower levels suffer untold hardships shuttling between departments and trying to accommodate themselves to contradictions at upper levels."[10]

Although these articles were published in the mid-1980s, the problems they identified were not new. Indeed, I will argue that the institutional changes of the post-Mao period somewhat improved policy coordination. Prior to the Cultural Revolution, most bureaucratic expertise was dispersed among functionally specialized agencies, particularly ministries. Although a few coordinating institutions existed—the State Council staff offices, the commissions, and a few leadership small groups—at best these helped to address the coordination problem within a broad functional area, such as the economy, or foreign affairs, but not to bring about coordination across those "systems" (*xitong*). Although the commissions, such as the State Planning Commission (SPC) and the State Science and Technology Commission (SSTC), had a broader mandate than most ministries, they have been criticized for acting too much as "administrative" bodies, suggesting that they did little to analyze or supplement the input from the ministries. It appears that policy-making in the Maoist era was generally a functionally specialized process, in which the main ministry involved often acquired a *de facto* monopoly on the information supplied to the top leaders about potential policy decisions. This dispersed expertise created a fragmentation of authority and the inability to coordinate policy. In science policy, for example, prior to 1982 the budgeting process consisted of adding up the relevant requests from all the ministries; the relevant commission—the State Science and Technology Commission—possessed no real authority to evaluate or coordinate these requests (i.e., to make trade-offs between them).[11]

9. Commentator's article, "On 'Wrangles,'" in *Liaowang*, no. 38 (1986), in *FBIS*, 23 September 1986, K17.

10. Ibid.

11. Interview with Wu Mingyu (vice-chairman of the SSTC, and director of the National Research Center for Science and Technology for Development), Beijing, January 1986.

The post-Mao leadership recognized the need to improve policy coordination, both within and across *xitong*. The research centers discussed in this chapter were part of an effort to reduce the fragmentation of authority stemming from functionally divided information flows so as to permit the leadership to formulate policies based on an understanding of the trade-offs and complementarities among policy areas. They were not the only such effort. Bureaucratic restructuring, particularly in 1982, altered the formal authority of some institutions. Many new interagency units—particularly the leadership small groups discussed in chapter 4[12]—modified both the formal and the informal pattern of authority, as did new planning and budgeting procedures. The research centers, however, addressed most directly the problem of dispersed expertise and monopolization of information by the ministries. Although many different factors undoubtedly motivated the creation of these centers, the discussion below concentrates on their impact on information flows and the structure of authority within the bureaucracy. I examine in turn their role in providing the information, authority, and incentive components of a solution to the problem of coordination. Through this vehicle, I explore the broader questions of the structure of authority and bureaucratic behavior in China and of the relevance of different models of such behavior.[13] In conclusion I ask whether the findings of this chapter continued to be relevant after Zhao Ziyang ceased to be premier, and particularly in the aftermath of Tiananmen.

RESEARCH CENTERS: ORGANIZATION AND MISSION

Lieberthal and Oksenberg identify a set of bodies within or immediately subordinate to the Zhongnanhai (the command headquarters of the Party and government) that they label "Staff, Research, and Coordinating Offices."[14] Among the more prominent of these bodies are a set of research centers on economics, technology, and foreign affairs directly subordinate to the premier's office or to a leadership small group. Unlike the leading groups, these centers are not line organs; they are attached to the premier's office and do not modify the basic chain of command within the

12. Although a few such leadership groups existed in the Maoist period, in the post-Mao period these groups have increased dramatically in number, and some have a much more elaborate institutional structure.

13. Sources for this chapter include published sources cited in the notes and interviews with officials and staff of the research centers. To maintain confidentiality, I have not cited individual informants by name or position. Where possible, I have provided citations to written documents; undocumented facts in the body of this chapter are based on interviews.

14. Lieberthal and Oksenberg, *Policy Making in China*, 41.

bureaucracy. Six such research centers were established between 1980 and 1982: (1) the Economic Research Center (ERC); (2) the Technical Economic Research Center (TERC); (3) the Price Research Center; (4) the Economic Legislation Center; (5) the Rural Development Research Center (RDRC); and (6) the Center For International Studies (CIS). The first three were combined in 1985 into an Economic, Technical, and Social Development Research Center (ETSDRC). A similar type of research center, which also supplies some advice directly to the State Council, was created under the State Science and Technology Commission: the National Research Center for S & T for Development (NRCSTD). In the aftermath of Tiananmen, the RDRC has apparently been abolished, but the other centers remain in existence. The discussion below is based on data on the structure and workings of these institutions during the period from 1981 to 1986; accordingly, it is written in the past tense, although many of the findings may still be accurate.

As was suggested above, these research centers undoubtedly had several purposes. All were created during the period of Zhao Ziyang's tenure as premier and therefore reflected his purposes in both a policy and a power sense. As Michel Oksenberg has pointed out, the top leadership in China is relatively understaffed, and the research centers in effect provided the premier and other leaders with personal staff.[15] But the centers were not simply personal staff; several became sizable operations with a significant degree of autonomy.[16] Accordingly, even if Zhao established these centers primarily for personal political reasons, they were likely to affect the policy process in somewhat broader ways.

Improving the flow of information from the bureaucracy, permitting some independent evaluation of that information, and enhancing policy coordination were all among the stated goals for which these centers were established, goals reflected in the broader institutional restructuring undertaken since 1982. The official mandate of the centers established three general purposes for them (this varied somewhat according to the specific body): (1) as cross-departmental bodies, to provide an integrated perspective on policy problems; (2) to develop a more long-range planning perspective than would emerge from the bureaucratic rhythms generated by the annual and five-year planning cycles; (3) to serve as a general source of expert analysis and advice for the State Council. Policy coordination was most obviously a key task of the TERC (now the ETSDRC) and the NRCSTD; these two bodies were explicitly

15. Comment at the conference on "The Structure of Authority and Bureaucratic Behavior in China," Tucson, Arizona, June 19–23, 1988.
16. In particular, the ETSDRC, the NRCSTD, and the RDRC.

intended to integrate scientific-technological considerations with economic ones and to provide cross-departmental and interdisciplinary perspectives on policy matters.[17] But the coordinating role of all the centers was obvious in their attempts to build staffs with several types of specialists and in their need to draw upon the expertise of a range of functional agencies.

The centers, when established, were formally subordinate either to the premier's office or to a leadership small group. The ETSDRC, for example, was formally subordinate to the Finance and Economics leading group, although center officials stated that the leading group's supervisory role was minimal. During the period when Zhao Ziyang was premier, the centers apparently operated largely as government bodies; their connections to Party bodies were obscure.[18]

Each center had a small staff of researchers (ranging from thirteen in the case of the CIS to about a hundred in the case of the combined ETSDRC) but drew largely upon relevant researchers and staff from outside the center: in ministries, the Chinese Academy of Sciences (CAS), the Chinese Academy of Social Sciences (CASS), universities, and professional associations. The CIS, for example, had fifty affiliated researchers. When the TERC was established, fourteen units from CAS and CASS participated; these units served as a source of research support.[19] The centers established subordinate groups or divisions to address particular research topics or to handle particular types of tasks.[20] However, one of the major perceived advantages of these centers was their ability to organize diverse groups of experts for purposes of obtain-

17. See *National Research Center for Science and Technology for Development* (Beijing: n.p., n.d.), 7. An official of the ETSDRC also stated that Zhao Ziyang suggested the establishment of the TERC as a method of overcoming bureaucratic specialization and differences among the ministries.

18. In some cases there were formal ties to other bodies besides the premier's office or a leading group. The Price Research Center, for example, was originally subordinate to the State Price Commission; whether this remained true after it became a division within the ETSDRC is uncertain. The Center for International Studies was originally set up jointly under the State Council and the Chinese Academy of Social Sciences (CASS) and physically located within CASS, so that it could draw on the expertise in the eight institutes studying foreign affairs; after two years, however, its formal connection with the CASS was eliminated.

19. *Jingjixue dongtai*, July 1981, 5–6.

20. The ETSDRC, for example, had divisions on forecasting and development; technical economics (responsible primarily for project evaluation); economic levers (monetary and fiscal policy and economic development); the current economic situation; pricing problems; information and documentation; and a general office. The NRCSTD established eight divisions: development strategy research; technology policy research; R & D management research; system analysis research; information services; editorial and publication; office for professional affairs; administrative office.

ing interdisciplinary and interdepartmental expertise;[21] accordingly, the NRCSTD declared that research groups would be formed across divisional lines, according to the nature of the research project, and regrouped when the project was completed.[22] A major difference between the research centers and the commissions, which also cross functional lines, was the nonfixed nature of the former's available research personnel: because they drew on researchers from across the bureaucracy and academia, they could make use of whatever types of expertise were most valuable for analyzing a particular policy problem.[23]

Although they were intended to facilitate the flow of information between the ministries and the premier's office (thereby serving as a link between the two levels), their primary "constituency" was the premier's office, not the lower-level units. This was made clear by their formal location directly subordinate to the premier's office (or, in some cases, a premier-led "leadership small group"); by the fact that their agendas were set either by the premier's or the State Council's office or by the centers themselves;[24] by media discussions of their mandate; and by interviews with officials of the centers, who stressed their relationship to the premier. They thus differed from the many other advisory bodies in the bureaucracy subordinate to particular ministries, which were functionally specialized and tended to see their mission as producing expert analysis compatible with ministerial objectives.[25] Officials of the research centers saw their mission as helping the premier establish "good policy." They possessed an ideology of "neutral expertise" and saw themselves in competition with the more parochial ministries for the premier's attention and approval.

21. Ma Hong stated in 1983 that most advisory bodies at that time suffered from being too specialized; he advocated that in the future more such bodies (besides his own TERC) integrate social and natural scientists on their staff. "Guanyu jiaqiang shehui kexue he ziran kexue de jiehe, jiefu shehuizhuyi xiandaihua jianshe wentide jianyi," in *Kaizhuang shehui kexue yanjiude xin jumian* (Beijing: Zhongguo shehui kexue chubanshe, 1984), 297.

22. *National Research Center for Science and Technology for Development,* 10–11.

23. This was the reason given by Zhao Ziyang for setting up a Technical Economic Research Center instead of a Technical Advisory Commission. See Ma Hong, "Jiaqiang jishu jingji yanjiu, wei 'sihua' jianshe fuwu," in *Kaizhuang jishu jingji yanjiude xin jumian,* 207.

24. Officially, the "State Council and premier's Office" set the research agenda of the ETSDRC and other centers. However, media discussions and interviews both suggest that the centers not only were permitted to establish their own research projects but probably did so most of the time.

25. Apart from media discussions (e.g., *Jingji Ribao,* 18 March 1983, 1; *Jingjixue Zhoubao,* 21 March 1983, p. 4), this was made clear by interviews with individuals in research institutes subordinate to ministries, such as the Ministry of Foreign Affairs or the Ministry of Finance. These researchers clearly identified with the ministries' objectives, often speaking of the ministry and its research institute interchangeably.

The centers thus differed in three primary ways from other bodies supplying information and expertise to the top leaders. First, they were not as functionally specialized as those other bodies. The ministries are perhaps the most specialized sources of information, but even extrabureaucratic bodies on which top leaders can draw—research institutes of CAS and CASS and university departments—specialize along academic lines that most of the centers crosscut. Second, unlike the commissions, the centers lacked administrative responsibilities; they did not oversee any ministries or need to become immersed in the day-to-day details of policy implementation.[26] Their sole purpose was policy analysis. Third, of all the sources of information and expertise, the centers were the most wholly dependent on the person and office of the premier; as a consequence, they were the most likely to share his perspective on policy. That perspective included certain substantive orientations, such as a commitment to reform; it also included a broader and more integrated view of the country's needs than that possessed by any of the ministries. At the same time, it probably included the premier's political orientations or idiosyncratic desires, which might have little to do with developing coordinated policies. The post-Tiananmen decision to abolish the RDRC presumably reflects a belief that this center remained too closely tied to Zhao in both policy and political ways.

RESEARCH CENTERS: IMPACT ON THE COORDINATION PROBLEM

Information Effects

The research centers altered the information flow to the leadership in ways that facilitated coordination. They created new information on policy externalities and trade-offs by bringing together agencies with different functional responsibilities, as well as extrabureaucratic experts, for discussion of policy problems and solutions, so that information on trade-offs and complementarities emerged from their discussion. They also pooled functionally specific information collected separately within ministries, integrated it, and communicated it to the leadership. To a far more limited extent, the centers also used their own staffs to perform policy analysis, adopting a cross-departmental perspective.

A meeting convened jointly by the Technical Economic Research Center and the Shanxi provincial government in 1982 to discuss development of Shanxi's energy resources provides an example of this information-

26. Ma Hong's description of the TERC indicates this; he called it a research consulting organ under State Council leadership, not an administrative organ (like the SPC), and said that it had no formal administrative power. Ma Hong, "Kaizhuang jishu jingji yanjiu, wei 'sihua' jianshe fuwu," in *Kaizhuang shehui kexue yanjiude xin jumian*, 204–5.

generating function. The meeting brought together specialists from four-teen different units and discussed questions relating to management and coordination between government levels, the relationship between new and existing mines, problems of transportation, pricing, pollution, and so on. The TERC also held a similar meeting in March 1982 to discuss the feasibility of transporting coal by means of pipelines. This meeting brought together representatives of the SPC, the State Economic Commis-sion (SEC), State Capital Construction Commission, the SSTC, the minis-tries of Coal, Petroleum, Railroads, Water and Electricity, Machinery, Met-allurgy, the CASS, universities, and mines.[27] In March 1985 the Price Research Center organized a meeting to discuss "questions concerning the influence of sociopsychological factors upon reform of the price sys-tem"; it included researchers in psychology, sociology, politics, and eco-nomics, as well as some economic bureaucrats.[28] Meetings of this type provided a forum for interagency discussion, for the pooling of relevant information and expertise, and for consideration of policy decisions in a multidimensional and cross-disciplinary fashion. In this way they helped develop the information base needed for policy coordination, supplying a type of information not available before the Cultural Revolution when bureaucratic research bodies were essentially all functionally specialized.

Who decided, and on what basis, which agencies and types of expertise to include in such meetings is obviously crucial, as these decisions deter-mined to a large extent which types of policy externalities were consid-ered. Such decisions appeared to be left to the discretion of the centers, not determined by higher-level officials. Officials of the ETSDRC stated that when the State Council assigned the center a policy study, if it was a small question, they would sometimes decide simply to utilize their own staff (which consisted of a mixture of scientists, engineers, and econo-mists), but if it was a larger issue, they would convene a conference of relevant specialists from different units. The CIS went through a two-stage process in undertaking a policy study. The director, Huan Xiang, would first ask a staff member to organize the necessary experts. After discussion with relevant specialists, a preliminary working agenda would be drawn up listing the types of experts needed for the study. This then went to Huan for his approval. For particularly important matters, such as the drafting of the section on international affairs for the premier's Na-tional People's Congress (NPC) work report, Huan personally selected the relevant experts. The factors determining the types of agencies and ex-perts included in a study need to be further explored; however, it is clear that one important factor was the center's ability to gain the cooperation of

27. *Jingjixue Zhoubao*, 19 April 1982, 1.
28. *Jingji Ribao*, 15 March 1985, 1, in *FBIS*, 21 March 1985, K18.

different units. This aspect of the centers' work will be further explored in the next section.

Apart from generating information on policy trade-offs and complementarities relevant to particular projects or decisions, the centers also supplied new information through their role in organizing and conducting long-term planning studies. This was a formal part of the mandate of the ETSDRC (before that, of the TERC), and an important aspect of the NRCSTD's work. These long-term planning and forecasting studies served in part to add a ten- or twenty-year perspective on future developments and needs in the economy, science and technology, foreign affairs, and other areas to complement the more short-term focus of the planning commissions (the SPC focused on five-year, and the SEC on annual, planning until the two were combined in June 1988) and ministries. More important for the focus of this chapter, these studies were conducted in a manner that contributed to policy coordination by drawing in different types of experts and explicitly seeking a comprehensive perspective on the costs and benefits of different policies.

One such long-term planning effort was a thirteen-volume report on "China to the Year 2000" produced over a three-year period under the overall supervision of the TERC (later the ETSDRC). The TERC was able to draw in a much broader range of specialists than would a similar effort by the SPC, including hundreds of specialists who were members of the professional associations that form the China Association of Science and Technology.[29] Ma Hong, the director of the TERC, headed a research leadership group composed of representatives of the SPC, the SEC, the SSTC, the CASS, as well as the TERC. This group then allocated specific parts of the report to particular units: the S & T one to the SSTC; the report on the international situation to the CASS Institute of World Economics and Politics; the transportation one to the SEC and the Ministry of Railways. This allocation obviously made it possible for the study to be carried out in a functionally specialized way that took little account of policy externalities; this tendency was noted and criticized at an early symposium on the study, held in August 1983.[30] However, by drawing in a large number of units and specialists, it was also possible to produce a more multidimensional analysis than would normally be undertaken.

29. This was the reason given by Ma Hong in explaining why he rejected the argument of "some comrades" that the organization of the study of "China to the Year 2000" should be the responsibility of the SPC. Although Ma obviously had other reasons for wanting to keep control of this effort under the auspices of his own TERC rather than the SPC, his assessment of the consequences seems accurate. See Ma Hong, "Kaizhan '2000 niande Zhongguo' de yanjiu," in *Kaizhuang shehui kexue yanjiude xin jumian*, 117.

30. *Xinhua*, 31 August 1983, in *JPRS*, no. 84374, 21 September 1983, Economic Affairs, no. 384, 71.

A second such long-term planning effort, organized by the NRCSTD, was undertaken jointly by the SPC, the SEC, and the SSTC in 1983, and resulted in the issuing in 1986 of a "white paper" on general S & T policy, and twelve "blue papers" on specialized areas of technical policy. Descriptions of this planning effort emphasize that it involved a new approach, particularly in the manner in which it integrated scientific and economic planning. The process went as follows: First, the planning bureau of the SSTC suggested some preliminary research items, which were discussed by the three commissions. Nine general areas were selected, and after discussions with relevant departments, were allocated in the form of about fifty individual research questions to those departments. Each department then organized S & T and economics specialists to carry out the research and suggest appropriate technical policies. Following this, the three commissions held conferences to discuss technical policy in each of the nine areas and produce draft documents, and they "repeatedly did overall balance work." Following these meetings, the three commissions jointly drafted the documents, sought relevant opinions, revised them, and submitted them to the State Council for approval.[31] The NRCSTD played a large role in this process: helping to organize the studies, chairing the working groups, and overseeing the compiling and publication of the final documents.[32] While perhaps not essential for such a major research and planning effort, the existence of the NRCSTD at least greatly facilitated it.

This planning effort promoted coordination in several ways. First, the very fact of cooperation between the three commissions was pointed to as an innovation.[33] Second, the many meetings held during the research process, like the TERC meetings on project evaluation and policy issues, brought together diverse groups of specialists for discussion of technical issues from scientific, economic, and other points of view, thereby generating new information on policy externalities. Third, the more long-term planning perspective meant that aspects of a problem that might be fixed in the short run, and thus be easy to ignore in routine planning, could now be considered. For example, when the SSTC Department of Comprehensive Management worked out a plan for developing Chinese energy to the year 2000, it not only invited specialists to consider the technical aspects of energy planning, but also included many economists from the TERC and Price Research Center to discuss relevant pricing questions. Although the group organizing the study had been told by the

31. Zheng Qinghan and Xie Chengyan, "Guanyu yanjiu, zhiding, guanchi jishu zhengcide jige wenti," *Kexue guanli yanjiu*, no. 4 (August 1983), 23.
32. *National Research Center for Science and Technology for Development*, 10–11; and personal communication from a participant in the energy study.
33. Ibid., 21.

State Council that prices could not be changed in the short run, it recognized that this was something that must be done eventually. The longer time horizon of this study made it sensible to consider the pricing aspects of energy and the consequences of altering energy prices. Finally, when the white and blue papers were publicly promulgated in 1986, the newspaper reports emphasized that these authoritative policies both permitted and required coordinated action by different departments and localities, which had not been possible before—that is, that the increased information provided by the planning process had given leadership policies sufficient authority that coordinated *implementation* of policy was now possible.[34] From the perspective of those writing the reports, at least, the results of the planning effort had contributed to policy coordination.

The "China to the Year 2000" study organized by the TERC and the technical blueprints organized by the NRCSTD were not the first examples in China of efforts to develop long-term plans for particular sectors while taking account of other related policy considerations. In 1979 the Energy Research Association, under the joint direction of the SSTC, the SPC, and the SEC, began work on a draft "China's Energy Policy Outline Recommendations," which was completed in December 1982. This outline put forward recommendations based on sixteen considerations, including economics, S & T research, education, and environmental policies. However, the establishment of the research centers permitted such efforts to be organized in a more systematic and regular fashion.

Authority Effects

The research centers did not formally alter the structure of authority within the bureaucracy. As staff and not line organs, they had independent authority—to conduct studies, contract with other units, and perform other tasks related to their research mission (such as, in the case of the CIS, to make contact with foreign bodies without going through the Ministry of Foreign Affairs)—but they did not have formal authority over the ministries or commissions; they were of the same bureaucratic rank. Their relations with these horizontally equal units were thus *yewu guanxi* (professional relations). They could not demand the cooperation

34. A commentator's article in *Renmin Ribao*, 3 September 1986, 1, in *FBIS*, 5 September 1986, K5, emphasized that all departments and localities were required to carry out the policies, and that this was the business not just of S & T personnel, but also of economic workers and the government departments. The article stated that these policies should be carried out in drawing up S & T, economic, and social development plans, carrying out technical transformation, deciding on priority construction plans, and so on. Song Jian, head of the SSTC, argued that coordination among departments, specialties, and trades required correct (i.e., knowledge-based) policies; these blueprints, he suggested, supplied these. Song Jian, "March Towards a New Realm—Preface to 'Guide to China's Science and Technology Policies,' " *Renmin Ribao*, 10 September 1986, 3, in *FBIS*, 17 September 1986, K10.

of any other unit; they also could not prevent any ministry from sending its advice directly to the State Council rather than through the research center.

The vertical relationship of the centers with the premier and the State Council differed from their horizontal relationship with the ministries and commissions. Although formally the research centers' authority was equivalent, their informal authority, and the attention paid them by the premier, varied. As many have noted, the personal authority of the director appeared to be a primary source of such variation; this in turn was a function of personal closeness to the premier and general respect of the top leadership. Ma Hong's ETSDRC (and before that the TERC) appeared to be by far the most influential, and the respect that Ma Hong has enjoyed among top leaders for many years is undoubtedly a key reason. The quality of the center's staff appeared to be another source of variation in informal authority; the TERC possessed a young, energetic staff, most of whom had graduated from the CASS graduate school or top universities.

But these intrinsic factors did not wholly determine the impact of the centers. Persuasion and competition were both key to the kind of relationship the centers had with higher officials. The relationship cannot be characterized as one of bargaining; because their authority was essentially derivative of the premier, the centers did not have the resources necessary to bargain with these higher authorities and therefore had to engage in persuasion. The centers' ethos was also not one of bargaining; their personnel repeatedly emphasized that they simply advised the premier and that he could accept or reject their advice. These personnel also recognized that they were competing with other units that might offer the premier more persuasive advice. Accordingly, a better model of the relationship between the centers and the premier (and the State Council generally) is one of "competitive persuasion."[35] Only when they could

35. The centers clearly compete with each other and the ministries and commissions for authority and jurisdiction and for the premier's attention and support. One staff member of another center described Ma Hong's TERC as a "hegemon," saying that in addition to incorporating the ERC and Price Research Center, Ma had hoped also to bring the Economic Legislation Center and CIS under his domain. Although this effort failed, the TERC did not appear to have particularly good relations with the CIS: for drafting of the international affairs section of the "China to the Year 2000" report, Ma turned instead to the Institute of World Economics and Politics at CASS. The centers competed not only with each other but also with powerful ministries: Huan Xiang's CIS and the Ministry of Foreign Affairs (MFA) clearly saw each other as major competitors for policy influence with the premier. Nor were the centers necessarily more influential than the ministries; although Ma Hong's ETSDRC appears to have been very influential relative to the economic ministries (perhaps less so relative to the SPC), the CIS seemed, if anything, less influential than the MFA. More research is needed to establish the exact nature of competition between the centers and the ministries, and the sources of relative influence.

persuade the top leaders to accept their policy recommendations could they actually affect the nature of policy implementation and the behavior of other bureaucratic units.[36] Thus, to demonstrate their influence on policy outcomes, ETSDRC officials pointed to their ability to get their suggestions formally incorporated into the Seventh Five-Year Plan, and NRCSTD officials pointed to the authoritative promulgation of the white and blue papers.[37]

However, because the centers possessed limited staff, in order to make their arguments persuasive to higher authorities they had to gain the cooperation of horizontally equal ministries and other units with relevant expertise (although in some cases they were able to draw on foreign expertise).[38] The resources that the centers possessed to gain the cooperation of researchers in other units varied considerably, and in somewhat circular fashion, varied in part according to the perceived clout of the center. In this set of relationships, bargaining was a more relevant factor.

A key research center resource for gaining the cooperation of the ministries was the fact that the premier and other important leaders were known to pay attention to their reports. Thus, when the centers organized meetings or prepared studies, ministries wanted to participate so that their voices would be heard.[39] This was particularly true for a study like "China to the Year 2000," which was known to be personally

36. A possible example of how a research institute was able to affect the behavior of a ministry in a different functional sphere through "competitive persuasion" and not bargaining comes from the MFA's Institute of International Studies. When world oil prices fell, the Institute wrote a report arguing that China should slow her oil production and sent it directly to the premier. Zhao agreed, and ordered the ministry to slow down production. However, as Michel Oksenberg points out (personal communication), confirming that this instance actually fits the model of "competitive persuasion" will require knowledge of the other input into the decision.

37. Undoubtedly, strategies other than simply providing a compelling argument were used in the competition between advisory bodies for policy influence. For example, a member of the SSTC energy-planning group described how, as a (then) minority voice opposing construction of the Three Gorges Dam, the group was horrified to read in *Renmin Ribao* that construction was already beginning. In a call to the newspaper, they discovered that this was false information that reporters had "heard from someone." My informant thought it likely that this was a deliberate leak to the newspaper by someone trying to influence the policy outcome. I do not discuss these alternative bureaucratic strategies for gaining policy influence because I lack any meaningful data on them.

38. In a personal communication, David Zweig indicates that the RDRC drew heavily on the resources of the World Bank in performing some of its studies.

39. One official of the research institute under the MFA suggested that his institute was very happy to have research tasks allocated by the premier or the State Council office (a relatively rare occurence), because researchers then knew that this was an issue to which the leadership was paying attention, and thus that the chances of having some influence were greater.

sanctioned by Zhao Ziyang. High-level leadership attention was also evident in the technical planning process organized by the NRCSTD; according to a participant in the energy-planning group, when the group organized meetings of different specialists, often a vice-premier would attend and ask questions. Since leadership attention is a scarce resource, the centers' ability to deliver it provided a strong incentive for the ministries to cooperate in their studies.

The importance of perceived influence with the premier for gaining the cooperation of ministries and research bodies is clear from conversations with researchers in different bodies. An official of the NRCSTD specializing in agricultural research said that his center maintained good relations with the Rural Development Research Center, in part because the two centers had similar policy interests, but also because the RDRC had "a great deal of clout." Although I heard no stories of TERC or ETSDRC difficulties in gaining the cooperation of ministries or researchers, the relatively less influential CIS clearly did have such difficulty. Indeed, it appears that the CIS had to struggle to find units willing to cooperate with its studies and had to rely partly on *guanxi*, or a personal relationship with individuals in those other units.[40]

Finally, the centers utilized financial resources and exchange of services to gain the support of researchers in other units. Here they clearly came closest to "bargaining" with those units. The CIS provided funds to fifty affiliated researchers to undertake research projects. Likewise, the NRCSTD contracted for studies by other units; its charter provided that it could sign such contracts with foreign as well as domestic entities. Some of those contracts—such as one for a study of sand-sedimentation problems related to the Three Gorges Project—were allocated through a bidding system, in which institutes from CAS and CASS, universities, and the bureaucracy could participate. Financial resources and broad contacts within the bureaucracy and academia apparently could be just as important as *guanxi* with the leadership, making the NRCSTD a major challenger to the ETSDRC. The NRCSTD had the resources of the SSTC behind it; the SSTC, in cooperation with the SPC, allocated all central-government funding for civilian S & T research. Indeed, when

40. Originally, the CIS was supposed to rely heavily upon the CASS area studies institutes for research support, but these institutes did not prove very cooperative. Although the MFA shared its documents with the CIS and invited CIS staff to attend its biweekly *wuxuhui* ("meetings to discuss ideological guidelines," i.e., meetings for internal coordination purposes where policy issues are discussed and debated), it was unwilling to undertake joint research with the center. The CIS came to rely heavily upon the Institute of Contemporary International Relations (ICIR). According to Barnett, the ICIR was responsible to the CIS (implying an authoritative relationship); according to a Chinese source, however, the reason it was so cooperative was that the former director of the ICIR, Chen Zhongjing, was married to a relative of Huan Xiang's.

the CIS wished to carry out a quantitative study, it had to go to the SSTC for funds.[41] Greater financial and staff resources provided the NRCSTD with another major advantage over some other centers in gaining the cooperation of ministries; it had the ability to undertake consulting work for other agencies. An official of the NRCSTD stated that a desire to have the NRCSTD do research for them was one of the major reasons why the ministries were willing to cooperate in studies organized by the NRCSTD. The ETSDRC, on the other hand, had to turn down requests by other bureaucratic units to undertake studies on their behalf, because it lacked the necessary resources.

In general, then, the research centers' main source of bureaucratic authority was their relationship to the premier and the ability to persuade him and other officials to accept their advice (these two characteristics were related, but not perfectly). To persuade other units to cooperate with them so that they could carry out their studies and try to influence decision making, they offered leadership attention, financial incentives, and exchange of services. They also sometimes made use of *guanxi* in the pure sense of a direct personal relationship. But these resources, used to "bargain" with other units, only allowed them to conduct their research; they did not permit the centers, independently of State Council authority, to actually alter the behavior of ministries in ways that affected policy implementation.

Although the centers did not formally alter the authority structure of the bureaucracy, they nevertheless did so informally by shifting the balance of information and expertise between the top leadership and the ministries. As was discussed in the section on information effects, they collected information from ministries and other units and transferred it upward; moreover, they generated some limited analysis of their own (more in the case of some centers than others), and could help the leadership integrate and assess the information coming in separately from the ministries. Indirectly, therefore, the centers potentially diminished the fragmentation of authority by decreasing the ministries' relative monopoly of expertise.

However, because expertise had become a more important resource in the Chinese bureaucracy, this shift in relative expertise from lower-level units to the leadership proved unstable. The ministries and commissions subordinate to the State Council had an incentive to try to reverse that shift by enlarging their own sources of information and expertise. The SSTC may have created the NRCSTD partly with this in mind; the State Planning and Economic commissions also increased their expertise by

41. The SSTC also allocated funding for very different types of policy-related activities, such as a "Beijing Youth Forum" organized by the NRCSTD, which brought together thirty-to-forty-year-olds once a month for lively debate of various policy issues.

making use of a network of expert consulting groups organized under a "China International Engineering Consulting Corporation" to help evaluate the feasibility of different projects considered for inclusion in their five- or one-year plans. The announcement of the two commissions' plan to make use of the corporation stated that the corporation planned to "recruit foreign specialists to join its consulting business in the hope of providing the state with reliable data needed for correct decision making."[42] The State Planning Commission's enhancement of its capability to supply such expertise shifted the balance between the expert resources of the State Council (enhanced by the creation of the TERC, which was set up partly to advise the State Council on major projects, such as the ones included in the five-year and annual plans) and the SPC back toward the latter. Some ministries also acted to enhance their analytical capability, either by enlarging their research staff or by moving to increase their contacts with other relevant units and experts. Thus, the exact degree to which the centers altered the balance of expertise (and thus informal authority) between the leadership and the ministries and commissions is uncertain.

Incentive Effects

In the preceding discussion I suggested that the research centers provided policymakers with information illuminating trade-offs and complementarities between policy areas, and to some extent shifted the balance of informal authority toward the leadership by diminishing the ministries' relative monopoly of expertise in their functional area. In this section I ask whether the research centers also changed the incentives of researchers and ministries so as to promote coordination through altered research strategies or mutual adjustment between ministries—for example, bargaining or consensus building. The discussion is essentially analytical, suggesting some propositions that might be tested through interviewing researchers and ministerial personnel; thus far, I do not have the data to do more.

First, the research centers provided different incentives for research personnel than did the rest of the bureaucratic structure. As I have already noted, researchers organized into functionally specialized research institutes subordinate to ministries have little if any incentive to consider the impact of ministry actions on other units. The tendency of such researchers to produce research results oriented toward fulfilling the goals of their superior ministries has been noted often in the Chinese press. Researchers working for the research centers, on the other hand,

42. Lin Xi, "Important Capital Construction and Technological Transformation Projects to Be Examined by Consulting Organs Before Finalization," *Renmin Ribao*, 8 February 1986, in *FBIS*, 21 February 1986, K11.

had no such incentives; indeed, their incentives were to consider the impact of policies in the broadest possible perspective and thus to take account of externalities between agencies. By building staffs that included individuals with a variety of expertise and from multiple agencies, the research centers attempted to provide both the capability and the incentives for researchers to consider the interrelationship between policy areas. Of course, the primary incentives of those researchers were to respond to the priorities of the centers' directors and, ultimately, of the premier. Policy coordination was one such priority, but hardly the only one; accordingly, researchers in these centers could not be expected always to adopt such a perspective.

What effect did the establishment of the research centers have on the incentives of the ministries? One effect, discussed earlier, was to motivate them to increase their expert resources in an effort to maintain their relative authority vis-à-vis the center. However, this ministerial strategy need not necessarily promote policy coordination, and might even interfere with it. Don K. Price has suggested that a major source of fragmentation in the American bureaucracy is precisely the cultural tendency for special interests to appeal to "science" (or expertise) in support of their special goals.[43] The key question is whether the research centers created incentives for the ministries to seek out and provide information regarding policy externalities and to propose policies that took account of such externalities.

The research centers might have done so in three ways. First, without altering the incentive structure, the centers provided information necessary for the ministries to respond to already-existing incentives for coordinating behavior. That is, ministries always had an incentive to make clear the externalities for them of policies proposed by other agencies; prior to the establishment of the research centers, however, it appears that they often could not do so because policies were frequently considered in a unidimensional manner, with many potentially affected agencies being ignored during the decision-making process and not even aware that the policy was being considered until after its adoption. A major function of the research centers was to collect views on policy proposals from all relevant agencies. Thus, when a ministry proposed a major policy, other units were much more likely to be made aware of it and thus be able to provide information on the externalities of that decision for their particular policy jurisdiction.

Second, the research centers might actually have altered the incentives of the ministries to seek out information on policy externalities and to

43. Don K. Price, *America's Unwritten Constitution* (Cambridge: Harvard University Press, 1985).

adjust their policies to take other agencies into account. Because the centers supposedly provided an "unbiased" view, taking account of interdepartmental effects, any ministry wishing to argue against a research center's view would have to make a better case. This should have encouraged the ministries not only to enhance their analytical capacity (as we have already seen), but also to seek out information on other functional areas so that they could make a case that the policy was good, not only for them, but also for other agencies. This hypothesis about the incentive effects of the centers remains to be tested, however, through interviews exploring whether the ministries' behavior actually changed in this manner.

Finally, the research centers probably promoted bargaining among ministries. The meetings they organized provided an important forum in which such bargaining could occur. Although ministries could provide their own views independently to the State Council, they had every reason to believe that a document reflecting agreement among multiple agencies would carry more weight than one expressing the opinion of a single agency. It therefore would be in the interest of each agency to reach some kind of compromise with other agencies, unless it had reason to believe that it could do better on its own. The latter might be true either because the goals of the agency diverged so greatly from those of others that compromise seemed impossible or, alternatively, because it reflected a belief that the ministry's resources were large enough to allow it to prevail against the opinions of the research center and other ministries. The Ministry of Foreign Affairs, for example, appeared to feel secure enough in its influence to go directly to the premier rather than reaching accommodation with the CIS or other units; according to one of its officials, its suggestions were sometimes overruled but were accepted on other occasions. A researcher from the CIS argued, however, that the ministry usually managed to get its preferred policies adopted.

The centers promoted bargaining—in the form of logrolling or quid-pro-quos—between agencies in other ways than simply providing the forums in which such discussions might take place. The centers altered the nature of interdepartmental discussions in both horizontal (cross-departmental and even cross-system) and vertical (long-term planning) ways that, as Robert Keohane has argued for the effect of international regimes on cooperation between nations, made the striking of deals between ministries more likely. First, the centers organized discussions that "cluster issues." As Keohane argued about international regimes: "Clustering of issues under a regime facilitates side-payments among these issues: more potential *quids* are available for the *quo*. Without international regimes linking clusters of issues to one another, side-payments and linkages would be difficult to arrange in world politics; in the absence of a price system for the exchange of favors, institutional barriers would hinder the construction of mutually beneficial bargains."[44] The interdepartmental discussions organized by the centers may have served a similar function. Second, the ongoing discussions and particularly the long-term planning efforts altered the policy process in ways that effectively placed the participants in a repeated-game situation: they could expect to interact repeatedly with other agencies that formerly they might only occasionally have encountered. Incentives were thereby created to cooperate now in exchange for future cooperation. Moreover, some of that future cooperation could be institutionalized in the present when policy documents were formulated that planned ahead many years. Like policy clustering, long-term planning created more potential "quids."

If the meetings organized by the centers promoted bargaining between ministries, they clearly did not produce total consensus on policy. One would expect that agreement would be reached primarily in those cases where ministries could discover complementarities between their desired policies, or where they could obtain desired concessions from other agencies without making more costly concessions of their own. This did not necessarily always happen. Center officials speak of normally providing final documents to the State Council that laid out remaining areas of disagreement. That these meetings did not produce total consensus is not undesirable from the point of view of the leadership: where basic value conflicts were revealed, the leadership obviously would prefer to make the needed trade-offs itself.

CONCLUSION: THE STRUCTURE OF AUTHORITY AND MODELS OF CHINESE BUREAUCRATIC BEHAVIOR

The above discussion of the role of the research centers was limited to analyzing the impact of these new institutions on information flows within the bureaucracy and the ability of the leadership to adopt and implement coordinated policies. I suggested three ways in which the centers promoted policy coordination: (1) by increasing the leadership's information on policy externalities (through independent research and the pooling of ministry-collected data and analysis, the organizing of interagency discussions of policy choices, and long-term planning procedures) so that coordinated policies could be formulated; (2) by shifting the balance of informal authority between the leadership and the ministries (by diminishing the latter's relative monopoly of expertise) so that coordinated policies could be implemented; and (3) by altering the envi-

---

44. Robert O. Keohane, *After Hegemony: Cooperation and Discord in the World Political Economy* (Princeton: Princeton University Press, 1984), 91.

ronment of researchers and ministries so as to produce both new capacity and new incentives for coordinating behavior (causing the ministries either to take account independently of the impact of their policy proposals on other policy spheres or to reach accommodation through bargaining with other units).

Although the centers clearly did not eliminate the fragmentation of authority, unlike other institutional changes of the post-Mao era they generally promoted centralized authority, if centralization is measured by the ability of the leadership to adopt and implement coordinated policies. This does not mean that such centralization was sufficient to overcome the fragmenting tendencies produced by the dispersal of resources other than information; most likely it was not. But my analysis should steer scholars away from any simplistic assumption that the post-Mao reforms uniformly altered the structure of authority in favor of subordinate units.

I suggested above that the model of "competitive persuasion" more accurately describes the relationship between the research centers and the top leaders than does either the command or the bargaining model. The research centers' attempts to formulate persuasive arguments about appropriate policy, in competition with other agencies offering alternative advice, fits neither the command model, with its emphasis on lower-level units' obedience to leadership commands, nor the bargaining model, which focuses on exchange and mutual veto power between different levels. Instead, it suggests a political relationship in which personal relations and expert analysis both play a role.

The continuing importance of personal relations for the research centers' ability to persuade top leaders—as well as for their ability to gain cooperation from other units—has been noted several times. Even while Zhao Ziyang was premier, personal relationships were an important element determining the influence of the research centers. As I suggested above, the research centers' authority was largely derivative of their relationship to and influence with the premier; the centers' ability to gain the cooperation of other units depended partly upon this derived authority, but sometimes upon a personal relationship with the head of one of those units.

At the same time, personal relations appear to be only a partial explanation of the centers' influence on decision making. The centers' staff and officials believed that their ability to persuade the premier and other leaders depended greatly upon the quality of the advice they were able to offer. Moreover, fluctuations in the research centers' overall and relative influence, and even their formal existence (such as the decline in influence of the CIS, the expansion and rise in influence of the TERC, and the abolition of the RDRC), are only partly correlated with leadership change and the politics of Tiananmen. Both Li Peng, who replaced Zhao Ziyang as premier in 1987, and the new Party general secretary, Jiang Zemin, seemingly rely more heavily on other sources of expertise, which they regard as personally loyal and perhaps ideologically more in tune with their policy orientations.[45] However, according to a former member of the CIS, that center's loss of influence predated both the death of its original director, Huan Xiang, and the removal of Zhao Ziyang as premier; apparently the CIS lost out in bureaucratic competition with the Ministry of Foreign Affairs (although the latter reportedly tried, but failed, to have the CIS eliminated during the bureaucratic reshuffling of 1987–88). And although the RDRC is being dismantled, seemingly as a direct result of the politics of Tiananmen, the ETSDRC has steadily expanded its scope and influence and, if anything, seems to have become more powerful after Zhao's removal. The NRCSTD also appears little affected by the events at Tiananmen. The mixture of personal and rational factors underlying the research centers' influence means that the centers' authority has not, and probably will not soon, become highly institutionalized. But the reliance upon expert advice and the use of such advice to counterbalance the authority of individual ministries appears more stable than the influence of any particular institution.

The events at Tiananmen do not invalidate these conclusions about the role of the research centers and similar advisory bodies in promoting policy coordination. They do, however, suggest that we must recognize the limitations of any study of bureaucratic politics for illuminating and predicting the behavior of China's top leaders. In a crisis, those leaders are unlikely to consult either with bureaucrats or with members of their advisory institutions; indeed, even in noncrisis conditions, they may sometimes choose to ignore them. However, in ordinary decision making, bureaucratic considerations loom large, and in the post-Mao period, even after Tiananmen, the distribution of information and expertise is one important factor shaping the nature and outcome of bureaucratic processes and authority.

45. *New York Times*, 6 February 1990.

PART THREE

Bureaucratic Clusters

SIX

Structure and Process in the Chinese Military System

Jonathan D. Pollack

Among the major institutions buttressing the power of the Chinese state, the People's Liberation Army remains one of the least well understood. Despite its vast size, its proprietary claim on resources, and its pivotal role in the political history of the People's Republic, the army remains to most professional observers unknown and inaccessible. The armed forces retain a subordinate status in relation to the Chinese Communist Party and still serve as the Party's ultimate instrument of coercive control. At the same time, however, the army assumes a distinctive, autonomous organizational identity, and in numerous respects constitutes a virtual state within a state, exercising pervasive if minimally observable influence over the lives of millions of Chinese citizens.

The army is also in the throes of major change. Having long functioned on the basis of inherited prerogatives and procedures, the PLA in the 1980s found itself challenged from above, below, and within. The challenge from above came from Deng Xiaoping, whose assumption of the chairmanship of the CCP Central Military Commission in 1981 reflected the singular importance of this leadership post and also Deng's convictions about the failings of the military establishment. The challenge from below concerned the diminished stature of the military profession in an era of economic reform, with the army no longer serving as a promising channel for upward mobility. The challenge from within came from a far more capable and increasingly restive segment of the officer corps, which had grown dissatisfied with the highly circumscribed opportunities for professional advancement. By mid-decade the fitful

The opinions expressed in this chapter are my own and do not represent the views of RAND or its governmental sponsors. I am much indebted to Kenneth Allen for his helpful suggestions and comments.

movement away from the inherited military arrangements of the Cultural Revolution era started to jell, with an embryonic modern military system beginning to take shape.

This transformed military system entailed the formulation of rules and regulations for long-term institutional development and the professionalization of the officer corps. At the same time, the armed forces began to interact more fully with other Chinese institutions than at any point in the last thirty years, even as the PLA's relationship with the Party remained distinct and unique. Although the PLA was still accountable to the CCP, it also stood apart from it, given the army's specialized, quasi-separatist character. The military leadership identified two tasks for the longer term: first, to enhance the stature of a modernized, professional military system within China, and second, to balance the military's need for autonomous professional development against the continuing imperative of accountability and subordination to Party rule.

The concepts underlying the emergent military system, however, remain transitional and incomplete. Current norms and arrangements still reflect three singular formative influences: the pervasive role of Mao and his closest military colleagues in shaping the PLA's thinking, policies, and procedures; the lasting technological and bureaucratic imprint of Soviet tutelage in the 1950s; and the absence of regular mechanisms for leadership turnover. In addition, given the army's crucial role in maintaining social and political order during the 1960s and 1970s, there was a predominantly inertial character to institutional development, with few efforts to alter existing personnel arrangements, especially those deeply embedded in the day-to-day workings of the system. Numerous recent changes have concerned the reconfiguration of the old system, not a comprehensive introduction of new structures and processes. These hybrid arrangements often remain derivative of interpersonal relations, rather than professional norms, and leave unresolved the mechanisms and forms of bargaining and resource allocation within the military and across bureaucratic channels. But the pervasive grip of tradition has begun to loosen, and the outlines of a more modern, regularized military establishment are discernible for the first time.

The upheavals of the spring of 1989, however, again thrust the leadership of the armed forces into a pivotal position in Chinese political life. This has presented the PLA with a newfound opportunity to advance its corporate interests (e.g., through increased budgets and an enhanced social-control function), and it could well afford the army a decisive role in the post-Deng succession process. But it is a very mixed blessing. By becoming deeply embroiled in interpersonal rivalries atop the system, the actions of the military leadership intruded upon the professionalizing mission that many in the officer corps deem the army's paramount objective. Thus, the PLA in the early 1990s is not a cohesive, unified institution.

This chapter addresses the distribution of power within the Chinese armed forces. Specifically, where does power reside within the military system? What are the principal resources available to the military leadership (e.g., personnel assignment, budget resources, foreign technology, etc.), and who controls them? Are the criteria for determining the distribution of such resources predominantly personal or institutional? Three major issues are assessed:

1. What are the predominant characteristics of the inherited military system?
2. What are the principal changes that Deng and his allies have tried to introduce in the military system, and what have been the results?
3. What are the defining traits of the PLA's present leadership arrangements and institutional procedures?

THE INHERITED MILITARY SYSTEM

The Chinese armed forces represent a virtual way of life for large numbers of Chinese. Although there have been periodic efforts to curb the size of the military establishment, these attempts have focused on the PLA as a fighting force, rather than as a full service institution. The army's allocative and distributive reach within Chinese society and the economy is unusually broad. It employs, feeds, and houses millions of people. Its claim on the national budget, while much diminished at present, was virtually unlimited in previous decades, and its proprietary access to resources remains very great.

The principal anomaly in the power of the military is its understated leadership role. Except in the early 1950s and between the mid to late 1960s and the early 1970s, the PLA has not assumed power in an overt political sense. The army frequently achieved disproportionate representation in national and provincial-level leadership bodies, but rarely chose to exercise this power fully. The Party and the army achieved a compact or at least a tacit understanding: in exchange for its obeisance to CCP rule, the PLA remained emperor of a vast realm of its own. Except for post–Korean War cutbacks and the retrenchment following the "high tide" of military influence under Lin Biao, the Party leadership very rarely intruded upon the societal, organizational, and economic domains controlled by the armed forces.

By dint of these understandings, the power and prerogatives of the PLA became embedded deeply in Chinese administrative and economic life. The military's entitlements ranged very widely, including control of airfields, ports, air space, communications networks, and industrial facilities, as well as access to goods and services from abroad. These inherited assets and jurisdictional claims, being reserved for the near exclusive use of the armed forces, inhibited infrastructural and societal development as a whole.

Some of the most telling consequences were found in the Chinese defense industrial system. Created and designed under Soviet guidance in the 1950s, but subsequently cloned at Mao's behest in interior provinces during the 1960s, the defense economy kept millions employed.[1] Except for high-priority national defense projects, there were neither incentives nor opportunities for meaningful reform. The creation of "third line" defense industries frequently replicated the inefficiencies of existing plants and facilities, with these units granted proprietary claim on budgetary, technical, and manpower resources, as well as preferential access to industrial materials and energy supplies.[2] Gross inefficiency and the absence of effective innovation went hand in hand, with Chinese factories producing endless amounts of antiquated equipment at heavily subsidized state prices. A vast, highly duplicative defense industrial system produced on demand for a military hierarchy that sought only to keep all key organizational constituencies "well fed."

Few within the leadership ever challenged the army's entitlements. As a consequence, the army grew by accretion and inertia, bloated by a personnel logjam, especially at the upper reaches of the system. The army was rewarded for its loyalty and service to the state in successive national crises, garnering progressively larger forces and budgetary resources. But size did not beget organizational efficiency; military preparedness was deemed important only for elite national defense units.

Different levels of the military system, however, performed invaluable services for state and society. The PLA built bridges and railways, furnished personnel and facilities for internal security, maintained order at times of upheaval, contributed labor and materials to major national projects, and safeguarded national security. By its reach throughout the provinces and by the strategic positioning of key military units, it also served as the ultimate guarantor of political and social control. But these arrangements gradually transformed the military system into a person-

1. According to a survey on China's defense R & D undertaken in 1987–88, total employment in the defense industries amounted to 2.86 million workers, of whom 400,000 were scientists and technicians. Interview with Chinese military researcher, October 1988. According to this source, as much as two-thirds of this total work force is considered redundant or unnecessary for current defense tasks, with approximately one-half of the scientific and technical work force still needed.

2. See Xiao Min, "A Tentative Discourse on Readjusting the Setup of Industry in the Third-Line Region," *Jingji Ribao*, 14 July 1989, in *FBIS-China*, 2 August 1989, 32–36.

nel, administrative, and economic network of staggering and unmanageable proportions.

Thus, to conceptualize the PLA as a military establishment and guardian of national security is somewhat misleading; to many, it was a way of life, insulated from society as a whole and highly privileged and protected. At the same time, soldiers and civilians employed by the army generally enjoyed living standards superior to other institutions. Few incentives existed to alter this general pattern, and the Party leadership (mindful of its dependence upon the armed forces) granted the PLA effective control of its own realm. Deng Xiaoping sought to remake the Chinese defense establishment in the context of these practices and circumstances.

REVAMPING THE PERSONNEL SYSTEM

When Deng (as PLA chief of staff) first assumed responsibility for military affairs in the mid-1970s, he quickly concluded that the PLA was a deeply troubled institution. In his infamous characterization to a meeting of the Military Commission in mid-1975, Deng asserted that the PLA suffered from "bloating, laxity, conceit, extravagance, and inertia."[3] Deng's reform efforts of this period were aborted by his ouster from power in 1976. By dint of its pivotal role in displacing the "Gang of Four," the PLA completed its recovery from the trauma of the Lin Biao affair, with the leadership settling into a Brezhnevite "stability of cadres" orientation. Except for those directly implicated in the factional politics of the Lin Biao era or for those who were hopelessly decrepit, most disgraced military leaders were returned to comparable or higher positions than those from which they had been ousted. The predominant character of military policy-making was inertial and self-satisfied, and an uncertain, untested Hua Guofeng was only too willing to comply.[4]

The consequences of this complacency, however, were driven home by China's inept military performance in the "pedagogic war" against Vietnam. As *Jiefangjun Bao* observed much later: "War is the mirror of training. The war of self-defensive counterattack against Vietnam in 1979— this small mirror—reflected the state of PLA's training at that time. . . . A generation of military men . . . had been wallowing [in] the PLA's glorious history: We are backward, our weapons and equipment are

3. Deng Xiaoping, "The Tasks of Consolidating the Army," 4 July 1975, in *Selected Works of Deng Xiaoping* (Beijing: Foreign Languages Press, 1984), 27.

4. For revealing insights into military policy-making during the late 1970s, see Zhang Aiping's reminiscences of Luo Ruiqing, in *Renmin Ribao*, 3 August 1988, 4, in *FBIS-China*, 12 August 1988, 30–33.

backward, and . . . even more frightening . . . our military thinking and training ideas are backward!"[5]

Although there was no single explanation of these circumstances, the sorry state of the officer corps was a principal contributing factor. China's ratio of officers to enlisted men was (and is) the highest of any major army in the world. Many of these revolutionary veterans were simply not competent to lead a modern military force. Once Deng assumed chairmanship of the Military Commission in 1981, a major overhaul of the leadership and personnel system was one of his highest priorities. His goal was to induce accountability, responsiveness, and increased efficiency within a vast bureaucratic system that placed little value on any of these goals. As reforms slowly began to take root, new generations of young, technically competent personnel were recruited and educated, but they awaited job assignments appropriate to their background and training. Thus, senior officials needed to yield their posts, but without excessive disruption or alienation.

Deng's efforts took a long time to bear fruit. In July 1988 *Jiefangjun Bao* observed that "as early as 1980, Chairman Deng Xiaoping proposed that the system of military ranks should be implemented."[6] Beginning with the replacement of a number of regional military commanders, and proceeding to ever more ambitious attempts to overhaul the procedures governing the military system as a whole, a modern, regularized institutional framework slowly developed. It took nearly a decade for these policies to emerge with any clarity, suggesting the deeply entrenched character of the inherited system. Deng sought to replace hundreds of thousands of superannuated officers, but he proceeded in measured fashion, seeking to restructure the military without humiliating those losing status and power.

According to subsequent accounts, Deng's efforts "to build a powerful, modern, and regular revolutionary army" began in earnest in September 1981, three months after his election as chairman of the Military Commission.[7] But the record of events in the early 1980s is spotty.[8] Although there were limited cutbacks in manpower, reductions in the defense budget, and some transfers of military enterprises to the civilian sector, these steps did not yield major results. Deng is alleged to have

5. Jiang Yanghong, "Combined Arms Style Pervades the Barracks," *Jiefangjun Bao,* 18 October 1987, 1, trans. in *JPRS,* no. 88,006, 19 February 1988, 81.

6. "The Aspiration of an Army" *Jiefangjun Bao,* 4 July 1988, in *FBIS-China,* 19 July 1988, 30.

7. Editorial Department, "Major Achievements in Army Building over the Last Eight Years," *Ban Yue Tan,* no. 14, 25 July 1987, in *FBIS-China,* 14 August 1987, K2.

8. For a firsthand account of the process, see Yuan Houqun, "Brief Stories of the Chinese PLA Reorganization and Force Reduction Process," *Kunlun,* March–April 1987, 4–41.

urged "radical measures" during a 1981 speech, but these efforts bore little fruit. Deng remained preoccupied in a more immediate sense with economic and political matters and chose to limit his direct involvement in military affairs. At Deng's behest, Yang Shangkun in 1983 was given overall responsibility to develop policy options for military reorganization; Yang is alleged to have overseen all subsequent reorganization and manpower-reduction measures.[9]

The principal obstacle to institutional reform was the sheer size of the PLA. For all practical purposes, there were no retirement procedures for senior personnel. In a speech to an enlarged meeting of the Military Commission on November 1, 1984, Deng commented on the immensity of the PLA, concluding that such a "swollen" military organization was too cumbersome to conduct actual military operations, let alone organize an orderly retreat. To underscore his unhappiness, Deng observed that the principal shortcoming of the triumphal military parade of October 1 marking the PRC's thirty-fifth anniversary was that "the man who reviewed the troops is an old man of eighty years."

In his November 1 address to the Military Commission, Deng announced the decision to reduce the PLA's manpower by one million men. Reflecting the sensitivity of these measures, Deng observed: "Let me assume responsibility for offending some people on this matter. I don't want to oblige the new chairman of the Military Commission."[10] The issues were subsequently deliberated at an enlarged meeting of the Central Military Commission in May–June 1985, which declared a "strategic shift" in the army's orientation geared toward "structural reform, reduction in strength, and reorganization [as] the central projects for the armed forces during the next two years."[11] Hu Yaobang asserted that the policy changes followed "two years of repeated deliberation and a cool and objective analysis of the international situation and China's own defense capabilities."[12] Although the manpower reductions had a strategic rationale—that China did not anticipate large-scale war for the remainder of this century—this characterization served principally to justify cutbacks and leadership turnover, rather than to explain them.

The principal effects of the 1984–85 decisions were to initiate a reduction in the officer corps ultimately totaling nearly 600,000 men, to pare China's military regions from eleven to seven, and to revamp a hopelessly inefficient system for allocating men, equipment, and materiel. At

9. Yuan, "Brief Stories," 6–7.
10. Deng's reference to the need for a new Central Military Commission (CMC) chairman bespeaks the obvious failure of his succession arrangements, first with Hu Yaobang and subsequently with Zhao Ziyang.
11. *Xinhua*, 11 June 1985, in *FBIS-China*, 12 June 1985, K1.
12. *Xinhua*, 11 June 1985, in *FBIS-China*, 11 June 1985, H1.

the same time, other military units were abolished, deactivated, or transferred to the civilian apparatus, with different military headquarters in Beijing absorbing more modest cuts in personnel. The consequences of these decisions for the combat strength of China's armed forces proved minimal; the moves were intended principally to accelerate the retirement of senior officers, who had been generally exempted from the far more modest cutbacks of the early 1980s. The 1985 measures reached deeply into the leadership ranks of the Kunming, Wuhan, Fuzhou, and Urumqi military regions, each of which was absorbed into neighboring regions. All four military regions had in the past been judged vital to Chinese security planning, and the commanders of these forces evidently believed that they would be exempted from major cuts.

Little is known about the criteria employed by the Military Commission in dismantling "the four big temples." Although Deng and Yang appealed to the leadership of the affected units to keep the "overall situation" in mind and to accept the decisions of the Center, the transition was not smooth. Units purportedly sought to circumvent or subvert the commission's decisions by the squandering of funds, the theft of equipment and resources, and questionable job reassignments.[13] Although it is impossible to gauge the extent of these activities, such behavior reflected the threat to the prerogatives of a comfortably ensconced military elite. As a retired PLA officer observed during an interview, "The most difficult questions in China are those of personnel affairs."

Both publicly and privately, Chinese military officers treat the decisions of the late spring of 1985 as crucial to all subsequent steps toward institutional reform. Having achieved (or perhaps imposed) a consensus within the senior military ranks for a major organizational restructuring, Deng and Yang Shangkun launched a corollary series of steps. Two processes had to occur in tandem: the provision of psychic and financial compensation for those compelled to step down, and the specification of professional criteria for those moving into vacated positions, including the procedures and standards for future promotions.[14]

Different but simultaneous criteria were therefore devised for the two separate populations. For those stepping down from military service, the size of their pensions and their attributed status (in the forms of different categories of medals) derived principally from longevity—that is, the

---

13. Yuan, "Brief Stories," 9, 22.

14. The Chinese media responsible for these policies identified the relevant decision-making bodies as the All-Army Leading Group on the New Military Ranking System, and the State Council Leading Group for Resettlement of Demobilized Military Cadres. *Xinhua,* 6 July 1988, in *FBIS-China,* 12 July 1988, 27, and *Xinhua,* 12 July 1988, in *FBIS-China,* 14 July 1988, 28.

date of entry into the army and their rank as of 1965.[15] One interviewee (a recent retiree) described some of the steps in the process. The officer acknowledged that retirement was compulsory, not voluntary. Retirement is resisted because of the decline in status and the lack of protection against inflation. The pension arrangements entail a combination of criteria: cadre rank (there are twenty-one grades in the military), retirement bonuses, and a variety of miscellaneous allowances all form part of the package. In the estimation of this retiree, the burgeoning costs associated with the retirement system have yet to yield any of the presumed financial dividends of a smaller military establishment, since the preponderance of the budget is devoted to salaries and pensions, not weapons.

For those moving up, the passage of military-service legislation in July 1988 and the reestablishment of military ranks on October 1, 1988, marked major milestones. For the first time in nearly a quarter of a century, explicit procedures governing appointment, promotion, compensation, job tenure, and retirement were in place.[16] Irrespective of the age and technical competence of particular serving officers, all military careers had suffered from a two-decade-long interruption of standard procedures for professional mobility. When ranks were eliminated in 1965, the prospects for advancement for all officers were frozen. Unlike those in the Party and state bureaucracies, career officers had no independent validation of their position and status. This problem assumed even greater poignancy when (as was noted earlier) officers discredited during the Lin Biao era were reappointed at the same rank or higher, blocking upward mobility for younger officers. The problems in the PLA were compounded by a lower mandatory age for retirement. Thus, a division commander must retire at fifty-five (although this can be extended to sixty if the officer has earned an advanced degree), whereas civilians may work for another five to ten years. Even with these new procedures, the system remains extremely top-heavy and overstaffed, especially at the rank of colonel and senior colonel.

There is also a subtle but significant differentiation between the PLA's military and technical cadres. Military personnel serving in various technical capacities have a rank system nearly equivalent to that of line officers, but their rank designations are slightly lower than those of other active duty personnel. Although some technical officers still wear uniforms, they wear different insignia from the line officers, thereby differ-

15. According to an interviewee, there are neither medals nor retirement bonuses for postliberation cadres, including Korean war veterans, which is evidently the subject of resentment. For pension purposes, these post-1949 soldiers fall under the civil affairs department rather than the PLA.

16. For a text of the regulations on ranks, see *Xinhua*, 2 July 1988, in *FBIS-China*, 15 July 1988, 24–28.

entiating the two groups. Thus, there is a pecking order between soldiers and scientists. This mechanism is also an artful means of keeping the total number of line officers at lower levels. The reintroduction of ranks represented a significant turning point in Chinese military development. Positions in the PLA hierarchy would no longer derive principally from date of entry into the Red Army; rank and promotion would purportedly be linked with professional competence, merit, and technical expertise. The promulgation of these policies constituted a crucial transition in establishing explicit, institutionalized personnel arrangements for the military system as a whole, in the hope that the armed forces would again represent a highly desirable career option. Over time, therefore, the senior leadership hopes to recruit capable, well-educated officers who will view a military career with motivation, purpose, and long-term commitment. Should they fail to establish and institutionalize appropriate, predictable criteria for professional development, the prospects for creating a modern military establishment remain dim.

MILITARY COMMAND AND CONTROL

Increased interactions between Chinese military officers and foreign scholars have begun to yield a more differentiated picture of the structure of military decision making.[17] In addition, Chinese military researchers are openly discussing the continued viability of long-standing arrangements for military command. Rapid changes in information and communications technology are transforming the conduct of military operations and the administration of large, complex military systems on a worldwide basis, and Chinese specialists have studied these developments in earnest. At the same time, however, changes dictated by technological and organizational imperatives continue to clash with personalism and tradition deeply embedded in the military system.

The extant military system remains premised on centralized command and control, with supreme decision-making authority vested in the Military Commission of the CCP Central Committee. Appointments to the Military Commission are based on two principal criteria: status as a "military elder," or designated responsibility for one of four major spheres of organizational activity. Membership until late 1987 consisted of four elders (Deng Xiaoping as chairman, Yang Shangkun as perma-

17. This discussion derives from interviews conducted during 1987 and 1988 with participants in the Chinese defense-planning process. For an extremely useful compilation of changes in the leadership structure since 1949, see Lin Tong, "Forty Years of the Chinese People's Liberation Army," *Ming Bao Yue Kan*, no. 286, October 1989, trans. in *JPRS-CAR-90-005, China: People's Liberation Army*, 22 January 1990, 1–11.

nent vice-chairman and secretary-general, and Marshals Xu Xiangqian and Nie Rongzhen as vice-chairmen) and four senior military leaders with designated bureaucratic responsibilities (Yang Dezhi as director of the General Staff Department, Yu Qiuli as director of the General Political Department, Hong Xuezhi as director of the General Logistics Department, and Defense Minister Zhang Aiping as overseer for military research and development).[18]

Following the Thirteenth Party Congress, major changes in the top military leadership led to a reshuffling in the Party Military Commission. Although Deng remained chairman, Zhao Ziyang was appointed first vice-chairman, with Yang Shangkun continuing to serve concurrently as permanent vice-chairman and secretary-general. Under Peng Dehuai and Lin Biao, the minister of defense had served concurrently as first vice-chairman of the commission, with very significant power vested in this position. Xu Xiangqian and Nie Rongzhen—the only surviving marshals of the Chinese army—initially retained their titles as commission vice-chairmen. Although their positions appeared increasingly honorific, they maintained substantial personal influence through offspring serving in military capacities. For example, Nie's son-in-law, Ding Henggao, is the chairman of the Commission on Science, Technology, and Industry for National Defense, or COSTIND, better known as the *guofang kegong wei*. Ding's wife, Nie Li, is also a senior official within COSTIND; in addition, she assumes a coordinating role across a number of institutions concerned with high technology.

In early June 1988, Deng, in an audience with the visiting Polish premier, elaborated on the implications of these changes:

> You may have already noticed that there are two Vice Chairmen in the Central Military Commission, one is our Party General Secretary Zhao Ziyang, and the other is State President Yang Shangkun. . . . Why have both the Party General Secretary and State President become Vice Chairmen? Probably this is a Chinese-style arrangement (laughs heartily). *Nevertheless, this arrangement has practical significance because it actually means that I have handed over my duties and the Central Military Commission is now under the leadership of Comrade Zhao Ziyang.*[19]

Zhao's growing involvement in and responsibility for military affairs during 1988 underscored this seeming changeover in leadership. In his capacity as first vice-chairman of the Military Commission, Zhao undertook an unpublicized visit to the Sino-Vietnamese border during the

18. Zhang's membership on the Military Commission derived *not* from his position as Minister of National Defense, but from his status as overseer of military R & D, and his rank as a Senior General.

19. *Zhongguo Xinwen She*, 7 June 1988, in *FBIS-China*, 8 June 1988, 8. My emphasis.

Lunar New Year (accompanied by Yang Shangkun and Wang Zhen), delivered a major address in March on the impending tasks in military reform to a high-level military conference, and discussed China's transition to a "partial war" strategy and the parallel upgrading of the functions and responsibilities of the Ministry of National Defense.[20] Zhao's involvement with military planning appeared to indicate the PLA's acceptance of Zhao's role in the defense sector and contrasted markedly with Deng's inability to secure such acceptance for Hu Yaobang, who never received a formal leadership designation in the Military Commission. Zhao based his role on a "modernist" concept of the PLA—that is, that the armed forces would develop autonomous concepts and norms that did not depend exclusively on an organic bond with the Party.

An equally significant set of changes occurred in personnel assignments in the top military command posts following the Party Congress, and with it a reshuffling of the membership of the Military Commission. These changes testified to the extraordinary authority that Deng had delegated to Yang Shangkun. In November 1987 the heads of all three General Departments of the PLA stepped down, as did Defense Minister Zhang Aiping. Of these four senior generals, three (Yang Dezhi, Yu Qiuli, and Zhang Aiping) yielded their seats on the Military Commission, with Hong Xuezhi remaining as a deputy to Secretary-General Yang Shangkun. Liu Huaqing, previously commander of the Chinese navy, also assumed a post as deputy to the secretary-general; several interviewees confirmed that he had inherited Zhang Aiping's portfolio for military research and development. But the new General Department heads (Chi Haotian, Yang Baibing, and Zhao Nanqi) were not immediately confirmed in their predecessors' positions on the Party Military Commission, nor was the new minister of national defense, Qin Jiwei, voted comparable status.

The case of Qin Jiwei is the most revealing. Although a member of the Politburo, a commander with impeccable Second Field Army credentials, a Korean War hero, and a supposed favorite of Deng's, a ministerial appointment in the State Council is of decidely lesser import within the military system's job order rank. The minister of national defense commands no troops; indeed, for purposes of resource allocation within the State Council, he shares essentially coequal status with heads of the industrial ministries. To rectify this gap between the status of the defense minister and that of the General Department directors, the ministry was supposedly to be strengthened in its functions, personnel, and status. The upgrading of the general office (*bangong ting*) within the Military

20. See *South China Morning Post*, 26 February 1988, 1–2; Hongkong *Wen Wei Po*, 24 March 1988, 1, and 11 May 1988, 1.

Commission, headed by Lt. Gen. Liu Kai, was viewed by some as the precursor of an effort to establish an autonomous capacity for defense planning, allegedly to be vested in a more powerful defense ministry.

But substantial ambiguity persisted for some time over the precise membership of the Party Military Commission.[21] Chinese sources remain silent on the differences between Party and state military commissions, referring in somewhat generic fashion to the "Central Military Commission" (*zhongyang junshi weiyuanhui*, or *jun-wei*). The absence of a standarized membership list for the commission suggested the potency of the Party connection to the military leadership; the senior leaders were not prepared to ratify an autonomous role for the armed forces apart from the long-standing mechanisms of political control. In addition, the commission created a military legislation bureau (*junshi fazhi ju*) intended to formulate explicit rules and regulations for upper-level personnel policy where none existed before.

The selection of new leaders for the general departments and the promotions of Liu Huaqing and Qin Jiwei also attested to the persistence of personalistic criteria in senior personnel assignments. The appointments of Liu Huaqing and Zhao Nanqi appeared attributable to their predecessors (both had worked closely with them in these designated areas of responsibility over long periods of time, with Zhao serving as Hong Xuezhi's aide-de-camp during the Korean War). Qin Jiwei's long-standing links to Deng appear to explain his designation. Yang Shangkun assumed a familial prerogative in the designation of his younger brother as head of the General Political Department. Chi, having leap-frogged over a number of far more senior officers, including Qin Jiwei, owed his appointment to Yang, though the precise nature of this relationship remains unknown. The persistence of these personalistic criteria suggests that the very top leadership remains unwilling to relinquish its most important prerogatives in personnel assignment and may be equally reluctant to forego the PLA's special relationship with the CCP.

Thus, it remains extremely uncertain whether the State Military Commission will assume an identity distinct from its Party counterpart, especially in the aftermath of the political crisis of 1989. The creation of the State Commission in 1982 was intended to encourage a separation of functions between Party and government, but it has thus far totally failed to achieve its stated goal. During the late 1980s (i.e., during the "high tide" of the professionalizing ethic in the armed forces), there was an effort to create a separate set of responsibilities for the second body. One line of speculation suggested that slots on the State Commission would be reserved for service chiefs and others charged with responsibility for

21. My thanks to Michael Byrnes for his very helpful observations on these issues.

the transition to a more modern defense force—in other words, formalizing the separation between command and administration.[22] By implication, membership would also be extended to those within the military scientific and industrial apparatus, whose status in the hierarchy was not deemed equivalent to that of the general departments.

Designation on the CCP Military Commission remains the job that counts. Confirmation of promotion to this body for the defense minister and the new general department heads long remained obscure, testifying to the awkward relationship between older military generations and the younger generations promoted into senior command slots.[23] Of the three new general department heads, two (Chi and Zhao) were in their mid to late fifties. Their appointments signified the bypassing of military leaders in their sixties and early seventies, who "rightfully" expected to succeed to top posts. Deng, mindful of the need to invigorate the military establishment at all levels, had insisted that the top command slots be filled by much younger men, thereby explaining why Qin Jiwei did not receive his logical promotion—that is, chief of the general staff. Yang Baibing, who is in his late sixties, represents an exception to this trend, with his appointment made solely on personalistic grounds.

Promotion to membership on the Party Military Commission required a rank congruent with such status. According to the available information, commission members must hold a rank no lower than major general (*shao jiang*).[24] The only confirmed promotion to the commission during 1987 was that of Liu Huaqing, who had achieved the rank of major general prior to the abolition of ranks in 1965. At best, Chi, Yang, and Zhao held this rank, or (more likely for Chi and Zhao) that of senior colonel (*da xiao*). However, Qin Jiwei already held the higher rank of lieutenant general (*zhong jiang*). To achieve congruence in status, all were among the seventeen senior officers receiving promotion to the rank of general (*shang jiang*) when ranks were formally reintroduced in September 1988.

The designation of seventeen full generals in September 1988 provided the best indicator of the allocation of status and power within the high command.[25] Deng, Zhao Ziyang, and Yang Shangkun were not

22. See, for example, *Far Eastern Economic Review*, 24 December 1987, 7.

23. For evidence that appeared to confirm promotion for new senior commanders to the CCP Commission, see *Xinhua*, 14 September 1988, in *FBIS-China*, 15 September 1988, 27.

24. For a detailed discussion of the rank system, see the article by Fu Meihua in *Kuang Chiao Ching*, 16 May 1988, 10–14, trans. in *FBIS-China*, 20 May 1988, 20–24.

25. *Xinhua*, 14 September 1988, in *FBIS-China*, 15 September 1988, 27. Retirements of several of these generals in the spring of 1990 (Hong Xuezhi and Li Desheng) and unconfirmed retirements of several others leave vacancies on the list of full generals, but no promotions to the rank of full general have yet been reported.

designated with any military rank. Below them, appointments reflected a mix of bureaucratic responsibility, party links, seniority, and personal relations: two deputy secretary-generals of the Military Commission; the defense minister; the three General Department heads; the deputy chief of staff responsible for foreign affairs and intelligence; the secretary and second secretary of the Discipline Inspection Commission of the CMC; the political commissar of the Academy of Military Science (but not the president); the president and the political commissar of the National Defense University; the political commissars of the Beijing and Chengdu Military Regions (but not the commanders); the commander of the Nanjing Military Region (but not the political commissar), the political commissar of the navy (but not the commander), and the commander of the air force (but not the political commissar).

Despite these personnel shifts, a CMC executive committee or leading group continued to maintain overall responsibility for military affairs. This group consisted of those identified as vice-chairmen or members of the Secretariat, plus the senior serving military officer.[26] When circumstances warranted, this group forwarded its recommendations to Deng Xiaoping, who remained the supreme arbiter on military matters. In a speech in late May 1989 following the imposition of martial law, Yang Shangkun came close to confirming such an arrangement, even if it discredited Deng's remark of June 1988 asserting that he had already bequeathed leadership of the commission to Zhao Ziyang:

> Now some people ask: As there are three chairmen [*sic*] in the Central Military Commission, how could Deng Xiaoping alone order the movement of the troops responsible for enforcing martial law? These people do not understand the military service in our country at all. . . . In our army, we pursue a commander responsibility system. Such people as I only play a counseling role in assisting the chairman. When he made the decision, he had not only talked with me, but had also talked with Xuezhi, Huaqing, and Minister Qin as well. Why could he not issue the order?[27]

The heads of the general departments represent a second tier of the military leadership. During the crisis of 1989 this group may not have participated in all critical decisions, although some were undoubtedly responsible for policy execution. But their capacity to wield power continued to derive principally from personal relationships, not institutional positions. A third concentric circle—those probably included in enlarged

26. This arrangement seemed implicit in the September 1988 announcement of the appointments of full generals. Hong Xuezhi, Liu Huaqing, and Qin Jiwei were all listed separately from the General Department heads as "members" of the Military Commission.

27. Yang's remarks are excerpted from his speech to the CMC "emergency enlarged meeting," 24 May 1989, in *Ming Pao*, 29 May 1989, in *FBIS-China*, 30 May 1989, 17–22.

meetings of the Military Commission—encompasses those miilitary chiefs above the army level. These would include service heads, commandants of the Academy of Military Service and the National Defense University, the seven military region commanders, and the political commissars from the above organizations.

The larger organizational constituencies represented on the Military Commission shed additional light on the allocation of power within the PLA. Each of the PLA's three general departments oversees a set of subsidiary institutions responsible for the full spectrum of activities incorporated within the military system. The reach of the General Staff Department is the largest, since this department is responsible for the separate force commands (air force, navy, strategic rocket forces, artillery, and armored forces), and it presides over other important organizational functions, including procurement, operational planning, and intelligence.[28] The General Political Department, although historically responsible for the system of political control and direction of the military propaganda apparatus, has played a lead role in redrafting the PLA's rules, regulations, and responsibilities. The Political Department has the largest voice in the reassignment of military personnel, including the designation of military ranks and the establishment of the retirement system. Thus, it subsumes most of the functions conducted within the CCP by the Organization Department. The General Logistics Department oversees the financial, supply, transportation, and maintenance network entailed in sustaining the operation of PLA units. This responsibility extends to the allocation of funds for equipment purchases and to the provision and maintenance of all nonlethal military equipment and ammunition stocks.

A lesser-known but increasingly important suborgan is the Discipline Inspection Commission (*jilu jiancha weiyuanhui*, or *jiwei*) of the CMC. First identified in Chinese sources in 1984, the Discipline Inspection Commission has been assigned many of the political control functions previously associated with the General Political Department, although its responsibilities also very likely extend to broader personnel matters. General Guo Linxiang, a Long March veteran, serves concurrently as secretary of this group and deputy director of the General Political Department, although recent reports suggest his retirement from his post. The Discipline Inspection Commission was also unusually visible in the period immediately

---

28. As a consequence of the streamlining and reorganization undertaken since 1985, there have been important changes in force commands. According to one official source, the artillery, armored, and engineering commands have been subsumed as departments under the General Staff headquarters. *Jiefangjun Bao*, 25 July 1987, 2. There is no separate ground force command. By tradition, however, the chief of the General Staff is drawn from the ground forces.

following the imposition of martial law in May 1989, confirming its Party watchdog or oversight function within the armed forces. Although the secretary's position remains procedural rather than policy-oriented, he reports directly to the CMC secretary-general, thereby potentially vesting critical powers in the post.

The Commission on National Defense Science, Technology, and Industry (which until late 1987 reported to Zhang Aiping) is charged with overseeing, evaluating, coordinating, and approving plans for military research and development. It has also served as the principal point of contact for countries and firms engaged in negotiations with the Chinese government over transfer of military technology. In theory, the commission's responsibilities extend across all State Council ministries involved in military production, as well as into the various service commands. The commission sees itself integrally involved in all long-range planning for high technology, with a mandate cutting across civilian as well as military jurisdictions. For reasons to be discussed further, its bark appears more imposing than its bite. But its influence remains substantial, both as a consequence of the prestige and position associated with its high-level patrons (Nie Rongzhen and Zhang Aiping) and by virtue of interpersonal connections that extend into various high-technology sectors.

The Military Commission sits atop this interlocking network of bureaucratic fiefdoms, and, at least nominally, it seeks to adjudicate (if not eliminate) the competition for manpower, budgetary, and technical resources within the system. As one interviewee indicated, however, the commission has a very small, dedicated staff and does not oversee a formally constituted system for defense planning; its power resides in the authority and prestige of individual leaders, rather than in the institution per se, and in its ability to tap expertise within an extensive research-and-planning apparatus.[29] Deng, in the early 1980s, delegated day-to-day responsibility for military affairs to Yang Shangkun, providing Yang with a decisive role in discharging the commission's responsibilities. The frequency and regularity of commission meetings remain unknown. In some instances, the commission has served as a "court of last resort" for disputes that cannot be resolved at lower levels, including major decisions on weapons acquisition. In addition, the commission retains the power of appointment to and dismissal from senior military posts, with the decision subject only to pro forma ratification by the Central Committee.

Differences between wartime and peacetime planning entail additional complexities. In conjuction with the service commands who serve

29. I will make only passing mention of the military-science research system. For a useful overview of the state of Western knowledge of this system immediately prior to the first opening of its doors to foreign scholars, see Tai Ming Cheung, "Trends in the Research of Chinese Military Strategy," *Survival*, May–June 1987, 239–59.

as "staff officers" under the General Staff Department, the Military Commission serves as the supreme deliberative body over the use of force. However, forces from the different services that are deployed "in theater" during peacetime report to the regional military commanders, who are responsible for coordinating and integrating all military assets available to them.[30] Interviewees explicitly described this arrangement in terms of the *tiao-tiao kuai-kuai* dynamic. The chief of staff in Beijing has authority over all operational forces in wartime, but in peacetime he delegates substantial responsibility to the regional commanders. Thus, the regional commander does not have the power to make decisions to initiate the use of force, since this responsibility attaches exclusively to higher-level authorities in Beijing. The role of the regional military commander therefore becomes especially sensitive. On the one hand, he cannot make the decision to go to war; on the other hand, he needs to make "on the spot" decisions based upon his own understanding of central directives. Thus, his responsibilities extend to crucial decisions at both the tactical and the operational level.

It is useful in this context to compare Chinese operational procedures with those followed in defense planning in the United States. In U.S. practice, the president and the secretary of defense (assisted by the joint chiefs in a staff role) deal directly with the unified regional commands. The service chiefs are therefore able to perform their principal responsibility—the management of day-to-day policy in their separate bureaucratic systems. Recent reforms, however, have shifted more power to the joint chiefs, with the chairman assuming an authoritative "centralizing" function, including powers that span the jurisdictional domains of the services and compel more "jointness" among the services.

Prior to the crisis of 1989, the PLA appeared to be headed in multiple directions. Chinese military researchers were increasingly questioning the relevance of a unitary system that combined command and administration, and they appeared to be searching for institutional mechanisms to divide these responsibilities.[31] Under these arrangements, military command and military management would be separated, creating a dual system that differentiated operational control of military forces from responsibility for manpower and materiel allocation, training, procure-

30. When asked whether comparable arrangements applied to command and control of nuclear weapons, my respondents emphatically insisted that all such forces were fully controlled by military authorities in Beijing through channels distinct from the regional military commands.

31. For one account of these deliberations, see Zhu Baogang, "A Trend in the Change of the National Defense System," *Jiefangjun Bao*, 6 March 1987, trans. in *JPRS*, no. 87,030, 95–97.

ment, and defense construction. But a differentiation between command and administration, although beneficial for the rationalization of functions within the armed forces, may also contribute to unwarranted complexity in bureaucratic channels, given the potential bifurcation of defense policy-making.

The prospects for military reform have been rendered much less certain in the aftermath of the 1989 crisis. Innumerable policy statements have reemphasized the singular importance again attached to political control, with an unmistakable effort to curtail efforts to encourage autonomous professional development. As was noted in an important *Jiefangjun Bao* editorial, "Over a certain period the leading advocates of bourgeois liberalization deliberately called for 'separating the Army from the Party' and 'preventing the Army from interfering in politics' in an attempt to shake off the Party's leadership over the army."[32] Pending a more conclusive determination of the CCP's future political directions, the development of autonomous institutional norms within the armed forces is likely to be far more curtailed, with renewed importance to personal relations atop the system.

Deng's resignation from the chairmanship of the CCP Military Commission in November 1989 and his replacement by the Party secretary-general, Jiang Zemin, further underscore these conclusions. Coincident with Jiang's appointment, Yang Shangkun was elevated to Zhao Ziyang's previous position of first vice-chairman, Liu Huaqing was promoted to vice-chairman, and Yang Baibing succeeded his brother as secretary-general, with Qin Jiwei (reflecting his political difficulties following his alleged support for Zhao in the spring crisis) now serving as a member of the commission without executive responsibilities.[33] But Jiang's powers appear more fictive than real: he lacks the stature and personal authority that has been associated historically with the chairman's position. As with Hua Guofeng in the late 1970s, no one seriously believes that Jiang wields supreme power in the armed forces: such capacities remain invested in Deng Xiaoping and his designated first vice-chairman, Yang Shangkun. Taken as a whole, China's military command arrangements still seem an uneasy mix of personalistic and professional considerations. The closer to the acme of the system, the less command derives from specified rules and norms, a judgment amply driven home by the events of the spring of 1989. The persistence of traditional norms amidst a serious, sustained effort to professionalize the Chinese military establishment seems likely to remain a continuing source of long-term conflict within the policy-making process.

32. "Uphold the Party's Absolute Leadership, Ensure That Our Army Is Always Politically up to Standard," *Jiefangjun Bao*, 1 October 1989, in *FBIS-China*, 18 October 1989, 38.
33. See *Xinhua*, 9 November 1989, in *FBIS-China*, 9 November 1989, 18.

THE BUDGETARY AND RESOURCE ALLOCATION PROCESS

The political and economic changes of the past decade have sharply altered the role and scope of military involvement in the Chinese system, with the armed forces no longer enjoying pride of place in centrally allocated budgetary, technical, and manpower resources. The PLA's diminished stature is reflected in its reduced leadership role: only two military leaders (Yang Shangkun and Qin Jiwei) serve on the Politburo elected at the CCP's Thirteenth National Congress, and military membership in the Central Committee has continued its slippage, evident since the Ninth Party Congress.[34]

There have also been sharp reductions in the defense budget. In the immediate aftermath of the Sino-Vietnamese War of early 1979, defense expenditure increased by 5.5 billion yuan, much of it replacement costs for the heavy losses of equipment and weaponry sustained during the war. This action proved the last major "out of cycle" surge in the military budget. The predominant thrust has been to reduce military manpower and defer major procurement decisions, in the hope of decreasing the military's operating budget in both absolute and relative terms. The announced increases of 15 percent in the 1990 military budget (much of it supposedly allocated for equipment purchases related to internal security needs) therefore represents a marked departure from this trend.[35]

As was noted earlier, however, the introduction of a retirement system has sharply increased near-term personnel and pension costs, effectively denying the PLA the surplus funds it hoped to generate by reducing the size of the armed forces. Moreover, a 1988 Central Intelligence Agency study estimated that total PLA manpower at the time of Deng's return to top military leadership may have been nearly double the prevailing estimates. Although much of this surplus manpower may not have been uniformed personnel, these individuals remained on the army payroll. According to this estimate, China "has reduced its armed forces by about 3 million men since 1977 . . . [and] China's military operating budget . . . has declined by about one-fifth over the last eight years." As the Chinese budget as a whole has grown, defense expenditures have shrunk from approximately one-third of total state expenditure in 1978 to about one-

34. Military membership on various central committees is as follows: 28.2% (1956); 44.1% (1969); 30.4% (1973); 30.9% (1977); 21.5% (1982); and 12.6% (1987). Li Cheng and Lynn White, "The Thirteenth Central Committee of the Chinese Communist Party," *Asian Survey*, April 1988, 385.

35. Daniel Southerland, "China Increases Spending of Military By 15 Percent," *Washington Post*, 22 March 1990, 33.

fifth in 1987. The share of gross national income in the same period declined from 12 percent to 5 percent.[36]

These trends have convinced numerous observers that the military has lost much of its previous "clout," generally embodied in the view that national defense is "the last of the four modernizations." This judgment is more assertion than fact. Of the other "three modernizations," two (industry and science-and-technology) are linked integrally to the enhancement of military power, with the PLA still able to exert substantial influence in both domains. In addition, Chinese strategies unequivocally view the modernization of military power as essential for China's credibility as a world power in the next century. In his address commemorating the sixtieth anniversary of the founding of the PLA, Yang Shangkun drew attention to the need to guarantee China's "status as a world power" (*shijie jiangguo diwei*) by the middle of the twenty-first century.[37] Huan Xiang, the late international-affairs strategist, insisted that China could not rest content with the position of "being a second-rate power or merely a regional power," arguing that the nation must aspire to a status (if not a strength) equivalent to that of the United States and the Soviet Union.[38] Thus, the curtailing of the acquisition of major weapons systems is intended to shift attention toward enhanced technological and industrial capabilities as a whole rather than weaponry per se, with the armed forces very well endowed in scientific and industrial resources, especially in high-technology areas.

The movement away from a central allocative system has also opened a wide array of commercial opportunities for portions of the military system, with some parts of the military doing very well in recent years. In particular, the automony permitted to various military organizations to buy and sell goods and services has transformed the PLA's position and role. Although it is no longer business as usual for the armed forces, it is very much a time of business, with more entrepreneurial segments of the military establishment testing the marketplace for financial gain, thereby recouping many of the losses sustained in central budgetary allocations. The generation of such export earnings (Chinese weapons sales abroad

36. Central Intelligence Agency, Directorate of Intelligence, *China: Economic Policy and Performance in 1987* (Report submitted to the Subcommittee on National Security Economics of the Joint Economic Committee, U.S. Congress, 21 April 1988), 17–18. CIA estimates of the Chinese defense budget are more than double those issued in Chinese statistical releases, with a 1986 estimate of 45 billion yuan, in contrast to an announced budget of 20 billion yuan.

37. *Jiefangjun Bao*, 1 August 1987, 2.

38. Huan Xiang, "The Future International Environment and Our National Defense Construction," *Guofang Fazhan Zhanlue Sikao* (Beijing: Jiefangjun Chubanshe, 1986), especially 23–26.

for 1988 were estimated at $3.1 billion in a U.S. congressional study) constitutes a new and potent source of power within the PLA.[39]

Although many levels of the military system initially appeared sluggish or resistant in responding to these new "rules of the game," the armed forces ultimately proved more adaptive. The defense establishment has been disabused of its somewhat complacent attitude toward its status and power relative to other functional sectors, and it is far more intent on developing strategies for enhancing institutional interests. But these commercial opportunities have disproportionately benefited those within the defense sector with the requisite connections to effect these transactions. It remains to be seen whether and when the military as an institution (as distinct from powerful individuals within the defense establishment) will realize gains appropriate to the scale of these activities.

The PLA remains an extremely powerful bureaucratic actor, a power reinforced by its coercive functions, by its responsibility for defense of the realm, and by its still potent access to technology and resources. But the military's capacity to retain or augment its financial and manpower assets was greatly challenged by various reform measures undertaken in the mid and late 1980s. At a time of budgetary stringency, the PLA confronted a growing gap between China's military-technological capabilities and those of its external rivals and potential adversaries. As Yang Shangkun observed at a Military Commission meeting in late 1986, "The principal contradiction in our army building is the contradiction between the objective requirements of modern warfare and the low level of modernization of our army."[40]

Paradoxes and contradictions nevertheless persist in the defense research-and-development sector. The Commission on Science, Technology, and Industry for National Defense nominally presides over a vast, interlocking network of institutions devoted to the specification, appraisal, and application of advanced technologies for national defense. These functions comprise the four major tasks of research, development, testing, and evaluation. In theory, COSTIND oversees this sprawling, unwieldy apparatus, coordinating requests from the services for particular technologies, evaluating budgetary requirements of project proposals, and forwarding recommendations to the Military Commission for approval. COSTIND also oversees China's missile launch sites and satellite tracking facilities, thereby providing it control over important resources for which it has no bureaucratic competitor.

39. Robert Pear, "U.S. Weapons Sales to Third World Increase by 66%," *New York Times*, 1 August 1989.

40. Yang is cited in Pan Shiying, "Have a Sober Understanding of the Principal Contradiction in Army Building," *Jiefangjun Bao*, 11 September 1987, in *FBIS-China*, 24 September 1987, 19.

Considered as a whole, China's defense technology apparatus combines the logic of centralization and coordination with the reality of fragmentation, duplication, intrabureaucratic competition, and the frequent absence of effective oversight.[41] Thus COSTIND lacks the manpower resources required to undertake a more comprehensive bureaucratic role; its immediate professional staff numbers only seven hundred. But its small size is symptomatic of two larger problems: the absence of a viable concept of defense-resource management through which the commission can direct the R & D process, and the diffusion of effective control over budgetary and technical resources within the defense industrial system.

In a certain sense, COSTIND is a victim of the success of the Chinese nuclear weapons program. This program stands as vivid testimony to the capabilities of Chinese scientists and engineers, and the Chinese are legitimately proud of its accomplishments.[42] But the history of this program has also had an inhibiting effect, since the circumstances that contributed to its success cannot be replicated in the defense-modernization process as a whole. The principal ingredients included a virtually unlimited budget, consistent support from the highest levels of the political system, a relatively large pool of scientists and engineers trained abroad in the requisite areas, substantial infrastructural and technological assistance from abroad in initiating the program, a limited number of required end products, and urgent, compelling pressure to produce rapid results.

In 1982 COSTIND was formed by merging its predecessor (the Commission on Science and Technology for National Defense) with the National Defense Industries Office, which oversaw defense industrial production within the numbered machine building industries.[43] By combining the research and production functions in one organization, a single body was expected to wield power that a more limited organization could not. COSTIND's mandate and authority were provided through its principal sponsors in the military leadership, Marshal Nie Rongzhen and Senior General Zhang Aiping, both of whom had been intimately involved in the nuclear weapons program. The power of the nuclear weapons and space bureaucracy was entrenched within the commission, but it was subsequently extended through senior person-

41. These paragraphs derive from discussions with Chinese military R & D personnel during 1987 and 1988.

42. See John Wilson Lewis and Xue Litai, *China Builds the Bomb* (Stanford: Stanford University Press, 1988).

43. For a useful overview of the institutional evolution of defense R & D, see Benjamin C. Ostrov, "Reforming China's National Defense Science and Technology Organs," *China News Analysis*, no. 140 (15 May 1990): 1–9.

nel appointments to the reconstituted industrial ministries that at least nominally "own" the plants that produce China's weapons.

These arrangements have guaranteed a pivotal role for COSTIND in the planning process and reflect a continuing effort (first put forward by Zhang Aiping in 1983) to maintain oversight and direction of major R & D decisions. Recalling the nuclear program, Zhang argued:

> In 1956 the CPC Central Committee decided that developing guided missiles and atomic energy were the two key projects in our national defense modernization. . . . Facts have proved that this was a completely correct decision. . . . Our work in developing guided missiles and atomic bombs started relatively late but the speed of development was relatively quick. One important reason for this is that we centralized our organization, vigorously carried out coordination and cooperation, gave priority to key tasks, and concentrated our resources of labor, materials, and funds.[44]

The difficulty in applying this concept more widely in defense R & D reflects the highly disparate technological and engineering demands imposed by the full array of military needs (especially products or components that require serial production), the absence of a guaranteed internal customer for the items produced, and the lack of requisite experience in incorporating more advanced technologies within an outmoded defense industrial structure. As a result, the Chinese still produce military equipment that improves only marginally on Soviet designs provided to China three decades ago. Although there are prototypes and limited production runs of some systems that incorporate more advanced technologies, China's indigenous capability for R & D innovation and diffusion remains quite limited.

Under the "old" R & D system, where the industrial ministries were virtually guaranteed an annual allocation of materials and funds and where few if any pressures existed for technological innovation, the inertial tendencies were substantial. Factories steadily produced large quantities of military equipment (there are over five thousand aircraft in the air force inventory alone), but with very little attention given to its relevance to potential combat needs. Under the "new" R & D system, the customers (i.e., the services) either no longer want the product or cannot always guarantee the funds needed for manufacture and procurement.

Thus, those officers responsible for miltary procurement (housed principally in the Armaments Department of the General Staff) believe that their power and status within the system have been greatly undermined, and they are actively seeking to reassert their power and prerogatives. Their efforts are aided by the existence of an informal "middle-age

44. Zhang Aiping, "Several Questions Concerning Modernization of National Defense," *Hongqi*, no. 5, 1 March 1983, trans. in *JPRS*, no. 83–318, *China Report*, 22 April 1983, 37.

boy" network, many with familial or personal ties to senior Chinese leaders, who are able to secure large quantities of surplus weaponry lying unused in army warehouses. These arrangements tend to cut across institutional lines of authority, suggesting that informal, personal relationships remain the glue to numerous commercial transactions within the military system. By marketing this equipment (some of it upgraded with Western technology) at bargain rates, Chinese suppliers earn substantial foreign exchange. Thus, financial power has passed to those who control the disbursement of surplus equipment and weaponry and show an aptitude for marketing these items.

The proliferation of trading companies that market Chinese military items attest to these changing conditions, with some companies also serving as purchasing agents for foreign military components or systems desired by end users.[45] There appear to be three principal types of actors: (1) companies associated with central R & D planners (i.e., COSTIND); (2) those linked to the industrial ministries (most prominently, North China Industries, or NORINCO); and (3) those associated with either the General Staff Department or the General Logistics Department (most prominently, Polytechnologies, which serves as the marketing arm of the General Staff's Armaments Department). COSTIND appeared to take the lead in negotiations at a government-to-government level (for example, the now-aborted Sino-American avionics agreement for the J-8 II aircraft); the ministries deal principally with collaborative arrangements with foreign firms, especially related to coproduction or technology transfer; and the services (as represented by the general departments) deal predominantly in Chinese sales to foreign governments and firms.

Of the three actors, the General Staff Armaments Department has garnered the largest amounts of hard-currency earnings. Partly because of its success but probably more because of the particular leaders involved in these transactions, it appears to have the most latitude in conducting such exchanges. The observable patterns, however, do not follow predictable institutional lines, but instead derive from the close family connections of these military entrepreneurs. The most frequently cited cases concern He Ping, a lead official in Polytechnologies and the son-in-law of Deng Xiaoping, and He Pengfei, director of the General Staff's Armaments Department and the son of He Long. Both organizations work under a cloak of secrecy, frequently working through umbrella import-export organizations such as the China International Trade and Investment Corporation (CITIC). The success of these officials demonstrates the capacity of different parts of the bureaucracy to "end run" the indus-

45. For a useful overview of this activity, see Bai Si Yeng, "Understanding the Chinese Defense Industry," *Military Technology*, March 1987, 36–52.

trial ministries by defense marketing activities, enabling the services to retain export earnings that would otherwise be unavailable to them. The precise portion of earnings retained by the services or the General Staff, and the uses to which these earnings are put, are subject to widely divergent estimates. But a profit-oriented military establishment reflects the sharply altered rules of the game. An entrepreneurial system does not necessarily produce a more technologically innovative defense force, but it does underscore the shifting locus of power within the armed forces.

A clear task for future research is to attempt to examine the effects of the weapons-sale process on the military system as a whole. The key questions include these: Where does financial control reside within the military system? Who allocates which resources, and are the purposes and consequences predominantly personal or institutional? Are these shifts in military behavior likely to manifest themselves over time in the form of increased demands for more sophisticated weapons systems being produced in Chinese factories? How has the incentive structure changed for both consumer and producer, and are there means by which profit motivations and military needs can be reconciled?

Another illustrative case concerns the canceled J-8 II avionics transaction with the United States. The total package, undertaken through the Foreign Military Sales (FMS) program, was to have totaled $550 million. One close observer of this process likened the scale of the project to the B-1 program in the United States. Although this probably overstated the costs for China, it was a major undertaking and by far the largest collaborative agreement with the United States in the defense sector. Yet the agreement was not well received by all portions of the military R & D apparatus, especially within the aviation industry, since the project did not entail the transfer of production know-how for the complex electronics packages that represented the heart of the transaction. From a service perspective, however, the prospect of the acquisition of more advanced avionics—even for a limited number of a prototype aircraft—was judged worth the risks and uncertainties. The project's cancellation in May 1990 reflected the escalating costs that the Chinese deemed unacceptable; some in China also appeared to believe that the United States was simply unprepared to implement the full scope of the agreement.[46]

Despite the cancellation of the project, this effort at foreign collaboration reflects the diminished power of China's indigenous military industrial system. Confronted by specific commercial and technological opportunities, the top levels of decision making slighted the interests of the ministries. As a result, numerous enterprises that previously concen-

46. Jim Mann, "China Cancels U.S. Deal for Modernizing F-8 Jet," *Los Angeles Times*, 15 May 1990; Lena H. Sun, "China to Drop Army Deal with U.S.," *Washington Post*, 16 May 1990.

trated on defense production now devote principal attention to civilian manufacture. Many defense enterprises, however, remain uncomfortable with the civilian market and have sought ways to sustain their military production capabilities. In one of his major commentaries on national defense modernization while overseer of the R & D process, Zhang Aiping spoke of the need to establish "a state mobilization working system for wartime." Zhang concluded:

> While carrying out national economic construction, we should consider the way to make peacetime construction conform with the material needs during future warfare. Peacetime construction . . . should make necessary preparations for meeting the demands of war. Otherwise, once war breaks out, there will not be enough time to build factories and institutes for manufacturing various kinds of weapons and facilities or to build roads and bridges. . . . We should do our best to integrate peacetime and wartime demand.[47]

Such comments leave unsettled the readiness of all portions of the military system to shift conclusively away from its long-standing practices and habits.

Despite these uncertainties, those responsible for long-term planning viewed the more constrained budgetary and investment climate as an opportunity rather than a problem. In an environment much less supportive of open-ended, frequently duplicative military allocations, the separate components of the military R & D process acquired incentives to collaborate rather than compete. This is the logic of more centrally coordinated and administered planning arrangements. In the deliberations over the Seventh Five-Year Plan, defense procurement fared very poorly. Since that time, senior defense planners have sought to introduce for the first time mechanisms geared toward long-range military planning. This effort is in contrast to the annual and five-year planning cycles and explicitly seeks to coordinate research and development activities to the year 2000 and beyond.

According to interviews with those involved in this process, the PLA is endeavoring for the first time to create a mechanism across all relevant bureaucracies to guide defense-technology planning from concept to final implementation. This effort entails a coordinated effort in all areas of potential military need (both technology related and service oriented), with subsequent reports purportedly serving as guidance for decision making and resource allocation. This effort is coordinated by COSTIND, with extensive participation by all relevant military bureaucracies. Even conceding the incentives for constituent organizations to inflate their im-

---

47. Zhang Aiping, "Peacetime National Defense Buildup," *Jiefangjun Bao*, 25 August 1987, 1–2, in *FBIS-China*, 17 September 1987, 16.

portance and needs, the very fact of such an exercise may prove more important than its actual results.

To the extent that this planning effort clarifies choices among alternatives and erodes a tradition of separatism widespread within the military, it seems likely to prove a valuable exercise. Regardless of any specific policy outcomes, it will help prepare the defense R & D system much more fully and effectively for the next five-year plan. Indeed, some military spokesmen openly hint at expectations of receiving an increased "return" on the deferral of major procurement decisions during the 1980s and see the next decade as a more promising period. The PLA's vital support for Deng and his political allies in the crisis of 1989 assumes obvious importance in this regard, with the announced defense budget increases for 1990 representing a "down payment" for services rendered by the military.

SOME PRELIMINARY CONCLUSIONS

The Chinese armed forces are in the midst of major challenge. Spurred by Deng Xiaoping's belief that the PLA had lost much of its credibility as an institution and was degrading China's claim to great-power status, the army (at Deng's behest) began to explore different directions. Part of these changes were a consequence of the gradual passing of a legendary generation of revolutionary-era generals, but Deng's determination was the principal spur to change. To achieve his goals, Deng required a senior military leadership accountable to him, a long-term plan to achieve necessary institutional reforms (especially in the personnel system), and the creation of pockets of innovation on which these changes could build.

Deng's accomplishments in these areas proved measurable, especially during the mid and late 1980s. But these new directions bred different problems and pressures. Elements of more traditional patterns of power and authority continued to abound, even as younger generations of officers were restive and increasingly resentful of arrangements and understandings at the top. The military became more professionalized and regularized, but there was still no escape from personalism, especially at the apex of the system. The familial ties within the military system suggest that advancement in the army may remain a matter more of inheritance than of competence.

At the same time, major uncertainties persist about the PLA's longer-term relationship with the Party. Even as the military leadership sought to impart a new organizational ethos, political control remained paramount, inhibiting truly autonomous institutional development. As the events of May and June 1989 amply demonstrated, organization charts and formal lines of authority proved very imperfect indicators of the structure of power in China. The declaration of martial law and the subsequent resort to force derived from ad hoc arrangements rather than any regular decision-making procedures. Military command and control under crisis circumstances served as a telling reminder that China remains devoid of institutionalized mechanisms to constrain the exercise of power.

Five dimensions of PLA behavior during the crisis of May and June 1989 illustrate the absence of such mechanisms: (1) the nonutilization of available procedures (for example, the convening of a regular rather than an "enlarged" Military Commission meeting) that could be expected to govern military behavior under extreme circumstances; (2) the intrusion of leaders without formal military responsibility (in particular, Premier Li Peng and the leadership of the Beijing Municipal People's Government) into armed forces channels, especially through the Martial Law Command organized by Chi Haotian; (3) Deng Xiaoping's absence from direct participation in numerous key military decisions, although nearly all actions appeared to have his concurrence, with Yang Shangkun serving as the transmission belt and executive agent; (4) Deng's extraordinary action of redeploying troop units from other military regions (especially Shenyang and Jinan) to Beijing and its environs, thereby assuring compliance with directives issued in the name of the CMC; and (5) the predominant reliance of the martial law authorities on main-force units and strategic reserves, effectively bypassing Beijing-based units, whose political loyalties and willingness to comply with leadership directives were judged more questionable. By resorting to these extralegal arrangements justified through quasi-statutory procedures and regulations, the proponents of martial law totally outmaneuvered those Party and army leaders who voiced reservations about the possible use of force.

The critical issues of the crisis pertained, however, not to legality or procedure, but to a preemptive bid for power by forces opposed to Zhao Ziyang's ultimate assumption of supreme decision-making authority. It seems entirely possible that a majority of the then extant executive committee of the Military Commission (Zhao Ziyang, Yang Shangkun, Hong Xuezhi, Liu Huaqing, and Qin Jiwei) would have opposed or seriously questioned the decision to impose martial law. Deng and Yang very likely knew they were outvoted, which compelled them to resort to "out of channel" arrangements that preempted the opposition.

At the same time, the use of force (drawing heavily but not exclusively from units of the Twenty-seventh Army that were totally unprepared for crowd control) underscored the unstinting loyalty of mobilized PLA units to Deng and Yang's orders, no matter how abhorrent the circumstances. Despite persistent reports of impending civil war between rival forces, very few units balked at implementing the orders of the martial law commanders. Even under extreme duress and confusion, the system held, and no collapse in state power took place. It remains to be seen whether comparable loyalty could be guaranteed in another leadership crisis. The near-total turnover of regional commanders in the spring of 1990 (with most new commanders brought into their assignments from other military regions) suggests a greatly heightened effort to assure loyalty and responsiveness to orders from the top, and to avoid manifestations of localism.[48]

In the aftermath of the Tiananmen crisis, the basis of the authority in the Chinese armed forces needs to be carefully reassessed. Personal loyalties and relationships proved decisive in the 1989 upheavals, with recent efforts to introduce regular channels and procedures for decision making shelved. Although it is too early to judge the longer-term consequences for the attempted institutionalization of military policy, the system in crisis reverted to a preexisting form, calling into question the true extent of organizational change. Even as the age of the regional and district commanders continues to decline and their professional skills continue to improve, political loyalty to the Center remains the paramount criterion for career advancement.

With the inevitable passing of Deng, Yang, and other senior leaders, however, the pressures for change will increase, especially from younger officers with a large stake in the future development of the armed forces. The capacity of the supreme military leadership to effect this transition without engendering a major crisis will remain crucial to the future of the Chinese political system.

48. See *Directory of People's Republic of China Military Personalities* (Hong Kong: Defense Liaison Office, U.S. Consulate General, June 1990), chapter 2.

SEVEN

The Educational Policy Process: A Case Study of Bureaucratic Action in China

Lynn Paine

Some bureaucracies are strong; others are weak. Education is a weak bureaucratic actor. Why is this so? How does the education sector cope in an environment dominated by more powerful organizations competing for scarce resources? These are the questions of concern in this chapter.

What makes the education bureaucracy weak? There are many factors, including the devastating legacy of the Cultural Revolution (which disproportionately affected education); the history of debates over education's very functions, which therefore remain unclear; the continued absence of a powerful champion for education; and the power of noneducators—especially the Party—to set the education agenda and determine boundaries for action.

Political explanations aside, important economic factors also contribute to education's relative weakness. Education is often considered a nonproductive sector. Schooling in China was long perceived as consumption (Yuan 1988, 26). Despite current exhortations to recognize education as valuable investment, it is at best an investment that only pays off in the future, after a generation of students graduates from an improved system. Yet the resources necessary to upgrade education significantly need to be provided now and on an enormous scale. In making

I wish to acknowledge the support of the Committee for Scholarly Communication with the People's Republic of China and Michigan State University for making possible the field research on which this chapter is based. Thanks go to David M. Lampton and Kenneth Lieberthal, other participants in the ACLS-sponsored conference The Structure of Authority and Bureaucratic Behavior in China, participants in the University of Michigan Contemporary China faculty seminar, and an anonymous reviewer for comments on an earlier draft of this chapter. I also appreciate help from Brian DeLany, DaeBong Kwon, Mun Tsang, and Zhang Naihua in gathering data, preparing charts and graphs, and commenting on revisions.

a case for this position, education bureaucrats suffer from an inability to guarantee their "product," since education's technology is unclear (that is, it is not clear how to "produce" the ideal student, if there were even agreement about what that student would be like).

These ambiguities and uncertainties help keep education spending low and fuel the continued debates about funding for education. While that funding in recent years has increased, education expenses in the 1980s have stayed well below 4 percent of GNP, a low figure internationally. What for China represents a high-water mark in educational spending—32.1 billion yuan budgeted in 1988—amounts to only about 32 yuan per person (*ZGJYB,* 4 April 1989, 1). Annual expenditures per pupil are very limited: 128.5 yuan for general secondary school students and only 47.3 yuan for elementary students in 1985 (*Zhongguo shehui tongji ziliao* 1987, 172). And these very "limited outlays and educational construction actually decrease" in value in the current period of inflation. Economically, the education bureaucracy is constrained (Yuan 1988; *ZGJYB,* 18 August 1988, 4).

Finally, organizational fragmentation further weakens education in the political struggle. Who is the education bureaucracy? Officially, education is represented by the State Education Commission (SEdC), yet SEdC-administered schools represent only a part of the nation's education activity, since other ministries fund and to a large degree control their own educational institutions. (In fact, their funds in 1987 represented 13.73 percent of government allocations to education.)[1] Further, the majority of precollegiate education is funded and directly administered by provincial or local (municipal, county, or township) educational authorities.[2] As a result, the formal-education bureaucracy of the SEdC must share authority horizontally and vertically.

These constraints burden the contemporary education bureaucracy. Yet today and in the future, education must play a central role if China's modernization is to progress. Today, approximately one-fifth of China's population is in school (*ZGJYB,* 18 August 1988, 4), and whether in strengthening science and technology, in raising worker productivity, or in training management, education is important.

Against this backdrop of weakness confronting enormous tasks, how

1. This figure includes budgets of the SEdC, educational capital construction, and other ministries. In 1987 the allocation to education in the SEdC budget was 22.63 billion yuan, while other ministries and departments allocated 2.0 billion (*ZGJYB,* 18 August 1988, 4).

2. The role of local authorities in funding and administering education continues to grow in light of a policy of delegated authority and official encouragement of external (nonstate budget) funding for schooling (Zhang Chengxian 1986, 4; *ZGJYB,* 27 October 1987, 3, and 4 April 1989, 1–2).

does education cope? How does it try to improve its situation? I argue that China's institutional environment requires much strategic action, consensus building, and, where possible, persuasion.

The policy process in education involves much interaction and negotiation up and down the hierarchical system and many alliances across sectors. Bureaucratic action proceeds through a groping process reminiscent of Cohen, March, and Olsen's garbage can model (1972). Within that process, participants at all levels have some power, yet each is constrained. The patterns of interaction of these participants reveal that the education bureaucrat relies on multiple coping strategies.

Hence, to talk about Chinese educational policy we must look both horizontally across ministries and vertically from central organs to provinces, municipalities, districts, and even the basic bureaucratic unit of individual colleges and schools. While education's resource dependence reduces the possibility of bargaining among equals, there are ways in which the education bureaucracy exerts pressure internally and on other sectors. Taking advantage of what Gustafson (1981, 51) calls the open window, the education bureaucracy has achieved some policy victories through forged alliances and the pressure of symbolic action. The limits of the education bureaucracy's authority and its coping responses are the topics of this chapter.

THE ISSUE: POLICY RELATED TO TEACHERS

Since the 1978 Third Plenum of the Eleventh Central Committee, education has been at the center of debates about China's development strategies. The "strategic focal role" of education has been stressed with increasing energy in central-level plans, and teachers have been a frequent topic of public debate and policy reform. Perhaps the most significant example of this is the placement of teachers on the list of targets of the landmark 1985 Education Reform Decision (the *jiaoyu tizhi gaige jueding*, hereafter called the Education Decision). In the wake of that Decision and the 1986 Compulsory Education Law, central leaders, education bureaucrats, and education researchers argued that teachers—better qualified, in larger numbers, and more highly rewarded—are an essential part of these reforms. Changes in the condition and ranks of teachers are viewed as a precondition for national education reform and, thus, for broader economic and social reform.[3]

Yet even in this purportedly supportive climate for education, one

3. For early post-1978 discussion, see *Jiaoyu gaige* 1986. For 1980s discussion, see Gao 1980; Deng 1983; Gu 1982, 1983a, and 1983b. With respect to the Education Decision and its aftermath, see *Jiaoyu gaige* 1986, 26–27, and, for example, *FBIS*, 3 April 1986, K2, and 4 April 1986, K7.

finds evidence of education's limits. The education system's bureaucratic weakness, its interdependence with other sectors, as well as its multiple coping strategies, can all be illustrated through examination of policies related to teachers. This issue area provides a window on broader aspects of bureaucratic behavior and educational policy formation.

Below I outline the structural constraints on the education bureaucracy as preparation for discussion of four interrelated features that describe dominant patterns of bureaucratic behavior in China's educational system. These features, described through analysis of two case studies of teacher policy, include (1) the groping process of policy activity; (2) the power of subordinates to shape policy; (3) the multiple coping strategies sought by participants in the educational policy process; and (4) the necessity of cross-sectoral work to support sectoral interests.

FORMAL AND INFORMAL STRUCTURES IN TEACHER POLICY

The formal bureaucratic home of educational policy, the State Education Commission, is itself an acknowledgment of the weakness of the education bureaucracy. Initially, the Ministry of Education (MOE) headed up the education sector. The MOE was functionally on a par with other ministries in competition to obtain scarce financial resources and official attention. But, as the then head of the SEdC, Li Peng, explained, this arrangement made it "very difficult for the Ministry of Education to map out an overall plan for education as a whole" (*FBIS*, 14 June 1985, K7).

The weakness of the MOE's position often undermined efforts regarding teachers. One MOE official I interviewed in 1983, for example, described how the MOE by itself could not solve the problems of the teaching profession. Instead, the ministry had to rely on the State Council, but had to compete with advocates of other sectors for State Council support, attention, and action. While he believed that central leaders like the then premier, Zhao Ziyang, understood the problem, the official said it would take much persuasion before teachers' situations could be improved. "Those of us doing education push education. . . . But other ministries have their problems as well."

The creation of the SEdC in 1985 was intended to address directly this problem of cross-ministry competition for money and attention. The goal was to improve the education system's persuasive position. Appointing members to sit concurrently on the SEdC and other ministries or commissions was to facilitate coordination across ministries and simplify structural arrangements. In addition, naming someone with the stature of Li Peng as head was to lend credibility (and symbolic clout) to the claims about the importance of education.

Yet although these structural changes, designed to reduce fragmentation, have occurred, interviews with officials in 1986 and 1987 suggest that education bureaucrats still must work regularly with other ministries, at times competing with them for attention and support. The presence of the concurrent members on the SEdC leadership group may have facilitated cross-ministry and cross-commission communication, yet it has not obviated the need to persuade policymakers outside the SEdC to cast their lot with education (as the second case study illustrates). Senior SEdC officials say that they still have to call on superiors to intervene in cross-sector bargaining. Though the SEdC may have more clout through its organizational structure than its predecessors, it must nevertheless negotiate with other bureaucracies.

Though the SEdC's role overlaps with other ministries, commissions, and the State Council, I focus chiefly on the SEdC organization and its role. It is the SEdC that bears the responsibility for studying and articulating major educational concerns, preparing guidelines for schools, overseeing the administration of much of higher education and—at a distance—the direction of precollegiate schooling, and the organizing of educational reform.[4]

The Formal Organization: A Horizontal View

The education sector, as formally represented in the central government by the SEdC, is connected to its organizational environment. That is, it is organized to include representation from other ministries and commissions whose work affects the education system. In 1987 the SEdC was headed by a leadership group consisting of its head (then Li Peng, and since 1988 Li Tieying), eight vice-ministers, a former vice-minister of education, and vice-ministers from the State Planning Commission (SPC), the State Economic Commission (SEC), the Ministry of Finance, the Ministry of Labor and Personnel, and the State Science and Technology Commission.

The SEdC is composed of some thirty-five departments and bureaus (*si* and *ju*), with various offices (*chu, shi*), and, below them, sections (*ke*). Policy issues often cut across several departments or bureaus in the SEdC. An issue area is typically the responsibility of a vice-minister; in the case of teachers, Liu Bin was responsible in 1988. (He also was responsible for precollegiate education and minority education.) He oversaw the extensive cross-department work that is required for teacher-related policies. The majority of teacher-related work comes

4. *FBIS*, 18 June 1985, K1. There is a need for systematic data collection regarding the administrative role of other ministries with regard to education. This sort of work would augment our knowledge of how education takes place and who bears responsibility, and it could help answer questions about the relative weakness of the former MOE and the current SEdC.

under the authority of the Teacher Education Department (*shifansi*), which is responsible for tertiary-level teacher-education institutions (that is, normal colleges and universities), their secondary equivalents (teacher-training schools), in-service training of teachers, and teaching materials. Teachers' work conditions are the concern of the Precollegiate Education Department. While these two departments shoulder the chief responsibility for teachers, some aspects of teacher-related policy come under the purview of other SEdC departments: the Political and Ideological Education Department, for example, and the bureaus of Capital Construction and of Planning and Financial Affairs.

At the same time, the policy process in education is not restricted to the SEdC. Teacher-related policies require contact and cooperation with other ministries. One SEdC official in 1987 explained that the SEdC necessarily has "closer relations" with the Ministry of Finance (for funding issues), the Ministry of Labor (for policy on personnel and salaries), and the SPC, the SEC, and the State Science and Technology Commission (SSTC). The presence on the SEdC of vice-ministers from these sectors is an acknowledgment of the interdependence among tasks.

The Vertical View

The formal description of the education system's bureaucratic actors portrays the focus of policy activity as being at the SEdC, albeit with active collaboration with or coordination of other ministries and commissions. But the educational policy process also involves much vertical movement. The State Council needs to approve major policy and, at times, mediate disagreements between participants. Provinces, counties, municipalities, and individual schools also are centrally involved. And there is substantial autonomy at the lower levels.

What is the relative power of these different levels within the educational system? Most generally, the central-government level (SEdC) is seen as having the greatest power, though provincial and local levels also have responsibilities that give them power over schools. It is the SEdC that determines broad policies, provides the outline for curriculum in precollegiate education, determines texts, and, to a large extent, runs higher education (through its control of the university entrance-examination system and the determination of academic majors). Provincial education authorities run the secondary education system (through their control of the secondary school entrance exams), provide some financing of precollegiate education, and control some aspects of the nonkey sector of higher education (its financing, student recruitment, and, in part, job assignments). Local governments provide the majority of funds for local elementary and secondary schools.

It should be noted also that the power of different levels of the education bureaucracy is complex because of overlap in the function of central, provincial, and local levels; regional variation; range in types of policy and kinds of resources that connote power; and the distinction between state-run and community-run (*minban*) schools. Power over funding, for example, depends on the level and type of school (e.g., key or nonkey). Power over the curriculum is also somewhat influenced by more than one level and varies by place: though in the 1980s the SEdC controlled a nationally unified curriculum, provinces and localities had the authority to supplement that curriculum (and varied greatly in the degree to which they did so). In the late 1980s Shanghai used its own experimental curriculum in place of the national curriculum. Finally, depending on the type of education policy (e.g., curriculum, funding, administrative structure), even individual schools can exert a kind of veto power in their ability to obstruct, delay, or reinterpret policy.

In short, the pattern of power within the education system is complex. The pattern has also changed. Over the 1980s there occurred nationally an increase in the relative strength, autonomy, and influence of the local bureaucratic level and individual school units as greater responsibility for finance devolved to local levels and schools were encouraged to rely on entrepreneurial solutions to many operational problems. At the same time, in policies regarding the admissions systems, bureaucratic structures, rules, and standards of evaluation, educational reforms have tied schools more closely to unified plans or central authority. The result of this two-sided change is the increased autonomy of lower levels of the educational system within a more circumscribed boundary of action.

With respect to teacher policy, the patterns of fragmented power parallel those described above for education generally. Formally, the departments responsible for teachers at the central level (in the SEdC) have provincial counterparts in the Bureau of Education (BOE).[5] These provincial offices have power over teacher policy through provincial administration of teacher education,[6] through direct administration of provincially run secondary schools, and indirectly through the oversight of county and district education offices, where the bulk of elementary and secondary schooling is administered. Provinces, like the counties and

5. As of late 1987, provinces varied in the location of a bureaucratic home for education. In some cases there was still a provincial Bureau of Education (*jiaoyuting* or *jiaoyuju*), in other places a provincial Education Commission; and in other places (such as Shanghai and Tianjin) there was an Education and Culture Commission (*jiaokewenwei*).
6. The majority of preservice teacher education occurs at provincially administered teacher-training colleges, since nationally only six come under the SEdC administration.

districts below them, play a noticeable role in interpreting and in effect shaping educational policy.

In this structure there is much delegation of discretionary authority. The Center decides that teacher competence must be assured, but municipalities choose the subjects in which to test their elementary teachers (*ZGJYB*, 10 November 1987, 1). The central government announces a 10 percent wage increase for teachers, but provinces and localities are authorized to find the money and make decisions about the actual allocations (*ZGJYB*, 3 December 1987, 1). And the former Ministry of Education announced that teacher education would be upgraded, but local institutions had to decide what that meant in curricular terms (Paine 1986).

Nonetheless, stopping with the observation that there is delegation of discretionary authority assigns too much rationality, foresight, and decisive clarity to the central education bureaucracy. Instead, closer examination of the process of educational policy formation suggests less rationality, more interaction, and iteration. Horizontal and vertical interactions produce a process and a set of policies that are at one time more responsive, vaguer, more heterogeneous, and slower than the delegation or discretion model suggests.

Two cases of policy formation—one regarding a regulatory issue, the other distributive in character, are analyzed below. While each illustrates the profoundly interactive nature of the process, the two differ in the locus of and approaches to authority and influence. The first concerns regulations for teacher competence. Through this case we see the groping process, the powerful role of subordinates, and the variety of coping strategies invoked. The second case concerns efforts to improve the social, economic, and political situation of teachers. Here we observe the limits of the education sector and the subsequent need for cross-sector alliances and cooperation.

CASE STUDY I: STANDARDS FOR TEACHERS

The Problem of Standards and Quality

Central to the discussions of teacher policies and educational reforms is the issue of standards for teachers. By the time of the 1978 Third Plenum a teacher shortage greater than that experienced before the Cultural Revolution existed quantitatively and in terms of credentials and competence. As figure 7.1 suggests, the rapid expansion of precollegiate education since the 1950s had not seen a commensurate growth in teacher education or trained teachers. The national shortage in 1977 was estimated at 3.45 million elementary and secondary school teachers (Cui 1979, 31). According to leaders, quality was a bigger problem than quan-

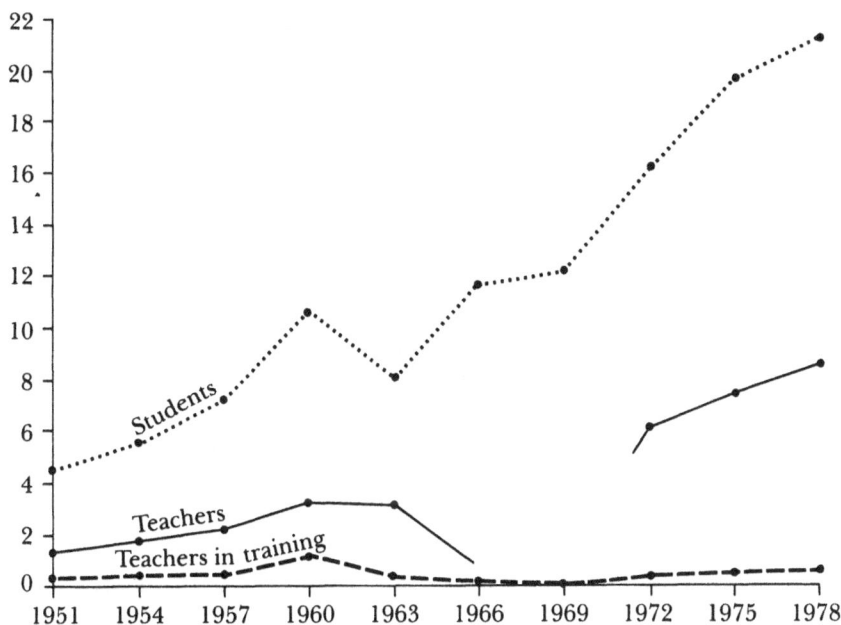

Fig. 7.1. Elementary and Secondary Expansion, 1951–78

NOTE: Figures for teachers represent the total number of teachers (qualified and unqualified) working in elementary, general secondary, and specialized secondary schools. Where data for elementary teachers were missing (1966–71), no estimates of the total teaching force are used. The numbers of teachers in training refer to students enrolled in either teacher-training schools or colleges. These numbers, as well as those for teachers, are plotted in millions. The numbers of students are represented on this graph in tens of millions.

SOURCE: Department of Planning 1984.

tity. The Chinese indicate that quality—as measured in terms of qualifications (teachers' academic credentials)—fell over the years, as is seen in table 7.1.[7]

If China was to reach its broader educational goals, there had to be a strengthening of standards. Yet given the vigor of the attacks on teacher education and professionalism during the years of the Cultural Revolution, the urgent need to coordinate and regulate the establishment of professional standards for teaching posed a major policy challenge. The study of bureaucratic behavior and the use of authority that were called

7. The standard formula assumes, for example, that elementary teachers need to be at least graduates of secondary school or a secondary teacher-training school, while junior high school teachers, for example, need at least the equivalent of a *zhuanke* degree following two to three years of postsecondary training, and senior high school teachers should have completed a four-year college program.

TABLE 7.1. National Percentage of
Academically Qualified Teachers

Year	Elementary	Junior High	Senior High
1965	81.6[a]	71.9	70.3
1977	66.0[b]	14.3	33.2
1987	68.2	35.6	39.6[c]

SOURCES: Cui 1979, 32; Department of Planning
1984, 222; Wu 1983, 82; *ZGJYB*, 31 December
1988, 1; *Zhongguo shehui tongji ziliao 1987* 1987,
161.
[a]Based on a survey of 2,601,400 teachers in 1963
(Department of Planning 1984, 222).
[b]Based on a survey of 5,216,600 teachers in 1978
(Department of Planning 1984, 222).
[c]This figure represents the percentage of qualified
senior high (*gao zhong*) teachers nationally in
1985, but does not include teachers in specialized
secondary schools (*zhongzhuan*).

on to meet this policy challenge illustrates three aspects of the process of
educational policy formation within the vertical educational policy system: its slow, reactive, and groping character; the power of subordinates;
and the limited authority available to education bureaucrats and the
resulting strategies they adopt.

The Groping Pace of Bureaucratic Action
Bureaucratic wrestling with the issue of teacher policy has occurred outside any routine temporal cycle. In the case of teacher standards, superiors have placed *no* deadline. (Contrast this with what an SEdC official
described as the one-year deadline the Central Committee gave the SEdC
for formulating the draft of the "Education Decision.") Instead, the regulation of teacher standards appears to be a case of an issue looking for a
policy, what Cohen, March, and Olsen might describe as "issues and
feelings looking for decision situations" (1972, 2). What we see is a practice of management through groping (Paine 1986; Behn 1988).

The policy process in this case involved the simultaneous occurrence
of goal setting, discussion, and implementation.[8] Goal setting began in

8. My description of this process and its local manifestations is based on field research in
1982–84, 1986, and 1987. As part of that work I conducted extensive interviewing, observa-
tion, and library research at Beijing Normal College, Beijing Normal University, Beijing
Education Institute, Changchun Teachers College, Changchun Education Institute, Dong-
bei Normal University, Fujian Normal University, Harbin Teachers University, Huadong
Normal University, Huazhong Teachers College, Jilin Education Institute, Jilin Teachers
College, Liaoning Education Institute, Liaoning Teachers University, Shanghai Education
Institute, Shenyang Education Institute, Shenyang Teachers College, and Siping Teachers
College.

1978 with "problem recognition" (Kingdon 1984, 19): the shortage of qualified teachers was identified as a policy problem at the 1978 National Education Work Conference, the 1980 National Teacher Education Work Conference, and in numerous articles published during this time. National leaders and high education officials gradually formulated a set of goals and principles for the reform of standards for professional preparation and practice,[9] yet these statements have been distinguished by their vagueness and breadth. The most frequently cited statement of goals, for example, simply claims that teachers (1) "must study hard and become more erudite; (2) they must seriously study and grasp the science of education and understand educational laws; (3) they must have a noble moral character and a lofty spiritual realm and must be worthy of the title teacher" (*FBIS*, 30 June 1980, L1).

While national political and education leaders gradually announced policy goals, discussion of teacher standards and teacher education reforms grew. Since 1978 the topic got increasing scholarly and popular attention. Over one hundred articles were published on teacher education between 1978 and 1982 (Tan, 1983), and at least six new teacher-education journals were started between 1982 and 1984. Nonetheless, the discussion did *not* become markedly more specific. Instead, the discussion was mired in epistemological and fundamental questions, with the most discussion of teachers' professional standards (accounting for 46 percent of the literature) concerning the need for increased attention to be given teacher education and its "special characteristics" (Tan 1983).[10]

Despite the absence of clearly defined goals, individual institutions, sometimes acting independently and sometimes acting in concert with the MOE or other schools, carried out numerous changes in all major areas of professional teacher preparation. Repeatedly in my interviews with school administrators, faculty, and education officials, respondents referred to this as a process of "groping" (*mosuo*), conveying a sense of exploration, trying to find something out, trying to accomplish something. In the Western literature we might prefer the phrase "muddling through" (Lindblom 1959).[11]

9. See, for example, Deng Xiaoping 1983; Gao 1980; Gu 1983a, 1983b.

10. While there grew to be more talk about the need to strengthen professional standards of entry, there was a noticeable absence of discussion of how teachers can best be trained or standards evaluated. A spate of articles in 1983–84 calling for clarification of the mission of teacher education offer a noteworthy contrast to Gao's 1980 assertion that the "basic mission" of teacher education programs is clear (Deng Liqun 1983; Gu 1983a, 1983b).

11. Behn (1988, 649) distinguishes "groping along" from "muddling through." He argues that Lindblom's concept implies choosing " 'among values and among policies at one and the same time,' " whereas "groping along" focuses on public management of various

The practice of management-by-groping results in an unevenness of policy activity. For example, during the 1980s bureaucratic and structural changes internal to the system of teacher education and its institutions occurred in a rather swift and uniform way; throughout the country, educators were promoted as leaders in teacher-education institutions, new institutions were established, and the system became more coordinated.[12] Yet other responses to policy discussion—especially regarding curriculum, admissions, and job allocation—were more idiosyncratic, uneven, and even problematic. Curricular change is a particularly illustrative example of three key features of management-by-groping: local interpretation, mutual adaptation, and policy fluidity.

As early as 1978, schools turned to their curricula to experiment practically with how quality could be assured. Formally, the changes appeared to be carefully controlled by the ministry, with the announcement of precise policy formulations about professional preparation in 1978 and 1980 (through MOE-published *jiaoxue jihua*, or teaching plans for eleven departments in teacher-training colleges, and *jiaoxue dagang*, or teaching outlines for 140 courses offered at normal colleges.)[13] Yet both the plans and the outlines are "reference" (*cankaoxing*) documents, which act as guidelines rather than as regulations. Without enforcing power, the guidelines allow for some measure of autonomy for individual institutions of teacher education.

Schools experimented with curriculum reform, and the plans of most schools deviated in some way from the MOE guidelines. Local experimentation varied, but beginning in 1978 it generally tended first toward expansion of and specialization within the academic curriculum and the reduction of course work in politics and education and time spent in student teaching.

Alteration of the central policy subsequently occurred, demonstrating

---

paths one could take to reach the desired goal. In my use of "groping" I agree with Behn that long-range, broad goals may be clear, but I find that these goals, once enacted, take on different meanings in the process of negotiation and the experience of trial and error.

12. By the mid-1980s an extensive "teacher education network" of programs and resources was established. Previously uncoordinated institutions now worked in a comprehensive, highly differentiated, and well-articulated system. This included six regional centers coordinating preservice efforts and taking responsibility for research and sabbatical training of provincial and local-level teacher educators; 218 provincial, district, and municipal education institutes (*jiaoyu xueyuan*) for retraining secondary school teachers; 2,174 teacher-refresher schools (*jiaoshi jinxiu xuexiao*) for elementary teachers; correspondence programs; and by 1986 a national education television station and its "television teacher-training college" (*zhongguo dianshi shifan xueyuan*) (*Zhongguo jiaoyu nianjian* 1986, 104–5; *ZGJYB*, 22 December 1987, 1; *RMRB*, 5 August 1986, 3; *FBIS*, 28 January 1987, K20).

13. The plans list courses and placement in a student's program, while outlines specify the topics and their sequence for each course.

the interactive quality and mutual adaptation that are at the core of the groping policy process. In the keynote address to the 1980 National Teacher Education Conference, Gao Yi, as a central-level representative, warned against an overly academic curriculum. This served as a response to the experimentation of local units and represented pressure from the Center (Gao 1980). Reorientation of teacher-education programs followed. According to department chairs interviewed, some departments reduced their elective offerings, and others shifted the course content away from theoretically advanced work to "fundamentals." The political-theory core sequence was strengthened, and a new required course in moral education and an extra year of physical education were added. And the MOE, in refusing the request by some normal colleges to expand to a five-year, academically more extensive B.A. program, like those that Beijing Normal University and East China Normal had established, asserted the limits of acceptable reform.

In sum, then, under the guidelines of these vague policy discussions, this reform policy has had fluidity that allowed it to change over time. Typical of the groping process, the current standards represent an evolutionary compromise between the broad objectives of the central bureaucracy (that is, upgrading teacher standards) and specific experiments of local experience. Policy is recast by those carrying it out, somewhat akin to Manion's "policy remakes" (see chapter 8 in this volume), yet different in that here those involved are relatively weak actors with limited power to revise policy. Groping is characterized by responsiveness, as implementation proceeds alongside the process of continual formulation. This policy process is iterative. Thus, the broad goals and principles for strengthening professional standards have not changed, but the boundaries of acceptability shifted after a certain amount of local experience was collected. Reformulation continues.

Actors in the Process: The Power of Subordinates
At the Center the SEdC has moved to regulate and strengthen standards for teachers by improving teacher education—through the promulgation and revision of curricular guidelines and the establishment of an elaborate network of in-service and preservice teacher-education programs—and by introducing a system of professional examinations and certificates.[14] Yet, we need to be wary of attributing too much leadership to the

14. See *GMRB*, 2 October 1986, 1. The system of testing and credentials at the end of the decade remained in an early phase, having produced anxiety in the teachers. The education bureaucracy has had to spend some time responding to their fears and complaints. (See, for example, *ZGJYB*, 9 July 1987, 2.) When the system was tried out in six provinces, autonomous regions, and municipalities in 1987, only between 22 and 27 percent of the 430,000 secondary school teachers passed (*ZGJYB*, 10 November 1987, 1). In

MOE and the SEdC. A review of participants highlights the limits of the Center and the resultant power of subordinates within the education bureaucracy.

The MOE and the SEdC are constrained horizontally in ways that weaken their efforts: the upgrading of teacher education depends first on attracting students of higher quality, something the MOE could not do on its own. Vertically constrained as well, the Center is limited in the extent to which it can direct and supervise activity. In the early 1980s, for example, the MOE's Teacher Education Bureau had a staff of only six. Shorthanded, it was only able to convene meetings with representatives from normal colleges to "exchange experience" and hold up for emulation the exemplary activities of individual programs. Its staff made occasional school inspections, but regular systematic review of all programs was impossible.[15]

The result is a kind of autonomy that is rationalized as education intelligence: responding to local needs, encouraging grass-roots initiatives, and so on. While the references in the Education Decision to reforms in higher education grant official legitimacy to this, my 1982–84 interviews at eighteen higher-education institutions indicate that this constrained autonomy predated the Decision.

The autonomy outlined above lends strength to the influence and power of lower-level units. Subordinates have participated in the policy process in four main ways: experimenting, interpreting, and undermining policy, as well as reshaping policy conceptualization.

Experimentation. Local and provincial education authorities exert their power to shape policy by initiating experiments that later are disseminated provincially and nationally. In 1984, for example, a provincial official told me about one province's reforms in job assignment, which included movement toward more contractual arrangements in hiring recent graduates in teacher education. Because the reform was described as an "experiment," it did not require MOE approval.

This situation—played out in provincial, municipal, and institutional practices—illustrates the significance of local experimentation. Many times local and provincial officials and school administrators talked

---

implementing the formal exam system, the SEdC will design the test for secondary teachers, but each province is determining the test for elementary teachers (*ZGJYB*, 26 December 1987, 1; *FBIS*, 29 December 1987, 43).

15. Instead of close supervision, according to a ministry official in 1984, special topics were chosen or a sampling of regional sites selected for investigation. University people, like MOE officials, were open about the lack of tight coupling. One university administrator in 1983 said that although the MOE "should come to understand our situation," they do not, because of the small staff.

about reforms they had initiated "as experiments"—in admissions to teacher education, curriculum, and professional standards. A commonly told story line runs like this: Some change in practice occurs that will serve the interests of local institutions, enterprises, or the local community's educational needs. An agreement is worked out, later noticed and encouraged by provincial or central officials, and finally widely implemented as a new development of the policy.

The process of experimentation, when it is successful, becomes one form of policy formation. The central bureaucracy, in fact, is organized to support that sort of persuasion-through-successful-experience. The teacher education and the teachers' conferences convened by the SEdC serve this function, as do the regularly featured stories of "successful" experiments of schools and local education authorities described by the education press, particularly *Renmin Jiaoyu* and *Zhongguo Jiaoyubao*. The value given to experimentation strengthens the negotiating position of local-level units. The recent distribution of rewards for reforms further encourages this.[16] Speaking of the power of grass-roots experimentation, one provincial official explained in 1984, "In recent years the big reforms in teacher-training colleges have come mainly from the teacher-training college itself."

Interpretation.   The influence of local institutions is also made possible in part by weak connections within the educational bureaucracy. Loose coupling between the Center and local areas has its parallel within individual institutions and schools. A de facto delegation of authority has important consequences for the power of lower-level actors to interpret and redefine policy.

The Dean of Studies office (*jiaowuchu*), the unit responsible for overseeing academic work within the normal college, like the SEdC, conducts only limited regular close inspection of its charges. The *jiaowuchu* typically has only a few staff members in each of four or five sections. Given personnel shortages and weak or nonexistent hardware for management in most of these schools, these offices, like the SEdC, are kept busy simply reviewing department schedules and plans and doing occasional in-depth sampling. Even during the 1980s reforms they could not afford to do regular lengthy studies of program quality, the impact of standards, or the fate of curriculum programs in use. There is no regular feedback mechanism. As a result, the *jiaowuchu* must delegate much

16. See, for example, the SEdC and Finance Ministry's award of 200,000 yuan to thirty-seven counties (*ZGJYB*, 10 September 1988) and the Shandong Provincial Government's decision to give the Pingdu County Education Commission a 100,000 yuan bonus and four individuals involved a 2,000 yuan bonus and a salary raise ("Zhonggong Shandong-shengwei Shangdongsheng renmin zhengfu" 1988.)

supervisory authority to leaders of each academic department. What occurs is the regular delegation of responsibility to lower levels—whether from ministry and provincial bureau to the grass-roots institution or from the institution to its academic departments.

Given this delegated authority, departmental-level interpretation of central-level policy is significant. Personalized decision making enters in. Within institutions there were unclear goals, little sense of how they were to be achieved and of who should make decisions. As a result, who participated in the decision in each department was significant, as the arrival of a "problem" allowed participants to match the problem to their pet solutions. The decisions, therefore, varied from unit to unit.

One example of this personalism and the range in policy interpretation comes from the Center's effort to provide more qualified teachers to rural and remote areas. The *dingxiang* (fixed destination) program of admissions and job assignment was introduced nationally in 1983 as a means of filling rural teaching positions with rural graduates and thereby avoiding urban students' resistance to rural teaching assignments. Although the program officially commenced in 1983, interviews in 1983–84 with eleven department chairs at one teacher-training college revealed a range of interpretation of the policy and consequently of its implementation. Some department chairs described plans to implement the policy, others assured me that they were not planning to do so, and one leader said that he did not know what the policy was.

Undermining Policy.   A third pattern of participation is to undermine or contradict policy. A variant perhaps of Manion's concept of "policy remakes" (see chapter 8 in this volume), this autonomy allows grass-roots actors to willfully recast policy according to their interests. This policy process can produce reforms that are inconsistent and at times conflicting.[17]

Reforming professional standards offers a good case of contradictory action. At one institution, one part of the curriculum was undermined by another, as each department interpreted "higher quality teacher educa-

17. In this way and others the phenomena I describe differ from Manion's examples of remaking policy, for the final outcome in the teacher standards case—uncoordinated policy and policy sabotaged—is not necessarily the desire of any actor or group of actors, but instead is a by-product of relatively weak actors, each exerting limited power to recast policy in their interest. Of course, another significant difference is in the resources and power possessed by individuals involved in the process: Manion's cadres as individuals bring more strength to their negotiations than these departmental leaders, who are not really negotiating but are simply trying to cope in self-interested ways with policies handed to them.

tion" as meaning expanding its own course hours and offerings. In effect, departmental plans that simultaneously called for strengthened preparation in education and more advanced work in the students' major fields produced an increase in specialization at the expense of professional training in education. In the school's 1980 course plan, for example, education courses for all departments constituted only 2.7–5.8 percent of student course hours, in contrast to an earlier 10–20 percent. Struggles within colleges demonstrate ways in which lower-level units deflect decisions in ways they find congenial.

Shaping Conceptualization of Policy. In addition to provincial and university or school actors in the teacher policy process, researchers and consultants play an increasingly important role. Halpern (see chapter 5 in this volume) describes the growing role of research centers and experts as one of "competitive persuasion." In education the influence of researchers and consultants is evident in their ability to shape the conceptualization of policy.

The SEdC conducts its own research within each of the various bureaus and departments and assigns responsibility for policy research to its Office of Policy Study and its Educational Development and Research Policy Center. The Policy Center researchers, as described by one educator, write for "leaders" in ways contrasted with the "more open" ability to "expose problems," which the many recently established research centers possess.

The contribution coming from these research institutes and consultants outside the SEdC grew in the late 1980s. The SEdC frequently called on researchers based at university research institutes to serve as consultants on teacher policy. At one university, for example, the SEdC asked one research group to prepare a paper on the academic specializations appropriate to teacher education, another to investigate the qualifications of all teacher educators involved in teacher-training institutes, and a third to analyze teacher standards in other countries. While noting that it is still "authority-driven policy," not "research-based policy," that is developed, researchers claim that the role of research in the policy process has increased since 1978. They find themselves called on more often for a wider range of tasks.

There seemed to be a common formal interpretation of the policy process: the administrative and political center raises an issue, the SEdC responds, and researchers get consulted. Still, this passive or reactive version of the consultant's role does not entirely coincide with the evidence of frequent and informal interaction between key researchers and SEdC officials. In 1987 several different researchers mentioned being consulted by phone by newly appointed SEdC vice-ministers,[18] called by an SEdC official to spend a morning talking about teacher education and this researcher's own research, and appointed on short notice to a small SEdC task force to evaluate the success of the reform efforts.

These phone calls, conversations, and last-minute committee assignments all suggest a rather close, informal, and personal network of scholars and officials, one that has grown stronger and perhaps tighter in recent years. Implicit in these anecdotes is the sense that the knowledge of and familiarity with academics is not insignificant in SEdC work. The expansion of the consulting role appears closely related to status— institutional status, personal connections, and status accrued from time overseas. (In teacher policy, researchers from Beijing Normal University and East China Normal appear to be most frequently consulted by SEdC officials.) As these ties grow, researchers also stand to influence policy— particularly the conceptualization of policy issues. As Kingdon found for the United States, these consultants are more likely to affect "alternatives" than national agendas (1984, 58).

Multiple Coping Strategies

The groping process of teacher policy described above rests on the interaction of several levels of actors. Each influences policy, although each is also constrained in its ability to form and carry out policies regarding standards for teachers. Acting with few material resources and both organizational and political constraints, education bureaucrats have pressed for their interests by relying on a range of coping strategies.

Many of the constraints on the education bureaucracy can be explained in organizational terms. In the absence of sufficient personnel and regular feedback mechanisms, weak articulation of central and local levels within the education system reduced the Center's ability to inspect performance at the grass roots. But local-level actors were also constrained, given their reliance on approval by the Center, which sets boundaries for acceptable action. All levels within the system are further constrained because the resources available to education are limited, with a budget representing 11.17 percent of government outlays (Yuan 1988, 24).

External factors also impose significant constraints on bureaucratic options within the educational system. The political, social, and economic climate for schools discourages talented people from entering and staying in teaching, and this situation profoundly limits the ability of the

18. Recall that although some of the vice-ministers—*fuzhuren*—come with academic administrative experience, they are not education scholars. As one education researcher in late 1987 pointed out, these new people (the group of vice-commissioners which began in 1986) "don't know the research community yet."

SEdC to make standards for teachers (Paine 1986). A popular phrase sums up the problems about teachers: "You can't get them, can't use them, and can't keep them" (*jinbulai, yongbushang, liubuzhu*) (Gu 1983a). Teacher-training colleges, despite reforms, are unable to recruit top students.[19] Assuring that well-qualified graduates of teacher-preparation programs end up teaching in elementary and secondary schools has likewise proven a formidable task. Despite heightened attention to the issue, there remain many ways in which universities and their students can conspire to escape high school assignments, especially as nonteaching units hire normal-college graduates. The central education bureaucracy's inability to determine and enforce hiring policies (that is, which units employ graduates of teacher-education programs) and the reward structure for teachers simply compounds the difficulties.[20]

Limited as they may be in resources and by the context in which they work, education bureaucrats use a range of strategies to achieve their policy aims. Three of the most common are linking to other agendas, piggybacking other education reforms, and spreading success stories.

Linking To Other Agendas.   Kingdon (1984) argues that changes in the "political stream" and, more important, agendas are significant. Changes in China's national agenda gave force to the reforming of teacher standards. Education actors were keen to link their interests with those of national reform. It is noteworthy, for example, that in an authoritative book on major policy documents of the educational reforms, the 1984 Economic Reform Decision and the 1985 Science and Technology System Reform were included (*Jiaoyu gaige* 1986). The reform of education is regularly and symbolically connected to other broader changes. Teacher-education respondents frequently related the bureaucratic reforms within their system to changes in economic enterprises or the agricultural responsibility system. For administrators at the grass-roots level there was a keen awareness that the bureaucratic changes associated with reforming teacher standards were part of a

19. Reforms include early university admissions for teacher education applicants and the continued use of stipends to teacher-training students despite the elimination of stipends in much of the rest of higher education. (See, for example, *GMRB*, 13 January 1985; *FBIS*, 28 July 1986, R1; Liu Bin 1986, 6; *ZGJYB*, 12 July 1986, 1, and 6 June 1987, 1; Xue 1986). The early-admissions program, for example, was described by SEdC, provincial BOE, and university admission officials as effective in attracting a stronger student-to-teacher preparation, yet all noted the limits of this approach. As one university official explained in 1986, the candidates were "not the best, but [academically] upper-middle students."

20. The SEdC vice-commissioner Liu Bin argued that recently there has actually been a decrease in the proportion of graduates entering precollegiate teaching, with some schools only managing to send 50 percent and others only a few percent (Liu Bin 1986, 6).

larger national agenda. For them, this connection gave persuasive power.

Thus, many of the changes at the local educational institution intended to raise the quality of teachers corresponded with the restructuring of political economic patterns nationally. As part of the process of policy change in teacher standards, for example, autonomy in some areas of educational work increased: using the rhetoric of decentralization, some provinces were able to vary from the national plan to institute early-admissions policies in teacher education that were to increase their chances of attracting strong candidates into teaching. This phenomenon of increased autonomy was justified by the renewed emphasis on expertise and decentralization elsewhere in the system.

Using Momentum of Other Educational Reforms.   If grand national changes in the political economy's landscape justify changes in education policy, even more forceful pressure for reform in teacher standards came from other educational reforms. Advocates for higher standards for teachers were able to use the 1985 Education Conference and subsequent Education Decision to increase the pace and specificity of their reforms far beyond what had occurred during the broad discussions in 1978–85. In December 1985 attention focused on teacher examinations, preservice and in-service teacher education, and restrictions on teacher mobility ("Yao zhuajin" 1986, 2–3). Soon after, in March 1986, the SEdC made specific recommendations regarding curriculum, admissions, and job assignments—areas that had previously experienced experimentation but no clear SEdC mandate.[21] Similarly, policy for teacher standards gained momentum with the April 1986 Compulsory Education Law's discussion of teacher testing and certification; this has encouraged a subsequent increase in both the level of attention and the degree of specificity of policy regarding teacher standards, with the SEdC and provinces moving ahead in developing and administering tests of teacher knowledge.[22]

Closet Reforms and the Spreading of Success Stories.   The groping and incremental quality to the policy change and the constraints felt by individuals at all levels encouraged official conservatism and unofficial experimentation. In the early unfocused stages of reform, the tendency to interpret policy literally and the vulnerability of educational institutions

21. These recommendations were made in the "Opinion on Strengthening and Developing Teacher Education." For more, see "Guojia jiaowei yaoqiu" 1986, 9; *RMRB*, 22 April 1986, 1.

22. See "Zhonghua renmin gongheguo yiwu jiaoyufa" 1986, 2; *FBIS*, 4 April 1986, K7; "Quanguo gaodeng shifan jiaoyu yanjiuhui" 1987; "Gaodeng shifan jiaoyu ruhe shiying" 1987; *ZGJYB*, 10 November 1987, 1, and 17 December 1987, 2.

generally encouraged a wait-and-see attitude. Many university officials whom I interviewed expressed this by saying that local reforms depend on reforms elsewhere; they did not feel that their school could go alone in its reform. (It is also clear, however, that higher-status organizations and individuals acted more boldly in interpreting reforms on their own.)

Despite this general conservatism, however, I observed a striking creativity among subordinates as departments or faculty conducted what I call "closet reforms." These reforms often represented significant changes from previous practices, yet their creators seemed to avoid publicizing them until informal support was gathered horizontally (at other institutions) or vertically (in the MOE, the SEdC, or the provincial BOE). An example would be one normal college's early revision of admissions practices before the *dingxiang* policy was created. The university, faced with graduates unwilling to teach at the secondary level, began to take proportionally more students from the countryside because they had, in the words of one administrator, fewer "conditions" and were more compliant. Within the space of one year the rural share of the entering class jumped from 40 percent to 60 percent. Soon after, the *dingxiang* program was introduced nationally. The experimentation observed at the local level was generalized as a popular coping strategy for the education sector as a whole.

In sum, the case study of teacher-standards policy represents many common qualities of the educational policy process. This groping process was shown to be interactive and slow and to involve many levels of the educational system. The SEdC, the BOE, institutions, and researchers all have some influence, but each is limited and is therefore forced to rely on multiple strategies for achieving their policy goals. The strategies vary with the unit's location in the structure of the education system's hierarchy, yet generally three kinds of strategies stand out: linking to changes in the political stream, riding the coattails of other educational reforms, or disseminating successful experiments.

CASE STUDY II: IMPROVING THE LOT OF TEACHERS

Teacher-standards policy illustrates many important aspects of the education bureaucracy's behavior and authority structure. A second case involves policy related to improving the living and work conditions of teachers. It offers us a second vantage point on educational policy by illustrating horizontal connections, rather than vertical links. This case represents a distributive decision, as opposed to the regulatory quality of teacher standards.

Despite these differences, these two cases share many qualities. Each has evolved slowly, outside recurrent rhythms of yearly work confer-

ences or the patterns of annual budgets. They involve the Center and
localities groping for and experimenting with solutions to complex and
pressing problems. Each demonstrates the surprising power of lower-
level actors, as well as the need to try multiple avenues toward the SEdC's
goals. Finally, each reveals the severe constraints under which education
policy is made. Below I quickly outline the policy problem in the second
case and specify the process of response. This chronology reveals an
ever-widening circle of involvement and the need for cross-sectoral cooperation, in this case culminating in a 1987 agreement that was intended to produce a 10 percent wage hike for teachers. Nonetheless, the
weakness of the education sector is very apparent in this story.

The Problem

Economically, teachers ranked among the lowest-paid professionals in
the country during the post-Mao years (*Zhishifenzi Wenti Wenxian Xuanbian* 1983, 136; *ZGJYB*, 6 September 1988, 1). Politically and socially,
their position—never high—was very low. Professionally, they represented poorly trained and demoralized individuals. The resultant problem of recruitment, noted above, coupled with school expansion, has
produced shortages, especially in rural areas, particular subject areas,
and vocational and technical education, clearly an impediment to national efforts to transform the once virtually uniform academic secondary school system into a highly differentiated, multitrack system in
which a majority of students receive vocational or technical training.[23]

Compounding the problem is teacher attrition. Particularly since
1978, discouraged teachers have left teaching in large numbers. Of
special concern is the fact that departing teachers tend to be strong,
experienced, middle-aged faculty, known as "backbone teachers" (*gugan
jiaoshi*). Though aggregate national figures are not available, frequent
reports from individual provinces, counties, and districts suggest that
the scale of the problem is large.[24] Between 1985 and 1988, 100,000

23. At the 1985 National Work Meeting on Elementary and Secondary School Teachers,
He Dongchang listed history, geography, biology, physical education, music, art, foreign
languages, and political science as areas of particular concern and estimated that one
million new elementary, 750,000 new junior high, and 300,000 new senior high teachers
would be needed over the next five years (*ZGJYB*, 23 November 1985, 1). For more on
vocational education, see *RMRB*, 7 July 1986; *ZGJYB*, 30 August 1986; Zhou 1985;
Jiningshi jiaoyuju 1985; and *ZGJYB*, 2 October and 15 November 1986. For more on the
reform of the secondary system, see Rosen 1985.

24. *ZGJYB*, 23 November 1985. In Liaoning, for example, more than 6,300 teachers left
or retired between 1979 and 1984, and about half of these were "backbone teachers."
Between 1980 and 1984 one small city in the province had more than 2,000 teachers leave
their jobs (Zheng Guanjian 1984). Recently in Hunan 3,850 "backbone teachers" changed
jobs or were transferred (*FBIS*, 27 June 1986, P5). In just the Dongcheng district of
Beijing, 103 of the teachers assigned upon graduation have already left their jobs (Chen
1988).

secondary school teachers a year (or approximately 3–4 percent of that group) have left their jobs (Xiang 1989). Of the remaining teachers, it is estimated that only 37.5 percent are qualified ("Zhongxue xiaozhang" 1988, 17).

The SEdC described this situation as a major obstacle to education reform and diagnoses the problem as having social, political, and economic roots (*ZGJYB*, 23 August 1988). The prescription has been a series of policy moves aimed at reversing the devaluing of teachers. But, as the narrative below suggests, horizontal or cross-sectoral action has been essential. Only when the SEdC could move the issue onto the agenda of other ministries and the State Council has any substantive progress been made.

Strategies for Improving the Teacher's Lot

Social Work. The common explanations for teachers' problems are social—lack of prestige and respect, as well as repeated instances of violence against teachers.[25] These incidents have received increasing publicity; consequently, one of the SEdC's first targets for change has been the social position of teachers.

Several specific efforts have been made by the central education bureaucracy to change social attitudes toward teachers. The most visible of these has been the institution of a national holiday to honor teachers. Inaugurated on September 9, 1985, with much publicity and elaborate public ceremonies, Teachers' Day honors the teaching profession and individual teachers. The message in the stories, reports, poems, and photographs of the day is clear: teachers play a valued role in society; they are supported by the country's top leaders; and they are appreciated by ordinary people.[26]

Similar themes appear in other socially oriented reforms as well. These range from the "respect teachers, love students" campaign (*zunshi aisheng*), to the 1986 Compulsory Education Law's stipulation to prosecute assaults on teachers, to the establishment of a system of honors for exemplary teachers (*mofan jiaoshi* and *teji jiaoshi*) (Cai 1985, 8; *Zhongguo jiaoyu nianjian 1949–1981* 1984, 200).

25. Even after the establishment of policies to improve the treatment of intellectuals, teachers in recent years have been beaten, killed, and publicly humiliated. (See, for example, *RMRB*, 31 May 1984, 3; *FBIS*, 20 August 1985, O1; *Zhongguo jiaoyu nianjian 1982–84* 1986, 351; *ZGJYB*, 24 October 1987, 19 April and 31 December 1988.) Instances of abuse have continued despite joint action taken by the MOE, the Public Security Bureau, the Judiciary Department, the People's Supreme Court, and the People's Supreme Inspection Court in 1983 (*Zhongguo jiaoyu nianjian 1982–84* 1986, 103). The Chinese Education Union reported that in the first nine months of 1987 there were several hundred reported instances of serious attacks (*ZGJYB*, 31 December 1988).

26. See, for example, *FBIS*, 10 September 1985, K1–8; 11 September 1985, K1–6; and 12 September 1985, K1–5.

Each of these efforts, initiated by the SEdC, has been largely symbolic and used few material resources (although, in the case of teacher awards, the actual recipients do get material benefits). Yet there has clearly been the hope that these symbolic gestures would both placate teachers and remind the general public of the importance of teachers' work. My interviews with teachers suggest, however, that while these symbolic gestures have been somehow comforting to "backbone teachers," they have provided little solace to young teachers and little attraction to people considering teaching (Paine 1987). Teachers interviewed noted both cryptically and cynically that these social reforms were "not hard to carry out."

Political Efforts.   A second area of relatively early attention, often discussed in connection with social efforts, centered around political gestures. These have required the cooperation of a wider range of units and individuals, have ultimately required going beyond symbolic action, and have proven more difficult.

The goal has been to confer political legitimacy on teachers. The two major efforts involve (1) the lending of credibility to the teaching profession and its work by state and Party and (2) the acceptance of teachers into the Party. Within the activities of the state bureaucracy there is evidence of success. Teachers interviewed often cited Teachers' Day, the 1985 National Meeting on the Work of Elementary and Secondary School Teachers, and the transformation of the Ministry of Education into the State Education Commission as important state activity.

A more direct yet less successful attempt to improve the political status of teaching is seen in the efforts to recruit teachers to the Chinese Communist Party. This has occurred as part of the Party's active recruitment of intellectuals (*Jiaoyu gaige* 1986; Zheng Lizhou 1986). Moreover, teachers have been the specific object of recruitment efforts: Party leaders have been urged to go to schools to encourage strong candidates to apply for Party membership. Despite official policy, however, reports indicate that local areas sometimes continue to experience resistance to the political legitimation of teachers. A 1984 study found that 15.7 percent of teachers complained of being denied Party membership after many years of testing, and some schools had stopped recruiting new Party members (He 1985). More recently, inadequate support from the Party was listed as a key concern for 62.5 percent of rural teachers surveyed in Ningxia and Inner Mongolia.[27] The experience of political efforts demonstrates again the SEdC's use of symbolic policy, but the difficulties encountered in implementing nonsymbolic aspects of the policy (such as Party recruitment) illustrate the limits of the SEdC in overseeing compliance.

27. Ma, Wang, and Chen 1987. See, for additional examples, *GMRB*, 25 March 1984; *RMRB*, 10 July 1984; Zu 1985; *Jiaoshibao*, 29 June 1986 and 7 July 1986.

Economic and Material Reforms.   Reforms in this area can be grouped into four major categories: housing, health, family economic security, and income. One notes certain patterns across these: the difficulty the SEdC has had in procuring resources; its tendency therefore to delegate responsibility for these changes to lower levels of authority; and its work to persuade other sectors to take part in these efforts.

Housing shortages in urban China are notorious. Teachers (particularly at the primary and secondary levels) are more vulnerable to this problem than almost any other urban workers, since schools—unlike factories, enterprises, and government offices—typically have not been able to provide dormitory housing for their employees. Researchers in 1985 estimated that nationally 32.3 percent of urban elementary and secondary teachers lacked housing (Li 1985), and in Beijing the principal of a prestigious high school reported that 80 percent of his faculty had housing difficulties ("Zhongxue xiaozhang" 1988). Acute housing problems count as an important reason for the current instability of the teaching force.

Therefore, the central government has encouraged provincial and municipal initiatives to solve the problem. The SEdC has primarily played a facilitating role, with an SEdC vice-minister in 1986 explaining that teachers "need to rely chiefly on local areas" for help (*Jiaoyu Tongxun* 1986, 16). The SEdC organized national meetings to coordinate discussion of teachers' housing problems and publicize local successes (Zhang Hongju 1985, 5–6). There has followed increased provincial and local activity. In one province, an education official interviewed in 1986 illustrated the changes: during a two-year period (1984–86) there was a fourfold increase in funds set aside for housing, with 24 million yuan allocated in 1986. Jinzhou's range of strategies, held up nationally as exemplary, typified many local solutions. These included directing 2 percent of the annual city and town housing investment to construction of housing for elementary and secondary teachers, returning to the provincial BOE (rather than other departments) the housing of teachers who leave, using income from school factories to buy housing, and, in cases of couples where one person is a teacher and the other not, relying on housing allocated to the nonteaching spouse. Nationally, housing problems had been resolved for some 90,000 families of teachers by 1986, but, according to SEdC vice-minister Peng Peiyuan, this was "still very far from what we need" (*Jiaoyu Tongxun* June 1986, 7).

Solutions to the housing problems, like those in Jinzhou, have tended to come from local initiatives and cooperation with noneducation sectors. Bargaining by school leaders with other units has been one important means by which housing (and other problems) of teachers has been addressed. In one instance, for example, high school leaders I interviewed explained that they negotiated with a nearby factory to admit a set number of its workers' children in exchange for construction and money. In another case secondary school administrators agreed to exceed their student enrollment quota to admit, for a fee, local students with lower entrance exam scores. Each "high-priced student" brought 2,000 yuan to the school. In both cases a portion of these earnings was allocated to teachers' housing.

These contractual agreements and informal bargains have been applauded by superiors as examples of how the grass roots can cope with scarcity. They represent some increase in decentralized authority and highlight the value of personalized ties, as well as the tendency for bureaucrats to negotiate in ways that support the needs of their institution. The increase in entrepreneurial solutions to educational problems illustrates the need for negotiation with organizations outside of education and the importance of Party policy in legitimating bureaucratic action. Certainly the heavy engagement of school principals in "creating income" as a solution to teachers' problems is only possible through its congruence with the Party's agenda for national reform.

The issue of health insurance and health care for teachers, in contrast to housing, is more a rural teacher problem, but it has been addressed in much the same way. Teachers hired by the state as public teachers (*gongban jiaoshi*) have the same benefits as employees in Party organs and cadres in enterprises. But *minban* teachers, who are hired by rural communities to work in community-run schools, do not automatically have comparable benefits. For these 3.6 million teachers, the situation is bleakest. Moreover, recent increases in the costs of health care are worrisome for the *minban* teachers, given their lack of guaranteed insurance. The patterns of bureaucratic action are familiar: reforms have been encouraged by the central government, but resources and action are expected to come from local areas.[28]

A third problem for teachers involves family economic security. Teachers, unlike their colleagues in factories and enterprises, have few ways to assure their children of a secure and desirable job. Though the problem is of concern to the SEdC, the commission serves chiefly as an information clearinghouse, spreading "success stories" to help local areas learn how other areas have addressed the problem. An SEdC report claimed that cooperation with the Ministry of Labor and Personnel was needed for more direct action (*Jiaoyu Tongxun*, 10 June 1986).

Finally, and most significant for this discussion, are reforms in wages and bonuses. This issue has been at the heart of discussion concerning

28. See, for example, *Jiaoyu Tongxun*, 10 June 1986, 6; "Liaoning jiejue jiaoshi gongfei yiliao" 1985, 5; "Minban jiaoshi dao gongren yiliaoyuan liaoyang" 1985, 23.

the treatment of teachers. Unlike many other areas, this issue could not be handled with symbolic gestures, the delegation of authority, or the spread of success stories. SEdC efforts alone were insufficient. For wages and bonuses, cooperation with other sectors has been essential.

There has been clear state action in recent years. For most elementary and secondary school teachers, there have been three wage increases in the ten years between 1977 and 1987: in 1977, in 1978, in 1980 or 1981.[29] The 1985 wage-system reform also resulted in higher wages. That reform replaced the previous system, based solely on rank, with a wage structure reflecting the sum of a basic wage, a wage for the years of employment, and a "teacher's years of service" wage, or *jiaoling*, which is money included only in salaries of teachers, computed on the basis of years of service in education.[30] This reform favors job stability for teachers and, in the formal wage structure, rewards teachers over and above other urban or industrial workers. Finally, as in the industrial sector, there has been room for bonuses within schools. While the presence, size, and allocation methods vary greatly by school, my interviews suggest that, in all cases, bonuses are a smaller percentage of the total income for teachers than for industrial workers.

These wage increases, the restructuring, and bonuses represent attempts by the central government to prompt provincial and local governments and schools to improve pay. Nonetheless, the ability of the central education bureaucracy to effect economic improvement for teachers has been very limited, being constrained by the entire national economy. Wage changes for teachers have not kept pace with improvements experienced by workers and, especially in the late 1980s, with inflation. My interviews reveal that teachers were frustrated as their recent wage increases, although ostensibly aimed at redressing inequities, were followed almost immediately by comparable and even greater increases in the wages for workers and others. The official teachers' union journal took a critical stance in assessing the problem: "Generally speaking, the economic and social situation of teachers has continued to rise. . . . But it is still not enough. . . . In recent years when teachers had their salaries

29. Wage increases to teachers have typically been given to categories of teachers, such as all those in a certain grade range ("China Education Almanac" 1986, 90). One can therefore only discuss general trends in teachers' wages. "Generally, salaries were raised by 10 percent in 1977," and most teachers have received two additional increases since then (Cleverly 1985, 225).

30. This seniority bonus, or *gongling*, is worth 0.5 yuan for each year of work, up to a total of 20 yuan, while the *jiaoling* is worth 5 yuan per month for people having taught 5–9 years, 7 yuan for 10–15 years of teaching, and 9 yuan for more than 15 years. Xiang (1989) reports, however, that some provinces have not complied with the policy of distributing *jiaoling*. An SEdC official estimated that the reform in the wage structure produced an average increase of a little less than 23 yuan in teachers' monthly wages.

raised a level, soon after other fields would also raise theirs a level, and the disparity in incomes which had just been reduced was once again created" (Zhu 1985, 20).

In addition, as a Ministry of Education official explained in 1984, "with expanded enterprise autonomy and workers in enterprises having increased bonuses . . . secondary and elementary teachers' salaries have dropped in comparison" (Zhang Wensong 1985, 3). Bonuses in 1986, for example, accounted for 13.4 percent of the total wages of staff and workers in state-owned units, but a 1988 study shows that bonuses contributed only 3.4 percent and 3.2 percent to the average secondary and elementary teacher's income (State Statistical Bureau 1987, 101; Wang 1988). Opportunities for augmenting wages with outside income, one feature of the 1980s reforms, have been quite limited for teachers, with Beijing teachers ranking lowest of twelve occupational groups for outside income generated (Xiang 1989, 15). Workers' income is thus often three times that of teachers (Wei 1985).

The wage changes have also failed to keep pace with inflation. Inflation in the mid and late 1980s cut sharply into increases in allocations to education. One Beijing principal, for example, showed that the 7.3 percent increase in budget allocations to Beijing education and the 7.8 percent increase to Beijing's Xicheng district fell below the official Beijing inflation rate of 8.7 percent, a rate he and others saw as an underestimate ("Zhongxue xiaozhang" 1988, 14). In 1987 the nation's teachers received only a 5.8 percent increase in wages, whereas the industrial workers received 10.8 percent. Teaching's position relative to other occupations remains weak, and inflation contributes to the increasing disparity (ZGJYB, 6 September 1985). "With price increases in recent years the real standard of living of teachers has not only not risen but actually declined" (Yuan 1988, 25). Thus, whatever headway had been made in teachers' living conditions tended to evaporate with the combined impact of inflation and the relative increases in the actual income (wages, bonuses, and outside earnings) of workers in other sectors. A 1987 report found the average income of teachers ranking eleventh out of twelve occupations (Yuan 1988, 25).

It was not until late in 1987 that the SEdC was able to work out an agreement with other ministries that would allow a teacher-specific wage hike, this time for 10 percent across the board for teachers. The story of that wage hike, the most significant act in the ten-year history of the government's efforts to improve teachers' lives, indicates the high level of dependence of the SEdC on the cooperation of other sectors. Through long years of persuasion, the SEdC was able to achieve its objective, which, ironically, was announced in the name of another ministry (the Ministry of Labor). As one SEdC official explained, it was the

SEdC that called for the wage hike, but it did not have the power to do this on its own. Rather, they had to approach the Ministries of Finance and Labor, who agreed. Together they wrote the proposal for submission to the State Council. This project took about half a year's work, "since people agreed" on it.[31] The problem was not agreement about need, but resources—could the Finance Ministry get the money?

Several conditions appear to have contributed to the SEdC's apparent speed in bringing about the agreement on 10 percent wage increase. Together they created a "policy window" of opportunity that allowed the SEdC to get agreement on the salary raise (Kingdon 1984). First, as an SEdC official I interviewed implied, the Finance Ministry had to be convinced that there were sufficient resources. Second, social campaigns and partially successful political reforms had done little to solve the problem of teachers' conditions. The inadequacy of these symbolic actions made clearer teachers' demands. Further, it is likely that the persistence of frustration among teachers about wages, the increasing sense of relative deprivation, and the subsequent attrition problem all contributed to the sense that this raise was necessary. The passing of the "Education Decision" and the Compulsory Education Law (with its scheduled deadlines) added legitimacy, specificity, and pressure to the need to raise teachers' salaries. Finally, that the education reforms (and, indirectly, much of the modernization drive) hinge on getting and keeping good teachers at their jobs gave urgency to the policy. There was a policy fit with the national mood and agenda.

The change in wage-increase policy is significant for what it tells us of the SEdC's need to seek alliances and to persuade other ministries, particularly those with resources. Like the teacher-standards issue, policy regarding teachers' conditions shows the value of piggybacking on other important reforms and being perceived as pivotal to their success. But the policy change is also important for what it may suggest about the ability of constituents to plead their case or apply pressure from the grass roots—even if through negative action.

31. The apparent agreement met by this decision has not been as solid as the interviewee suggested. By the end of June 1988 the wage increase had still not been implemented in many places; only sixteen provinces, autonomous regions, and municipalities had promulgated specific regulations for implementing the increase (*ZGJYB*, 7 July 1988, 1). According to one educator, disagreement includes an initial controversy within the State Council on the ways in which the money would be distributed. While the SEdC approach, which eventually won out, favored an even 10 percent hike across the board for all teachers, the Ministry of Labor argued (unsuccessfully) for a 10 percent hike that could be distributed unevenly to compensate for previous inequities. Although the SEdC version of the wage hike became official policy, the actual implementation of the salary increases has gotten caught in discussions at the provincial level, for it is the provinces who ultimately take responsibility for the increases.

Finally, the story of the teachers' wage increase may tell us more of the education bureaucracy's failures and limitations than it does of its success—the wage increase may simply be one more symbolic gesture. Announced in 1987, the distribution of the increase by late 1988 was still being hammered out in provincial and county-level debates (*ZGJYB*, 6 September 1988). Moreover, basing the increase on a percentage of an already low wage is little solace too late for most teachers. Given inflation rates of that year (the year of China's steepest price increases since 1949, with food costs in large cities rising 20–30 percent) the 1987 raise represents an actual decline in standard of living (He 1987). And with provincial-level delays in the increase being distributed to teachers, the actual value of the increase has declined further.

SUMMARY AND NEW DIRECTIONS FOR EDUCATION POLICY

The process of educational policy moves in a constrained, iterative fashion. It is an interactive process vertically and one that requires intersectoral cooperation. For the education bureaucracy, symbolic action is clearly the easiest to provide. For many other issues, a piecemeal incrementalist approach that delegates much responsibility to local levels must do. The management of teachers' housing problems and the establishment of teacher-preparation curricula are examples of this. In the most important cases, however, these strategies have proven insufficient. To raise teachers' salaries, as we saw, the SEdC had to wait for the right moment in terms of fiscal resources and national agendas. At that point, with an open policy window, the symbolism, public concern, and submerged professional protests worked together to thrust forward the issue of teachers' wages. Even with this, only partial success was possible.

Consensus building, negotiation, and persuasion are central features of much of the education policy process, yet they take different forms, depending on whether bureaucratic interaction occurs within the education system or across sectors. The vertical connections within the system are such that teacher policy is negotiated and defined through a process of local-Center interaction and mutual adaptation. Connections to national agendas or other education reforms speed the process of policy implementation locally. At the same time, local experimentation, interpretation, and contradictions eventually shape the SEdC's view of appropriate practice.

If the loose coupling within the education bureaucracy gives a distinctive cast and pace to educational change, cross-sector negotiation represents horizontal connections and characterizes the formation of major education policies. Because it is not a productive, income-generating ministry, the SEdC has to turn elsewhere for resources. In general, the education bureaucracy has little to bring to the negotiating table. It must forge alliances with more powerful actors. The case of teacher salaries suggests that there are some forms of persuasion available to education, though they are slow to be expressed. While the education bureaucracy had little clout with which to influence other ministries, unorganized but persistent signs of a grass-roots boycott (through teacher attrition and the withholding of their labor) may have lent persuasive pressure to the discussion of teachers' wages.

The teacher policy case suggests several ways that the education bureaucracy copes. In the past, this bureaucracy has relied heavily on symbolic action. This is dangerous, inasmuch as people will only accept symbols for a finite period. One new strategy, however, focuses on education itself as a valuable commodity. In today's negotiations the resource that education can call on is the service it provides. In the late 1980s the Party's emphasis on scientific and technological development added to education's prestige, and changes in the bureaucracy and society began to create a credential market with tighter links between education and the labor market. As a result, at the level of the individual consumer (the student or parent), education has come to be seen as a form of investment in human capital. For the present, education, though still a weak bureaucratic actor, is enjoying a favorable moment.

An important consequence of education's new exchange value is the recent trend of the educational bureaucracy and its institutions to highlight and rely on economic activity. It is likely that current patterns we observe today will continue in ways that strengthen ties between educational institutions and enterprises.[32] With little inherent financial clout or productive capacity, the education bureaucracy can now gain some internal leverage through lucrative arrangements with factories and enterprises. For educational institutions this has become a significant way to augment state support and offers one avenue for local solutions to policy problems (like teachers' welfare). Education institutions such as schools or local (or provincial) education authorities can bargain with other (noneducation) units for exchanges that benefit their own constituencies and organizational interests; training can be offered in exchange for fees, goods, or services. Within the education system the resources that these cross-sector negotiations make possible alter the landscape in varied ways and reshape the traditional divisions of power. Already it is clear that some local units benefit from these bargaining possibilities more than others (since they are able to strike bargains their counterparts cannot), and some local units therefore now can be less reliant on or more persuasive with superordi-

32. See, as recent examples, stories about the enterprising activities of institutions as chronicled in *ZGJYB*, 10 October 1987, 1; 26 October 1987, 3; 17 December 1987, 3; 4 August 1988, 1; and *FBIS*, 5 April 1988, 34.

nate bureaucratic organizations than they had been previously. The basic entrepreneurial principles underlying these new strategies in cross-sector work have been endorsed by the SEdC (*ZGJYB*, 4 August 1987, 1). At the same time, education institutions have been warned against becoming an "economic center" (*jingji zhongxin*) by chasing after funds.[33]

It is this tension between looking for sources of power and staying within acceptable boundaries that characterizes much of the education bureaucracy's behavior. Anthony Downs talks about the crucial influence of the "power setting" (1967, 44). The case of education reveals the powerful role of the Party in delineating the boundaries of the acceptable. Education's relative position is greatly influenced by the Party agenda. The SEdC does not have autonomy in setting the direction of education policy but reflects instead broad goals outlined by the Party. In the late 1980s the education sector had greater autonomy, allowed for wider experimentation, relied more on expertise, and encouraged greater fiscal independence than previously. Yet these developments were only made possible by Party-approved policies. While the case studies demonstrate an interactive process of policy change, the education bureaucracy remains a vulnerable actor in a complex political landscape. Given the power of the framework surrounding the policy process, education therefore remains weak in ways that force it, both horizontally and vertically, to be responsive, flexible, and active in forging compromises.

REFERENCES

Behn, Robert D. 1988. "Management by Groping Along." *Journal of Policy Analysis and Management* 7:643–63.

Cai Bangcui. 1985. "Sichuan caiqu shiji cuoshi qingzhu jiaoshijie" (Sichuan takes concrete steps to celebrate Teachers' Day). *Shifan Jiaoyu* (October), 8.

Chen Siyi. 1988. "Zhongxue jingfei he shizi duanque youwu chulu" (Are there solutions to secondary school funding and teacher shortage problems?). *Liaowang* 32:30–31.

"China Education Almanac." 1986. *Chinese Education* (Fall): 7–111.

Cleverley, John. 1985. *The Schooling of China.* Sydney: George Allen and Unwin.

Cohen, Michael D., James March, and Johan P. Olsen. 1972. "A Garbage Can Model of Organizational Choice." *Administrative Science Quarterly* 17 (March): 1–25.

Cui Yangshu. 1979. "Tuchu shifan jiaoyu tedian tigao shifan jiaoyu zhiliang" (Make prominent the special characteristic of teacher education and raise the quality of teacher education). In *Banhao Shifan Jiaoyu Fazhan Jiaoyu Kexue*, edited by Quanguo Jiaoyuxue Yanjiuhui, 28–40. Beijing: Renmin Jiaoyu Chubanshe.

---

33. This caution was raised, for instance in a 1985 report of the CPPCC ("Zhengxie diaochazu tan gaoxiao gaige" 1985).

Deng Liqun. 1983. "Gaohao shifan jiaoyu shi fazhan putong jiaoyu de diyiwei gongzuo" (Doing a good job of teacher education is first priority work for developing precollegiate education). *Guangming Ribao*, 1 December, 1.

Deng Xiaoping. 1983. *Deng Xiaoping wenxuan* (The collected works of Deng Xiaoping). Beijing: Renmin chubanshe.

Department of Planning, Ministry of Education. 1984. *Zhongguo jiaoyu chengjiu 1949–83* (Achievements of education in China 1949–83). Beijing: Renmin jiaoyu chubanshe.

Downs, Anthony. 1967. *Inside Bureaucracy*. Boston: Little, Brown.

Foreign Broadcast Information Service Daily Report: China (FBIS).

Gao Yi. 1980. "Banhao shifan jiaoyu tigao shizi shuiping wei sihua jianshe peiyang rencai zuochu gongxian" (Run normal education well, raise the level of teachers, train talent to make a contribution toward the construction of the four modernizations). *Jiaoyu Yanjiu* 4:6–12.

"Gaodeng shifan jiaoyu ruhe shiying shehui zhuyi jianshe shiye de fazhan" (How tertiary teacher education can adjust to the development of socialist construction). 1987. *Shida Zhoubao* (Beijing Normal University), 4 December, 2.

Guangming Ribao (GMRB).

Gu Mingyuan. 1982. "Jiaqiang shifan jiaoyu shi fazhan jiaoyu shiye de genben" (Strengthening teacher education is basic to developing education). *Jiaoyu Yanjiu* 11:37–40.

———. 1983a. "Gaige shifan jiaoyu de jidian yijian" (Several opinions on the reform of teacher education). *Guangming Ribao*, 2 December, 3.

———. 1983b. "Jiaqiang shifan jiaoyu shi kaichuang jiaoyu xin jumian de tupokou" (Strengthening teacher education makes a breakthrough for initiating a new situation of education). *Guangming Ribao*, 4 November, 3.

Guojia jiaowei yaoqiu dali fazhan he jiaqiang shifan jiaoyu" (SEdC calls for major development and strengthening in teacher education). 1986. *Renmin Jiaoyu* 6:9.

Gustafson, Thane. 1981. *Reform in Soviet Politics*. New York: Cambridge University Press.

He Bin. 1985. "Dui jiaoshi de kunnan yu xuyao de diaocha fenxi" (A survey and analysis of teachers' troubles and needs). *Jiaoyu Lilun yu Shijian* 1:16–22.

He Daofeng, Duan Yingbi, Yuan Zongfa. 1987. "Lun woguo tonghuo pengzhang de fasheng jizhi he jiegou biaoxian" (On the development mechanism and structural manifestation of our country's recent inflation). *Jingji Yanjiu* 1: 21–28.

Jiaoshibao (Teachers' News).

Jiaoyu gaige zhongyaowenxian xuanbian. 1986. Beijing: Renmin jiaoyu chubanshe.

Jiaoyu Tongxun (Education Bulletin).

Jiningshi jiaoyuju. 1985. "Ruhe xuanpei he tigao nongye jishu zhongxue de zhuanye jiaoshi" (Selecting and improving specialized teachers for technical agricultural secondary schools). *Zhiye Jiaoyu Yanjiu* 3:34–36.

Kingdon, John W. 1984. *Agendas, Alternatives, and Public Policies*. Boston: Little, Brown.

Li Kegang. 1985. "Lun jiaoshi de laodong baochou" (On teachers' work rewards). *Jiaoyu yu Jingji* 1:34–37, 46.

"Liaoning jiejue jiaoshi gongfei yiliao baogan wenti" (Liaoning solves the problem of responsibility for teachers' health insurance). 1985. *Jiaogong Yuekan* 10:5.

Lindblom, Charles. 1959. "The Science of 'Muddling Through.' " *Public Administration Review* 19 (Spring): 79–88.

Liu Bin. 1986. "Jiaqiang hongguan guanli tigao jiaoyu zhiliang" (Strengthen macro management, raise the quality of education). *Renmin Jiaoyu* 1:5–8.

Ma Denghai, Wang He, and Chen Wentai. 1987. "Nongcun zhongxiaoxue jiaoshi jingsheng yu wuzhi xuyao de diaocha" (A survey of the spiritual and material needs of rural elementary and secondary school teachers). *Ningxia Jiaoyu Xueyuan Xuebao* 1:31–34.

"Minban jiaoshi dao gongren yiliaoyuan liaoyang" (Locally hired teacher goes to convalesce at workers' sanitorium). 1985. *Jiaogong Yuekan* 9:23.

Paine, Lynn. 1986. "Reform and Balance in Chinese Teacher Education." Ph.D. diss., Stanford University, Stanford, California.

———. 1987. "Lessons from Rapid Reform: The Changing Context of China's Teaching Profession." Paper presented at the annual meeting of the American Educational Research Association, Washington, D.C.

"Quanguo gaodeng shifan jiaoyu yanjiuhui zai woxiao juxing chenglihui" (Inaugural meeting of national tertiary teacher education research association held at our school). 1987. *Shida Zhoubao* (Beijing Normal University), 27 November, 1. *Renmin Ribao (RMRB)*.

Rosen, Stanley. 1985. "Recentralization, Decentralization, and Rationalization: Deng Xiaoping's Bifurcated Educational Policy." *Modern China* (July): 301–46.

State Statistical Bureau. 1987. *China: A Statistical Survey in 1987.* Beijing: New World Press and China Statistical Information and Consultancy Service Centre.

Tan Renmei. 1983. "Jiji kaichuang shifan jiaoyu yanjiu de xin jumian" (Actively create a new situation in teacher education research). *Shifan Jiaoyu Yanjiu* 1:18–22.

Wang Li. 1988. "Lun jiaoshi laodong baochang" (On compensation for teachers' labor). *Zhongguo shehui kexue* 4:83–95.

Wei Dianhua. 1985. "Qieshi tigao zhongxue jiaoshi de shehui diwei" (Raising secondary school teachers' social status). *Jiaoyu Yanjiu* 1:17–21.

Xiang Yaonan. 1989. "Dui jiaoshi gongzi zhidu gaige de yixie shexiang" (Reflections on the reform of the wage system for teachers). *Jiaoyu Yanjiu* 2:15–17.

Xue Daohua. 1986. "Shifan yuanxiao zhaosheng tiqian dandu luquhao" (A separate early admissions for teacher-training institutions is good). *Gaojiao Zhanxian* 5:34–35.

"Yao zhuajin jichu jiaoyu de shizi duiwu jianshe" (Work on the development of teachers for basic education). 1986. *Renmin Jiaoyu* 1:2–3.

Yuan Liansheng. 1988. "Lun woguo jiaoyu jingji kuique" (On the shortage of China's educational funds). *Jiaoyu Yanjiu* 7:23–26, 31.

Zhang Chengxian. 1986. " 'Yiwujiaoyufa' biaoshi woguo jichu jiaoyu jinru le xinde lishi jieduan" (The Compulsory Education Act: Symbol of a new historical phase in the development of basic education in China). *Jiaoyu Yanjiu* 6:3–5.

Zhang Hongju. 1985. "Jiejue jiaoshi zhufang wenti dayou xiwang" (Great hopes for solving teachers' housing problems). *Renmin Jiaoyu* 2:5–6.

Zhang Wensong. 1985. "Lingdao zhongshe tongyi renshi gefang zhichi zuzhi luoshi" (Leaders have a united view on various sides' supporting and carrying out the organizational policy). *Renmin Jiaoyu* 2:3.

Zheng Guanjian. 1984. "Wending jiaoshiduiwu de yixiang genbenxing cuoshi" (A basic measure to stabilize the teaching force). *Liaoning Shida Xuebao* 6:25–30.

Zheng Lizhou. 1986. "Integration with Intellectuals Should also Be Advocated." From *Renmin Ribao* 8 January 1983. In *Policy Conflicts in Post-Mao China*, edited by John Burns and Stanley Rosen, 129–32. Armonk, N.Y.: M. E. Sharpe.

"Zhengxie diaochazu tan gaoxiao gaige" (CPPCC investigation group discusses higher education reform). 1985. From *Renmin Zhengxie*, 22 January 1985. In *Jiaoyu Wenzhai* 5:2.

Zhishifenzi Wenti Wenxian Xuanbian (Selected Documents on the Problems of Intellectuals). 1983. Edited by the Central Committee Document Research Section. Beijing: Renmin Chubanshe.

"Zhonggong Shandongshengwei Shandongsheng renmin zhengfu guanyu biaoyang Pingduxian fazhan jiaoyu shiye wei jingji jianshe fuwu de jueding" (The decision of the Shandong Province Party Committee and the Shandong Province People's Government to commend Pingdu County on developing education to serve economic construction). 1988. *Shandong Jiaoyu* 6:2.

Zhongguo Jiaoyubao (ZGJYB).

Zhongguo jiaoyu nianjian 1949–1981. 1984. Edited by the Chinese Education Yearbook Editorial Group. Beijing: Zhongguo dabaike quanshu chubanshe.

Zhongguo jiaoyu nianjian 1982–84. 1986. Edited by the Chinese Education Yearbook Editorial Group. Changsha: Hunan jiaoyu chubanshe.

Zhongguo shehui tongji ziliao 1987. 1987. Edited by the State Statistical Bureau Social Statistics Section. Beijing: Zhongguo tongji chubanshe.

"Zhonghua renmin gongheguo yiwu jiaoyufa" (The compulsory education law of the People's Republic of China). 1986. *Renmin Jiaoyu* 5:2–3.

"Zhongxue xiaozhang zuotanhui" (Secondary school headmasters' panel discussion). 1988. *Keji Daobao* 5:22–24. In *Fuyin Baokan Ziliao* G3, 11:13–18.

Zhou Ning. 1985. "Jiejue shizi wenti de jianyi" (Suggestions on solving the teacher problem). *Zhiye Jiaoyu Yanjiu* 6:27–28.

Zhu Yuanxing. 1985. "Yao tigao jiaoshi jingji daiyu he shehui diwei" (Teachers' economic and social position needs improvement). *Jiaogong Yuekan* 2:20–23.

Zu Shanji. 1985. " 'Zuo' de pianjian neng kefu jiaoshi rudang jiu bu nan" (If the "leftist" influence can be overcome, it will be easy for teachers to join the Party). *Jiaogong Yuekan* 2:8–9.

EIGHT

The Behavior of Middlemen in the Cadre Retirement Policy Process

Melanie Manion

In the decade since 1978 top leaders in Beijing have introduced policies that seem to mandate important changes in virtually every issue area. Policy outcomes vary widely. Many policies have failed to produce the prescribed levels of change, and some have failed even to produce change in the prescribed directions. What accounts for such differences in the transformation of policies into actions? Taking their cues from work on implementation in developed and other developing countries, studies of post-Mao reform have described the twists and turns of policy that occur after its formulation and have suggested a number of explanations.[1] This chapter builds on those case studies that investigate the behaviors of different individuals and organizations and extrapolate to the Chinese policy process generally and, often less explicitly, to relations of authority in the Chinese bureaucracy.

One line of argument focuses on behaviors of the policy-making elite. Rosen's study of the policy to restore key secondary schools after 1976 points to a leadership divided on basic developmental strategies as the

I am particularly grateful to the following conference participants for their helpful comments on an earlier version of this chapter: Nina Halpern, Ken Jowitt, David Lampton, Kenneth Lieberthal, Michel Oksenberg, Susan Shirk, and Andrew Walder. The Joint Committee on Chinese Studies of the American Council of Learned Societies and Social Science Research Council funded the research I conducted in the People's Republic of China in 1986–87. The Dean's Office of the Rackham School of Graduate Studies of the University of Michigan provided funding for a second trip in 1988.

1. See, for example, the chapters in Elizabeth J. Perry and Christine Wong, eds., *The Political Economy of Reform in Post-Mao China* (Cambridge: Council on East Asian Studies of Harvard University, 1985); and see especially David M. Lampton, ed., *Policy Implementation in Post-Mao China* (Berkeley and Los Angeles: University of California Press, 1987).

main explanation for how the policy was implemented. The original policy had built-in contradictions, reflecting conflict between the goals of popularization and the raising of standards in education. Policy implementation was similarly conflictual, until the political conflict at the top was resolved in favor of the reformers.[2] Solinger's work on the attempt to use price controls in 1980–81 also emphasizes elite divisions. Policymakers disagreed about the extent of inflation and about how to deal with it. Even after the decision was reached to enforce a price freeze, leadership differences persisted. These differences were reflected in policy directives and accompanying documents. Lower levels reacted differently to the signs of elite discord, and the result was great variation in local implementation.[3] Lampton also finds disagreement at the top in his study of long-range water policies. He focuses less on the conflicts than on the process for resolving them—consensus building. Lampton documents the extensive consultation and negotiation that policymakers promoted and tolerated in a quest for consensus. This consensus orientation and the large number of players that were involved in the wrangling over solutions ultimately resulted in ineffective implementation.[4]

Another set of explanations focuses on behaviors of the ultimate targets of policy. Naughton examines the post-1978 effort to reduce the share of decentralized investment and finds that the localities thwarted this effort by consistently deflecting central-government decisions toward their own interests. They implemented policies selectively, taking an active stance only toward policies that gave them a greater degree of control over resources. The result of this pragmatic approach to policy implementation was persistent overfulfillment of the decentralized investment plan.[5] Walder describes successful efforts by workers to resist wage and incentive policies in state enterprises in 1978–82. Workers withdrew efficiency in the face of attempts to increase productivity through higher work norms and performance-based bonuses and wage raises. Managers responded to the efforts by workers to defend their interests. For example, they distributed as bonuses the maximum amount permitted by policy and relaxed the link between performance

2. Stanley Rosen, "Restoring Key Secondary Schools in Post-Mao China: The Politics of Competition and Educational Quality," in *Policy Implementation in Post-Mao China*, ed. Lampton, 321–53.

3. Dorothy J. Solinger, "The 1980 Inflation and the Politics of Price Control in the PRC," in Lampton, *Policy*, 81–118.

4. David M. Lampton, "Water: Challenge to a Fragmented Political System," in Lampton, *Policy*, 157–89.

5. Barry Naughton, "The Decline of Central Control over Investment in Post-Mao China," in Lampton, *Policy*, 51–80.

and reward. This diverted policy from its original goals and affected the outcome of the industrial reform program.[6]

The analysis presented in this chapter investigates variation across time in the transformation of one policy into actions and finds evidence of the influences reviewed above: underlying leadership conflict, unwillingness or inability to impose solutions on subordinates, a selective approach to policies, and pressure at the grass roots. Analytically, it links up explanations that give priority to policymakers at the top and those that pay more attention to policy targets at the bottom. I situate the analytical perspective between top and bottom in the policy process by asking about the behavior of middlemen—the individuals and organizations charged with implementing policy. Investigating the policy process from this perspective proves useful, not only because middlemen are major players in the process but also because it requires an explicit consideration of the relative effects on policy outcomes of those at the top and bottom.

My specific empirical focus is implementation of cadre retirement policy—the policy to institute regular retirement of political and administrative functionaries, professionals, and specially skilled personnel.[7] The time period is 1978, when the policy was introduced, through 1986, a period in which policy outcomes varied significantly and intelligibly. Briefly, in 1978–81 cadre retirement was a policy that did not yield results, essentially because it was not implemented; beginning in 1982, cadre retirement policy began actually to be implemented, but not without serious deviations. I organize my analysis around three simple questions about middlemen in the cadre retirement policy process. Why did they effectively ignore policy for more than three years? What caused them ultimately to begin to implement policy? And what explains their choice to deviate from official policy in the course of implementing it?

I find that three factors help explain why cadre retirement was a policy without action implications in 1978–81. First, middlemen confronted conflicting signals from policymakers, reflecting a lack of consensus at the top. Second, middlemen were charged with executing a policy of cadre restoration that in practice contradicted retirement policy and gave them a legitimate alternative to retiring cadres. And third, retire-

6. Andrew G. Walder, "Communist Social Structure and Workers' Politics in China," in *Citizens and Groups in Contemporary China*, ed. Victor C. Falkenheim (Ann Arbor: Center for Chinese Studies of the University of Michigan, 1987), 45–90.

7. The Chinese have defined cadres in different ways, and definitions have changed over time. A recent Ministry of Labor and Personnel publication on labor and personnel statistics provides a very clear definition for the compilation of statistics. See Laodong renshi bu ganbu jiaoyu ju, ed., *Laodong renshi tongjixue* (Beijing: Laodong renshi chubanshe, 1985), 111–29.

ment policy did not contain objective decision criteria such as mandated retirement ages to constrain middlemen to take action. A formal revision of policy in 1982 changed this situation. As a result, middlemen began then to implement policy. Policymakers revised cadre retirement policy in ways that both encouraged and constrained middlemen to implement it and made it easier to implement. The Party organization joined the government in support of the policy, sending a single clear signal to middlemen in place of previous conflicting signals. The policy of restoring veteran cadres to power was dropped and was replaced with campaigns to streamline bureaucracies and rejuvenate leading groups. Both campaigns had objectives that were consistent with those of cadre retirement policy. Policymakers constrained middlemen to implement policy by making age the basic criterion for retirement decisions and by specifying ages of retirement for all cadres. And policymakers changed the incentive structure, to make retirement more attractive to cadres. This made retirement policy easier to implement.

Middlemen implemented policy, but not without serious deviations. The nature of those deviations provides insight into their underlying cause: deviations consisted of increasing incentives for cadres to retire. Middlemen thus proved to be unwilling or unable to implement policy successfully without providing a retirement deal better than that stipulated in official policy. In implementing policy, they proved keenly responsive to policy targets at the grass roots, as well as to policymakers at the top.

These answers suggest some tentative conclusions about the actual consequences of the formal structure of bureaucratic authority and about the constraints and incentives not represented in that organizational design. I discuss those conclusions and consider their generalizability in the final section of the chapter.

SOURCES

The information in this chapter derives mainly from the following sources: collections of official documents, a self-administered questionnaire distributed to retired cadres, interviews with retired cadres, interviews with younger cadres, and interviews with government leaders.[8]

Of official documents consulted, the most useful were those reproduced in two collections of Party and government documents on veteran cadre work, published by the Central Organization Department and the

---

8. For a more thoroughgoing discussion of sources and methods I employed in researching cadre retirement, see M. Manion, "Building a Norm: Cadre Retirement in the People's Republic of China, Post-Mao" (Ph.D. diss., University of Michigan, 1989).

Ministry of Labor and Personnel in 1983 and 1986.[9] These constitute my main source of information about formal policy. I also obtained some such information in interviews with government officials in charge of cadre retirement policy in 1986 and 1988.

Interviews with retired cadres and younger cadres supplied useful information on how retirement policy was implemented at the workplace. I conducted thirty-six loosely structured interviews with retired cadres in Beijing in 1986–87. I also conducted structured interviews with a class of seventy-one younger cadres at Beijing University in 1988. They had been sent by their workplaces, representing nearly every province in the country, to obtain college equivalence in a special two-year course of cadre training.

In addition, I arranged for the distribution in 1987 of questionnaires containing closed-category items only, to a larger sample, consisting of all retired cadres in a small city in the northeast. A total of 250 questionnaires were completed and returned, an acceptable response rate of 38 percent. These questionnaires were an additional source of information on how policy was implemented.

PLAYERS AND ORGANIZATIONAL CONTEXT

Cadre retirement policy aimed to retire nearly 2.5 million surviving veteran cadres, revolutionaries who had joined the Communists during the wars of 1924–49.[10] It also aimed to replace an existing de facto lifelong tenure system for cadres with a regular retirement system. Consequently, veteran cadres were the immediate but not the only targets of retirement policy. Postrevolutionaries, those who had become cadres after the Communist victory in 1949, were also affected. Among them were 2,353,000 cadres who had been recruited in 1950–52,[11] many of whom were in their fifties when cadre retirement policy was introduced. These two groups, veteran revolutionaries and cadre recruits of the early 1950s, constituted the most important targets of cadre retirement policy.

9. *Lao ganbu gongzuo wenjian xuanbian*, vols. 1 and 2 (Beijing: Zhonggong zhongyang zuzhi bu lao ganbu ju laodong renshi bu lao ganbu fuwu ju, 1983 and 1986). Cited hereafter as *Gongzuo wenjian*, vols. 1 and 2. These sources are internal (*neibu*).

10. Of these, 10,000 were veterans of the Revolutionary Civil Wars (1924–27 and 1927–37), 300,000 were veterans of the Anti-Japanese War (1937–45), and 2,190,000 were veterans of the War of Liberation (1945–49). See "Selecting Young Cadres for Leading Posts," *Beijing Review* 24, no. 31 (1981): 3.

11. U.S. Department of Commerce, Bureau of Economic Analysis, Foreign Demographic Analysis Division, *Administrative and Technical Manpower in the People's Republic of China*, by John Philip Emerson, International Population Reports Series P-95, no. 72 (Washington, D.C.: Government Printing Office, 1973), 37. Obviously, not all 2,353,000 were postrevolutionaries; probably many had joined the Communists before victory in 1949 but had been recruited as cadres only after the Communists gained national power.

Middlemen in the cadre retirement policy process are defined here as people and organizations charged with executing the policy formulated at the top. These range from local governments that promulgated local regulations on cadre retirement to functionaries at the lowest level of the workplace who were charged with processing retirements. Their actions make more sense in the context of two features of the formal structure of authority: the differences between territorially based organizations and functional departments, and the exceptional Party domination of the issue area in which cadre retirement falls.

In the case studied here, as in many other issue areas, authority is formally structured in two separate hierarchies of territorially based organizations and two functional hierarchies. Both kinds of hierarchies have organizations at the top in Beijing and down to the county level. There are two of each kind of hierarchy because at each level are parallel Party and government organizations.

The key differences between the territorially based organizations and the functional departments are the span of authority and the nature of authority relations. The authority of territorially based organizations, the Party committees and governments at the various levels, extends to more than simply the cadre issue in territory at and below their respective levels.[12] This span of authority over many issues is reflected in the relation between a territorially based organization and the functional department responsible for cadres, in the Party or government hierarchy at any given level: the functional department is subordinate to the territorially based organization in a "relation of leadership" (lingdao guanxi), the most authoritative type of linkage between Chinese organizations. The relation between territorially based organizations at different levels of the hierarchy is also one of leadership. By contrast, the authority of functional departments spans separate, broadly defined issue areas which in principle do not overlap. The relation between superior and subordinate organizations in the functional hierarchy dealing with cadres is one of "professional guidance" (yewu zhidao), a relation more circumscribed than that of leadership.

Cadre retirement is one issue within the area defined as part of the organization-personnel "system" (xitong). This system is virtually solely responsible for all cadre work—which includes recruitment, staffing, training and education, various forms of assessment, and maintenance

---

12. Authority over the cadre issue is not to be confused with authority to approve appointments, promotions, transfers, and removals. The latter kind of authority belongs to the Party committee, and it extends to cadres at the next subordinate level. See M. Manion, "The Cadre Management System, Post-Mao: The Appointment, Promotion, Transfer and Removal of Party and State Leaders," *China Quarterly*, no. 102 (1985): 203–33; and John P. Burns, "China's *Nomenklatura* System," *Problems of Communism* 36, no. 5 (1987): 36–51.

of personnel dossiers.[13] The main Party organizations in the system are the organization departments at the various levels; their government counterparts are the personnel departments.[14]

Barnett in 1967 identified the system as the most important of the key "watchdog" mechanisms for ensuring Party leadership.[15] More recent studies concur with this view. The post-Mao trend in many issue areas has been toward a retreat of Party organizations from routine work, along with a decentralization of authority and the granting of more autonomy to government organizations in the conduct of administrative work. In the organization-personnel system, authority has been substantially decentralized. However, Party organizations continue to dominate even the day-to-day work.[16]

Within the organization-personnel system, the issue of cadre retirement is particularly important and, perhaps as a consequence, particularly dominated by the Party. This is revealed most clearly in the elaboration of structures to manage cadre retirement.[17] These are indicated in figure 8.1.

13. See M. Manion, "Cadre Recruitment and Management in the People's Republic of China," *Chinese Law and Government* 17, no. 3 (1984); Manion, "The Cadre Management System"; and Burns, "China's *Nomenklatura* System."

14. The Party organizations for managing personnel have been the same since 1949. Government organizations have been rearranged several times, five times in the post-Mao period alone. In 1978–80 the top government personnel organization was the Government Organs Personnel Bureau in the Ministry of Civil Affairs; in 1980–82 it was combined with the State Council Small Group Office on Settlement of Demobilized Military Personnel to form the State Personnel Bureau; in 1982 this bureau was combined with the General Labor Bureau, the Bureau of Scientific and Technical Cadres, and the State Establishment (*bianzhi*) Commission to form the Ministry of Labor and Personnel; and in 1984 the Bureau of Scientific and Technical Cadres was placed under the State Science and Technology Commission. See Cao Zhi, ed., *Zhonghua renmin gongheguo renshi zhidu gaiyao* (Beijing: Beijing daxue chubanshe, 1985), 426–32. This source is internal. The Ministry of Labor and Personnel was reseparated into two separate ministries at the First Session of the Seventh National People's Congress in March 1988.

15. A. Doak Barnett, *Cadres, Bureaucracy, and Political Power in Communist China* (New York: Columbia University Press, 1967), 20.

16. Manion, "Cadre Recruitment and Management" and "The Cadre Management System"; and Burns, "China's *Nomenklatura* System." Burns's recent study of the reforms proposed by the Thirteenth Party Congress (convened in November 1987) concludes that Party dominance is likely to change but not diminish in a significant way; see "Civil Service Reform in Post-Mao China," *Australian Journal of Chinese Affairs*, no. 18:47–84.

17. Documents calling for the assignment of personnel to manage veteran cadres and the establishment of specialized structures were issued as early as December 1978. See Some Views of the Central Organization Department on Strengthening Veteran Cadre Work (29 Dec. 1978), in *Gongzuo wenjian*, vol. 1, 80–88; State Council Temporary Regulations on Veteran Cadre Special Retirement (*lixiu*) (7 Oct. 1980), in *Gongzuo wenjian*, vol. 1, 32–36; Central Organization Department, Suggestions on Appropriate Handling of Veteran Cadres Who Have Stepped Down from Positions (2 June 1982), in *Gongzuo wenjian*, vol. 1, 192–95; Central Organization Department and Ministry of Labor and Personnel,

The importance of cadre retirement is evident in the status of veteran cadre departments at the provincial, prefectural, and county levels: the departments are not subordinate to the organization departments at the respective levels, but rather are equal to them in bureaucratic status. The organization departments relate to parallel veteran cadre departments by giving professional guidance. The Party committees exercise direct leadership over veteran cadre departments. Only at the top level is the Veteran Cadre Bureau a subordinate department of the Central Organization Department.

Party dominance is indicated by the virtual absence, until about ten years after the first regulation on cadre retirement was issued, of specialized structures for cadre retirement in the government hierarchy, except at the top level. As late as 1986, government organizations usually attended to cadre retirement work by assigning responsibility to one leading cadre in each of the personnel departments at the provincial, prefectural, and county levels. These cadres worked in coordination with the Party veteran cadre departments parallel to their personnel departments.[18]

Institutional arrangements for cadre retirement at the workplace have tended to depend on workplace size and the number of retired cadres. National and provincial departments have either bureau-level veteran cadre departments or division-level departments under the organizations (usually the organization department) responsible for cadre work. Smaller and lower-level workplaces do not usually have specialized structures for cadre retirement. Rather, this work is carried out by the Party and government cadres or organizations responsible for cadre work.[19]

What did this context mean for middlemen in the cadre retirement policy process? Those at the workplace were responsible for implementing a large number of policies in the organization-personnel system, and cadre retirement represented only one task among many. Those tasks were not always mutually complementary; in cases of policy conflict, middlemen had to choose which policies to implement and which to ignore effectively. Many factors determined how middlemen responded to this choice. Party domination of cadre management dictated greater

---

Trial Measures on Scope of Responsibility of Veteran Cadre Bureaus (and Divisions) in State Council and Central Committee Organizations (31 Dec. 1982), in *Gongzuo wenjian*, vol. 1, 222–23; and Central Organization Department, Summary of Forum of Nine Provinces (and City) on Veteran Cadre Work (25 Apr. 1983), in *Gongzuo wenjian*, vol. 1, 89–97. However, structures were not in place until 1982–83. Wang Xingming (deputy director of Cadre Retirement Division, Veteran Cadre Bureau, Ministry of Labor and Personnel), interviewed in Beijing, 24 November 1986.

   18. Wang Xingming, 1986.
   19. Ibid.

Party Hierarchy   *Government Hierarchy*

Central Committee ──────────────────────────── State Council

Central Organization   Ministry of Labor
Department   and Personnel

Veteran Cadre Bureau   Veteran Cadre Bureau

Provincial Party Committee ◄──────────► Provincial Government

Organization ──────► Veteran   Personnel Bureau
Department   Cadre
                                   Department

Prefectural Party Committee ◄─────────► Prefectural Government

Organization ──────► Veteran   Personnel Division
Department   Cadre
                                   Department
County Party Committee ◄──────────► County Government

Organization ──────► Veteran   Personnel Division
Department   Cadre
                                   Department

KEY: ────── Leadership
        ------ Professional guidance

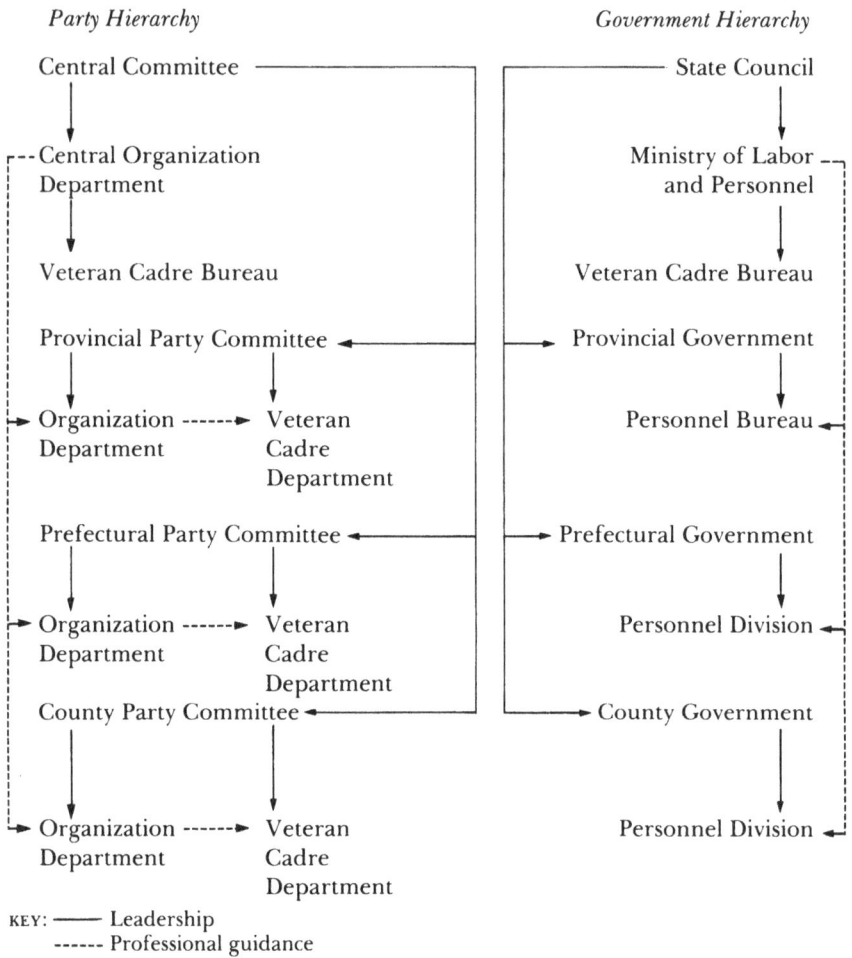

Fig. 8.1. Formal Structure of Authority in Veteran Cadre Work

attention to signals from Party organizations than to those from their
government counterparts. The interests of policy targets also came into
play. In making choices about transforming policies into actions, it made
sense for middlemen to consider the relative difficulty of their tasks.
Obviously, policies that challenged vested interests would not meet with
ready compliance. Thus middlemen could be expected to prefer to implement more-appealing policies over less-appealing ones. Cadre retirement disturbed what was seen as the norm in bureaucratic careers, and it
deprived cadres of positions and income. For these reasons and others,

many cadres were inclined to resist retirement. Further, immediate policy targets were generally those with the most seniority at the workplace. Virtually by definition they included those with the most clout, whether that was reflected in official position or not. These interests of policy targets made cadre retirement policy difficult to implement easily. Resistance of policy targets made it an unappealing policy for middlemen too.

POLICY WITHOUT ACTION IMPLICATIONS

From June 1978 through 1981, top Party and government organizations issued more than twenty documents regulating various aspects of cadre retirement. These organizations include the Central Committee and the State Council, as well as the Central Organization Department and the Ministry of Labor and Personnel. However, middlemen took little action to retire cadres in this period. Indeed, in the view of those for whom the policy can be expected to be most salient, those charged with executing policy and the cadres who were the policy's immediate targets, the post-Mao cadre retirement policy dates from 1982, not 1978. Why did what seems, from the flow of official documents, to be a policy not have action implications?

Before exploring this question, it is important to establish that the documents do, in fact, seem to articulate a policy to retire cadres. Taken as a whole, they combined proclamations of general principles with concrete measures that elaborated a comprehensive cadre retirement system.[20]

The documents established eligibility standards and pensions for three retirement statuses: regular retirement (*tuixiu*), "special" retirement (*lizhi xiuyang,* usually abbreviated to *lixiu*), and semiretirement to advisory (*guwen*) and honorary (*rongyu*) positions. Rank and revolutionary seniority determined eligibility for the different statuses and pension levels. Revolutionary seniority was measured as participation in the Communist revolution before four strategic turning points in the military struggle for power: 7 July 1937, the end of 1942, 3 September 1945, and 1 October 1949. Higher status and bigger pensions were allotted to higher-ranking cadres and those who had joined the Communists earlier rather than later. Eligibility standards and pension levels for special and regular retirement statuses are summarized in table 8.1. The vast majority of veteran cadres surviving in 1978–81 had joined after the defeat of the Japanese in 1945. These veterans of the civil war between the Com-

---

20. The most important documents establishing a systemic framework for cadre retirement in 1978–81 were: State Council Temporary Measures on Arrangements for Aged, Weak, Ill, and Disabled Cadres (2 June 1978), in *Gongzuo wenjian,* vol. 1, 17–31; and State Council Temporary Regulations on Veteran Cadre Special Retirement, 1980.

TABLE 8.1. Retirement Standards, Statuses, and
Pensions, 1978–81

Revolutionaries			
Period of Recruitment	Rank	Retirement Status	Pension (%)
1921–37	low, middle, high	special	100
1937–42	middle, high	special	100
	low	regular	90
1943–45	high	special	100
	low, middle[a]	regular	90
1945–49	high	special	100
	low, middle	regular	80

Postrevolutionaries		
Years of Service	Retirement Status	Pension
≥20	regular	75
15–19	regular	70
10–14	regular	60

NOTE: Rank standards are categorized as high for a rank at or above prefectural level, middle for a rank at or above county level but below prefectural level, and low for a rank below county level.
[a]In 1980 a middle-ranking cadre who joined the revolution before 1945 became eligible for special retirement status and the full pension.

munists and the Guomindang numbered 2,190,000 in 1980.[21] Most were eligible only for regular retirement status.

Veteran cadres in positions of leadership at and above the county level whose health prevented them from performing normal duties of office but who were still able to do some work could semiretire to advisory or honorary positions.[22] This was termed retirement to the "second line" (di er xian).[23] Evidently, the second line was introduced to permit cadres to transfer leadership duties gradually and continue to play a role while

21. "Selecting Young Cadres for Leading Posts."
22. Central Committee and State Council Decision to Establish Advisors (13 Aug. 1980), in Gongzuo wenjian, vol. 1, 14–16.
23. The notion of retirement to the second line was not new. It dated from 1959, when Mao had withdrawn as head of state as the first step in a gradual disengagement from duties, at least partly to allow other leaders to develop the skills and prestige of leadership. See Roderick MacFarquhar, The Origins of the Cultural Revolution, vol. 1, Contradictions among the People, 1956–1957 (New York: Columbia University Press, 1974), 105–7, 152–56, and vol. 2, The Great Leap Forward, 1958–1960 (New York: Columbia University Press, 1983), 32–33, 173.

taking into account their age and health. But of all aspects of the cadre retirement system elaborated in 1978–81, this status was least explicitly articulated. For years after their introduction in 1978, the actual role of cadres on the second line remained unclear, even to those who had designed the system.[24] Documents never defined the role of cadres in honorary positions. They defined the role of advisers, but in very general terms. Advisers were to engage in investigation and study, maintain familiarity with the overall situation, help leaders originate and develop ideas, provide counsel, and transmit to younger generations the Party's traditions and style of work as well as their personal experience and knowledge.

Documents established special retirement status for some veteran cadres in poor health and unable to continue work. Before 1978 the term *lizhi xiuyang*, literally "leave of absence for convalescence," had referred to a practice of permitting veteran cadres to retire from office temporarily, on full salary, to convalesce. The practice dated from 1958.[25] When the term *lixiu* was revived two decades later as a special form of permanent retirement, it retained its earlier connotation of privileged status and its provision of full salary.[26]

Cadres who did not meet the standards for special retirement could retire with regular retirement status, on less than full salary. Special retirement and regular retirement became retirement to the "third line" (*di san xian*). Standards for regular retirement included age guidelines, generally fifty-five for women and sixty for men, but no rank guidelines. Standards and pensions for cadre regular retirement were the same as those established for worker retirement. Only age guidelines differed, and those only for women.[27] Pensions for regularly retired cadres ranged from 60 to 90 percent of salary, depending on period of recruitment to service. Veteran cadres were eligible for 80 or 90 percent of salary, while postrevolutionaries were eligible for 60 to 75 percent.

The documents issued in 1978–81 not only detailed arrangements for pensions but also outlined provisions on health care, housing and relocation subsidies, participation in political study, access to informa-

24. See Zhonggong zhongyang zuzhi bu yanjiu shi, ed., *Zuo hao xin shiqi de ganbu gongzuo* (Beijing: Renmin chubanshe, 1984), 201–3.

25. Cao, *Renshi zhidu gaiyao*, 382–83.

26. One example of this status was the continued use after 1978 of the term *gongzi* (salary) to refer to pensions for cadres with special retirement status. However, the term *lixiu fei* (special retirement fee or payment) also came into use. *Fei* was the term used for pensions of cadres with regular retirement status. Ibid., 396.

27. The retirement age for women workers was set five years below that for cadres. State Council Temporary Measures on Worker Retirement (2 June 1978), in Laodong renshi bu zhengce yanjiu shi, ed., *Zhonghua renmin gongheguo fagui xuanbian, 1985* (Beijing: Laodong renshi chubanshe, 1986), 337–40.

tion, and leisure activities. They discussed broader issues as well, such as how to promote respect and concern for retired cadres in society at large.

The articulation in official documents of a policy to retire cadres was buttressed by a thoroughgoing critique of the cadre lifelong tenure system, conducted in a wide range of periodicals, mostly in 1980. Critics associated lifelong tenure in the span of world history with economic backwardness and political autocracy, claimed no support for lifelong tenure in the Marxist classics, and found lifelong tenure directly or indirectly responsible for a number of serious defects in the exercise of power in communist systems generally and the Chinese system in particular.[28]

Why did what seems to be a policy to retire cadres not have action implications for middlemen? First, policymakers at the top had not reached a consensus on cadre retirement policy, and they communicated their ambivalence to middlemen in a number of ways. Party documents and government documents differed in nuance: the Party organization did not express unambiguous support for a policy to retire cadres in 1978–81. And because cadre management is a particularly Party-dominated issue area, it is not surprising that the lack of clear Party support for retirement blunted any action implications of government documents. Second, policymakers gave middlemen another policy to execute, one that conflicted with cadre retirement. Middlemen had a legitimate alternative to retiring cadres. And finally, cadre retirement policy contained no stipulations such as mandated retirement ages that could serve as objective measures of success or as constraints on middlemen to execute policy.

According to Chen Yeping, writing in 1983 as the prospective Central Organization Department head, there was consensus among top leaders on the principle of a cadre retirement system. However, leaders dis-

---

28. See Yan Jiaqi, "Lun feizhi 'zhongshenzhi,' " *Xin shiqi*, 1980, no. 3:5–7, and excerpt in *Renmin ribao*, 12 June 1980, 5; Gao Fang, "Feichu ganbu zhiwu zhongshenzhi de weida yiyi," *Renwen zazhi*, 1980, no. 4:7–10; Jia Fuhai, Cheng Jie, and Wei Yi, "Lue lun zhongshenzhi," *Shehui kexue*, 1980, no. 4:10–15; Xiao Guangming et al., "Lun feichu ganbu lingdao zhiwu zhongshenzhi," *Jiangxi daxue xuebao*, 1980, no. 4:20–28; Peng Xiangfu and Zheng Zhongbin, "Shi tan feizhi ganbu zhiwu zhongshenzhi," *Lilun yu shijian*, 1980, no. 5:8–11, excerpt in *Renmin ribao*, 3 June 1980, 5; *Gongren ribao*, 15 July 1980, 4; *Nanfang ribao*, 20 Sept. 1980, 3; Special Commentator, *Renmin ribao*, 28 Oct. 1980, 5, and excerpt in *Beijing Review* 23, no. 46 (1980): 20–23; Wu Liping, "Ganbu zhidu shang yi xiang zhongda de gaige," *Hongqi*, 1980, no. 11:6–10; Bao Jirui, "Tantan zhongshenzhi wenti," *Guizhou shehui kexue*, 1981, no. 1:29–34; and Wen Kang, "Ganbu zhidu de yi xiang genbenxing gaige: tantan feizhi zhongshenzhi de wenti," *Qunzhong*, 1981, no. 5:8–11. In 1984 Yan Jiaqi elaborated the critique in *Zhongshenzhi yu xianrenzhi* (Shenyang: Liaoning renmin chubanshe, 1984).

agreed on the urgency of replacing old cadres with younger ones. In a series of speeches beginning in 1979, Deng Xiaoping argued that generational succession was a very urgent matter and that younger cadres should be apprenticed while taking on main responsibility, with older veterans providing guidance as required. Deng's opponents on the issue contended that generational succession could be taken more slowly and that veteran cadres could exercise primary responsibility for a number of years.[29]

This ambivalence among policymakers probably accounts for the difference in priorities reflected in Party and government documents and the failure of the Central Committee and the Central Organization Department to demonstrate clear support for a policy to retire cadres. Not until February 1982 did the Central Committee issue a partner document to the many State Council initiatives on cadre retirement.[30] The strongest Central Committee show of support for cadre retirement in 1978–81 was a general resolution, passed in February 1980, to abolish the de facto lifelong tenure system for cadres.[31]

Party documents on cadre retirement contained a message that effectively replaced the policy to retire cadres with a policy to restore to power veteran cadres who had been purged or demoted during the Cultural Revolution. Probably the first document on veteran cadre work issued by a Party organization in 1978–81 was a February 1978 Central Organization Department statement of views on veteran cadre work.[32] Its main content was the importance of restoring veteran cadres to power. It stated that those able to work were to be assigned suitable work as soon as possible. Those with long experience in positions of leadership were to be assigned main positions of leadership. Indeed, the document instructed subordinate organization departments to promote the core role of veteran cadres in modernization. As an example of the scope and nature of restoration, the party journal *Hongqi* publicized the work of the organization department of Hunan province. In Hunan, of the surviving cadres managed by the provincial Party committee before the Cultural Revolution, 98 percent were assigned positions ranked equivalent to or higher than their former positions. The rule adopted was this: so long as

29. Chen Yeping, "Baozheng dang de shiye jiwang kailai de zhongda juece: xuexi Deng Xiaoping wenxuan zhong guanyu xin lao ganbu hezuo jiaoti sixiang de tihui," *Hongqi*, 1983, no. 16:2–6.

30. Central Committee Decision to Establish a Veteran Cadre Retirement System (20 Feb. 1982), in *Gongzuo wenjian*, vol. 1, 1–13.

31. Communique of the Fifth Plenary Session of the 11th Central Committee of the Communist Party of China (29 Feb. 1980), *Beijing Review* 23, no. 10 (1980): 8.

32. Some Views of the Central Organization Department on Strengthening Veteran Cadre Work (29 Dec. 1978), in *Gongzuo wenjian*, vol. 1, 80–88.

they are able to work, they are assigned work; those unable to work are permitted to retire upon request.[33]

In principle, restoration of veteran cadres as a strategic short-term policy was not inconsistent with retirement. The younger generations of cadres the regime sought overall to promote included most who had been recruited and had risen under the influence of radical leftist standards thoroughly discredited by the end of 1978. Policymakers sought the cooperation of veterans in selecting and training suitable successors. This was not simply a task of recruiting qualified managers of modernization, but one of weeding out those whose politics were suspect in the changed political climate.[34] In practice, however, veterans restored to power did not actively create the conditions for their own retirement by preparing successors.[35]

Finally, even the government documents that established a cadre retirement system did not clearly impel middlemen to execute policy. The main reason is their failure to set objective criteria for decisions on retirement. In turn, there were no such criteria to evaluate the performance of middlemen or to constrain them to retire cadres.

If retirement is defined as an explicit direct relationship between old age and employment, then government documents introduced neither the principle nor the practice of cadre retirement in 1978–81. Retirement-age guidelines were set for regular retirement status, but these determined eligibility for benefits and in no sense mandated retirement at specified ages. More to the point, old age was not intrinsically a reason to retire cadres. Retirement was for those whose state of health precluded performing normal work. Documents acknowledged that old age generally brought with it some decline that could affect the ability to work, but the rationale for cadre retirement was two vague intervening variables: state of health and the ability to work normally. Old age per se was not linked to retirement until 1982.

It is instructive here to compare the language in the first and most comprehensive post-Mao government document on cadre retirement

33. Zhonggong Hunan sheng wei zuzhi bu, "Zhengque shixing laozhongqing san jiehe de yuanze," *Hongqi*, 1978, no. 6:46–50.

34. The essentially political character of the role was openly acknowledged. See especially Special Commentator, *Renmin ribao*, 19 Feb. 1978, 1; and Huang Baowei, "Lao ganbu zai xuanba zhongqingnian ganbu zhong de lishi zeren," *Lilun yu shijian*, 1981, no. 8:32–33.

35. See Commentator, *Renmin ribao*, 29 Oct. 1980, 1; Song Renqiong, "Renzhen jiejue gongzuo mianlin de xin keti," *Hongqi*, 1980, no. 16:2–9; Special Commentator, "Lao ganbu de yi xiang zhongda zhengzhi zeren," *Hongqi*, 1980, no. 19:2–5; Huang, "Lao ganbu zai xuanba zhongqingnian ganbu zhong de lishi zeren"; and Shi Yan, "Lao ganbu de di yi wei de gongzuo," *Xin changzheng*, 1981, no. 9:18–20.

with a document on worker retirement issued at the same time.[36] The State Council Temporary Measures on Arrangements for Aged, Weak, Ill, and Disabled Cadres applied to cadres whose "age and state of health preclude continuing normal work." The document on worker retirement applied to "old workers and workers who have lost the ability to work because of illness or disability." Cadres meeting standards specified "could retire." Workers meeting standards specified "should retire." Even the title of the document on workers, the State Council Temporary Measures on Worker Retirement, suggests the contrast. In 1980 the State Council did issue a document stating that cadres who were unable to work "should retire."[37] Yet that document applied to cadres for whom no retirement-age guidelines had been set. And even with the stronger language, inability to work normally rather than old age per se was given as the reason for retirement.

Yet another contrast is provided in a government document protesting the pro forma nature of some worker retirements, with formally retired workers remaining employed at their posts.[38] No comparable protest was contained in documents on cadre retirement in 1978–81. Also, workers who did not retire according to regulations were to have their salaries stopped.[39] No comparable arrangement existed for cadres.

One retired cadre summed up the situation in 1978–81 in the following way: "It was very difficult to distinguish who should retire from who should not retire. If it is too flexible, it is the same as not having it at all." Without age guidelines as the basic decision rule for retirement, decisions could be made only through case-by-case deliberation on the applicability of vague subjective standards to particular cadres. These standards were open to interpretation and did not constrain middlemen to retire cadres.

EXECUTION OF POLICY

The formal revision of policy in 1982 transformed a policy without action implications into a policy that middlemen executed by retiring cadres. Four features characterize this change. First, policymakers gave middle-

36. State Council Temporary Measures on Arrangements for Aged, Weak, Ill, and Disabled Cadres, 1978; and State Council Temporary Measures on Worker Retirement, 1978.

37. State Council Temporary Regulations on Veteran Cadre Special Retirement, 1980.

38. State Council Notice on Strict Implementation of Temporary Measures on Worker Retirement (7 Nov. 1981), in *Zhonghua renmin gongheguo fagui huibian, 1981* (Beijing: Falu chubanshe, 1986), 294–97.

39. "Guanyu gongren tuixiu tuizhi shixiang de wenda," *Banyuetan,* 1981, no. 23:10–11.

men clear and coherent signals of their commitment to cadre retirement. In particular, middlemen in the Party-dominated organization-personnel system no longer faced the ambivalent situation of government initiatives and Party disinclination on cadre retirement. Second, middlemen no longer had conflicting policy goals that gave them a legitimate alternative to executing policy. Rather, policymakers established a number of objectives that were mutually reinforcing: retiring cadres helped middlemen achieve success in the campaigns to streamline bureaucracies and rejuvenate leading groups. Third, retirement policy was revised to constrain middlemen to execute it. Policymakers set the objective criterion of age as the basis for specific decisions to retire cadres. Decisions not to retire cadres who had reached the relevant ages became exceptions to the general rule, requiring justification. Finally, policymakers made compliance with retirement policy more attractive to a large proportion of potential retirees. Consequently, middlemen faced less resistance from the ultimate targets of the policy.

It is plausible that policymakers reached agreement to revise cadre retirement policy only by changing the incentive structure for themselves and other leaders: some key revisions applied to leaders at the top and were probably the result of a negotiated settlement. Thus a changed incentive structure may have been not only a feature but also an explanation of the radical shift in policy in 1982.

The revised policy exempted from retirement leaders at the very summit of power. The elimination of these leaders as targets of cadre retirement policy was announced in a Central Committee document in February 1982 and aired in *Hongqi* in March 1982:

> Our party is a big party, our country is a big country. We need a few dozen veteran comrades with international prestige, who are capable of careful and long-term planning, who maintain a comprehensive view of the situation, and who are still in good health. [We need them to remain] in positions at the core of leadership in the party and government, to help stay the course. Other veteran cadres must gloriously retire from service at the ages specified, in keeping with regulations.[40]

A second indication of a compromise was the creation of a new institution for retired top leaders: advisory commissions at the national and provincial levels.[41] The commissions were given an estimated life span of ten to fifteen years, enough time to ease into retirement a generation of

40. Editorial Board, "Jigou gaige shi yi chang geming," *Hongqi*, 1982, no. 6:5. The document announcing the exemption was the Central Committee Decision to Establish a Veteran Cadre Retirement System, 1982.

41. See Constitution of the Communist Party of China (6 Sept. 1982), chap. 3, art. 22, and chap. 4, art. 28, in *Beijing Review* 25, no. 38 (1982): 15–17.

senior veteran cadres.[42] These changes in the retirement-incentive structure at the very top seem to have been the key to reaching agreement on the revised policy that emerged in Party and government documents beginning in 1982.

In February 1982 the Central Committee issued a Decision to Establish a Veteran Cadre Retirement System, indicating its support of earlier government initiatives and sending a clear signal to middlemen to begin to execute policy. The signal was not only symbolic. The document explicitly assigned tasks to the Central Organization Department. Nearly twenty more documents were issued by Party and government organizations in 1982 alone, treating various aspects of cadre retirement: establishing accurately revolutionary seniority, determining changes in retirement status, detailing formal procedures for retiring cadres, introducing honorary certificates of retirement, discussing the role of retired cadres, and instructing veteran cadre departments in their responsibilities. For the first time, Party and government documents were speaking the same language on cadre retirement.

Policymakers linked retirement to campaigns to streamline bureaucracies and rejuvenate leading groups, begun at the national level in 1982 and carried out at the provincial and lower levels in 1983–84.[43] Streamlining bureaucracies involved a reduction in personnel and departments in the Party and the government, with the objective of improving policy coordination. The rejuvenation of leading groups aimed to improve the quality of leadership by promoting more highly educated, professionally competent, and younger cadres. Quotas were set for both campaigns. Unlike the policy of restoring cadres to power, which had conflicted with retirement goals, these two campaigns complemented the policy to retire cadres. Middlemen no longer had a legitimate alternative to retiring cadres. Indeed, retirement was virtually a prerequisite for success in the campaigns.

Policymakers also constrained middlemen to execute policy, by replac-

42. Deng Xiaoping gave these estimates in speeches made on 30 July 1982 at an enlarged meeting of the Political Bureau and on 13 Sept. 1982 to the Central Advisory Commission. See "Deng Speech on Setting Up Advisory Commissions," Foreign Broadcast Information Service, *Daily Report: China*, 22 July 1983, K8–K9; "Zai zhongyang guwen weiyuanhui di yi ci quanti huiyi shang de jianghua," *Xinhua yuebao*, 1982, no. 9:65–68.

43. See William deB. Mills, "Generational Change in China," *Problems of Communism* 32, no. 6 (1983): 16–35; Keith Forster, "The Reform of Provincial Party Committees in China: The Case of Zhejiang," *Asian Survey* 24, no. 6 (1984): 618–36, and "Repudiation of the Cultural Revolution in China: The Case of Zhejiang," *Pacific Affairs* 59, no. 1 (1986): 5–27; Hong Yung Lee, "Deng Xiaoping's Reform of the Chinese Bureaucracy," in *The Limits of Reform in China*, ed. Ronald A. Morse (Boulder, Colo.: Westview Press, 1983), 19–37; and Kenneth Lieberthal, "China in 1982: A Middling Course for the Middle Kingdom," *Asian Survey* 23, no. 1 (1983): 26–37.

ing the vague and subjective standards of good health and the ability to work normally with age as the criterion for decisions on retirement. Flexibility was built into the policy in two ways. A supplementary rule stated that those whose health prevented them from working normally could retire early, and those who were needed at work and whose health was good could postpone retirement, with the approval of the relevant Party committee. Also, retirement age guidelines differed by rank and sex: in general, higher-ranking cadres retired later than lower-ranking cadres, and men retired later than women.[44]

Even with the opportunity to exercise discretion introduced in the supplementary rule, the 1982 revised policy constrained middlemen to retire cadres. The policy introduced a direct link between age and retirement, making age per se a reason to retire cadres. And it reversed the relative importance of the objective standard, age, and subjective standards. Health and ability to work normally were no longer an integral part of all decisions on retirement. With retirement at fixed ages as the general rule, decisions to retire cadres were essentially standardized. Whereas in 1978–81 middlemen had had to interpret and apply ambiguous guidelines in order to retire cadres, beginning in 1982 a decision not to retire cadres was the one demanding an interpretation and explanation.

Policymakers also changed the incentive structure to make retirement more attractive to cadres and, presumably, easier for middlemen to execute successfully. Beginning in April 1982 all veteran cadres became eligible for special retirement status and its full pension.[45] For the 2,190,000 veterans of the 1945–49 civil war, pensions increased from 80 to 100 percent of salary. For all veteran cadres, then, retirement no longer brought about a loss in salary. And for those who had joined the Communists before 1945, policymakers provided a retirement bonus,

44. A retirement age of fifty-five for women and sixty for men was set for most cadres. A retirement age of sixty-five, regardless of sex, was set for main leaders of Party and government departments (ministries, commissions), provincial Party committee first secretaries, and provincial governors. A retirement age of sixty, again regardless of sex, was set for deputy leaders of Party and government departments (ministries, commissions), provincial Party committee secretaries (other than first secretaries), provincial deputy governors, main and deputy leaders of provincial Party committees and provincial government departments, prefectural Party committee secretaries and deputy secretaries, and prefectural commissioners and deputy commissioners.

45. Strictly speaking, most but not all veteran cadres were eligible for special retirement status. The general formulation was this: cadres who before the founding of the People's Republic of China had participated in revolutionary wars under the leadership of the Communist Party, had not engaged in productive labor and had been paid in kind through the Communist Party supply system, or who had engaged in underground revolutionary work for the Communist Party were eligible for special retirement status once they reached the age specified for retirement for their rank and sex. Detailed regulations were issued to clarify this general formulation.

equivalent to one to two months' salary, conferred annually after retirement. Amount of bonus depended on period of recruitment to service.
These changes are summarized in table 8.2. Policymakers did not change
the retirement incentive structure for postrevolutionaries. And by extending special retirement status to all veteran cadres and providing
bonuses to some, they exacerbated the gap between veteran cadres and
postrevolutionaries. Whereas in 1978 the smallest difference in pensions
for the two groups had been 5 percent of salary, in 1982 it became 25
percent. The biggest difference became 57 percent.

While the four features discussed above made cadre retirement a
policy with action implications, middlemen proved unwilling or unable
to execute it with its formally established incentive structure. They subtly
changed the policy in the course of executing it, by increasing incentives
to retire. This was a deviation from official policy.

DEVIATION FROM POLICY

In salary terms the 1982 revised incentive structure eliminated the material disincentive to retire for veteran cadres and provided a small incentive for some. Postrevolutionaries still lost 25 to 40 percent of salary after
retirement. However, middlemen provided incentives to retire, above
those stipulated in official policy, to veteran cadres and postrevolutionaries. At the workplace, middlemen engaged in bargaining with
potential retirees seeking a better retirement deal. At the provincial
level, governments issued temporary regulations increasing stipends to
postrevolutionaries. In both instances, middlemen responded to pressure and passive resistance from older cadres, the targets of the policy,
even when doing so deviated from policy. In short, better incentives
seemed to be necessary to get cadres to retire. Middlemen proved themselves unwilling or unable to execute policy successfully, given the official
incentive structure. They did not enforce compliance so much as induce
cadres to comply.

In an economy where goods and opportunities are scarce and the
market mechanism inoperative in distributing them, as is true of the
People's Republic of China, the power to obtain things is not always
strongly linked to cash income. It is linked also to rank and, more generally, to being a member of a workplace.[46] For these reasons, even a full
pension was unlikely to compensate cadres adequately for postretire-

46. See Gail E. Henderson and Myron S. Cohen, M.D., *The Chinese Hospital: A Socialist Work Unit* (New Haven: Yale University Press, 1984). Also, Andrew G. Walder provides an excellent discussion of these issues, but with reference to workers. See especially *Communist Neo-Traditionalism: Work and Authority in Chinese Industry* (Berkeley and Los Angeles: University of California Press, 1986).

TABLE 8.2. Retirement Standards, Statuses,
Pensions, and Bonuses for Veteran Cadres, 1982

Period of Recruitment	Status	Pension (%)	Bonus (%)
1921–37	special	100	16.6
1937–42	special	100	12.5
1943–45	special	100	8.3
1945–49	special	100	0

NOTE: Pensions are expressed as a percentage of preretirement salary. Bonuses are expressed as percentages of annual preretirement salary and are conferred annually after retirement.

ment losses. Thus the types of benefits potential retirees sought were often different in nature from those the official policy offered.

Although the age criterion provided an objective means of singling out cadres for retirement, middlemen at the workplace did not usually instruct cadres to retire. They engaged in discussions with potential retirees, in the course of which cadres voiced requests to improve their situation in some way. Cadres generally referred to this process as one of "bargaining" (shangliang). In the description of one retired cadre:

> Retirement decisions come from the organization department at the workplace. It has records of how old cadres are and who should retire. To get people to retire, the organization department cadres come to talk to you. Cadres bargain with them. They may say: "First you resolve my housing problem or my son's employment problem, and then I will retire." Before the Cultural Revolution, people did whatever the organization told them to do. They went wherever the organization decided they should go. Now, people are not so obedient. The organization has to bargain with them.

Some of the things often bargained for were better housing, a preretirement salary raise, and employment for a son or a daughter. Table 8.3 shows preretirement requests that questionnaire respondents made to middlemen at the workplace. Nearly 85 percent of respondents made such requests. Among them, employment for a son or a daughter was the most common: including those who made more than one request, more than half of all respondents made this request. Providing employment for a son or a daughter was not strictly permissible, but younger cadres interviewed indicated that it was widely practiced. For ordinary cadres especially, with fewer perquisites of position than high-ranking cadres, providing such an incentive could induce early retirement. In Guizhou province, for example, eight thousand cadres had retired early

TABLE 8.3. Preretirement Requests to
Middlemen
(Questionnaire Respondents)

Request	No. of Responses	%
Salary	22	9.2
Housing	34	14.2
Employment for son or daughter	113	47.3
Other	7	2.9
No request	37	15.5
>1 request	26	10.9
Total	239	100.0

NOTE: Of those with >1 request, there were 15 requests about salary, 21 requests about housing, 20 requests about employment for a son or daughter, and 3 other requests.

by the end of 1983. Of these early retirements, more than half involved providing employment for a son or a daughter.[47]

Yet another incentive middlemen provided to potential retirees was pro forma retirement, which some cadres referred to as "retirement without leaving the workpost" (*lixiu bu li zhi*). Essentially this meant that cadres worked regular hours, at the workplace, attending to the same kind of work as before their retirement. It seems not to have been as common as another postretirement practice: reducing work hours and time spent at the workplace and attending to special projects unconnected with regular work. For example, among questionnaire respondents, 21 percent indicated they spent most of their time after retirement doing work for the former workplace and returned to the workplace at least several times every couple of weeks.[48]

That these efforts served the interests of potential retirees is obvious. However, middlemen also had an interest in providing incentives. Middlemen had an interest in retiring cadres to fulfill campaign quotas to cut staff and promote younger cadres. Even pro forma retirement eliminated cadres from the authorized personnel complement (*bianzhi*) and gave workplaces time to find and train replacements. Providing incentives for early retirement was also in the interest of middlemen. Because the practice of lifelong tenure had prevented regular personnel renewal, those directly in line for promotion at middle levels were themselves not young. Part of the campaign to promote younger cadres involved short-

47. Foreign Broadcast Information Service, *Daily Report: China*, 23 Sept. 1983, Q1, and 2 Dec. 1983, Q1.
48. With missing data excluded, $N = 224$.

cutting the regular career ladder and skipping over cadres in their fifties. This created a morale problem among these cadres, whose careers
were frozen.[49] Early retirement with a better retirement deal was one
way to handle this problem. A postretirement work relation with the
workplace was another.

By the end of 1985 more than half of all surviving veteran cadres had
retired.[50] However, more than two million cadres had been recruited in
1950–52. In September 1984 Jiao Shanmin, a deputy head of the Ministry of Labor and Personnel, noted that hundreds and thousands of
postrevolutionaries had reached the ages of retirement but were not
retiring.[51] He cited the discrepancy in pensions between veteran cadres
and postrevolutionaries as the main problem, stating that pensions for
postrevolutionaries were too low and that retirement seriously affected
their standard of living. He concluded that the problem was a serious
obstacle to rejuvenating the cadre ranks.

Policymakers had fixed pensions for postrevolutionaries at 60 to 75
percent of salary in 1978, and these had not been changed in 1982.
The 1982 increase in pensions for veteran cadres had exacerbated the
difference between veteran cadres and postrevolutionaries. In addition,
beginning in 1982 there was considerable propaganda on veteran cadre
retirement, which very likely increased awareness of that difference.
Not surprisingly, there was resentment among postrevolutionaries. As
one postrevolutionary explained: "We are all working together—then
this distinction. Of course, to distinguish between special retirement
and regular retirement is not unreasonable. These veteran revolutionaries deserve some special treatment. But why must it be so much? People
are upset not with the distinction itself, but with the size of the gap."
Postrevolutionary questionnaire respondents too revealed their dissatisfaction with the difference. As is indicated in table 8.4, 71 percent of
postrevolutionaries (18 percent of veteran cadres) considered it unreasonable (*bu heli*).

Workplaces in the public sector considered here do not themselves
finance the retirement of their cadres. Middlemen at the workplace could
not take the initiative to actually increase cadre pensions. Most of the

49. The policy was to promote only a small minority of cadres in their fifties, with the
majority either remaining at the same level until retirement or being replaced by younger
and better-qualified cadres. See "Yao zhongshi fahui wushi duo sui ganbu de jiji xing," in
Zuo hao xin shiqi de ganbu gongzuo, 209–16.

50. A total of 1,380,000 veteran cadres had retired. Chen Liang (deputy director of
Special Retirement Division, Cadre Retirement Bureau, Ministry of Personnel) and Wang
Wenbo (director of Cadre Retirement Bureau General Office, Ministry of Personnel),
interviewed in Beijing, 7 Nov. 1988.

51. Jiao Shanmin, "Youguan renshi zhidu gaige de jige wenti," in *Laodong gongzi renshi
zhidu gaige de yanjiu yu tantao*, ed. Laodong renshi bu ganbu jiaoyu ju (Beijing: Laodong
renshi chubanshe, 1985), 279–96. This source is internal.

TABLE 8.4. Evaluation of Equity of Pension and
Benefits Differences for Revolutionaries and
Postrevolutionaries, by Recruitment Category
(Row Percentages)
(Questionnaire Respondents)

	Evaluation		
Recruitment Category	Unreasonable	Reasonable	Totals
Revolutionaries	18.4	81.7	100% (158)
Postrevolutionaries	71.0	29.0	100% (69)
Totals	34.4 (78)	65.6 (149)	100% (227)

NOTE: Percentages may not add up because of rounding.

Pearson chi-square value: 59.049
Probability: .000

financial burden for retirement is borne by local governments. Through-out 1986 twenty-five provincial governments adopted measures to increase pensions for postrevolutionaries.[52] The measures adopted, often called temporary regulations, technically did not revise central regulations on retirement. Rather, they provided subsidies or additional maintenance stipends (*shenghuo butie*) from provincial budgets for regularly retired cadres.

It is interesting to consider the case of Beijing, a provincial-level municipality and an anomaly in the local revision of cadre retirement policy. The municipal government of Beijing did not issue regulations to increase pensions for regularly retired cadres. Some interview subjects offered as an explanation the view that proximity to the national government meant that Beijing was more likely to act according to official policy. However, middlemen at workplaces in Beijing had their own way of dealing with this issue: they postponed the processing of the retirement of postrevolutionaries, in the expectation that policymakers at the top would soon ratify the informal changes in policy made by virtually all provincial governments. As with other informal deviations, postponement constituted a way of "taking into consideration" (*zhaogu*) the interests of targets of the policy. One retired cadre described the situation at the end of 1986 as follows:

> [Retirement] has been postponed . . . because of the dissatisfaction among cadres about differences in material benefits between special retirement

52. Wang Xingming, 1986.

and regular retirement. Cadres who do not meet the standards for special retirement are dissatisfied about accepting a smaller pension than cadres who do meet these standards. There is no question or complaint about veteran cadres deserving the title of veteran revolutionaries and some honorary status, but there is grumbling about their extra material benefits. So the workplace is putting off processing cadre retirement, because there is a sense that the policy will probably change soon, and the workplace wants to show consideration for the cadres who do not meet special retirement standards but are at the age of retirement. New regulations may come out soon. People are waiting.

Policymakers may have unwittingly sanctioned the deviations by middlemen at the workplace and by the provinces. For example, middlemen could view the concern about low pensions for postrevolutionaries that Jiao Shanmin voiced in 1984 as granting legitimacy to the provincial subsidies. Providing a better retirement deal was consistent with a policy guideline to take into account the special needs of veteran cadres, especially in matters of general well-being.[53] And policy guidelines on the role of veteran cadres in training successors and those on promoting an active postretirement role for veteran cadres seemed to support a continued relation with the workplace after retirement.[54] The blanket exclusion from promotion of all cadres in their fifties was officially criticized, but guidelines suggested that even those in good health should step down if younger, better-qualified candidates for office were available.[55] Even providing employment for a son or a daughter was not entirely without a basis in official policy. It was a corruption of the principle of employment substitution (*dingti*), which, under certain circumstances, allowed the workplace to hire one son or daughter of a retiring worker. Employment substitution was not applicable to cadres, however.[56]

Nonetheless, these were, in fact, deviations—not simply permissible interpretations and adaptations of official policy. In September 1983 the Central Committee sharply criticized the extension of employment substi-

53. See Trial Measures on Scope of Responsibility of Veteran Cadre Bureaus (and Divisions) in State Council and Central Committee Organizations, 1982.

54. See Suggestions on Appropriate Handling of Veteran Cadres Who Have Stepped Down from Positions, 1982.

55. See, for example, Li Rui, "Xin xingshi yu ganbu gongzuo," *Xinhua yuebao*, 1985, no. 2:31–35.

56. On employment substitution, see Cao, *Zhonghua renmin gongheguo renshi zhidu gaiyao*, 406–9 (n. 14 above). When a retired cadre had no children living in the locality, it was generally permissible to relocate one and provide employment. See Ministry of Labor and Personnel, Opinions on the Handling of Concrete Problems in Implementing "Some State Council Regulations on the Veteran Cadre Special Retirement System" (10 Dec. 1982), in *Gongzuo wenjian*, vol. 1, 48–55. Deborah Davis discusses employment substitution among workers in "Unequal Chances, Unequal Outcomes: Pension Reform and Urban Inequality," *China Quarterly*, no. 114 (1988): 223–42.

tution to cadres and placed stringent restrictions on its application, even among workers.[57] The stipend increases for postrevolutionaries were treated somewhat differently. They were clearly viewed as a violation and an irregularity, but in the end policymakers took the local government measures as a signal to review the policy. The State Council issued a report in early 1987, pointing out that the subsidies had created a heavy financial burden on the state and that departments were studying the matter to recommend policy revisions. It asked the localities to take into account the financial burden and the adverse effect of the increases on building a cadre retirement system. However, policymakers did not explicitly demand a repeal of the increases.[58]

CONCLUSION

For a number of reasons, cadre retirement policy was a policy without action implications in 1978–81. Policymakers gave middlemen conflicting signals, reflecting a lack of consensus at the top. Party and government organizations issued documents with different nuances, and the lack of clear Party support for a policy in a Party-dominated issue area was especially important. Also, middlemen were given another policy to execute, the goals of which conflicted with cadre retirement policy. And policymakers did not constrain middlemen to retire cadres with an objective criterion, such as mandatory retirement at specified ages.

In 1982 middlemen took action to retire cadres. A number of factors explain this. Policymakers signaled agreement at the top and, in particular, Party support of retirement. They eliminated conflicting policy demands on middlemen and introduced mutually reinforcing demands by starting up two campaigns, in which cadre retirement was virtually a prerequisite for success. And they constrained middlemen to retire cadres by making retirement at specified ages the general rule. Policymakers also made the policy easier to execute, by increasing incentives for a large proportion of older cadres to retire.

However, in executing policy middlemen took the interests of potential retirees into consideration. They increased incentives to retire—even when doing so deviated from policy. Thus middlemen proved unwilling or unable to enforce policy. Instead, they induced compliance by making retirement more attractive.

57. State Council Notice to Strictly Rectify Recruitment of Sons and Daughters of Workers and Staff Regularly Retired and Retired for Extraordinary Reasons (3 Sept. 1983), *Guowuyuan gongbao*, 1983, no. 20:931–33.

58. Chen Liang and Wang Wenbo, 1988; Ministry of Finance and Ministry of Labor and Personnel, Report on Strictly Controlling the Unauthorized Increase of Regular Retirement Benefits (10 Jan. 1987), *Guowuyuan gongbao*, 1987, no. 5:195.

The evidence presented points toward a number of conclusions about the choices middlemen make after policymakers formulate policy. These can be simply summarized as choices about taking risks, justifying actions, and using resources. When there is a lack of consensus among policymakers, what middlemen do or do not do is a choice that reflects a stand—and potential political risk. Further, middlemen are in positions of responsibility toward policymakers and of authority over ultimate targets of a policy. This means they must justify their actions to both, with reference to policy. Finally, middlemen have a number of tasks in their issue area at any given time. Anything they do consumes limited resources (such as personnel), and when they face contradictory demands they must choose to use resources on one task or another. Because of these choices they make, middlemen are more likely to execute policy or execute it successfully to the degree that policymakers reduce their risks, constrain their actions, and coordinate demands on them.

However, this does not appear to be enough to ensure successful execution of policy. Middlemen need an attractive policy to execute. Ultimate targets of the policy seem to be, not passive policy takers, but discriminating consumers. Middlemen will find ways to make an unattractive policy attractive, even if this means deviating from official policy. The nature of their deviations is inhibited and shaped by both policy content and the formal structure of authority. The degree of latitude for interpretation in policy and the kinds of actions that appear to be sanctioned by policy affect how middlemen make policy more attractive. And middlemen are limited by their formal authority: thus middlemen in one issue area cannot take authoritative actions that span different areas, but local governments can take such actions.

What does this imply about the actual consequences of the formal structure of bureaucratic authority in the policy process? To begin with, the formal structure is meaningful in a couple of ways. First, the distinction between Party and government organizations has action implications in the policy process. When conflicting signals are issued by policymakers at the top, middlemen weigh those signals differently. In the extraordinarily Party-dominated issue area of cadre management, Party signals were taken as the meaningful guidelines for action. Second, the officially defined span of authority over issue areas channels how policy is implemented. The ways middlemen deviated from formulated policy were constrained by whether their formal authority was limited to one issue area or extended to many.

In short, formal authority relations matter. But much of the behavior of middlemen cannot be explained with reference to those relations. In particular, the nature of deviations in the course of policy implementation reveals an informal structure of constraints and incentives at the grass roots. Middlemen proved clearly unwilling or unable to implement what was considered by older cadres to be an unattractive policy. Thus middlemen are keenly responsive to interests of policy targets who have little or no place on charts delineating official authority relations in the policy process. That responsiveness, not represented in the formal organizational design, has a real impact on how policies are transformed into actions.

The actual scope of these generalizations is essentially an empirical matter. However, there are a few features of this case that may restrict its generalizability to other policies. In particular, the tendency of middlemen to provide additional incentives to potential retirees may be quite atypical. Cadre retirement is an unusual policy because of the lack of legitimate precedent for it, the relative absence of risk for targets of the policy in resisting it, and the special resources possessed by these potential retirees.

First, cadre retirement lacked a supportive legacy on which to build. Indeed, Chinese Communist experience attached stigma to exit from office: movement in and out of official position has typically been the result of natural death, political error, or consolidation of personal power from the top. Cadre retirement policy was a new attempt to change a de facto lifelong tenure system that had been in place since the 1950s. This system not only had the legitimacy of habit, but also had been explicitly legitimated as an entitlement of revolutionaries for their role in the Communist rise to power. The notion of cadre, then, was not one of bureaucratic career, but rather one of revolutionary calling. Retirement represented a reinterpretation of what it meant to be a cadre.

In these circumstances, the interests of potential retirees, especially veteran cadres, could not easily be dismissed as illegitimate. Both the magnitude of the change involved and the policy's lack of legitimate precedent were probably influences on the policy process, making it more likely that middlemen would take the interests of potential retirees into consideration. An example of a comparable kind of policy in the same issue area is the elimination of job security for workers and cadres.

Second, and somewhat paradoxically, older cadres could resist retirement and press for an increase in pensions and benefits without major risk. The organization-personnel system is important precisely because it is the system through which the Party controls life chances. Cadre retirement is an atypical problem in this issue area because, to a considerable degree, retirement involves an exit from this system of control. Potential retirees had less to lose in resisting retirement policy, because the outcome was a career end point in any case.

Finally and relatedly, older cadres could draw on resources that targets of other policies might not be expected to possess. This was especially true of veteran cadres. Most potential retirees were not leaders and, therefore, did not have a lot of power in the usual sense. However, they had years of Party membership, tenure in office, work experience, and networks of contacts. Veteran cadres restored to office also had prestige, because they were associated with the Party's greatest achievement to date—gaining power. As well, they were often victims of the Cultural Revolution and untainted by the policies of that repudiated period. They were symbols of the Party's better face, at a time when the Party was facing a crisis of faith. Given this situation, middlemen could ill afford to provoke the resistance of potential retirees. They could be expected to adopt a less authoritarian and more concessionary style of executing policy.

NINE

Hierarchy and the Bargaining Economy: Government and Enterprise in the Reform Process

Barry Naughton

Before economic reform China ran a command economy, and economic decisions were made and evaluated within a hierarchical bureaucracy. Because decision-makers were not directly subject to competitive pressures or external review, decisions generally emerged from a process of negotiation and bargaining within the bureaucracy. Bargaining in the upper reaches of the bureaucracy determined the choice of investment projects, and bargaining between enterprises and their superiors over planned targets determined current production levels. This system permitted inefficient decisions to be made repeatedly because the costs of wrong choices were not borne by any single individual or work unit, but were instead diffused through the economy as a whole. From the beginning, one of the hopes of reform was that it would reduce the scope for decision making by bargaining, substituting instead an objective "discipline of the market."

In fact, economic reforms *have* transformed the nature of bargaining relations in China's industrial economy, changing the bargaining positions of superiors and subordinates, transferring control over large blocks of resources, and introducing elements of market competition into the decision-making process. But the hope that reform would somehow diminish the overall importance of bargaining within the bureaucracy has been sorely disappointed. Instead, reforms have caused bargaining relations to become more complex and even more pervasive. Within the state sector the maintenance of the administrative hierarchy has preserved the basic precondition for the bargaining relationship, while the increasingly complex and diversified economic environment has enriched the content of the bargains that can be struck. In this new bargaining environment the roles of the central government and state enterprises have been recast, without, however, solving the question of what those roles should be.

The new bargaining relations are the result of changes in the forces that shape the bargaining environment. Changes in two areas are particularly striking. First, the relative strength of different parties in the hierarchical bargaining process—determined primarily by their control over resources and information—has shifted. The central government has been weakened by a decline in the volume of resources under its direct control, but strengthened by an increase in information and skills and by a broader range of instruments at its disposal. In certain respects this combination has led to an unexpected increase in the strength of the central government. Second, the coexistence of plan and market sectors has led to bargains with increasingly complex and diverse contents. There are simply more economic variables to be bargained over than there were in the past. From the enterprise standpoint, this aspect of change has been crucial. While enterprises have more resources at their disposal, they also face a vastly more complex bargaining environment, and bargaining has shifted from predominantly plan bargaining to a complicated mixture of plan, exchange, and redistributive bargaining. The combination of ambiguous shifts in power relations and increasing complexity in the economic system has resulted in an increased prominence for bargaining overall in economic decision making. This is ironic, for we might have supposed that it would be precisely in the economic realm that market relations would replace the give-and-take of bureaucratic politics at an early stage of the reform process.

In the first section of this chapter I introduce the conceptual framework by describing a pure "command-bureaucratic" economy. Stress is laid on the closed, monopolistic nature of the system and on the degraded character of information flows within the bureaucracy. The prereform Chinese economic system is described with reference to these characteristics. The second section begins the discussion of the contemporary Chinese environment by examining the role of the central government in Beijing in the investment process, stressing changes in bargaining strength. The third section examines the changing bargaining environment at the enterprise level. This necessarily involves a discussion of the "two-track" strategy for economic reform and of the nature of enterprise response to the new risks and opportunities facing them. In the fourth section, I examine the basic structural conditions that serve to maintain and reproduce the bargaining relationship at the enterprise level: I stress the continuing bilateral monopoly that prevails between enterprises and their superiors. Some of the implications of this way of looking at the Chinese reform process are presented in a brief concluding section.

THE COMMAND-BUREAUCRATIC ECONOMY

The economic system China operated before reform is often called a "command economy," and this term accurately captures the nature of most economic decision making in such a system. Information is collected from production and consumption units; the information flows upward through bureaucratic channels; decisions are made on the basis of this information; and commands are issued down through the same bureaucratic channels to determine production decisions. Vertical flows of information and command are thus the basis of the system. The label "command economy" applies to the economic system as a whole because the "commands" issued by superiors are the central features that organize the system. Just as the flow of energy through an organism or a machine determines the physical form of that system, so the flow of commands through the bureaucracy determines the characteristic forms of the command economy. Individual incomes are determined by the extent to which commands are carried out (degree of plan fulfillment); input purchases and output sales are planned to enable production commands to be fulfilled; and financial flows are set to accommodate those planned tasks. Moreover, various planning exercises are expected to mesh into a single integrated plan that expresses the will of those who command. Thus, the command economy is "monomorphic," or uniform: all economic decision making is organized in such a way that it replicates and is subordinate to the basic "command" relationship. Similarly, economic organizations generally have the same internal structure regardless of their rank in the hierarchy, because all organizations serve the same functions of relaying commands and information. This monomorphism characterizes the command economy regardless of whether it is highly centralized or relatively decentralized.

The command economy is also monolithic. That is, there are no significant organizations outside the planned economy that compete with units inside. Because of the lack of competition and markets, prices do not carry much information useful in economic decision making. Instead, important information flows mainly through a few narrow channels connecting lower and higher levels. The importance and scarcity of official information channels means that they become the focus of interest of many different individuals. Those at lower levels, for example, have an interest in retaining information so that they can use this scarce resource to advance their own careers. The same superior-subordinate relations are used to structure information gathering and to issue commands, so the incentives to manipulate and distort those relations are very great. Bargaining within the bureaucracy is concentrated on the level of commands coming down the bureaucratic chain and the type of information going up: it is predominantly "plan bargaining."

In ordinary times this bargaining takes the form of "hiding reserves." Lower-level units wish to conceal capacity from their superiors in order to obtain plans that are easy to fulfill. In that way, they can be assured of a quiet life and an adequate income. Thus, the economic system as a whole tends to sink into a low-level equilibrium of low productivity and low effort. The situation is neatly captured by an epigram from Eastern Europe: "They pretend to pay us, and we pretend to work." In this respect, the command economy resembles any bureaucratic system, which may fall into this low-level trap when morale is low, tasks routinized, and external checks weak. The basic problem is that the narrow channels connecting subordinates to superiors become clogged with pseudoinformation, which is often intentionally distorted. While the system continues to report thousands of "bits" of data, the actual information content is quite limited. Production data are abundant, but these reflect merely an institutional consensus about appropriate levels of effort, rather than actual information about attainable levels of output. Uniformly organized production units all report more or less adequate performances, and it becomes impossible to know, for instance, the potential savings in energy usage that could be achieved by a drastically reshaped enterprise. Because of this impoverished information flow, it becomes difficult for leaders to get the kind of response from the "command economy" that they desire. The "command economy"—a model of subordination to the leader's will— becomes instead the "bureaucratic economy"—a model of unresponsiveness. It would be best to characterize these systems as "command-bureaucratic economies" to capture both the authoritarian flavor and the sense of unresponsiveness which the word *bureaucratic* has come to carry in daily language.[1]

One of the curiosities of the command economy is the tendency of the system to generate an opposite, superresponsive kind of behavior during certain exceptional periods. During exceptional "forward leaps" a different response emerges, which we can call Stakhanovite after the Soviet coal miner who hewed 104 tons of coal—fourteen times his output quota—on one particularly good day in 1935. During these periods the incentive structure is altered to reward exceptional achievements, and production workers and units begin vying to overfulfill their plans by ever more astonishing margins. Suddenly, all the desire to conceal reserves is abandoned: in the context of a revivalist spirit, the worker-hero

1. Charles Lindblom characterizes these systems as having "strong thumbs, no fingers." See *Politics and Markets: The World's Political-Economic Systems* (New York: Basic Books, 1977), 65–75.

shatters the stagnation of the bureaucratic system. Certainly the most spectacular example of this behavior shift was the Great Leap Forward in China, when it seemed for a period that all the laws of nature had been repealed. In 1958 cadres eager for recognition reported spectacular grain harvests, leading the central leadership to believe that China's total harvest had increased by a miraculous amount. The commands that followed included instructions to reduce the acreage sown to grain and increase deliveries of grain to the state, thus leading directly to disastrous famine.[2] While Stakhanovite leaps forward seem to be the opposite of the bureaucratic economy, they are really just the flip side of the same phenomenon. In both cases, the tangling of the incentive system and information flows creates a distorted and degraded flow of information; the indeterminacy of the whole system, because of the absence of external checks, permits the most outrageous outcomes to appear acceptable for a period. The extremes of stagnation and Stakhanovite leaps forward are *both* more likely when central planners have a weak and uncertain grasp over concrete decision making in the economy.[3]

What determines the level of effective control over the economy exerted by central planners? The size and complexity of the economy play a major role, and Chinese planners would face a formidable control problem under any conceivable system. More specifically, however, effective control basically depends on two factors. The first is the direct control over resources—particularly investment resources—exercised by planners, and the second is the quality of the information available to planners. In both these respects, Chinese planners were exceptionally weak before reforms. Even before reforms, financial control over one-third of investment had been decentralized, and only two-thirds of investment was disbursed directly through the government budget. Slightly less than half of state investment went for projects that were included in the central-government investment plan. Moreover, central-government resources were tied up in the misguided "Third Front" development strategy, leaving central planners with little freedom to shift resources in

2. The process of misinformation can explain policy mistakes through late 1958, but it cannot, of course, explain the criminal continuance of the Great Leap Forward after such misinformation was recognized, probably by the beginning of 1959, and certainly after the Lushan Plenum in summer 1959.

3. In a recent analysis, the Stakhanovite movement in the Soviet Union has been explicitly linked to a radical attempt to shake up a system sinking into bureaucratic stagnation. See J. Arch Getty, *Origins of the Great Purges: The Soviet Communist Party Reconsidered, 1933–1938* (New York: Cambridge University Press, 1985). As individuals, Stakhanovite workers received substantial material rewards and, on occasion, high political office. P. Krivonos, the leading Stakhanovite in the railroads, parlayed his achievement into a position on the Ukrainian Central Committee. John Armstrong. *The Politics of Totalitarianism: The Communist Party of the Soviet Union from 1934 to the Present* (New York: Random House, 1961), 91–93.

response to changing priorities.[4] Even more striking was the decline in the quality of the information available to planners. During the Cultural Revolution the State Statistical Bureau was reduced sharply in size, and most of its functions were incorporated into the planning commissions at all levels. This meant that the government sacrificed a semiautonomous source of information and became completely dependent on information channeled directly through the industrial hierarchy. Moreover, the whole scope of statistics gathering changed. Previously, the Statistical Bureau had been charged with gathering data about the entire economy, but as control over significant blocks of resources was decentralized, the data-collection network shrank to cover only those areas directly under central control. Thus, when control over "technical transformation" investment was decentralized, the government ceased to collect information about this important component of investment. The government literally did not know how much total investment was taking place.[5] Similarly, materials that were under local control and "balanced" by local authorities were not incorporated into the central-government balancing process at all. Of course, the government continued to collect output figures, but it made no effort to coordinate sources and uses of this important portion of total output. Finally, the decimation of the technically skilled economic bureaucracy meant that only relatively crude direction of resource flows could take place. Only a few hundred commodities were centrally planned, whereas in the Soviet Union several thousand such commodities are planned. With limited skills and limited information, the central government was unable to exercise detailed control over even those portions of the economy where it nominally possessed absolute authority.

China's economic system before reform was unquestionably a "command economy," but it is of only limited value to describe it as a centrally planned economy. While the Center had enormous formal authority, and while the ultimate centralization of the Communist Party and other aspects of the political system cannot be neglected, the Center was extraordinarily weak compared with other planned economies. As a result, the industrial economy was unresponsive to attempts to regulate daily decision making but was at the same time vulnerable to recurrent periods of

4. For the central-government investment plan, see the Appendix. For the other points, see Barry Naughton, "The Decline of Central Control over Investment in Post-Mao China," in *Policy Implementation in Post-Mao China*, ed. David M. Lampton (Berkeley and Los Angeles: University of California Press, 1987), 51–80; and "The Third Front: Defense Industrialization in the Chinese Interior," *China Quarterly*, no. 115 (Autumn 1988).

5. See Wang Yifu, ed., *Xin Zhongguo Tongji Shigao* (A Draft History of Statistics in New China) (Beijing: *Zhongguo Tongji*, 1986), 165–82; Planning Section, Fushun Colliery, "How We Unified Statistical Work for Technical Transformation," *Tongji*, 1981, no. 4:11–12.

leaping forward. One case that occurred on the eve of economic reform is symptomatic of the weakness of central control. In November 1977 the State Council approved a proposal to build at Baoshan in the Shanghai suburbs an advanced iron mill, to be imported from Japan and capable of supplying 5 million metric tons (MMT) of iron annually. Within six months of approval, the cost of the projected plant had approximately quadrupled, as it was expanded to a comprehensive steel mill producing 6 MMT of iron and 6 MMT of steel, plus continuous hot and cold steel rolling mills. Yet at this time no blueprints or construction plans had ever been submitted to the central Planning Commission. In July 1978 the Planning Commission finally obtained and approved blueprints, but the discovery that the designs submitted incorporated a further expansion of the project and still more cost increases led to escalating doubts. Subsequent rethinking led to the recognition that the project was deeply flawed, but by that time contracts had been signed with Japanese suppliers that basically locked the government into the proposal. Ultimately, the government proceeded with a project with a total cost of over 20 *billion* yuan (over $4 billion at today's exchange rates), in spite of the fact that planners had not possessed any detailed information about the project until it was already under way.[6] Surely few decisions of this magnitude have ever been made on such a flimsy information base. We can speculate that cases like this, occurring after the door had been decisively closed on the Cultural Revolution era, forced China's leaders to recognize the weakness of their bureaucratic decision-making process and made them more receptive to the possibility of economic reform.

THE CENTRAL GOVERNMENT AND THE CONTROL OF INVESTMENT

The early stages of economic reform in China were dominated by a process of decentralization. But while decentralization was taking place, a countervailing movement that improved the skills, information, and control available to the central government can also be discerned. This accumulation of skills was not in any sense contrary to the ideals of reform; indeed, increased sophistication of central officials was a key objective of reform in China, as in other socialist countries. Improved government skills would be necessary to guide the economy through the complexities of an increasingly marketized economy open to the outside world. However, in the face of constant change and recurrent crises,

6. Liu Jingtan and Hong Huiru, "Report on the Baoshan Steel Mill," *Gongye Jingji Guanli Congkan*, 1981, no. 2:29–32; Martin Weil, "Baoshan: A Symbol of Change in China's Industrial Policy," in *China Under the Four Modernizations*, ed. U.S. Congress Joint Economic Committee, 1:365–93.

central leaders have understandably used their newly available skills and information, and this has involved the central government in new activities despite the general decentralization process. Moreover, the two-track or "piecemeal" reform process in China has left a wide range of activities potentially open to central-government involvement. As a result, while the volume of resources directly under the control of the central government has declined, the Center's bargaining position has in other respects been enhanced by its greater access to information and the wider range of tools at its disposal. These contrasting trends can be seen most clearly through an investigation of the crucial focus of government activity in a command economy, the investment process.

By acceding to a dramatic reduction in its direct control over investment resources, the central government created the economic space that allowed reform to proceed in the late 1970s. Enterprises were given direct control over a substantial portion of profits and depreciation allowances that had previously been drawn into the state budget, and the government budget shrank as a proportion of the economy. The clearest indicator of direct government control over investment resources is the amount of investment that is funded directly through the government budget (shown in figure 9.1 as a proportion of national income [net material product].) Between 1978 and 1981 budgetary investment fell by half, from almost 15 percent of national income to slightly over 7 percent; moreover, the decline was persistent, with budgetary investment declining each successive year. This is an extremely unusual phenomenon, virtually unprecedented in the experience of centrally planned economies.[7] Between 1981 and 1984 budgetary investment stabilized. While it rose slightly as a proportion of national income to above 8 percent, it continued to decline as a proportion of total investment, which was increasing rapidly. After 1984 budgetary investment again entered a declining phase and fell below 6 percent of national income in 1987.

In the early reform years the central leadership acceded to this diminution in its direct control and began rebuilding the institutions that would improve the quality and volume of its information about the economy. At this point central planners had little choice, since they quite literally had no central plan: the existing planning procedures, as of the late 1970s, had produced only the grandiose Ten-Year Plan, which was widely recognized as unrealistic and had been discarded. The rebuilding of information networks began with the rehabilitation and strengthening

7. I discussed this phenomenon in 1983 in "The Decline of Central Control over Investment in Post-Mao China," in Lampton, ed., *Policy Implementation*. This section is an extension and revision of the analysis presented there.

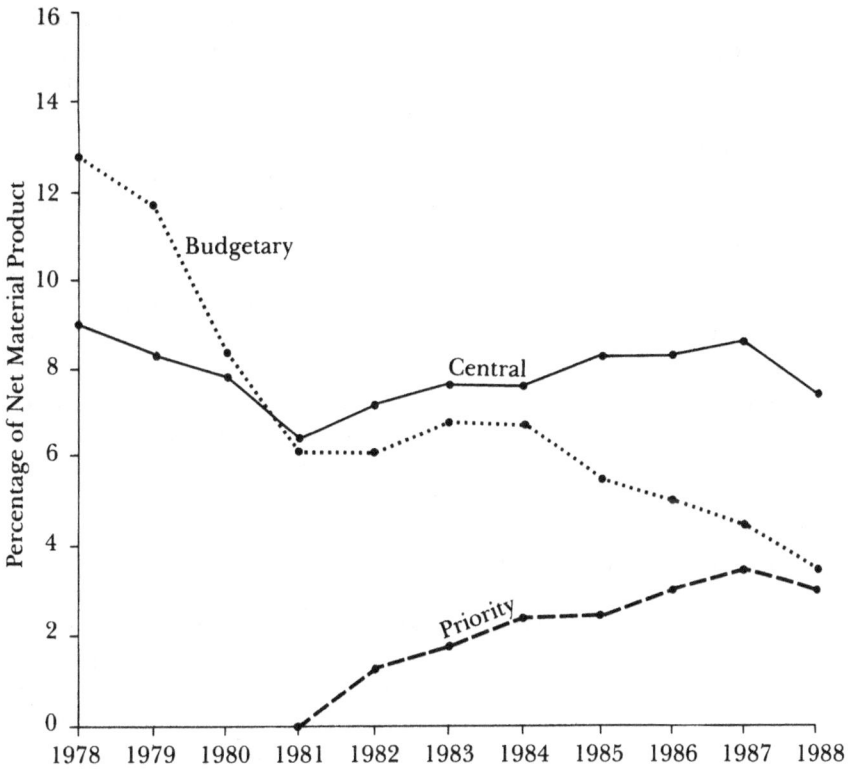

Fig. 9.1. Fixed Investment: Budgetary and Central Government

of the State Statistical Bureau. The Statistical Bureau then gradually expanded the coverage of its data-collection network, improving the reliability and meaningfulness of data. In the sphere of investment the Statistical Bureau gradually progressed from collecting information only about capital construction within the state economy to collecting information about all kinds of fixed investment economy-wide, including that carried out by individual households. Computerized information centers under the State Council now regularly collect data from all large industrial enterprises. Several new research institutes labor with increasing sophistication to interpret and analyze the available information.[8] As the available information base improved planners began to engage in a series of long-range projections of the future of the economy, projections

8. See chapter 5 in this volume, and "Fixed Investment Statistics," *China Statistics Monthly* (University of Illinois at Chicago), 1988, no. 2:1–2.

that became gradually more meaningful and specific.[9] Even as direct central control over investable resources declined, a gradually more sophisticated process of economic strategizing led to increased demands that investment accord with central-government priorities.

As central planners gradually developed a coherent vision of future economic development, they began to engage in a continuous tug-of-war with local interests. Generally speaking, central planners tried to increase the flow of investment to key bottleneck sectors, particularly energy and transport. Local governments and enterprises, by contrast, tried to develop industries with high profit rates and prospects for rapid growth. Because China's distorted price system keeps the profitability of energy low, and projects in this sector require large-scale investments often beyond local capabilities, the energy sector was rarely targeted by localities. They gambled instead that bottlenecks in transportation and energy would ultimately be taken care of by the central government, and that localities with the most promising early development of profitable industries would be able to hold on to those assets.

From the beginning of the reform process, the central government repeatedly stressed the need to develop energy production, but energy investment nevertheless stagnated between 1978 and 1982. This stagnation came about in part because central planners simply did not have workable plans for energy development. They had not carried out the detailed work of selecting sites and projects, drawing up blueprints, and working out supply arrangements. For a period they hoped the foreign multinationals would solve some of the problems by developing offshore oil fields, but this hope was disappointed. Priority to energy and transportation remained a long-range goal rather than a concrete task for operational plans. In addition, planners felt they could temporarily survive by allowing the industrial structure to shift toward a lighter, less energy-intensive pattern. The new decentralized funding mechanisms that were devised were used predominantly for light-industry investment. For example, when new programs of bank lending for fixed investment were initiated, 13 billion yuan worth of fixed investment were funded by bank loans, and of this, 68 percent went for light industry (mid-1979 through mid-1982).[10] During this period even central-government projects were frequently in light and consumption-goods industries. Ultimately, however, the growing economy would need more investment in energy and transport.

9. Carol Hamrin, *China and the Challenge of the Future* (Boulder, Colo.: Westview, 1990). Barry Naughton, "China's Experience with Guidance Planning," *Journal of Comparative Economics* 14, no. 4 (December 1990): 743–67.

10. Zhu Tianshun, "Medium Period Equipment Loans Make a Big Contribution," *Zhongguo Jinrong*, 1982, no. 22:1–3, translated in JPRS Economic Affairs, no. 303, 4–6.

During the early 1980s the central government gradually created a menu of projects in the energy and transport sectors that it wished to carry out. The result was a steady revival in the importance of the central investment plan. Statistics are shown in figure 9.1 on investment spending on all projects included in the central-government investment plan. (For a description of the data, see the appendix to this chapter.) Between 1978 and 1981 spending on central-government projects declined substantially but not as much as budgetary investment. Spending on central projects declined from slightly over 10 percent of national income to just below 8 percent, a reduction of 2.5 percent of national income—a very substantial change, but quite a bit less than the decline in budgetary investment. In 1978 spending on central projects was significantly less than budgetary investment. If we think of the central government as simultaneously establishing an investment-funding mechanism and a program of investment projects, these two activities in conjunction yielded a substantial surplus in 1978, equal to slightly over 4 percent of national income. Thus, after spending on central projects was complete, budgetary funds were still available to fund projects planned by local governments.

From 1981 through 1984 budgetary investment and spending on central-government projects were roughly equal. This does not mean that all budgetary investment went directly to central-government projects: some central projects were funded in whole or in part through bank loans, and some through extrabudgetary retained funds; conversely, some budgetary investment went to local-level projects. Netting out these flows, central-government projects and budgetary investment were roughly in balance, with a slight deficit amounting to about 1 percent of national income. In order to fund central-government projects the central government would have to draw in extrabudgetary funds or bank loans equal to about 1 percent of national income, even if no budgetary funds went to local-level projects.[11] During this period, household and enterprise saving was rising rapidly, so drawing on surplus funds was not difficult, and no serious economic problems arose.[12] After 1984 the spending trend for central-government projects diverged from that of budgetary investment.

11. Note that this deficit in the central-government investment program is entirely separate from, and in addition to, the government budget deficit. The budget deficit measures the borrowing necessary to fund actual government expenditures; the investment program deficit measures the borrowing necessary to complete the investment program after actual government expenditures have been used.

12. See the important flow of funds data given in Macroeconomic Research Office, Economic System Reform Research Institute, "The Macroeconomy in the Process of Reform: Distribution and Use of National Income," *Jingji Yanjiu* (Economic Research), 1987, no. 8:16–28. The data from this article are reproduced and discussed in Barry Naughton, "Macroeconomic Management and System Reform in China," in *From Crisis to Crisis: The Chinese State in the Era of Economic Reform*, ed. Gordon White (London: Macmillan, 1990).

While budgetary investment dropped further, spending on central-government projects climbed steadily; by 1987 it had surpassed 10 percent of NMP (net material product), regaining the 1978 level. In order to fund this substantial investment program, the central government, by 1987, had to borrow funds equal to 4 percent of national income. Thus, while the central government surrendered direct control over economic resources, it did not reduce its aspirations in a corresponding fashion. By the second half of the 1980s a significant disparity had developed between what the central government wished to accomplish and the resources at its disposal. The central plan had been reborn, but whereas before reform the central government had directly disposed of the resources to carry out this plan, it now had to devise additional mechanisms to draw resources into planned projects.

Central-government planners evolved three complementary strategies to attain their investment objectives: they concentrated their own resources on priority sectors; they harnessed the financial resources of the banking system to those priorities; and they drew on local financial resources through a version of "matching funds." While the first of these strategies was merely a rationalized version of the old planned system, the other two involved the central government in bargaining exercises with local officials and enterprises. Each of these strategies will be examined in detail.

The most important single component of the central government's concentration of its own resources has been the creation of a special program of priority projects. A gradually increasing number of projects had been planned with "rational time-tables and guaranteed supply of materials." These projects have first claim on materials still under state control. This is a kind of plan within the plan, and its significance can be seen from the figures in table 9.1. The priority-investment program has grown steadily, both in absolute terms and as a proportion of national income. Moreover, all these projects have access to in-plan materials provided at subsidized prices, so that real resources are concentrated on the priority program to an even greater extent than the financial data indicate. In essence, the central government is subordinating the surviving elements of the material-allocation system to its development strategy. Before reforms the material-allocation system was charged with the nearly impossible task of delivering resources to all state-run factories for all production needs. But as reform has deepened and the economy has diversified, the allocation system, now much smaller relative to the economy as a whole, has increasingly been targeted to this investment program. The central government no longer has nominal control over all the materials in the economy; but the remaining control over materials is now used almost exclusively to carry out central-government priorities.

TABLE 9.1. Central Government Priority Investment

Year	No. of Projects	Investment (B. Yuan)	% of Total Capital Construction	% of NMP
1982	50	6.30	11.3	1.47
1983	70	9.41	9.9	1.97
1984	123	15.90	13.4	2.79
1985	169	19.83	18.5	2.64
1986	190	27.99	23.8	3.37
1987	206	36.19	27.3	3.95

SOURCES: 1986 *Jingji Nianjian*, V-12; *Zhongguo Jiben Jianshe*, 1986, no. 5:25; 1987, no. 7:9–10; 1988, no. 2:8.

The priority-investment program also differs from the old central plan in the quality of the design and planning activity. Unlike the Baoshan steel mill, symbolic of the low quality of planning prior to reform, today's priority projects are carried out with reasonable preparatory work, feasibility studies, and complete sets of design documents. Indeed, a number of the projects utilize international funds, such as those from the Japanese Development Bank and the World Bank, and thus have to comply with international standards for project appraisal and implementation, including competitive bidding for some parts of the work. The central plan has thus been strengthened in a technocratic sense; with a better understanding of the economy as a whole and better utilization of trained manpower, the economic returns of these projects will generally be higher than those of projects during the 1970s before reform. This is true both because individual projects are better designed and because the program as a whole is targeted more effectively on bottleneck sectors. At the same time, priority status and access to materials serves to ensure the completion of the projects. In 1987 the capital-construction expenditure plan for these projects was 109 percent fulfilled, while the remainder of the plan was only 90.5 percent completed.[13] Although this is an improved version of the central plan, relative to what China had before, it still suffers from the inherent liabilities of central planning, as was discussed in the preceding section.

In order to carry out the broader central-government plan (including the priority plan as one component), the government still needs access to additional financial resources. As central plans grew, bank lending was harnessed to the needs of this plan. By 1985, at the latest, this had worked a fundamental change in the composition of both central-government investment and the use of bank loans. Figures are presented in table 9.2 on the proportion of different types of capital-construction investment going to three bottleneck sectors—energy, transport, and heavy raw-materials

13. *Zhongguo Jiben Jianshe* (China Capital Construction), 1988, no. 2:8–9.

TABLE 9.2. Percentage of Capital
Construction Going to Energy,
Materials, and Transport

By administrative level	
Central	62
Local	19
By primary funding source	
Budgetary	49
Bank loans	62
Retained (extrabudgetary)	28

SOURCE: Song Guangrong, "An Analysis of
Investment in Bottleneck Sectors," *Zhongguo Jiben Jianshe*, 1988, no. 8:27. Transport
includes telecommunications.

industries—in 1985. Table 9.2 shows the striking difference between the
composition of central and local-level investment and confirms the reluctance of local governments and enterprises to invest their own money in
bottleneck sectors. According to the same source, 80 percent of electricity
investment in the past few years has been on central-government projects.
Even more striking is the extent to which bank lending conforms to
central-government priorities. Originally introduced to permit flexible,
decentralized financing of consumer goods industries, bank lending
for fixed investment has increasingly been reshaped to serve central-
government investment projects. While 68 percent of fixed-investment
lending went to light industry in 1979–82, 62 percent went for a
subcategory of heavy industry and transportation in 1985.[14] Given the
division of responsibility over different sectors, this means that the central
government effectively preempts most fixed-investment lending, and local governments and enterprises have correspondingly fewer financial
resources. The banking system is unable to serve as an independent,
decentralized funding source, for it is squeezed between the demands of
the central government and local officials. Banks are obligated first to
fund central-government projects; subsequently, they are placed under
enormous political pressure to put remaining resources in the service of
projects favored by local governments.

The second source of additional financing is the retained funds of

14. There are no direct data on the proportion of bank loans going to central projects.
(Cross-tabulations of investment categories are not generally published.) Also, the comparison is not precise, since the 1979–82 figures include all fixed-investment lending, whereas
the 1985 figure includes only capital construction, excluding technical-transformation investment. This biases the comparison somewhat, but I have been unable to locate additional
data on the sectoral composition of technical-transformation lending.

localities and enterprises. Increasingly, the central government requires localities to contribute "matching funds" in order to see critical infrastructure projects in their regions. For example, while the projects in electricity generation are overwhelmingly central, the money for them comes to a significant degree from the localities. Through the end of 1984, twenty-six large-scale electricity-generation projects had been carried out in the central plan, but using the joint resources of central and local authorities; the localities had provided 3.5 billion yuan, or 51 percent of the total cost.[15] Thus, the central government resolves the disparity between its limited financial resources and its responsibility for crucial sectors of the economy by negotiating for additional resources project by project. In this negotiation the central government is quite powerful: it possesses the design resources and seed money needed for large-scale energy development, and it possesses enormous leverage over the economic system as a whole, including the material-allocation and banking systems. Yet it also requires the cooperation and financial resources of local governments and enterprises. Thus, the Center and local governments are now involved in a classic bargaining situation: each has something the other needs. It is in the interests of both parties to get together, and it is in the interests of each to shape the resulting bargain to their own advantage.

One example of this bargaining process is presented by the province of Shandong.[16] Shandong is a large, slightly above-average coastal province, which has grown rapidly in recent years and has also experienced significant energy shortages. It is estimated that energy supply is 20 percent below demand. Shandong is the site of 11 of the 190 central-government priority projects, and it accounted for 8.5 percent of 1986 national priority-investment expenditure. Shandong thus receives substantial central-government support, and central projects include two large power plants, a very large ethylene plant, and two ports. Shandong's development strategy is therefore inextricably bound up with its relations with the central government.

To obtain central-government investment projects, Shandong makes—and publicizes—major contributions to those projects. Shandong provides a significant portion of the money for these projects, and must also organize land requisition and purchase; supply of water, electricity, and transport; supply of local building materials (cement, bricks, stone, and sand); and design and construction services. Thus, a substantial part of

15. *1985 Zhongguo Baike Nianjian* (China Encyclopedic Yearbook), 226.

16. The following discussion is based on the Sixth Five-Year Plan for Shandong, *Dazhong Ribao*, 2 May 1983, and a series of articles in *Zhongguo Jiben Jianshe* (China Capital Construction), 1986, no. 9:22; 1986, no. 12:35; 1987, no. 1:18–19; 1987, no. 2:10–11; 1987, no. 5:18–30; 1988, no. 1:12.

Shandong's investment policy consists of coordination and support for central-government investments. An important reason for this support is to demonstrate to the central government that the locality is making a contribution, thus ensuring a future flow of central resources to Shandong. A significant public relations effort goes on to reassure the central government that its money is well spent. Yet these contributions are also a substantial burden to Shandong. The central-government financial contribution to a project covers only a portion of total cost and is generally fixed at the beginning of the plan year, leaving the locality to deal with the frequent cost overruns, while quantitative controls on investment strictly limit the province's total investment. Moreover, the province has to pay taxes on its investment spending—even when that spending goes to central-government projects—whereas the central government itself is exempt from construction taxes.

The province's strategy is to publicize all contributions to central-government projects while seeking ways to minimize the actual burden of those projects. Shandong authorities argue for tax exemptions and additional investment authority in order to carry the burden of central-government projects; at the same time, their own projects have been further "decentralized," placed under the nominal control of rural collectives so that they disappear from the provincial investment quotas. Every investment decision is thus shaped by the desire to draw in the largest possible amount of central resources (including centrally approved bank loans) while simultaneously protecting local resources as much as possible. Compared with the prereform system, Shandong is much less a passive agent of central-government plans; yet its more active role is shaped by obligations as much as opportunities and is still dominated by the need to draw resources from the central government. Shandong follows a particular strategy of high-visibility support for the central government, which is consistent with its generous endowment of central projects. Other localities follow a low-profile strategy of quietly draining resources from central projects, hoping that, ultimately, the Center's commitment to those projects will insure their completion. In this way, local projects that have little protection in case of policy changes can be completed as quickly as possible.[17] The bargaining relation between Center and locality is here in full flower.

Local governments find themselves squeezed between the Center and their enterprises. On the one hand, they must bargain with the Center to maximize central-government investments in their territory; on the other hand, they seek to retain as much as possible in the way of re-

17. This strategy is described in Huang Kai, "Macro-control of the Scale of Fixed Investment," *Zhongguo Jinrong* (China Finance), 1986, no. 2:60.

sources and finances. They must promulgate their own development strategies, but they typically find themselves highly constrained by lack of expertise and experience. The obvious source of additional resources is the locality's own enterprises, which it can tap for a range of voluntary and involuntary contributions. But localities must strike a balance between drawing the resources they need from enterprises and allowing them sufficient resources for growth. This generally ends with local governments assuming a paternalistic, somewhat benevolent attitude toward all their enterprises, protecting them from the vicissitudes of the marketplace and encouraging their development, without regard for any particular development strategy. The relation between enterprises and their superiors will be discussed further below (see also chapter 11 in this volume), but it should be apparent that the difficult position in which localities find themselves will be reflected in their relations with their subordinate enterprises.

By following the three strategies described, the central government has managed to engineer a rebound in energy and transportation investment. Such investment was at a peak in 1978 before the initiation of reform. Energy investment as a proportion of total state fixed investment reached a low point in 1982 and since then has climbed to approximately the 1978 proportion (22–23 percent of investment); transportation investment has displayed a similar pattern, declining until 1981 and recovering since to 13–14 percent of investment. Measured both by the proportion of national income going to central-government projects and by the proportion of total investment going to central-priority sectors, central direction of investment appears as strong now as it was in 1978 before reforms began.

From the aggregate numbers, it would appear that the central government has simply been scrambling to get back to where it was in 1978. In fact, its economic role has been strengthened by access to three types of superior information. The Center's coordination of technical information has improved, so that individual projects are better. Much of the energy investment in 1978 was actually wasted; this is particularly clear in petroleum and is evident in other central-priority sectors as well, such as steel. Second, the central government has utilized better information about the economy as a whole, including long-range forecasting, to concentrate on areas where the case for central coordination is stronger. Generally leaving smaller-scale, consumer-oriented production to the localities and enterprises, the Center has focused on large-scale infrastructure projects, which often span provincial boundaries. These two factors together have caused a gradual improvement in the provision of energy and transport services; while these sectors have remained bottlenecks, industrial growth has nevertheless accelerated, and the shortages persist relative to a much larger volume of output. Finally, the Center's increased information about local-government activities permits it to engage in specific bargains with localities about individual projects. It is this last type of information that ultimately has allowed the Center to subordinate the banking and material-allocation systems to its objectives, using the resources in those systems as bargaining chips to shape local behavior.

Nevertheless, these factors must always be seen in the context of the decline in direct central control over resources. Central planners are arguably stronger, and certainly more capable, than before reform, but they must deal with a vastly more complex economic environment in which many different agents have control over resources. This environment constantly threatens to overwhelm central-government actions. Although central actions have increased the investment share of priority sectors, the results still fall quite a bit short of central-government objectives. The Sixth Five-Year Plan, covering 1981–85 but drawn up only in 1982, called for the completion of 400 large and medium-sized investment projects, but in fact only 235 (59 percent) were completed by the end of 1985. In 1987, 63 out of 74 planned large projects (85 percent) were completed on schedule.[18] The sustained central-government focus on energy and transportation has just barely offset the bias toward light-industry investment created by decentralization of resources.

Examination of the investment process thus shows a complex set of changes. Although the central government's direct control over investment resources has been unambiguously reduced, it has been able to use its authority over the economic system as a whole, in combination with substantially enhanced information about the economy, to increase its indirect control over investment. But the nature of the central government's "indirect control" instruments is still highly imperfect: rather than manipulating objective economic levers to control the market environment and thus shape lower-level decisions, central planners instead achieve indirect control by engaging with lower levels in a case-by-case bargaining process. In an immediate sense, this works: it has increased the flow of investment resources into bottleneck sectors. Yet this strategy is clearly a second-best alternative to more fundamental reforms, including increases in the relative price of energy and transport. The central government's expedient policies draw local governments into further complex bargaining relations with the central government, rather than confronting them with more rational costs and opportunities for their own investments. A modest recentralization of finances, bringing financial capabilities in line with central-government ambitions, combined

18. Hu Changlin, "When Will the System of Allocating Blocks of Investment and Lending to Functional Departments Be Reformed?" *Zhongguo Jiben Jianshe* (China Capital Construction), 1986, no. 12:7–8; 1988, no. 3:41–42.

with price rationalization and greater autonomy for those controlling decentralized finances, would be preferable. In this way, energy shortages could be addressed without enmeshing all parties in an overly complex bargaining relationship.

More generally, the strategy that has been followed does not seem capable of resolving the fundamental problems of the command-bureaucratic economy. While the Center has better information about local activities and can bargain with localities about a relatively small number of large-scale projects, it still lacks detailed knowledge and control of the bulk of economic decisions. In a sense, the central government can achieve certain objectives precisely because those objectives are circumscribed in scope, while the economy as a whole is just as resistant to specific manipulation by administrative means as it always has been. The new bargaining relations can only compensate for some of the deterioration in authority relations. Moreover, as the central government must cover a deficit in its investment program equal to 4 percent of national income, it competes for savings and pressures the banking system to create credit at an excessive rate. The central government is powerful but needy, and this tends to destabilize the system.

ENTERPRISES AND THE TWO-TRACK SYSTEM

At the opposite end of the hierarchy from the central government, enterprises are the building blocks of the industrial economy. A few basic principles have guided enterprise reforms from the beginning. Reformers held that enterprises should cease to be administrative subdivisions of the government bureaucracy and should instead become economic entities making independent decisions based on price and profitability. Enterprises would become "relatively autonomous commodity producers," responsible for their own profits and losses, and economic—rather than administrative—means would be used to accomplish economic objectives. Most reformers envisage a continuing activist role for government, but that role is carried out through the manipulation of "economic levers," such as interest rates and prices.[19] Evidently, such principles require a reduction in direct government interference with enterprise decision making and imply a limited and indirect role for government that requires substantial sophistication.

These principles are too broad to serve as a specific blueprint for the reform process. The concrete strategy that has dominated the Chinese reform process has been that of allowing a gradual expansion of markets

19. All these principles can be found in the basic urban reform charter, passed by the Central Committee in October 1984. "Zhonggong zhongyang guanyu jingji tizhi gaige de jueding," (20 October 1984) in *Zhongguo Jingji Nianjian 1985*, I/1–I/13.

outside the confines of the planned economy. The planned economy survives, but its size has been held roughly constant, while the regular growth of the economy has steadily swelled the proportion of economic activity carried on outside the plan through the market or marketlike exchanges. The leadership hoped that this evolutionary process would result in the gradual marketization of the economy, while the maintenance of a planned sector would anchor the system during the period when leaders were learning to use "economic levers" and indirect market regulation. This reform strategy has often been referred to as a "two-track" system combining both traditional planning and market operations. One of the essential features of this strategy—and one that gives the Chinese system its great novelty—has been that the two-track system is applied not only to the economy as a whole but also to each individual enterprise. Thus, nearly every state-owned factory operates with a portion of its output planned by government and a portion produced according to market demand.

At its best, the two-track-system strategy of reform held the promise of introducing market forces into the state-run industrial system at a rapid pace. Rather than waiting years for a comprehensive rationalization of prices and taxes, enterprises would be confronted with the opportunity of operating in the marketplace immediately. The command economy would persist, but its scope would be strictly limited. As a result, the monomorphism that made all decision making subject to the command relationship would be broken, since enterprise decisions about the growing portion of the economy would be made on the basis of profitability considerations determined by market prices. At the same time, the growth of a market sector would shatter the monolithic state economy; state-run enterprises operating out-of-plan would compete with collective and private enterprises, and markets would provide information and competitive pressures that could be used to reshape the state economy. Alternately stated, if plan targets were frozen, enterprises would face market prices on the margin, and the enterprise's plan would serve as a lump-sum tax, having no effect on current operations. The administrative economy would thus be gradually dissolved by market forces, and the bargaining economy progressively replaced by the objective rule of the market.

In this framework it is essential that the planned "track" be frozen. If the size of the planned economy is not fixed, then enterprise decision making cannot be fully freed to depend on the market. If the enterprise expects that its market-oriented behavior will have repercussions on the level of planned targets or inputs, it will inevitably take those repercussions into account in its decision making. As a result, advocates of the two-track system have tended to oppose using the old command-economy structure to solve problems, even to the extent of opposing price reforms within the administrative economy. This position has been bolstered by a perception of the bureaucratic economy as a clumsy and unresponsive system, evident in a recent article by advocates of the two-track system:

> The debate over whether it is better to adjust planned prices or to simply decontrol stems from different assessments of the ability of the government. Those who advocate price adjustment believe strongly in the ability of the government to control the price reform process . . . [while we believe that] there is a serious contradiction between highly centralized price adjustment and the decentralized structure of interest groups. The central government will never be able to calculate the impact of each individual price change as accurately as the localities and . . . enterprises, and the ultimate burden of price adjustment will inevitably be shifted onto the state treasury.[20]

In other words, advocates of the two-track system felt that the flows of information in the command economy were too crude and distorted to be useful in a rationalization of economic relations. A bureaucracy with weak information-gathering capabilities and correspondingly limited management abilities had no choice but to rely on the expansion of markets outside the system to realize its ideals of reformed enterprise behavior. The strategy of freezing a clumsy bureaucracy—rather than trying to rationalize it—implied that the financial and authority relations linking enterprises to their superiors would persist, though, one would hope, in fossilized form.

Unfortunately, this strategy has not yet been adequate to make the enterprise-reform principles into reality. It has been impossible, first of all, to freeze the planned "track" of the economy. The overall size of the command economy (the scale of central-government production and allocation plans) has indeed stayed relatively constant, declining steadily as a proportion of total economic activity as the economy grows. Yet from the perspective of an individual enterprise, plans are anything but stable. Some enterprises experience shrinking plans and are uncertain about the speed of shrinking. Other enterprises discover that their plan is increasing, and they may welcome this when it promises access to cheap inputs. For example, when the foreign joint-venture automobile companies, such as Beijing Jeep and Guangzhou Peugeot, ran into problems with raw-material supplies, the government provided them a special benefit: incorporation into the plan. The overall constancy of the plan thus conceals considerable variation in plan targets at the enterprise level.

20. Hua Sheng, Zhang Xuejun, and Luo Xiaopeng, "Ten Years of Reform in China: Retrospective, Rethinking, and Prospects," *Jingji Yanjiu*, 1988, no. 9:16.

Moreover, in the traditional command economy, input supplies are subordinate to the production plan, so that only the level of the production plan itself is important. However, in China, as bureaucratic capabilities declined during the Cultural Revolution, and as the system became less regularized during the reform process, there began to be substantial discrepancies between production plans and the allocation of inputs. Enterprises today cannot necessarily get the full quota of inputs required to fulfill their compulsory plan. Thus, even for a given production plan, enterprises face differential supplies of low-price inputs, and ultimately supply depends upon the nature of enterprise relations with their superiors. Here, paradoxically, the deterioration of bureaucratic capabilities makes it harder to freeze the bureaucratic portion of the economy, because the bureaucratic system is incapable of generating a single parameter to represent the level at which the plan should be fixed. Only enterprises that have obtained administrative recognition of their priority status can hope to receive a full complement of subsidized inputs.[21] The individual enterprise cannot regard the plan as being fixed in any meaningful sense. A persuasive case to a superior might always make a difference; "plan bargaining" persists in the two-track system.

Outside the plan, the environment in which enterprises operate is still not a pure market environment. Indeed, in general, enterprises do not sell their outside-plan output at market-clearing prices. In most cases, outside-plan output is sold at a higher price than planned output, but the price is kept low enough that shortages continue to arise and the enterprise must decide to whom to deliver its products.[22] This is a very curious phenomenon that requires explanation: Why do enterprises not exploit their apparent ability to charge higher prices? There seem to be three mutually reinforcing causes of this type of enterprise behavior. First is the government effort to restrain price increases in the inflationary environment that has prevailed since 1984. The old bureaucratic networks persist and are used to pressure enterprises to refrain from raising prices; in this sense, the failure to charge market-clearing prices is simply a result of the failure to free the enterprise from the old authority relations. Such pressures vary greatly from region to region and from sector to sector, depending upon the bureaucracy and type of good involved—producers of certain consumer goods are subject to more

21. This generalization is based on a sample of twenty-two enterprises visited in the summer of 1988. Individual enterprises reported receiving anywhere between 20 percent and 100 percent of the main inputs required for in-plan production.

22. Of twenty-two enterprises visited (see n. 21), each was selling some outside-plan output at a higher price. However, only two were selling at a price that equated supply and demand, and all the others practiced some type of informal rationing.

pressure, as are factories in "conservative" provinces with active price-control efforts.

The second factor is that enterprises find it in their own interest not to charge high, market-clearing prices for their output. When enterprises sell their output at the highest possible price, they receive all the benefit from the sale in overt, monetary form: high profits. Profits are highly visible, and they are highly taxed. As a result, although the enterprise may reap greater paper profits from such a sale, it may find itself with little real benefit after delivering taxes and other revenues to its superiors. When the enterprise chooses to sell its output at a lower price, it forgoes some money income but receives something else in return. Most commonly, it receives access to other goods at a concessionary price. If these are consumption goods, the enterprise benefits directly: the goods can be sold to the enterprise's workers without any overt subsidization and without restrictions. It appears to be a pure market transaction and is thus subject to no taxes and no quantitative limits. (If the enterprise had taken the income in money form and then distributed it to its workers, that distribution would have been subject to limitations on bonuses.) Furthermore, the enterprise creates a hedge against future supply and price uncertainties by creating a long-term cooperative relationship with another enterprise. Current income forgone is "saved" by accumulating capital in the form of *guanxi* (connections). By building up *guanxi* the enterprise obtains greater flexibility and security: *guanxi* can be used to shift income from one period to another, or to guarantee supplies of materials when the need is critical. For the enterprise to forgo *guanxi* for some short-run financial advantage would be shortsighted indeed.

Finally, the benefits received by forgoing enterprise profits can accrue to individuals, particularly managerial and sales personnel. This can take the form of a slightly lavish dinner and a carton of cigarettes, or it can involve major bribery. The danger of corruption is, of course, endemic to a two-track system, because of the existence of more than one price for any given commodity. Overt bribery and illicit sale of in-plan goods, however, can be extremely dangerous and seem to be relatively infrequent. A far more common pattern is the creation of long chains of buyers and sellers, each of whom raises the price of a good by, say, 10 percent, just enough to cover "handling charges." The individual privileged enough to be one of the links in this chain earns a moderate cash reward and acquires the gratitude of the individual who is the next link. No unambiguously illegal activity has taken place, and everyone involved has profited, except the original enterprise. Only at the end of this long chain does the good sell for something like a true market price.

For these three reasons, enterprises and their superiors collaborate in complex exchanges at other than market prices. On occasion, an enterprise may dispose of goods at market prices when it has no "connection" with the purchaser, and logically even the longest chain of buyers and sellers has a final link, so market prices exist. But it is extremely difficult to determine what those prices are, and difficult to object when transactions take place at other prices. Thus, there is a kind of "exchange bargaining" that goes on between enterprises and also affects enterprise relations with their superiors. Enterprise managers try to maximize a complex mixture of sales revenues and outside-sales benefits, and this leads them into elaborate bargaining arrangements.

When all the enterprise's supplies have been purchased, and all the output has been sold at various prices, the enterprise's ultimate profit is still far from determined. The final bargain that must be struck is that which determines the financial relations that link enterprises to their superiors. These have remained unregularized and subject to a bewildering array of inconsistent provisions. In part, this is due to the failure to successfully implement new fiscal systems, such as the "tax for profit" system and the consequent prevalence of the "contracting" (*chengbao*) system. Under the contracting system, enterprise financial obligations to superiors are determined as part of a multiyear contract negotiated between the two sides. Such a system is designed to provide high-powered incentives to enterprises by allowing them to retain a high percentage of their incremental revenues. At the same time, the contracting system indicates the inherent difficulty of the two-track system: the multiyear contract is an attempt to "freeze" the financial tribute the enterprise pays annually to its superiors. The fact that such a freeze has to be specified in a negotiated contract between the enterprise and its superior simply demonstrates that the planned track of the economy was not frozen to begin with. Quite the contrary, the financial relations between enterprises and superiors have been subject to constant, virtually annual, changes between 1978 and 1988. Unavoidably, each time financial provisions are altered, every aspect of the enterprise's economic health, behavior, and relations with its superiors enters into the process of adjustment. The striking of a deal dividing up enterprise revenues, which Kornai has described in Hungary and labeled "redistributional bargaining,"[23] is prevalent in China as well.

Redistributional bargaining in China is peculiarly unconstrained because of the absence of clear fiscal and financial regulations. Almost any parameter can be altered through negotiation between superiors and subordinates. For example, there is uncertainty as to whether bank loans

23. Janos Kornai, "The Hungarian Reform Process," *Journal of Economic Literature*, 24 (December 1986): 1691–1701.

should be repaid before or after taxes, so the authority to repay before taxes thus becomes a benefit that superiors grant enterprises. Actually, the discretion available to superiors is virtually unbounded; at one plant visited in 1988 the superiors had decided that the enterprise was having legitimate difficulties in fulfilling its profit-remittance contract because it had such a large volume of loans to repay. The superiors simply allowed the enterprise to count 50 percent of the loans it repaid as remitted profits for the purpose of calculating the revenue split, so that the enterprise succeeded in fulfilling its contract. In this case, the contract fulfillment was entirely imaginary. Taxes are slightly more difficult to alter, since the central government has repeatedly insisted that taxes, particularly those on cigarettes and liquor, should not be forgiven. Nevertheless, tax forgiveness is very significant. In Jiangsu in 1986 local authorities forgave taxes equal to a remarkable 12 percent of total budgetary revenue.[24] Every financial parameter is subject to negotiation and thus subject to constant change.

An additional aspect of redistributional bargaining links it to my earlier discussion of the central government and its investment plan. I noted above that, before reform, enterprises retained some funds for investment purposes, but that the central government collected no data on this investment and had no way of controlling it. Local governments and enterprises, in collaboration, were thus completely autonomous users of these funds. In the current period, enterprises control substantially more funds, but the central government no longer closes its eyes to their use. Instead, the government by the mid-1980s had promulgated a plan for enterprise-level investment in technical transformation. This plan, which includes projects for about half of all large enterprises, classifies enterprises and projects according to level of priority and establishes technologies and processes that are to be introduced.[25] This is not a detailed central investment plan, like the priority capital-construction program described above. However, it is the basis for central-government involvement in redistributional bargaining. Enterprises with authorized and high-priority investments are supposed to retain more profit and have easier access to bank loans than other enterprises. Thus, the central government uses this planning exercise to reach down the administrative hierarchy and shape the bargain between the enterprise and its direct superior in ways that reflect central-government priorities. Clearly, enterprises can benefit by appealing to patrons at the central level.

24. Tian Yuan, "Price Reform and the Transference of Property Rights," *Jingji Yanjiu*, 1988, no. 2:15.

25. "Strengthen the Long-range Planned Categorization of Large Enterprise Technical Transformation," *Zhongguo Jiben Jianshe* (China Capital Construction), 1985, no. 7:4–7.

The enterprise is thus enmeshed in a complex bargaining relationship with its superiors. Plan bargaining, exchange bargaining, and redistributional bargaining are all taking place simultaneously; in fact, along with the face-to-face personal relationships involved, they are woven into a single inextricable chain of bargains—repeatedly struck and constantly reopened—between enterprises and their superiors. No wonder, since both enterprises and superiors face a vast realm of indeterminacy, in which everything—price, plan, supply, tax, credit—is subject to change and negotiation. All these parameters can be altered by the enterprise's superior, and only an extraordinarily bold, or extraordinarily foolish, enterprise manager would choose to operate "on the market" as if the wishes of his superior did not matter. Conversely, only an exceptionally obtuse manager would ignore the opportunity to improve his lot and protect himself against adverse outcomes that is possible by the appeal to his superiors. The astute enterprise manager will always keep open the channels to his superiors that permit him to reopen the bargaining relation at any time.

What is true at the enterprise level is also true one step higher in the bureaucratic hierarchy. Local government officials must always be aware of the possibilities involved in currying favor with their superiors. Indeed, since there is no final blueprint for reforms, localities must be given the freedom to experiment and must be supported in this experimentation process. Localities learn very quickly that it is in their interest to have some kind of reform pilot project.[26] Localities receive special benefits to operate pilot projects, and if one is deemed successful, local officials will undoubtedly receive a career boost. As a result, reform "experiments" proliferate; at the end of 1986 there were seventy-two cities that were "comprehensive-reform pilot cities," sixteen "medium-size city administrative-reform pilots," twenty-seven banking-reform pilots, thirteen producers-goods-marketing pilots, fourteen housing-reform pilots, plus labor-reform pilots, coastal development zones, and so forth.[27] In each of these "experimental cities" local authorities could hope to obtain benefits and preferential treatment from the central government by extending benefits and preferential treatment to their subordinate enterprises. Thus, just as local governments were squeezed by the central government in the investment-allocation process, so do they squeeze themselves into the system-reform process. The reform process, and the real distribution of benefits within the state sector, evolve from this constant contention and interplay of interests.

26. An expression has arisen: "Whoever has a pilot project, benefits" (*shei shidian, shei deyi*).

27. *Zhongguo Baike Nianjian 1987*, 201–2.

BILATERAL MONOPOLY

By itself, the indeterminacy of so many economic parameters cannot explain the persistence of bargaining relations at the enterprise level. Indeed, given the rise of marketlike institutions in China during the past ten years, the question is why market forces do not in the long run eliminate the indeterminacy. Ultimately, the crucial factor is that state enterprises are in a relationship of bilateral monopoly with their superiors. The two-track reform strategy implies the retention of the administrative hierarchy, and because of the retention of the administrative hierarchy, enterprises cannot escape the influence of their superiors, while superiors cannot escape their ultimate reliance on the productive capacity of their enterprises. The importance of the retention of the hierarchy is thus not primarily that the enterprise remains subject to arbitrary commands from its superior (though this is sometimes a factor). Rather, the importance lies in the fact that the enterprise and its superior are forced to make a deal with each other. This is a special case of the general problem of small numbers exchange: one buyer confronts one seller and there are no competitive forces to drive the two into competitive equilibrium. The transaction takes place, given there are gains to be realized, but the benefits are divided between the two parties according to their relative bargaining power.

Within the state sector relations between the enterprise and its superior body are always situations of bilateral monopoly. Within any given urban area there is always a sector-specific bureaucracy that has responsibility for a certain type of production. For example, production of machine tools in Taiyuan will be subject to the Taiyuan machinery bureau, or to a similar provincial or national body. That bureau has the authority to permit or prevent production of machine tools by anybody in the city of Taiyuan, and this type of authority is universal and entirely formalized. It is impossible that "nobody" could be in charge of a certain kind of production in a certain locality; every locality and every type of production is automatically established as a monopoly.

Two particular aspects of the Chinese economic system affect the way these local-sectoral monopolies are managed, but they do not change the basic monopoly condition. First, it is a curiosity of the relatively decentralized Chinese system that industrial production in rural areas is controlled, not by sectoral bureaucracies of broad geographic scope, but by local bureaucracies with authority over a broad range of industrial sectors. Since there are so many local bureaucracies (more than 2,000 county-level governments), urban producers cannot be completely protected from competition arising in a nearby rural area. Indeed, markets in which rural producers play a role are the most competitive markets that exist in China. In most cases, though, rural industries have limited technological capabilities and produce goods of poor quality. Although this is gradually changing, competition from rural factories does not yet significantly change the market position of most modern urban factories, particularly in an economic environment characterized by excess demand and inflationary pressures.[28] Urban producers of a given product would be far more threatened by the threat that another urban factory would cross sectoral boundaries and produce a competing product, and it is precisely this danger from which they are protected by the monopoly power their superiors exercise over their own product lines.

Second, the enterprise may be subject to a number of different supervisory bodies that make its task more difficult. For instance, the municipal labor bureaus, tax offices, and banks may intrude from time to time on enterprise decision making. Even worse, during certain periods the enterprise may be subject to "dual leadership" in which authority is shared by local and national authorities. These peculiarities make the job of running a factory much more difficult, but they do not fundamentally alter the enterprise's position. Except for brief periods following on administrative reorganization, an enterprise always has an immediate superior (*zhuguan bumen*), which is clearly identified. The fact that individual decisions must be made taking into consideration the opinions of various "related administrative agencies" (*youguan bumen*) makes the deal-making process more complex and onerous. However, this does not change the basic situation, which is that the enterprise must procure the assent of its superior organ to *every* significant decision, while additional approvals may still be required for some of these decisions. Quite frequently the enterprise's superior organ negotiates with the related administrative agencies in place of the enterprise. In all cases the one permanent and inescapable relationship every enterprise has is the one with its superior organ.

Conversely, the enterprise possesses significant task-specific capital, which cannot be easily exploited by other parties. The superiors cannot simply dispense with the existing enterprise and its workers and hire somebody else to produce machine tools. Because of China's decentralized management system, most enterprises are subordinate to authorities in the city in which they are located; this means that superior authorities have under their control only a handful of enterprises, or

28. Competition from rural factories depends on the ability of competitors to transport their products across administrative boundaries. That condition is not always met in China. In the final analysis, though, state enterprises are more often protected by the difficult technological requirements of certain goods, especially heavy industrial products, than by barriers to interregional flows.

even a single enterprise, capable of producing a given product. Because their span of control is narrow, it is difficult for the superior to monitor enterprise performance by comparing it with other enterprises, and difficult to apply severe sanctions to the enterprise because there are few alternate sources of supply. Ultimately, bureaucratic superiors must deal with the existing enterprises, which are their only viable sources of money and output. Bureaucratic superiors in China worry constantly about the possibility that subordinates will restrict output, substituting perfunctory performance (or nonperformance) for hard work and frustrating the objectives of superiors by slowdown and egregiously sloppy work. The relationship between superiors and enterprises is thus the same as that between management and workers within the Chinese enterprise, and for the same reason: top and bottom are locked into a relationship that neither can escape. The ultimate bargaining power of those at the bottom derives from the fact that they can frustrate the deal-making process so that both sides lose. Because those at the top are aware of this power, they strive to keep those on the bottom mollified and part of the bargaining process. This one-on-one bargaining process is thus the inevitable outcome of a basic condition of bilateral monopoly, in which neither side can do without the other.

This state of affairs is perpetuated by the financial and pricing policies that the central government carries out. By maintaining low prices on energy and basic foods; by subsidizing capital (interest rates) and social security and health benefits; and by protecting factories from import competition, the government ensures that the great majority of state factories turn a paper profit regardless of their economic efficiency. The large stream of accounting profits generated in industry—industry accounts for over 80 percent of budgetary revenues—ensures that there will always be a deal to be struck over enterprise revenues. Both superiors and subordinates have a major incentive to stay in the bargaining process so that they can reap a share of these accounting profits. The bilateral monopoly persists because neither party would be likely to gain by breaking up the relationship, even if that were possible. We might say that the monopoly power exists, not to keep the two sides in the bargaining relation, but rather to keep other parties out. Having between them the disposition of the surplus generated in industry, the two sides then bargain over the precise distribution of benefits.

Market forces cannot yet dissolve this monopoly relationship, because there is always some combination of concessions and benefits the superiors can grant that will enable the enterprises to survive even the fiercest competition. State enterprises have large buildings and extensive arrays of equipment for which they pay little; and they have access to substantial financial resources at very low cost. It is not difficult for even a very inefficient enterprise to "out-compete" his potential rivals from rural industry. No superior will acquiesce in the collapse of a sector under his control, because that will shut him out of the stream of benefits generated by that sector. Thus, both parties remain locked into the hierarchical structure and the bilateral monopoly bargain that goes with it. One consequence is the maintenance of the monomorphic organizational form from the command economy. The internal organization of the enterprise is standardized to match that of its superior organs: functional departments within the enterprise report to—and bargain with—parallel departments in their superior organs, as well as management in their own enterprise. According to a survey of 170 managers of large factories in Liaoning province, the two greatest sources of discontent were the lack of control managers had over personnel decisions, and their inability to alter the organizational structure of their enterprises.[29] Given this state of affairs, Chinese industry is unable to reap the efficiency gains that come from idiosyncratically specialized organizational forms, or those that come from diversified multiproduct corporations with significant economies of scale.

Finally, the maintenance of the administrative hierarchy and the underdevelopment of outside-of-plan markets has meant that the monolithic character of the state economy has not been fundamentally changed. In the discussion of the central-government role in investment, it was argued that the information available to central planners had been greatly increased. Planners had better technical information for project design and long-range projections, and more timely and complete information about the behavior of the economy as a whole. These generally can be understood as improvements and rationalizations of the information-gathering facilities that normally characterize command-bureaucratic systems. That is, even for a command-bureaucratic system, China had an exceptionally weak information-coordinating capability before reforms, and this weakness has been partially rectified. However, if market-oriented reforms are to work, whole new channels for the circulation of information must be created. These channels operate through the market mechanism itself to provide information to decentralized agents (not just to central planners) about economic opportunities. In this respect, the Chinese reform has not

29. Liaoning Statistical Bureau, "The Opinions of Managers of Large and Medium Size Enterprises on Several Problems of Reform," *Tongji*, 1987, no. 3:32–33. These opinions are more striking in that the managers were not anxious to escape from the authority of their supervisors in other respects: 37 percent wanted a larger compulsory plan; 33 percent thought the plan was about right; only 30 percent wanted a smaller plan. On the organizational form of enterprises, see also the discussion in Max Boisot and Xing Guoliang, "The Nature of Managerial Work—Chinese Style," paper presented at the International Conference on Management in China Today, Leuven, Belgium, June 19–21, 1988.

really transformed the state-owned sector. Indeed, the two-track system has in some respects impeded the circulation of information in the economic system. Since enterprises do not regularly sell above-plan output at market prices, it is difficult to tell what market prices are. This—combined with rapidly changing market prices in an inflationary environment—has meant that market prices cannot really serve as readily available "shadow prices" that could be used to assess state enterprise performance. At the same time, each enterprise's capital stock and inputs are purchased at widely varying prices. As a result, an enterprise that purchased its fixed capital at low state-set prices will show a much higher profit rate than one that purchased machinery outside the plan; enterprises dependent on high-priced inputs may show losses while less well run factories in the same sector generate profits because of access to subsidized inputs. These factors are too complex to allow systematic calculations at the higher level to correct for them. For instance, who can say whether textile production is more efficiently carried out in small-scale rural factories or in state urban factories? Certainly the central government has no information at its disposal that would permit a ready answer to such a question.

Because of the weakness of markets, both central planners and local agents continue to base much of their decision making on pseudoinformation. Nominally profitable enterprises are propped up or expanded, without accurate information about the actual comparative productivity of those enterprises. Local monopolies are perpetuated because it is impossible for governments or enterprises to devise alternative strategies based on mutually beneficial specialization and trade. While technical information available to the Center has been enhanced, local information on economic choices has not been qualitatively improved. The two-track system has thus not been able to change the fundamentally hierarchical nature of the system, and this has perpetuated the basic bargaining relations of that system.

CONCLUSION

The reform strategy of a two-track system has opened up the monolithic command economy somewhat by allowing private and collective enterprises to play an increasingly important role. However, it has not altered the fundamental authority relationship that ties enterprises to their superiors and perpetuates the bilateral monopoly between them. As a result, the monolithic and monomorphic nature of the state-run economy has been preserved to an important extent. Enterprises and their superiors continue to be entangled in complex bargaining relationships. One of the most obvious and immediate consequences is that enterprises can never be held fully accountable for their operations. Every aspect of enterprise performance is related in some way to the bargains the enterprise has struck; an enterprise therefore always has someone in the administrative hierarchy to share the blame for unfavorable outcomes. Conversely, any unfavorable outcome has a possible remedy somewhere in the bargaining process; some negotiated package of concessions and benefits is always potentially available. The lack of accountability naturally reproduces the "soft budget constraint" characteristic of bureaucratic economies. Pressures to raise efficiency are correspondingly reduced, and destabilizing types of behavior are encouraged.

At the same time, the central government has returned to the investment arena with a renewed program for development of priority areas, but without direct control over the resources needed to implement that program. As a result, the national government increasingly competes with enterprises and local governments for available investment resources. The central-government investment deficit combines with the "investment hunger" created by soft budget constraints at the enterprise level to generate significant macroeconomic pressures. In order to accommodate the demands of central and local governments and enterprises, the banking system is continuously prodded to provide more loans to finance investment. The result is a continuing expansion of total demand in the economy and—since the expansion in demand outpaces the expansion in supply—a serious inflation problem. By the middle of 1988 the economic system and reform strategy were in the midst of a major crisis brought about by steadily accelerating inflation.

In a general sense, this crisis can be attributed to the continuation of the bargaining economy. The central government uses the bureaucratic apparatus to reach for more than it could accomplish with its own resources. The enterprises rely on the bureaucratic apparatus to shield them from losses and to avoid stark pressures to economize. These two forces collide in an escalation of demands that the economy cannot accommodate. The continuation of the bureaucratic economy means that the cost of wrong decisions can still be shifted onto society as a whole, rather than being borne by individual decision-makers. The difference today is that such costs are increasingly visible. During the period of the command economy, the monolithic economic structure was able to hide the effects of poor economic choices; there were few markets to register disequilibria, and poor choices became manifest only very gradually with a recognition that real growth and improvement in living standards were occurring much more slowly than seemed warranted. Today, the disproportion between total demand and total supply shows up quickly with the emergence and acceleration of inflation. This could be an advantage if central planners were able to respond quickly to signs of imbalance. In any case, though, a successful reform process demands a high degree of responsiveness in each individual market, as the system really starts to reward more efficient producers and cut down the flow of resources to the less efficient. The polymorphous bargaining relations that characterize China's industrial hierarchy today tend to deflect the impact of any positive or negative shocks, thus diffusing the pressure for better performance that those shocks would otherwise create. They also serve to disperse costs so that they are borne by the economy as a whole and show up as inflation. Although the system has been partially opened up, the prevalence of complex bargaining relations within the state-run industrial hierarchy is a symptom of the system's inability thus far to establish new principles of operation and decision making on which to base future development.

APPENDIX

The basic data sources are *Zhongguo Guding Zichan Touzi Tongji Ziliao 1950–1985* (China Fixed Investment Statistical Materials), 59, 64, 218–19; 1988 *Tongji Nianjian* (Statistical Yearbook), 564, 566, 605; 1988 *Tongji Zhaiyao* (Statistical Abstract), 67. In the table below, *technical transformation* includes "other" investment. Column (5) is the sum of columns (1) and (2), divided by *net material product,* and column (6) is the sum of (3) and (4), again divided by NMP.

Data on budgetary and extrabudgetary investment. The *capital-construction* figures are consistent and readily available. However, I wish to include foreign borrowing disbursed through the central budget in budgetary investment. This is available through 1985 in the first source cited, and 1985–86 figures are available in

Investment Composition
(Units: Billion Yuan, Percent)

Year	(1) Budget Capital Const.	(2) Budget Technical Trans.	(3) Central Capital Const.	(4) Central Technical Trans.	(5) Total Central % NMP	(6) Total Budget % NMP
1978	38.921	2.648	26.643	4.529	10.4	14.7
1979	39.692	4.364	27.320	4.749	9.6	13.6
1980	30.011	3.298	29.261	5.049	9.3	9.7
1981	22.262	3.488	24.103	6.088	7.7	7.1
1982	23.248	3.295	29.657	6.540	8.5	7.3
1983	29.597	4.083	35.503	7.493	9.1	8.2
1984	35.985	5.81	44.117	7.576	9.1	8.2
1985	38.118	3.54	57.524	10.482	9.7	6.5
1986	41.739	3.94	63.252	14.867	9.9	6.2
1987	43.852	5.32	76.166	17.909	10.1	5.7

1987 *Tongji Nianjian*, 467n. The 1985 figure thus given is 4.103 billion, and the 1986 figure is 3.003. The latter figure can be confirmed with reference to 1988 *Tongji Nianjian*, 564. However, the 1987 figure is not available. Since total state investment funded by foreign capital increased 31.2 percent during 1987, and budgetary foreign borrowing of all kinds increased 36 percent, while foreign direct investment increased 33 percent in *renminbi* terms (1988 *Tongji Nianjian*, pp. 565, 732–33, 762), I have assumed that foreign-funded investment channeled through the budget increased by one-third to 4.0 billion.

Figures for technical renovation are more complicated because data on "other" investment are sometimes included and sometimes separated, but separate data are never presented with the breakdown we require. Data are good for technical transformation, not including "other," for 1981–85 in the first source cited. However, the 1980 data are incomplete and seem unreliable. Figures for 1978–84 on financing for the category of technical transformation-including-"other" are available in the earlier Statistical Yearbooks, e.g., 1983, English, 360, and 1985, 452. These are used for those years. These show that budgetary finance of "other" investment was very small but not zero. The composition of "other" investment financing 1985–87 thus is the only remaining financing problem. Overall, the composition of "other" investment changes considerably through 1983, but is quite stable in the 1984–87 period. In 1984 it can be calculated that 1.25 billion, or about 10 percent, of "other" investment was funded from the budget. This proportion has been applied for the years 1985–87. In the calculation of budgetary and nonbudgetary shares of investment some approximation is required, but the possible margin of error is very small.

Data on Investment Included in Central and Local Plans. Data for capital construction are clearly presented in the first source cited. It is less clear what proportion of technical transformation and other investment should be counted as central government. The figures from 1981 through 1987 for technical transformation-excluding-"other" are good, but there are no figures at all for "other." Unfortunately, there is no alternate source where the proportion of technical transformation-plus-"other" that is included in the central plan is given. I have therefore assumed that *no* "other" investment is central. An alternate assumption would be that petroleum-depletion allowances, which account for a little over 50 percent of "other" in 1984–87, are also "central." This alternate assumption would raise the proportion of total investment included in the central plan in every year, but would have virtually no impact on the trends that are the subject of the analysis.

The other problem is determining the proportions of technical transformation that are incorporated in the central-government plan during 1978–80 (there was no "other" investment during those years: thus, this is implicitly technical transformation-plus-"other"). I simply assumed central projects were equal to 27 percent of technical transformation in those years, as they were in 1981. This is plausible because the proportion of capital construction accounted for by central projects is quite stable during the 1978–80 period, and we know that technical transformation investment at this time was predominantly under local control. The maximum error involved in this procedure would be if we undercounted central-government technical transformation projects by 2–3 billion in 1978 through 1980, which would amount to at most 1 percent of NMP in 1978, or ½ percent of NMP in 1980 (a more likely error, since bank lending for technical transformation starts to become important at that time, and that might fund central-government projects). Thus, there is a margin for error in the 1978–80 figures larger than that involved in the calculation of budgetary shares. Nevertheless, the margin is not sufficient to materially alter the qualitative conclusions presented here.

PART FOUR

Subnational Levels

.

TEN

Territorial Actors as Competitors for Power: The Case of Hubei and Wuhan

Paul E. Schroeder

The competition for power between Hubei province and its capital city, Wuhan, reveals Chinese political and legal systems little changed by urban reforms. These systems are still unable to determine how to handle the sharing of decision-making authority between different levels of government. The formula adopted by central leaders to spur regional economic growth, namely, the central-cities policy, offers only a carbon copy of the earlier Center-province decentralization, this time from provinces to central cities. The strategy offers no new political, constitutional, or legal formula by which new territorial competitors for power might more easily reach accommodation. Through all this, China's administrative system, with its multiple lines of authority that hold units and individuals under tight control, has shown a tenacity for self-preservation. Efforts to cut these lines of authority have resulted only in their multiplication.

In the absence of political, constitutional, or legal formulas that might guide the policy process, Chinese units engage in lengthy bargaining over the specifics of any general policy that is to be implemented. Such bargaining is done within certain limits. Bargaining positions can change over time and from issue to issue. Success often depends on the issue at hand, the context in which it is debated, and the nature of coalitions that form on either side of the bargaining table.

Such was clearly the case with Wuhan and Hubei. The 1984 policy decision to give Wuhan provincial-level status in economic affairs was taken only after the Center, siding with Wuhan, mediated extensive bargaining between the city and the province. From then until late 1988, when the province—with central backing—resumed authority in the face of economic retrenchment, a continuing stalemate between Hubei and Wuhan as to the definition of this new power revealed that bargaining, even in a system characterized by bargaining,[1] does have limits. The stalemate was caused by political and legal systems that lack proper definitions of authority and offer no formula for allowing those definitions to be developed. Definitions of the limits of authority are given by fiat and are often intentionally left vague.[2] China's legal system is not mature enough to permit development of legal definitions through the gradual building of any substantive body of case law. Nor is the court system mature enough to permit dispassionate settlement of disputes and the enforcement of those settlements. Given that the two actors in question are sitting on top of each other, the result is competition for power characterized by irrational policy proposals and the inertia that arises from an inability to find accommodation.

These factors are evidence that, though featuring many changes, late-twentieth-century China has changed little since the days of the Qin dynasty in terms of finding an appropriate balance of power between Center, region, and locality. Territorial actors in China are the key to the strength or weakness of any regime, and each of China's dynasties, including the Republic and the People's Republic, has struggled to find an adequate formula for determining the proper distribution of decision-making power between Center and region.

Following the economic and administrative reforms that began in China in late 1978, research has focused on the competition between provincial-level actors and the Center. This competition was heightened as the Center gave to these governments greater decision-making power and greater resources with which to implement their decisions. Provincially based commodity blockades, wars over export-commodity prices, resistance to resource sharing, and increased provincial financial resources have been documented since the reform era began.[3] In some respects, provinces, with autarkic tendencies, still seek to become self-

    1. David M. Lampton, "Chinese Politics: The Bargaining Treadmill," *Issues and Studies* 23, no. 3 (March 1987): 11–41.
    2. Interview File 6, Interview No. 6, April 30, 1988 (China): 1. This point is developed later in this chapter. Hereafter my interview sources will be abbreviated. For example: I.F. 6, no. 6 (30 April 1988): 1.
    3. For example, see Susan Shirk, "The Domestic Political Dimensions of China's Foreign Economic Relations," in *China and the World*, ed. Samuel S. Kim (Boulder: Westview Press, 1984), 60–64; and "The Politics of Industrial Reform," in *The Political Economy of Reform in Post-Mao China*, ed. Elizabeth J. Perry and Christine Wong (Cambridge: Harvard University Press, 1985), 195–221; *Foreign Broadcast Information Service* (hereafter *FBIS*), 21 November 1984, K2; and Barry Naughton, "The Decline of Central Control Over Investment in Post-Mao China," in *Policy Implementation in Post-Mao China*, ed. David M. Lampton (Berkeley and Los Angeles: University of California Press, 1987), 51–80.

reliant in as many areas as possible to reduce dependence on other Chinese provinces.[4]

Close examination of provincial-government activities, both with the Center and with lower-level governmental units and enterprises under their jurisdictions, provides a clearer picture of the nature of China's political system. The number of units with some authority in any functional setting, their interlocking connections with central leading organs (*tiao-tiao lingdao guanxi*) and local leading organs (*kuai-kuai lingdao guanxi*), the relative inability to obtain resources easily (what some blame on a scarcity of these resources), the complexity of decisions demanded by modern commercial activity, the lack of formalized decision-making rules, and weak institutions—all constrain policymakers. The Center, lacking the capability to enforce policy choices, is thus forced to issue implementation guidelines that are vague and open to broad, conflicting interpretation by implementing agencies. Things get accomplished more often than not by bargaining among the many actors involved.[5]

The research on interprovincial competition raises a second set of questions about the Chinese political system. Do territorial units within a province compete? If decentralization focuses power at the provincial level, do subprovincial groups attempt to have power decentralized further? Is the Chinese political system institutionalized enough to handle any further decentralization? Does the Chinese bureaucracy at different levels exhibit the same characteristics as bureaus found in other countries?

The case of Hubei and Wuhan shows that intraprovincial competition for power does exist. While provinces may view power as decentralized, subprovincial governments clearly do not. Writing in *Liaowang,* Wuhan's first Party secretary, Zheng Yunfei, linked the success of economic reform to political reform, which he said was needed to overcome "excessive centralization of power."[6] China's decision to make central cities a focal point for economic development during the Seventh Five-Year Plan (1986–90) provides an opportunity to examine the competition between city and province, the structural characteristics affecting implementation

4. Although this may gradually give way as China's economic reforms continue, the thinking that accompanies such activities will be hard to change. For example, an economist with the Hubei Province Economic Commission said, "Much of the packaged food in Hubei comes from Guangzhou and we don't like it. We have a hard time developing our own food industry because of this competition. These products are already here before ours can be produced. We need to upgrade our food industry more quickly or we'll lose out." I.F. 7, no. 1 (26 December 1986): 1.

5. Lampton, "Chinese Politics: The Bargaining Treadmill"; and I.F. 6, no. 6 (30 April 1988): 2.

6. Zheng Yunfei: "Ideas about the Next Step of Reform of the Political Structure in Wuhan City," in *Liaowang,* no. 33 (15 August 1988): 11, in *FBIS,* 29 August 1988, 46–47.

of this policy, the bureaucratic behavior prompted by this policy decision, and the structural changes required if the policy is to work. The competition between Hubei and Wuhan reveals much about the nature of bureaucratic behavior in China and the limits of Party cohesion when territorial interests are at stake. Strategies to minimize the conflict, such as problem solving, persuasion, or bargaining,[7] have given way to what Downs called "excessive territorial sensitivity" as both Hubei and Wuhan struggle for policy-making and policy-implementation autonomy.[8]

Though designed to push economic growth by decentralizing power to levels below provincial governments, the central-cities policy shows clearly the structural constraints that inhibit the development of the Chinese economy, no matter where decentralization stops. Without full implementation of the reform of the economic management system, without "smashing" the *tiao-kuai* lines of authority that bind all units and individuals, the central-cities policy has had and will have limited success. Indeed, Wuhan's Zheng Yunfei, referring to city and provincial governments, complained that these "have . . . become major obstacles [to] the perfection and development" of enterprise reform.[9] Before turning to the nature of the competition between Hubei and Wuhan, a brief discussion of structural reform and the central-cities policy is in order.

STRUCTURAL REFORM AND THE CENTRAL-CITIES POLICY

In China's unitary system, *tiao-tiao* lines of authority tie each unit vertically to superior organs of power at the Center, whereas *kuai-kuai* lines of authority tie them horizontally to local organs of power. In the Chinese scheme of things, both *tiao-tiao* and *kuai-kuai* authorities are to share power cooperatively according to a system of dual rule, or *shuangchong lingdao*. Problems that arise in this dual-rule scheme are supposed to be ironed out by the unifying authority of the Communist Party, *dang tongyi lingdao*, a hierarchical organization that theoretically has only a single leading organ at the Center.

This system, instituted after much debate in the decentralization drive of 1957, does not work as leaders at the time stated it would. There is no dual rule; instead, there is rule by either *tiao-tiao* or *kuai-kuai* authorities, depending on the issue at hand and the relative power of each. The relative power of *tiao-kuai* authorities changes with time and with differ-

---

7. J. G. March and H. A. Simon, *Organizations,* quoted in Anthony Downs, *Inside Bureaucracy* (Boston: Little, Brown, 1967), 217.

8. Downs, *Inside Bureaucracy,* 217.

9. *FBIS,* 29 August 1988, 46.

ent functional systems.[10] In the decentralization that followed 1978, provincial governments have gained considerable decision-making authority, thereby enhancing the relative power of these *kuai-kuai* leaders. These locally based authorities have shown themselves (as have *tiao-tiao authorities at the Center*) to be quite resilient despite efforts designed to curtail their authority (such as periodic recentralization of foreign trade), in large measure because the Center is relying on these same *kuai-kuai* (and *tiao-tiao*) authorities to implement the reform policies that would replace administrative authorities with economic networks.

The basic goal of China's urban economic reforms is to break the administrative lines of authority that bind China's economy and to replace them with market-logical ties that instill competition, make use of comparative advantages, allow for informational (market and otherwise) efficiency, and spur economic growth.[11] These governmental, bureaucratic lines of authority, the *tiao-tiao lingdao guanxi* and *kuai-kuai lingdao guanxi* already mentioned, tie each unit to multiple other units in fishnet fashion.[12] This makes it difficult for any single unit, or *danwei*, in any functional setting to act quickly enough to take advantage of opportunities as they arise—in short, to act economically. The entrepreneurship so essential to any economic-development plan is hampered by these artificial lines of authority.

For example, initial reforms designed to curtail governmental interference in economic activity and to spur horizontal economic ties across territorial boundaries resulted in the establishment of many new industrial corporations and research institutes. The Wuhan Hydraulic Cylinder Plant is one of twelve such factories that constitute the Wuhan Hydraulic and Pneumatic Industry Corporation. The plant had been the former Machinery Research Institute of the Wuhan Machinery Bureau. The name changed, but the personnel and facilities remained the same.

10. Kenneth Lieberthal and Michel Oksenberg, *Bureaucratic Politics and Chinese Energy Development*, (Washington, D.C.: U.S. Department of Commerce, 1987), 122. Also I.F. 11, no. 2 (1 May 1988): 1.

11. I.F. 1, no. 9 (21 October 1984): 2; and Li Chonghuai, "Pingjie 'liang tong' qi fei, ba Wuhan jiancheng wei 'nei lian huazhong, wai tong haiyang' de jingji zhongxin" (Rely on letting the two 'tongs' fly to build Wuhan into an economic center for internally building the central-China region and externally opening to the sea), *Wuhan Daxue Xuebao* (Shehui Kexue Ban), 1983, no. 6.

12. Nowhere is this lack of flexibility more evident than in Chinese efforts to purchase secondhand industrial equipment from abroad. This equipment is sold too quickly for the Chinese, who cannot act fast enough because it takes too long for a Chinese unit to gain the required approval from the many *tiao-kuai* authorities for making such a purchase. For detailed explanations of *tiao-tiao* and *kuai-kuai lingdao guanxi*, see Paul Schroeder, "Regionalism in China: Tiao-Tiao Kuai-Kuai Authority in the Chinese Political System" (Ph.D. diss., Ohio State University, 1987).

The new corporation is owned by the Wuhan Municipal Government and answers to the Wuhan Economic Commission.[13]

The aim here was to put the administrative bureaus onto a business footing, letting them make money, and, at the same time, to cut government spending by putting them on a profit-loss basis. Theoretically, this step was to cut *tiao-kuai* lines of authority and permit the growth of horizontal economic ties. Actually, the *tiao-kuai* lines of authority were increased rather than reduced. The twelve hydraulic factories under the Wuhan Machinery Bureau continue to answer to their original *tiao-kuai* authorities, but now they must also answer to the Hydraulic and Pneumatic Industry Corporation, which has what is termed *yewu guanxi*, or business authority, over them.

Many Chinese, however, see *yewu* lines of authority in terms of *tiao-tiao* and *kuai-kuai* authority. A Chinese economist explained *yewu guanxi* in theoretical terms as *tiao-tiao* "all the way to the Center. A pure administrative relationship is *kuai-kuai* up to the Center."[14] This theoretical approach, obviously, can lead to confusion because the line between administration and business is blurred in a Communist system. Business managers who deal not in theory but in the real world of determining to whom they answer tend to ignore the distinction.

In an interview, the manager of a rubber factory in Bengbu city, Anhui province, said his plant was attached to the Bengbu City Chemical Industry Corporation through *yewu guanxi*. "In some ways this is *tiao-tiao* because it connects us to similar corporations in Beijing. But this corporation is owned by Bengbu city's Economic Commission, which is our *kuai-kuai* authority. Actually, they both [the corporation and the Economic Commission] are *kuai-kuai* authorities. Nothing has been eliminated."[15]

Whether China's system is decentralized, then, depends on where one is within that system. Post-1978 China is certainly decentralized from the point of view of provincial governments, but to the manager of the Bengbu factory, and to Wuhan's Zheng Yunfei, it remains centralized, albeit at levels lower than Beijing.

In an atmosphere of continuing administrative interference, then, where economic management reform is not fully implemented, the Center, under Zhao Ziyang, listened closely to any proposal aimed at reducing the *tiao-kuai* network and instilling some economic logic into China's development strategy.

Such was the case in 1979 and 1980 as the era of economic reform got under way. The hierarchical nature of urban economies was dictated by

13. Interview with Mr. Yang Deyao, manager, Wuhan Hydraulic Cylinder Plant, 26 December 1986, and I.F. 5, no. 3 (17 October 1987): 1.
14. I.F. 4, no. 2 (31 December 1988, New York City): 1.
15. I.F. 10, no. 1 (16 October 1987): 1.

the Stalinist command-economy model chosen by China's Communist leadership in the 1950s. All trade within and between cities was monopolized by government agencies. The results of this—a collection of urban economies that were closed to each other, related only by administrative bureaus at the top of the governmental hierarchy—was seen as hampering China's development.

In 1980 economist Xue Muqiao promoted the idea of Chinese cities rebuilding the interurban economic networks that existed before the 1950s. The focus on cities as economic centers was given political life in 1982 by the then premier, Zhao Ziyang, at the Fifth Session of the Fifth National People's Congress, where it became one of his ten principles for economic development.

Then, in October 1984, at its Third Plenum, the Twelfth Communist Party Central Committee formally adopted the central-cities policy as part of its urban economic reform program. Large central cities would be given the necessary authority to break *tiao-kuai* control and act, as Solinger states, "as the nuclei of several large economic regional networks and markets across the nation."[16] Wuhan's participation in the central-cities strategy was first espoused in 1983 by Dr. Li Chonghuai, professor of economic management at Wuhan University.[17] In brief, this was an effort to tap the economic potential of larger cities in China's interior, which are not part of the coastal-cities program nor of the provincial-level cities of Beijing, Shanghai, and Tianjin. The *stated* goal, as in the creation of industrial corporations, was to cut *tiao-kuai* lines of authority and allow larger cities to act as economic magnets, building regional economies that would tap their respective comparative advantages, foster foreign trade, and thereby help build the national economy.

In 1983 Li put forward an overall central-cities strategy for Wuhan's economic development.[18] Among the twelve measures was an effort to "establish a rational economic network while implementing economic management reform." In discussing this step, Li went directly to the

16. Dorothy Solinger, "The Place of the Central City in China's Economic Reform: From Hierarchy to Network?" paper prepared for the First International Urban Anthropology-Ethnology Conference in China, Beijing, June 26 to July 2, 1989.

17. Li Chonghuai, "Pingjie 'liang tong' qi fei, ba Wuhan jiancheng wei 'nei lian huazhong, wai tong haiyang' de jingji zhongxin," in *Liang Tong Qi Fei* (Let the Two Tongs Fly) (Wuhan: Wuhan University Press, 1986), 28.

18. The twelve strategic measures were to strengthen communications and transportation, reform commodity-circulation systems, establish a rational economic network while implementing economic-management reform, reorganize industry, open up new municipal zones along the banks of the Yangtze River, develop aquatic products, help develop other Hubei cities, establish Wuhan as a financial center for central China, develop the service trade, develop the tourist industry, and better organize Wuhan's scientific, technological, and educational strengths.

heart of China's problem: "In China's current economic management system, the major abuse is too many centralized authorities, the failure to break *tiao-kuai* [lines of authority] and to separate government and enterprises so that we still cannot handle affairs according to economic laws. This is done not only in business but in all aspects of industry, planning, and finance."[19] Li pointed out that most enterprises in Wuhan were "under the direction" of the Center and the province. City-run firms were very few. The value of fixed assets for enterprises under city management was less than one-third of the total value of fixed assets for all enterprises within the city limits.[20] Using Wuhan's machinery industry as an example, Li said the 1,141 factories (in 1983) were "interlocked vertically and horizontally and subordinated to more than forty *xitongs* (functional systems) and departments at the five administrative levels of Center, province, city, district, and neighborhood. Vertically and horizontally they have no mutual relationship." The result was operation at only 30 percent of what local economists considered potential industrial capacity.[21]

Li's remedy was the central-cities policy. These cities, not their provincial authorities, should manage all economic activity within their borders. A city should be given "enough authority in economics, enabling it to be engaged in essential construction and technology and equipment renovation and transformation, to break *tiao-tiao kuai-kuai* fetters, and, according to economic needs, carry out cooperative ventures across regions, departments, and trade and organize regions in rational economic networks."[22] This was to be done through separate listing in the state plan, *jihua danlie.* Briefly, a city's annual plan would be given its own listing in the national plan separate from the provincial plan. Municipal officials would deal directly with central planners regarding the contents of the city plan. Without *jihua danlie,* a city's annual plan would be subsumed in the provincial plan. The city would deal directly with provincial planners in this case. With separate listing, municipal construction projects and products would be able to "enter the national plan" directly. Provincial leaders initially welcomed the idea but soon came to see it as a direct assault on their planning prerogatives, especially when Li coupled *jihua danlie* with greater autonomy and authority in finance and foreign and domestic commerce, giving central cities "ample economic strength to bring into play the effects of an economic center."[23]

19. Li Chonghuai, "Pingjie 'liang tong' qi fei," quoted in *Liang Tong Qi Fei,* 28.
20. Ibid.
21. Ibid.
22. Ibid., 29.
23. Ibid.

Li's formula, as I said at the outset, sought only further decentralization, this time from provinces to central cities, mirroring earlier efforts by provinces to decentralize from the Center. His strategy offered no new political, constitutional, or legal formula by which the new territorial competitors for power might more easily reach accommodation. Li pinned hopes for his strategy on successful implementation of the management system reform and decentralization to the enterprises, what one Wuhan economist called a long-term prospect, given the intransigence of both local and provincial authorities about giving up power.[24] But, as Zheng Yunfei wrote, this policy was blocked by a lack of political structural reform and clear definitions of the functions of Party, government, and enterprises.[25]

By simply decentralizing authority lower to the central cities without any fundamental change in *tiao-kuai* relationships, the bargaining inherent in the Chinese system was increasingly to be found in the localities as well as Beijing.

NEGOTIATION

Throughout early 1983 Li Chonghuai was busy publicizing his strategy for Wuhan's development. A series of articles in the local media and academic journals pushed the idea of Wuhan's relying on "liang tong," or *liutong*, meaning circulation (of commodities), and *jiaotong*, meaning communications.[26] Thus Wuhan should rely on its geographic position in China's center, equidistant along the main rail line from Beijing in the north and Guangzhou in the south and along the Yangtze River from Chongqing to the west and Shanghai to the east. By relying on this position, Wuhan could recapture the leading position it had early in the twentieth century as the core city of a central China economic region. It would once again become the "thoroughfare of nine provinces."

The central-cities program was a national policy, as was stated earlier. Separate listing in the state plan for central cities was not limited to Wuhan. Chongqing was granted *jihua danlie* in early 1983. Implementing the policy there, however, was much less difficult than in Wuhan because "Chongqing is not the seat of provincial government. Wuhan is, and that makes it much more difficult. The closer authorities are to each other, the more difficulties there are."[27] Wuhan was the first provincial capital to be

24. I.F. 11, no. 2 (1 May 1988): 1.
25. *FBIS*, 29 August 1988, 46–47.
26. *Changjiang Ribao* (Yangtze Daily), 26 May and 10 August 1983; and "Pingjie 'liang tong' qi fei" in *Wuhan Daxue Xuebao*.
27. I.F. 9, no. 1 (6 April 1988): 4.

given *jihua danlie* status and, as such, drew special attention from central leaders. By early 1989 twelve other cities, in addition to Wuhan and Chongqing, were granted *jihua danlie:* Guangzhou, Shenyang, Dalian, Chengdu, Harbin, Xian, Qingdao, Ningbo, Xiamen, Shenzhen, Nanjing, and Changchun.[28]

At the start it appeared that implementation would be easy. The Center and Wuhan both used bargaining strategies designed to convince Hubei officials of the policy's benefits for all concerned. While Center, province, and city watched developments in Chongqing closely, municipal officials and the State Commission on Restructuring the Economy communicated the need to approach Hubei about giving Wuhan separate listing in the state plan.[29] With prodding from the commission's vice-minister, Zhou Taihe, Wuhan sent Hubei a proposal, which provincial officials accepted. "Hubei didn't know what it would mean, so with Zhou's encouragement they accepted the plan gladly. Hubei sent the proposal to the Center, which acted immediately, something Beijing intended to do anyway. The Center had given clear hints to Wuhan of its support [in this issue] and the city seized the opportunity."[30] According to other sources, Hubei's initial acceptance of the policy was urged by the provincial first Party secretary, Guan Guangfu, and the then governor, Huang Zhizhen, close associates of the former PRC president Li Xiannian, a former Wuhan mayor.[31]

The bargaining strategies used here fit Lampton's classifications of "foot-in-the-door" and "a little something for everyone."[32] Theoretically, separate listing would lead to increased economic activity by Wuhan, which in turn would increase the financial returns for city, province, and Center, all of which "had little money."[33]

The decision to grant Wuhan *jihua danlie* was made in May 1984 and announced to the nation on June 3 in a statement that Wuhan would be a test-point for a variety of urban economic reforms, including provincial-level economic management status, the establishment of trade centers, the invigoration of transportation and the opening up of the Yangtze River, and the creation of horizontal economic ties with other regions in China.[34] Once the decision was made to permit *jihua danlie* for Wuhan, the city and the province had to work out how to implement the plan before the separation could be formalized by the State Council. During

28. See *Renmin Ribao*, 22 October 1987, 4; 13 June 1988, 2; and 19 February 1989, 1; and *FBIS*, 20 October 1988, 27.
29. I.F. 9, no. 2 (16 May 1988): 1.
30. Ibid.
31. I.F. 11, no. 2 (1 May 1988): 1.
32. Lampton, "Chinese Politics: The Bargaining Treadmill," 37–38.
33. I.F. 9, no. 2 (16 May 1988): 2.
34. "Wuhan jinzing jingji tizhi zonghe gaige shidian" (Wuhan conducts experiments in comprehensive reform of the economic system), *Renmin Ribao*, 3 June 1984, 1.

this period it was clear that separation would lead to a division of powers between city and province, which created a variety of problems to which Hubei objected. The Center, led by Zhou Taihe, had to negotiate a settlement between Hubei and Wuhan so the policy could be implemented beginning with the 1985 plan.[35]

At this juncture, the historically bad relations between Wuhan and Hubei became a critical factor. The major initial problem, determining what Wuhan's proportion of retained capital should be, along with what enterprises under provincial jurisdiction would be sent down (*xiafang*) to the city's jurisdiction, had to be negotiated in an atmosphere of mutual mistrust.

PROBLEMS IN RELATIONS

Standing behind the negotiations over separation was the continuing conflict between Hubei and Wuhan. The rub runs both ways. First, Hubei is fearful of Wuhan independence, given the latter's superior economic base. For many years it had been rumored that Wuhan would become a provincial-level city like Beijing, Shanghai, and Tianjin, and that Hubei would have to move its provincial capital to some other city, such as Huangshi or Shashi. "This rumor started in the Cultural Revolution. There was never anything to it, but it has persisted, so Hubei is afraid of any steps that could lead in this direction. That's why other Hubei cities always got more help from the province than Wuhan did."[36]

The result of this fear was what one city official termed Hubei's "reluctance" to consider Wuhan's development proposals for inclusion in the provincial plan that would itself become part of the national plan. This meant a gradual reduction in the amount of money going to Wuhan through Hubei. In the 1950s Wuhan received sizable investments for construction of such items as Wuhan Iron and Steel and the Yangtze River bridge. By the 1970s it was felt that investment should be made in other areas of the province.[37] Consequently, Wuhan requests for additional large-scale capital-construction projects (which had been made through the provincial planning process), despite benefits to economic development, were not included in Hubei's annual plans. An example of Hubei's reluctance in this regard is the construction of a new airport, which Wuhan proposed in each annual plan for nearly thirty years prior to separation. Citing lack of money, Hubei repeatedly cut the airport out of the city's annual plan.

Second, these bad relations were compounded by Wuhan's attitude as

35. I.F. 11, no. 2 (1 May 1988): 1.
36. I.F. 9, no. 1 (6 April 1988): 2.
37. Ibid.

the central-cities policy was debated and implementation was negotiated. Wuhan adopted an attitude that it was the biggest city in central China and that it could act as a development magnet for the entire region, not just Hubei. "From the beginning Wuhan thought its many functions had been ignored [by Hubei]. It tried to take too many steps too fast, too directly cutting itself off from Hubei. Wuhan thought it was Wuhan of central China and this made Hubei very unhappy. Shenyang took the opposite tactic, calling itself Shenyang of Liaoning. It put Liaoning first, even though it was breaking away from provincial bonds."[38] It was in this contentious atmosphere that the two sides began negotiations over the details of the separation. To help ease Hubei's concerns, Beijing, though pushing the central-cities policy, warned Wuhan that it would remain under Hubei's leadership.

FINANCIAL PROBLEMS

Before the policy could be implemented, the Center also had to find a way to assuage Hubei's worries about the prospect of losing sizable revenues to Wuhan. Thus the bargaining centered on two basic aspects of the proposed separate listing: assuring Hubei that Wuhan would not become a "province within a province,"[39] and more directly, finding an arrangement that would eliminate Hubei's objections to losing revenue.

Two key sources in the Wuhan city administration described what was at stake. Prior to separation, Wuhan was allowed to keep on average 20 percent of its revenue. Actually, this rate was "returned, not retained," as all revenue was sent to Hubei as the basic governmental accounting unit. Hubei kept 55 percent, (with 5 percent going to other Hubei local governments), sent the Center about 25 percent, and returned 20 percent to Wuhan with clear stipulations in each annual plan as to how the money was to be used.

This was the major sore point in the relations between Wuhan and Hubei. Revenue from the city accounted for about half of Hubei's total income, yet the rate of money returned to Wuhan was far less than the city contributed.

The effects of this treatment by Hubei continue to plague Wuhan, even after separation. During the negotiations leading to separation, the Center calculated the expenses and revenues of Wuhan for the previous five years, 1980 through 1984. It then said Wuhan could keep 19 percent while sending the rest to the Center. Expecting to be given between 30

38. I.F. 9, no. 2 (16 May 1988): 2.
39. *Renmin Ribao*, 4 April 1985, 5.

and 40 percent of its earned revenue, Wuhan objected. The Center finally agreed on a 20 percent retention rate. This was certainly to Hubei's advantage. If Wuhan were able to retain large portions of revenue and thus gain greater independence in key financial resources, the city might prove to be too strong a competitor. However, given the basically incremental nature of decision making at the Center in such instances, Hubei did not need to worry. "The Center has an unwritten rule to decide everything. It bases every decision on the previous few years' experience. The Center doesn't have enough money, so a comparison is a good way. Despite Wuhan's objections, the city was given only what it had been getting from Hubei. That's why Hubei could sit quietly and let the Center handle the problem."[40]

What Hubei did seek was some mechanism that would allow the province not to lose any revenue that had previously come from Wuhan and that would now go directly to the state. The Center agreed to permit the province to count Wuhan's retained portion as part of Hubei's annually planned payments to the Center, meaning that the financial arrangement between all three parties would not really change, except in accounting terms.[41] Separation, then, was something less than complete if one considers the many ways governmental units are interrelated.

This fits with Solinger's findings that the negotiated settlement that paved the way for implementing the central-cities policy saw changes in the accounting procedures but little loss of revenue for Hubei. Based on interviews with Wuhan economists, she found that Hubei got about 100 million yuan per year from the Center, the initial amount the province lost as a result of *jihua danlie* and decentralization.[42] At the same time, Wuhan gave the Center about 100 million yuan more than Hubei had been doing before the policy was implemented, in large part because of increased economic activity.

Wuhan officials feel cheated by these results, especially after the other cities granted *jihua danlie* are permitted to retain between 30 and 40 percent of their income. Wuhan had the lowest retention rate of any of the first seven cities (there were fourteen by 1990) given separate listing in the national plan, despite the city's connections at the Center through Li Xiannian. "Wuhan thinks it lost a great deal. It wanted to retain a lot more of its money. The reason it gets the least is because the Center based the amount on the previous five years' experience. This reflects

40. I.F. 9, no. 2 (16 May 1988): 2.
41. Ibid.
42. Dorothy Solinger, "City, Province and Region: The Case of Wuhan," paper prepared for the Third International Congress of Professors World Peace Academy: "China in a New Era: Continuity and Change," Manila, August 24–29, 1987, 11–12 and 62, n. 15.

the low status Wuhan was given by Hubei. The reason for this is the relationship between Wuhan and Hubei. It was very bad for a long long time."[43]

Despite the financial agreement, the Center announced that Wuhan was retaining 28 percent, with 72 percent going to the Center,[44] a point that was not appreciated by the city officials I interviewed. Three city-government sources said Wuhan's retention rate was 20 percent for 1985 through 1987. In 1988 it was decreased to 16.4 percent as part of tax system reform. This lower figure was determined by the Center as part of an incentive to increase production. It has nothing to do with separation, except that Wuhan started the tax reform from a lower retention-rate base.[45] This low retention rate is the key problem in Wuhan's development strategy. "We have a basic capital supply and demand problem. Local financing is very difficult. We have great need for money but a shortage of funds. This is an important reason why Wuhan is what it is."[46]

Despite the financial shell game and Wuhan's relatively low retention rate, the city benefited under *jihua danlie* because it could determine how to spend its money rather than getting approval from Hubei.[47] For example, Wuhan is now planning construction of a new airport in Tianhe, on the western outskirts of the city. In addition, Wuhan also gained the right to approve foreign investment and import projects up to U.S. $5 million, the same authority as Hubei. Further, city export revenues that had accrued to Hubei foreign trade corporations or were controlled by Hubei's foreign trade apparatus are now controlled by Wuhan's foreign trade organization. In 1984 total provincial revenues from exports was 1.46 billion yuan, of which 17.53 percent, or 256,320,000 yuan, came from Wuhan enterprises. In 1985, the first year that revenue went to Wuhan, the city's export income had increased by 16 percent, to 299,230,000 yuan, which accounted for 14.81 percent of total provincial export revenue.[48] Wuhan officials put the 1985 figure slightly higher, at 333,130,000 yuan.[49]

43. I.F. 9, no. 2 (16 May 1988): 2.
44. "Wo shi jingji tizhi zonghe gaige shidian shishi fangan" (Our city's trial of compre-hensive economic reform plan is implemented), in *Changjiang Ribao,* 13 October 1984, 1.
45. Ibid.; I.F. 11, no. 1 (29 April 1988): 2, and I.F. 12, no. 1 (29 April 1988): 2.
46. I.F. 11, no. 1 (29 April 1988): 2.
47. I.F. 9, no. 1 (6 April 1988): 1.
48. *Hubei Sheng Qing* (Hubei Province Conditions) (Wuhan: Hubei Renmin Chubanshe, 1987), 253.
49. *Wuhan Nianjian 1987* (Wuhan Yearbook 1987) (Wuhan: Wuhan Chubanshe, 1986), 562.

IMPLEMENTATION

Once the financial arrangements had been negotiated, the Center on 13 October 1984 officially announced that Wuhan would be granted *jihua danlie* beginning with the 1985 plan. The central documents state that "in *all* aspects of planning, finance, banking, taxation, *prices*, industrial and commerical *administration, labor* and wages, electric power, materials distribution, foreign trade and foreign economic relations, post and communications, environmental protection, medical administration and inspection, tourism, and so forth, Wuhan enjoys provincial-level status in *economic management power (xiangyou sheng yiji jingji guanli quanxian)*" (emphasis added).[50] This seems comprehensive. City officials took it at face value and proceeded to exercise provincial-level rights in all these areas, no doubt taking, as was mentioned above, "too many steps too fast." They interpreted the above statement to give Wuhan rights in economics *and* administration. Hubei officials, however, read this much differently. To them, Wuhan's rights are limited to economic management (*jingji guanli quanxian*) and do not include critical items of administration, such as distribution, pricing, and personnel.

The problem for both parties is the lack of any definition of where economics ends and administration begins in a planned economy. Hubei, therefore, has been able to block several Wuhan initiatives in policy areas that directly pertain to the city's economic development. As one economist with close ties to the city said, "In some areas Hubei continues to hold power. They simply refuse to give it up. The line where economics ends and administration begins is very, very thin. There is no definition and I don't know how long it will take before we can get one."[51]

According to a business source with close ties to Hubei and Wuhan, the central documents were purposely left vague. Without the resources to adequately enforce its will on lower levels, the Center is left with little choice but to set general guidelines and let the implementing parties involved bargain-out any disputes between them. "This vague writing is done purposely. They [the Center] are not stupid. They know it will cause problems. But what else can they do?"[52]

Given the already poor relations between the two governments, this differing interpretation has set the stage for a continuing series of prob-

---

50. "Guanyu Wuhan shi jingji tizhi zonghe gaige shidian shishi fangan de baogao" (Report concerning Wuhan's implementation of its plan for comprehensive economic system reform), report of the Central Party Secretariat and the State Council, reprinted in *Changjiang Ribao,* 13 October 1984, 1.

51. I.F. 11, no. 2 (1 May 1988): 1.

52. I.F. 6, no. 6 (30 April 1988): 1.

lems between them that require bargaining. Knowing this, both sides have established "leadership groups" to handle problems as they arise. When problems are too critical or solutions too difficult to obtain, the mayor and the governor become active participants in negotiating a bargain that would settle the issue.[53]

The problems caused by the new relationship between Hubei and Wuhan can be found in almost every sector, but brief discussions involving distribution, price setting and food subsidies, and personnel provide clear examples of the bargaining necessary when policies such as *jihua danlie* are adopted in the absence of the appropriate political and legal means to determine definitions of authority.

DISTRIBUTION

Critical to any planned economy is the need for adequate distribution of the inputs necessary for production. According to Wuhan's interpretation of the central documents granting *jihua danlie*, the city is to be given provincial-level rights in materials distribution. Though directly related to management of the economy, Hubei officials view this activity as proper governmental administration. The province has exercised its authority in this sphere, more often as a means to "get back at" upstart city officials.

As economic reforms have instilled some market forces into the allocation picture, Hubei has been able to use its distribution capacity as a bargaining tool with Wuhan. For example, Solinger found that Hubei was withholding cotton from Wuhan textile mills, thereby threatening their production.[54] Of course, market forces open up opportunities for Wuhan as well. When textile prices are high, Hubei has refused to allocate cotton to city mills, threatening production and forcing the city to buy from more expensive suppliers outside the province. But when textile prices are falling and Hubei wants to get rid of cotton quicker, Wuhan has refused and continued to buy elsewhere.[55] Despite this game playing, it is estimated that "nearly one third of Wuhan's textile productive capacity is idle because of the lack of cotton."[56]

Commodity speculation was encouraged by decentralization of the distribution system. By September 1988, with economic retrenchment under way, Hubei ordered ten measures designed to "rectify the eco-

53. Ibid.
54. Solinger, "City, Province and Region: The Case of Wuhan," 12–13.
55. I.F. 9, no. 1 (6 April 1988): 2.
56. Mao Zhenjua "The Predicament and the Way Out for Urban Jihua Danlie," *Jianghan Luntan*, no. 1 (1988): 44, quoted in Solinger, "The Place of the Central City in China's Economic Reform," 28.

nomic order" for the entire province, including Wuhan. Among these was the demand that provincial quotas for the procurement of grain, oil, and cotton be met and that speculation be stopped. Distribution was to be recentralized to the provincial level.[57]

PRICES

The central documents granting *jihua danlie* clearly state that prices are included in the areas now under Wuhan's competence. Yet Hubei has flatly refused to give the city any real authority in price management. "Hubei still sets the prices and subsidies for food. This is a sensitive problem and the mayor has to negotiate this directly with the governor."[58] For example, provincial and municipal authorities, fearful of "disorderly price increases," announced that basic monthly food subsidies would go up from 10 yuan per Wuhan resident to 13.50 yuan on April 1, 1988.[59] The city had sought to limit the subsidy's increase because inflation, combined with increasing population, makes it increasingly difficult to pay for them. Up until 1988 Wuhan was paying about 1 billion yuan per year for food subsidies. The province, fearful of adverse public reaction to inflationary pressures being felt for the first time in China in two generations, forced the city to accept a higher subsidy than it wanted. The city objected to what it sees as "direct interference" in its new authority, but it had little choice.[60]

By late October strong efforts to control inflation were being pushed by provincial authorities. With pressure from Hubei's first Party secretary, Guan Guangfu, Wuhan city Party secretary, Zheng Yunfei, publicly agreed to follow Hubei's price control index, abrogating city-approved price increases that were made after September 1. Further, the city agreed to forgo any price increases through spring 1989 and expansion of the scope and range of commodities with floating prices, and refused to allow any temporary price increases. Wuhan, at Hubei's insistence, agreed that no authority over prices would be delegated below the provincial level until some undetermined time in 1989.[61]

Wuhan's acquiescence to Hubei in these matters, in contrast to the 1984 effort to bargain with the province, indicates it lost the backing of

57. *FBIS*, 27 September 1988, 54–56.

58. I.F. 11, no. 1 (29 April 1988): 2.

59. "Wuhan shi shixing zhuyao shipin jiage biandong dingliang butie zhi" (Wuhan implements changes in main food product prices and rationing and subsidy systems), in *Hubei Ribao*, 1 April 1988, 1, and "Jinqi jianli zhuyao shipin jiage biandong an dingliang ji zhigong butie de zhidu" (Today establishes changes in main food product prices and workers' rationing and subsidy systems), in *Changjiang Ribao*, 1 April 1988, 1.

60. I.F. 11, no. 2 (1 May 1988): 1

61. "Hubei's Capital Acts to Control Market Prices" in *FBIS*, 31 October 1988, 56.

the Center on this issue. Indeed, it was the Center that pushed lower levels to, first, deal with public complaints about inflation and, when this failed, to bring it under control by means of the economic retrenchment. By early 1990 that program was clearly in place in Wuhan, where commercial activity was considerably less than that of mid-1988.

PERSONNEL

The rising costs of basic food subsidies has become a nagging problem for Wuhan. A severe cash shortage for reconstruction of badly needed transportation and communications facilities, factory equipment, and other basic city services is straining Wuhan's capacity to govern. The rising population, coupled with an annual inflation rate of at least 8 percent (in 1987), has meant that an increasing amount of city money has gone into what one disgruntled economist called "keeping the peace." In one year, from 1985 to 1986, the city's population rose by 116,000 to a total 6,199,600. To long-term visitors, the pressure this increasing population is putting on Wuhan's infrastructure is obvious.[62]

Facing increasing costs in food subsidies because of this and a provincial government unwilling to allow Wuhan to forgo raising the per capita subsidies in the midst of inflation, the city sought relief where it could. In autumn 1987 a municipal regulation was circulated through various city departments stating that, beginning on January 1, 1988, any unit bringing a new worker into the city would have to pay twelve thousand yuan. Though city planners hoped to make exceptions for certain skilled labor, the rules for which might take six months to formulate, the nascent Wuhan labor market came to a halt weeks before the January deadline. My business source said, "Even though the rules are still to be issued, many units are no longer accepting new employees because they fear they might have to pay."[63]

62. *Wuhan Nianjian 1987* (Wuhan Yearbook 1987), 36–37. Increasing population has compounded many of Wuhan's problems. For example, in 1984 a mid-morning car trip from Wuhan University in Wuchang to downtown Hankou would take approximately thirty minutes. In 1988 the same trip was taking nearly sixty minutes. A crosstown trip by public transit can take nearly two hours, depending on making connecting lines in time. By early 1990, in the face of the economic retrenchment program, a rush-hour car trip from Wuhan University to downtown Hankou took thirty minutes, reflecting, as provincial officials admitted, the decreased number of people coming into the city for commercial purposes from the surrounding countryside.

63. I.F. 6, no. 2 (22 November 1987): 1. News of the proposed policy was a serious blow to many Chinese who had been either trying to reunite family members living far away or, for those living in the city without municipal registration, trying to obtain a proper *hukou* to qualify for the subsidies. Chinese feared that the twelve thousand yuan fee would have to be paid by their family, not by the hiring work unit.

Based on information from three city sources, this policy's brief history clearly reflects the tension between Hubei and Wuhan. The city did not act alone but sought and obtained permission from a provincial vice-governor to implement the program. When the policy documents circulated around city departments, however, Hubei changed its mind. An official with the Wuhan administration put the issue into terms that reflect both the differing opinions as to the extent of the city's authority and Hubei's fears of Wuhan's independence: "Wuhan wanted to limit population growth, which we see as an economic problem. Wuhan would screen who was coming in and determine who would be exempted. A regulation was prepared for this procedure. Hubei said no. If Wuhan implemented the policy, Hubei might have trouble moving its people in and out of the capital city."[64]

STALEMATE

There is no doubt that the central-cities policy has permitted the growth of interurban economic networks. Solinger outlined the economic institutional framework built up in the Yangtze River Valley, centered at Wuhan, between 1984 and 1988.[65] This framework, if granted appropriate authority, could help transform the economy of central China from an administrative hierarchy into a regional economic network. The framework includes the creation of a wholesale marketing network; the creation of the Yangtze River Joint Transportation Company by thirteen cities along the river in 1984; establishment of sixty-four networks in commerce, materials supply, transport, and finance, plus the Wuhan Economic Cooperation Region by seventeen cities in Hubei, Hunan, and Jiangxi provinces; and creation of five capital markets to serve the region. Despite the creation of these various networks, the question was whether they would be permitted to act in their own economic interests or whether they would continue to be controlled by government agencies at the local, provincial, or central levels.

Since 1985, when *jihua danlie* was implemented, relations between Wuhan and Hubei have worsened. A stalemate ensued until China's overall economic situation worsened in the second half of 1988 and, as part of a national retrenchment program and Wuhan's loss of central backing in its efforts to negotiate with Hubei, the province was able to impose its will on Wuhan economic activity once again. Prior to the retrenchment program, however, Hubei continued to exercise authority in areas where Wuhan thinks it should have authority. Provincial and

64. I.F. 9, no. 1 (6 April 1988): 3.
65. "The Place of the Central City in China's Economic Reform," 18–23.

municipal leaders were locked in debate, largely in scholarly journals, about the efficacy of *jihua danlie*. The debate involved those who oppose separation and those who think it has not gone far enough. Although the scholars do not say for whom they are speaking, those opposed to *jihua danlie* are voicing Hubei's opinion while the other side voices that of city officials.[66]

Opponents base their argument on three basic factors. First, the goal of urban economic reform was to diversify into a market economy with limited planning. Separation strengthens planning by elevating another governmental actor to an active role in the planning process. Second, *jihua danlie* does decentralize enterprises from the province to the city, but in the absence of management system reform "nothing has changed except the grandmother."[67] And third, the only real result has been the creation of "new contradictions" between Wuhan and Hubei, making a bad situation worse.

In my work as trade representative for the state of Ohio, based in Wuhan, I was continually mindful of the growing competition between Hubei and Wuhan. For example, prior to *jihua danlie*, Wuhan was always included in trade shows and other Hubei efforts to find foreign markets. From 1985 until 1988, however, Wuhan representatives were conspicuously absent from Hubei-sponsored trade promotion events. In 1988 the two began an annual, jointly sponsored trade exhibition in an effort to show greater cooperation. The competition between Hubei and Wuhan foreign trade corporations, trading companies and officials, however, became all the more obvious at these events.

Further, with *jihua danlie* came a division of the Bank of China, Hankou branch (the provincial branch), to exclude the Bank of China, Jianghan branch, representing Wuhan city. The Hankou branch moved to new, fully automated quarters, leaving the Jianghan branch to the old bank building. Also, the Hankou branch would not permit the Jianghan branch to cash personal checks, written in U.S. dollars, above $134, or about 500 yuan in foreign exchange certificates, even with a credit card as collateral. The Hankou branch, meanwhile, gladly cashed personal checks up to $750 if a credit card was used. This was done to limit Wuhan's ability to earn foreign exchange.

In 1988 interviews in Wuhan, Solinger also found that, in an effort to boost provincial income and to cut Wuhan's, Hubei "forbade lesser cities in the province which are still under its immediate control to order goods—such as shoes or tape recorders—from Wuhan."[68]

Proponents of separation do not dispute the poor showing *jihua danlie*

66. I.F. 9, no. 1 (6 April 1988): 2.
67. Ibid.
68. Solinger, "The Place of the Central City in China's Economic Reform," 28.

has had so far, but lay the blame for this on Hubei's recalcitrance and not on the policy itself. To them, separation must include granting wider powers to the cities if the policy is to succeed. "It is clear Wuhan has not been given enough power. Society is a complex system of laws, administration and economy. . . . Presently administration is above law and economy. Administrative separation has not been given to Wuhan, only economic planning. Problems exist when there is a mix. It is hard to say which is which when both are present so Hubei claims the rights."[69]

The bargaining required to find a modus vivendi and to implement policies has become tougher. The result is a vicious circle of poor policy planning or backdoor deals that only heighten mutual mistrust. "When problems arise, everyone adopts a gentlemanly attitude and sits at the table. But when their interests are involved, the result is either no solution or under-the-table bargains and the creation of new contradictions that arise from them."[70]

My sources say it is more and more apparent that a successful negotiation will be difficult. Consequently, Wuhan has begun to ask the Center to mediate, a fact some Wuhan officials admit further alienates Hubei. Despite the Center's interest in pushing *jihua danlie*, it is apparent that Hubei continues to exercise authority and expects Wuhan to accept this fact. At a conference of Party and government leaders in August 1987, the provincial Party secretary, Guan Guangfu, pointedly told Wuhan it would not be permitted to go it alone: "By giving full play to Wuhan's multiple functions, the city should work in full cooperation with the whole province toward overall development. [But] . . . successfully developing Wuhan needs joint efforts by the province and the city."[71] Nine months after this admonition, however, Wuhan had yet to give up ideas of a more complete separation. My sources with the city agreed that reaching an accommodation under the original separation plan was hopeless.[72]

By spring 1988 Wuhan's various research organizations had developed five alternatives to the original separation scheme that could be presented to the Center at an appropriate and opportune time.[73] The first would make an effort to better define the limits of separation by making Wuhan a practice case for more local authority in administrative and legislative activities in addition to economics. Wuhan would still be attached to Hubei but would have more authority that would be better defined. The second plan would make large portions of the city a Special

69. I.F. 9, no. 1 (6 April 1988): 2.
70. Ibid.
71. *FBIS*, 3 September 1987, 19.
72. I.F. 9, no. 1 (6 April 1988): 4.
73. Ibid.

Economic Zone, similar to Shenzhen. This idea has been studied at length, with a section of Hankou along the north side of the Yangtze River in the city's northeast earmarked for it.

The third plan, which gives Hubei anxiety, is to make Wuhan a provincial-level city, like Beijing, Shanghai, or Tianjin. Both the second and third plans include the fourth idea, setting aside a Special Administrative Zone within Wuhan for the provincial government, allowing it to operate under its own authority without having to move the provincial capital. Finally, there is discussion about making Wuhan a test case for an entirely market-oriented economy with no planning and little government administration of economic activity.

Though these alternatives are being prepared by Wuhan's planners, my sources had no answer as to how these plans could ever be implemented, given Hubei's unwillingness to grant *jihua danlie* as stipulated and the Center's lack of enforcement powers. The proposals reveal, however, what Downs might call the "excessive territorial sensitivity" of Hubei and Wuhan, which make change more difficult because it leads to irrational policy choices.[74] Such sensitivity makes conflict between territorial actors likely. The bureaus involved, therefore, seek to minimize this conflict either by narrowing the scope of proposed actions or by ignoring their competitors and going for broke. Both reactions, which Downs calls the shrinking violet and superman syndromes, respectively, are irrational.

It is highly unlikely the Center would approve any of the final three plans, while Wuhan's financial problems eliminate the creation of a special economic zone in the near term. Given this, these options are irrational by attempting too much—that is, Wuhan planners are engaging in the superman syndrome. The first plan is more realistic, but, given China's administrative system, its lack of institutionalization and law in determining how power might be shared and how disputes are settled, it too is irrational.

CONCLUSION

China's clampdown on the prodemocracy movement on 4 June 1989 and the repression of participants afterward makes it quite clear that the political system has changed little in the ten-year reform period of Deng Xiaoping's regime. The regime's violent reaction to the movement could not be foreseen, especially because it involves the loss of international credibility so carefully nurtured by China. But there was clear evidence that the reforms aimed at separating Party from government and admin-

---

74. Anthony Downs, *Inside Bureaucracy*, 216–17.

istration from business were superficial: little had changed in the authority relations between various levels of government, especially below the province.[75]

Part of this evidence lies in the lengthy stalemate between Hubei and Wuhan over the limits of *jihua danlie*. Wuhan could not muster the strength, even with central backing, to convince the province to give up key economic decision-making power. The parameters of bargaining were set by Hubei. Ultimately, Hubei's ability to impose its will on Wuhan's economy in late 1988 doomed *jihua danlie* to failure. Reimposition of provincial authority came in the wake of inflationary pressure, as was discussed above, and after a January 1989 drop in industrial production in Wuhan and a number of other Hubei cities. Viewing Hubei's overall industrial production increase of 2.4 percent for January 1989 as fifth from the bottom nationwide (the national average was 2.8 percent), the vice-governor, Xu Penghang, noted that production in Wuhan, Huangshi, Shashi, Jingmen, and other areas actually declined. In a mid-February speech, he demanded that "all levels" and "all localities" arrange production in line with "lists . . . drawn up by the state and the provincial authorities."[76]

The implication here is obvious; the central-cities policy, as implemented in Hubei and Wuhan, failed. The policy's success, as Li Chonghuai wrote, depended on successful implementation of management reforms designed to cut *tiao-kuai* lines of authority. But management reforms have not been implemented. Changing the power relations configured by *tiao-kuai* lines of authority over economic activity requires reform of the political system, not just the economic system, something the events of June 4 have shown is not acceptable to the Deng regime.

Efforts to cut *tiao-kuai* through economic system reform alone, for example, by creating *yewu* lines of authority exercised by industrial corporations, has failed in this task. As in the case of the Bengbu City Chemical Industry Corporation, enterprise managers see *yewu* lines of authority in terms of *tiao-kuai lingdao guanxi*. The number of lines "tying enterprises hand and foot" have increased rather than decreased.

Efforts to decentralize authority, giving it to provinces in the late 1970s and early 1980s, to key cities in the mid-1980s, and, in some

75. The increased power of provincial governments in the reform period is well documented, as is the Center's inability to recoup some of the power granted to them. For example, see note 3 above, plus Daniel Southerland, "The Chinese Fear Economic Warlordism," *Washington Post,* 12 December 1988, 1; Nicholas D. Kristof, "Beijing Authority Being Challenged by Local Powers," *New York Times,* 11 December 1988, 1; and Ellen Salem, "Things Fall Apart, the Centre Cannot Hold," *Far Eastern Economic Review,* 27 October 1988, 38–40.

76. "Hubei Urges Industry Performance Improvement," *FBIS,* 15 February 1989, 60–61.

functional areas, to smaller cities in the late 1980s,[77] have reduced somewhat the power of *tiao-tiao* lines of authority but, by giving provinces and
some cities greater financial resources and authority over such items as
materials distribution and personnel, have increased the power and number of *kuai-kuai* lines of authority. "At the moment, *kuai-kuai* is tighter
than *tiao-tiao*. *Tiao-tiao* interference is still great. But the real problem is
kuai-kuai interference. At this level, the provincial level, there is no real
understanding of what needs to be done for economic development, or
at least no real willingness to do it."[78]

The results of *jihua danlie*, then, at least in Wuhan, have been tension
as Wuhan attempted to compete with Hubei for *kuai-kuai* authority. A
business source said that "Wuhan's *tiao-tiao* is the Center, its *kuai-kuai* is
Hubei. Now [after separation] Wuhan is trying to break its *kuai-kuai* from
Hubei and Hubei is very upset with this. There is a severe lack of cooperation between them. This is compounded by the confusion of the
reform period."[79]

The *tiao-kuai* lines of authority that constitute China's structural organization are, theoretically, supposed to cooperate in a system of dual rule
that never really did work.[80] In the absence of cooperation between the
two, the Chinese Communist Party is to act as the mediating, unifying
force, with leadership coming from the Center.

But how can officials who disagree while wearing their administrative
hats suddenly find the willingness to cooperate when they put on their
Party hats? They cannot, so *tiao-kuai* competition exists within the Party
as well, a mirror image of what is more easily seen in the government.
And, while Wuhan and Hubei vie for *kuai-kuai* power, their respective
Party committees are likewise engaged. This can be seen in the differing
points of view expressed by Hubei's provincial Party secretary, Guan
Guangfu, and Wuhan's Party secretary, Zheng Yunfei. The latter is also a
member of Hubei's Provincial Party Committee.

A business source, also a Party member, said, "In reality, Wuhan and
Hubei cannot cooperate at both the administrative and the Party level.
The split has created a *kuai-kuai* competition within the Party. There
always was *tiao-tiao* competition between the Center and local Party
branches."[81]

77. "Sheng zhengfu zhengshi jueding wosheng waimao tizhi gaige fangan" (The provincial government formally decides Hubei's foreign trade system reform plan), in *Hubei
Ribao*, 7 April 1988, 1.

78. I.F. 11, no. 2 (1 May 1988): 1.

79. I.F. 6, no. 5 (23 February 1988): 1.

80. Paul E. Schroeder, "Regional Power in China: Tiao-Tiao Kuai-Kuai Authority in the
Chinese Political System," chaps. 1 and 2.

81. I.F. 6, no. 5 (27 February 1988): 2.

Economically speaking, the central-cities policy is an effort to decentralize decision-making power closer to the point of production in order to maximize efficiency and flexibility and to push growth. Politically speaking, it is an effort to decentralize power to a key city that has become a competitor with its provincial government. The competition is a predictable result, given that there is no strong consensus about the policy's goals.

Herein lies China's Catch-22, put into terms of the Law of Countervailing Goal Pressures used by Downs: economic development requires innovation, which, especially in a planned economy, "creates a strain toward greater goal diversity in every organization." But Hubei's fear of losing power to Wuhan is based on its "need for control and coordination, [which] creates a strain toward greater goal consensus." Thus goal consensus "is a vital part of any true decentralization of authority."[82]

But the functional aspects of the central-cities policy encourages heterogeneous goals between the two territorial actors. The policy, with *jihua danlie,* is broad in scope. It has multiple, highly complex, and vaguely defined functions, which must operate simultaneously. There is considerable conflict about these functions as they relate to relative power between Hubei and Wuhan. All this presages conflict between the actors involved. Despite Wuhan's continuing efforts to wrest greater authority from Hubei, its *kuai-kuai* leader, in the absence of specific policy changes granting the city greater power, there has been no real decentralization of authority to the municipal level.[83]

When territorial actors compete for power in such an atmosphere of mistrust, under vague guidelines, and with no legal system that might mediate disputes, the result will be continual delay in making timely decisions because required policy action by those in authority, who are caught in the web of *tiao-kuai* hierarchies, needs to be bargained.

82. Anthony Downs, *Inside Bureaucracy,* 223–24.
83. Ibid., 226.

ELEVEN

Local Bargaining Relationships and Urban Industrial Finance

Andrew G. Walder

The term "bargaining" is used frequently to characterize bureaucratic behavior in socialist states. Political scientists have characterized policy-making and implementation as protracted processes of bargaining and accommodation among leaders of organizations.[1] Analysts of planned economies have come to see them as "infinitely flexible bargaining systems," in which production plans, material supply, prices, taxation, and credit are subject to protracted bargaining and renegotiation.[2] For the political scientist "bargaining" is an emblematic style of politics, said to be responsible for ambiguity and delays in decision making and for intractable problems of policy implementation. For the economist bargaining is a cause of soft enterprise-budget constraints, which in turn are said to explain the perennial inefficiency of traditional central planning and the protracted difficulties of industrial reform in Hungary, China, and elsewhere.

While these studies aptly characterize a style of bureaucratic decision

I wish to thank Kenneth Lieberthal, David M. Lampton, Barry Naughton, Michel Oksenberg, and Ezra Vogel for their detailed comments on the original version of this chapter.

1. T. H. Rigby, "Politics in the Mono-organizational Society," in *Authoritarian Politics in Communist Europe,* ed. Andrew Janos (Berkeley: Institute of International Studies, University of California, 1976), 31–81; David M. Lampton, "Chinese Politics: The Bargaining Treadmill," *Issues and Studies* 23, no. 3 (March 1987): 11–41; Kenneth Lieberthal and Michel Oksenberg, *Bureaucratic Politics and Chinese Energy Development* (Washington D.C.: Department of Commerce, 1986), chap. 4.

2. Janos Kornai, " 'Hard' and 'Soft' Budget Constraint," *Acta Oeconomica* 25 (1980): 231–45, is the most concise statement of the objects of bargaining and its consequences for the behavior of firms. See also Terez Laky, "Enterprises in Bargaining Position," *Acta Oeconomica* 22, nos. 3–4 (1979): 227–46; and Terez Laky, "The Hidden Mechanisms of Recentralization in Hungary," *Acta Oeconomica* 24, nos. 1–2 (1980): 95–109.

making and its consequences, there is a structural dimension to bargaining that has not received careful attention. With notable exceptions, political scientists have focused on the activity and strategy of bargaining, and economists on the consequences of bargaining, while neglecting the patterned relationships within which bargaining activities take place.[3] The bargaining that we see is a symptom, not a cause, of preexisting institutional structures. As Ellen Comisso observed, "Focusing on the bargaining process alone ignores the fact that the arenas within which bargaining occurs are strictly limited and the issues up for bureaucratic negotiation are tightly restricted. Further, the bargaining partners themselves (e.g., enterprises and ministries) do not determine these limits and restrictions; rather, the political leaders outside them do."[4] Bargaining is also constrained by peculiar kinds of resource dependencies and resource flows. It is accompanied by identifiable norms and is justified (or rationalized) by deducible values. The relationships in which bargaining activity is embedded are a neglected but vitally important subject. Here we focus, not on bargaining activity per se, but on *bargaining relationships.*

Nowhere are these relationships more evident, or more vital politically and economically, than in the government's fiscal and budgetary processes. In Chinese cities revenues come almost exclusively from taxes on enterprise profits. The proceeds are divided with the provincial or the central government, according to a negotiated formula. With its share, the city funds its social services, public works, and infrastructure development. Through its planning commissions and bureaus, the city government also redirects part of its revenues back into industry as credit and investment funds. Just as the retained share of its total annual revenues is renegotiated separately for every city, the city itself negotiates the proportionate annual flow of revenues between it and each enterprise.[5] These negotiations are especially important when the government approves a factory's investment project. Several local organizations are

3. Kornai himself, while certainly aware of their importance, treats bureaucratic relationships as outside the sphere of economics proper. His analyses are concerned with measuring and demonstrating the consequences of soft budget constraints. Lieberthal and Oksenberg, *Bureaucratic Politics,* chap. 4, is an important exception: the authors sketch the relevant web of bureaucratic relationships before analyzing bargaining behavior as a consequence of that context.

4. Ellen Comisso, "Introduction: State Structures, Political Processes, and Collective Choice in CMEA States," in *Power, Purpose, and Collective Choice: Economic Strategy in Socialist States,* edited by Ellen Comisso and Laura D'Andrea Tyson (Ithaca, N.Y.: Cornell University Press, 1986), 30.

5. Some units have had their negotiated formula fixed for a number of years as an incentive to raise more revenues. Guangdong province enjoyed this status from the early 1980s. Recently, many enterprises throughout the country have begun to sign profit and tax contracts for three-year periods. In these cases the renegotiation takes place less often.

310 ANDREW G. WALDER

involved continuously in these negotiations. Each of them plays a different role, and each has a different interest in the proceedings, but they
must all work out a viable compromise on each case.[6]
    In the summers of 1984, 1985, and 1986 I investigated these relation-
ships in a study of industrial planning and financial reforms in Chinese
cities.[7] I interviewed officials and executives from a total of sixty-one
government agencies and industrial enterprises (see the appendix to this
chapter) about production planning, supply and sales, and the present
subject, taxation and finance. These interviews underpin the analysis I
offer here.

CORPORATE TIES IN LOCAL INDUSTRY

One arresting image of China's huge bureaucratic polity is that of fragmentation. Lieberthal and Oksenberg specify the aspects of fragmentation that require such compensating integrative mechanisms as regular
meetings, document-transmittal systems, and personal ties, to give it
whatever cohesion it may possess.[8] But if one looks at only a part of the
whole, in this case a city's industrial system, what strikes the researcher is
not its fragmentation but its degree of integration. Here the problem is
less to compensate for fragmentation than to allow enterprises significant autonomy in important business decisions. From the mayor's office
to the enterprise, there is considerable integration in fiscal and budgetary matters within the municipality's own industrial system.[9] As I describe the relations among actors in the process of budgeting and finance, we shall see that a city's industrial system operates in ways that we
associate with large, diversified corporations: carefully regulating financial flows to subsidiaries and blurring organizational boundaries by intervening extensively in important decisions.

---

    6. My interview subjects most commonly used the terms *tanpan* (negotiations, talks) and
xietiao (coordinate, harmonize, work out) when referring to these negotiations. On occasion
they would also use such terms as *qiuqiu* (beg) and *chaozui* (quarrel, haggle).
    7. In 1986 my four-month stay in China was funded by a grant from the Committee on
Scholarly Communication with the People's Republic of China. I wish to thank that institution and my various hosts in China: the Institute of Industrial Economics, Chinese Academy of Social Sciences; the Liaoning Academy of Social Sciences; the Tianjin Academy of
Social Sciences; the Sichuan Academy of Social Sciences; and the Shanghai Institute of
Foreign Trade. None of these institutions are responsible for the conclusions expressed
here.
    8. Lieberthal and Oksenberg, *Bureaucratic Politics*, 117–33.
    9. Enterprises owned by ministries and provinces are also located within municipalities,
and they are party to a more complicated three-party arrangement with their superior
organs and the city government. Here I focus on the city's own industrial system.

Institutional Actors

There are six kinds of municipal institutions that participate in decisions on the extraction of revenues from enterprises, or the funding of their expansion or renovation. Some seek to support the development of enterprises under them; others seek overall balance in the growth of different industrial sectors—slowing it in some areas, speeding it in others. Some view investment in an enterprise purely from the financial angle; others must balance social utility and local advantage against narrow considerations of profit. Some seek to maximize tax revenues and maintain the city government's ability to guide local development. Others seek to keep resources in the enterprises and protect them against excessive demands from the government.

Enterprises. One of the most important tasks of factory directors and of department heads in charge of finance is to turn the flow of financial resources between their enterprise and the government increasingly in their favor. The greater the proportion of revenues they keep, the more prosperous will be their employees and the greater their ability to fund their own expansion. Such growth and prosperity will be viewed favorably by their superiors.[10] The *nominal* tax rate on enterprises in China is very high. Taxes on sales revenue or value added usually take from about 10 to 15 percent, and of the remaining "realized profit" (*shixian lirun*) there is a standard income tax (*shouru shui*) of 55 percent, an individually set adjustment tax (*tiaojie shui*) that usually is between 5 and 30 percent, and a variety of smaller local taxes and levies.

The remainder is kept by the enterprise and put into several funds in proportions decided upon by the finance bureau, with participation of their "leading organ" (*lingdao bumen* or *zhuguan bumen*)—either an industrial bureau (*gongye ju*) or a company (*gongsi*). Commonly, a portion is for employee benefits and bonuses, another for development of production, and a third for reserves. Only one of these funds, for bonuses and benefits, comes close to meeting perceived factory needs (though managers commonly feel pressure to enlarge this fund even further).[11] China's reformers also encourage enterprises to pay for more of their own expansion out of retained funds. From 1977 to 1984 the percentage of national investment paid for by enterprises increased from 38 to 44

10. See Andrew G. Walder, "Factory and Manager in an Era of Reform," *China Quarterly* 118 (June 1989): 242–64.
11. See Andrew G. Walder, "Wage Reform and the Web of Factory Interests," *China Quarterly* 109 (March 1987): 36–41.

percent.[12] But retained profits themselves cover only a fraction of enterprise investment funds: as late as 1982, enterprise depreciation funds were still double the amount of retained profits.[13] In short, enterprises must still rely upon public investment and bank loans to cover their projects, and they must have tax breaks in order to repay these loans.

Therefore, negotiations over investment projects and marginal changes in revenue flows have assumed central importance to the manager; they determine the prosperity and future vitality of the firm. Managers seek to reduce the effective taxation rate on their enterprises in both the long and the short run. Their primary opportunity to do so is when they are given permission to engage in a major construction or renovation project that expands plant capacity or increases the technical efficiency of the firm. When this occurs, the flow of funds must be renegotiated in the short term, because enterprises otherwise will be unable to repay their loans, and in the long term, because plant improvements or expansion can greatly affect the firm's ability to generate revenues. Almost every investment project is accompanied by a corresponding set of tax breaks. The task of the manager, therefore, is to get investment projects approved and to negotiate the most favorable possible tax treatment, both during and after the project. He must draw up financial projections, submit applications to leading organs, and persuasively present the project, both formally and informally, to the members of the city's industrial circles.

Industrial Bureaus.   Every industrial bureau manages a cluster of enterprises in similar lines of production. Their finance and planning departments are the ones most actively involved in decisions regarding investment projects and their tax treatments.[14] Whenever an enterprise manager wants to engage in an investment project, he must first get the approval of its industrial bureau. Every project must be approved and put into the city's construction or renovation plan. Small projects that are paid for entirely by an enterprise's own funds are routinely approved, but they must still be approved by the bureau and counted toward its city-delegated quota of industrial investment for the year. Anything

12. See Barry Naughton, "Finance and Planning Reforms in Industry," in *China's Economy Looks Toward the Year 2000,* vol. 1, *The Four Modernizations,* Joint Economic Committee, Congress of the United States (Washington, D.C.: U.S. Government Printing Office, 1986), 629.

13. See Barry Naughton, "The Decline of Central Control Over Investment in Post-Mao China," in *Policy Implementation in Post-Mao China,* ed. David M. Lampton (Berkeley and Los Angeles: University of California Press, 1987), 60.

14. Each department (*chu*) assigns an individual to take charge of a single enterprise or, in the case of smaller ones, several. These are often people who had worked in the enterprise in the past.

large enough to require a loan—all but the smallest projects—must be studied, approved by the bureau, and then taken to higher levels of government to arrange financing and put the project into the city's industrial-investment plans.[15]

For the enterprise, the bureau is the first and easiest step in a process that usually takes between three months and a year. Industrial bureaus generally support any project that will improve or expand the capacity of their enterprises. But they are limited by city investment plans, which ration investment projects to various lines of industry and cannot champion every proposal brought to them, at least not immediately. They therefore evaluate enterprise proposals and authorize full-scale feasibility studies for the ones approved, after which they go to other government agencies to get permission and funding. Enterprises whose initial proposals are rejected will work with the relevant officials in the bureau to come up with a better proposal in the immediate future.[16] The bureau's primary function in this area is to strengthen proposals that it forwards to higher levels, while keeping within the overall limits placed on investment.

Finance and Taxation Bureaus. These are the two "comprehensive bureaus" (*zonghe ju*), responsible for coordinating the financial activities of industrial bureaus and enterprises.[17] Although their relations are not always harmonious, municipal bureaus of taxation and finance perform closely related functions and indeed have been separated organizationally only in recent years. The scope of responsibility, and power, of the finance bureau is greater than that of the taxation bureau. The finance bureau is responsible for managing both revenues and expenditures for the city. It budgets industrial investments from city revenues to bureaus and enterprises, and it sets tax quotas for collection in the city as a whole and divides them among industrial bureaus, which in turn divide them

15. In the cities I studied, factories had the ability to decide upon projects under 1 million yuan, bureaus had the right to approve projects from 1 to 3 million; the city's planning commission, all projects between 3 and 10 million; central ministries, 10 to 30 million; and the State Planning Commission, all projects over 30 million.

16. Most industrial bureaus, on the order of the local planning commission, have a five-year program (*wunian guihua*) for construction and renovation, which allocates funding among its subordinate enterprises. For an enterprise to surpass its quota of investment, the bureau must reduce the quotas for other enterprises correspondingly. When an enterprise applies for an investment project, it is in effect getting in line for the investment already earmarked for it. Once it has approved the factory's plan, the bureau's responsibility is to put together a package of funding for the project and have it approved by higher-level agencies.

17. The other local comprehensive bureaus that deal often with industry are the price, materials management (or supply), and labor bureaus.

among their enterprises. While it is under the nominal leadership of the
Ministry of Finance and must conduct its business in accord with that
ministry's regulations and documents, the bureau is in fact an organ of
the city government that is directly under the city's planning and economic commissions and ultimately responsible to the mayor's office.[18]
The finance bureau must agree to all investment expenditures by enterprises, whether they are made out of city funds, loans from bank deposits, or their own funds. Public finance funds to be loaned to enterprises
must be placed in the city budget. The bureau must also approve any tax
breaks that are included in financing packages given to enterprises, or
any tax bailouts or subsidies of firms in financial trouble.

The taxation bureau was a department within the finance bureau
before the tax reforms of the early 1980s. Now it is a separate organ
responsible for fulfilling tax quotas set by the finance bureau. Although
it conducts its work according to guidelines and regulations sent down
from the General Bureau for Taxation in Beijing, the taxation bureau
operates under the guidance of local authorities: the finance bureau,
which sends down annual tax quotas that serve as targets both for enterprises and for tax collectors; the planning and economic commissions;
and ultimately the mayor's office. Its relationship with the finance bureau is an ambiguous one: in many cities, the rank of the bureaus is the
same, and their responsibilities overlap, whereas the scope of the finance
bureau's responsibility and power are broader. The two organizations
must agree to all tax breaks, but the responsibility is often blurred because of an overlap in functions. Many local tax bureaus have tried to
assert their independence in recent years and have precipitated discord
with finance departments over their mutual powers and responsibilities.
These disputes must be ironed out by planning and economic commissions, or by the mayor's office.

Local Bank Branches.   Local banks—primarily branches of the Construction Bank in the case of capital-construction (*jiben jianshe*) projects
that involve significant expansion of plant capacity, and the Industrial-
Commercial Bank in the case of technical renovation (*jishu gaizao*) and
equipment purchases—have sharply defined and different interests in
these matters than do the bureaus of taxation and finance. Banks study
every loan application from an enterprise for its financial prospects.
They want evidence that the firm's profitability will be significantly improved by the project (*xiangmu*) and that the firm can repay the loan

18. When mayors attend national or provincial financial work conferences in the fall of
each year, the head of the finance bureau accompanies him and bargains on behalf of the
locality for a larger share of collected revenues.

within the specified period of time *entirely from its increased profits.* Banks reject proposals that do not meet these financial criteria, *unless* the bureaus of taxation and finance, with the permission of the planning commission, are willing to cut taxes to allow the firm to repay. Since that is usually what happens, banks rarely end up killing investment projects.

The bank's attitude toward a loan application depends on the proposed source of funding. The great majority of funds for capital-construction projects are made through the Construction Bank and come not from bank deposits but from public finance funds or credits (*caizhengxing jinrong* or *xindai*) from the budget of the city or a higher level of government.[19] If the funding for the project is to come from the budget of the city or another level of government, it reaches the bank in the form of a grant earmarked for a specific enterprise. The bank manages the investment for the government, eventually returning all repaid principal to the public coffers while keeping the interest as a service fee. This practice is known as "loans from grants" (*bo gai dai*). In these cases the role of the bank is largely to inform the finance bureau of the prospects for repayment of the loan. It is up to the finance and tax bureaus to come up with a package of tax breaks to allow the firm to repay if that is necessary.[20] But whether the firm can repay does not greatly affect the bank, since its own credit reserves (*xindai jijin*) are not at risk.

In many cases, however, a firm's municipal sponsors would prefer to have the project funded with the bank's own funds. This is the case for the great majority of loans for technical-renovation projects made by the Industrial-Commercial Bank.[21] These loans, usually smaller than the

19. Of the total loans made by the Beijing branch of the Construction Bank in 1985, "most" (*da bufen*) were publicly financed (interview 107, July 1986); in Shenyang, 67 percent (interview 113, July 1986).

20. The manager of one enterprise oversimplified the issue, but he pinpointed the cause of banks' continuing lack of independence when he said, "Banks are supposed to be independent now but in reality they can't ignore the government. Investment loans are set by the planning commissions at various levels. Banks simply carry out their orders once the project is put into the plan" (interview 90, Beijing, May 1986). An economic commission official stated the matter more precisely: "The planning commission makes decisions on individual cases for all investment loans. The bank can offer objections, and theoretically has the right to refuse in the end, but the planning commission decides who should get how much and for what purpose. The bank cannot plan and distribute funds, only check and approve" (interview 92, Beijing, May 1986). Another factory director said: "Generally speaking, after the commissions have agreed, the bank won't block you. They have participated in these meetings all along" (interview 98, Beijing, June 1986).

21. Regardless of the banks that disbursed the funds, investment from public finance was 46 billion, and from bank funds 18 billion yuan in 1984. See Naughton, "Finance and Planning Reforms," 629.

construction projects but much more numerous, are made from the substantial deposits that this bank keeps as manager of the accounts of local industrial enterprises. On loans of this type the bank involved will inspect the application more carefully and object more pointedly if there is too much risk. From the bank's perspective, the finance system can risk its own funds on marginal projects but has no right to force the bank to use its own funds to do so. The bank's protection of its own funds affects the funding process in two ways. First, bureaus and planning commissions will generally send only the better projects to apply for bank funds. Second, recalcitrant bank officers need to be "convinced" by local officials—usually from the planning commission or the vice-mayor's office—to "think over" their denial. In almost all cases, the city "convinces" the bank by tailoring a package of subsidies and tax breaks that will virtually guarantee that the firm can repay.

Planning and Economic Commissions.   In the cities in which I conducted my interviews, these commissions are usually higher in rank than the local industrial bureaus, comprehensive bureaus, and banks, and their task is to coordinate the work of all of them to fit into an overall plan. Their exact division of responsibilities is often vague and varies from city to city. But in general, the planning commission is responsible for the long-term development of the local economy, which includes all aspects of industrial finance and planning, and it is directly responsible for coordinating the work of all of the comprehensive and industrial bureaus in the city. The economic commission, in contrast, is usually responsible for the immediate coordination necessary to iron out bottlenecks and delays that threaten the implementation of annual plans. The planning commission's departments for basic construction and industry (*jijian chu, gongye chu*) are responsible for budgeting and arranging funding for major investment items and for fitting these items into its longer-term plans for the development of local industry. The commission deals primarily with the various comprehensive bureaus, especially the tax and finance bureaus, and the banks. The economic commission, on the other hand, approves the technical-renovation projects, which are smaller but more numerous, spending most of its time trying to resolve urgent problems of materials supply, transportation bottlenecks, shortages in operating capital, and energy shortages. Because of its problem-solving role, the economic commission deals much more frequently with industrial bureaus and factory directors.

However they divide their responsibilities, both of these commissions see their mission as "managing local industry on behalf of the city government." Their immediate superiors are the vice-mayor in charge of local industry and, ultimately, the mayor himself.[22] The heads of the planning commission's finance and business department (*caizheng jingying chu*) act as both coordinators and participants in negotiations over individual investment items and tax breaks. In some cities they have organized coordination groups (*tiaojie xiaozu*) made up of representatives from each of the concerned comprehensive bureaus, to resolve disputes and come to decisions on contested items.[23]

The Mayor's Office.   The mayor's office is the ultimate source of authority for all decisions on investment and taxation. To be sure, there are regulations and guidelines regarding taxation and industrial investment issued by the Finance Ministry, Central Bureau of Taxation, State Planning Commission, and other central-government agencies. But these guidelines leave broad discretionary powers to local authorities, who have wide latitude in granting tax breaks and who have an abiding interest in directing investment to those sectors high on their development plans.

Unless the enterprise involved is substantially funded by a province or a central ministry, the mayor's office is the appeal of last resort in disputes over these issues. Usually it is only the largest or most controversial cases that are sent to the top for resolution. But such cases are brought to the top with enough frequency that in Dalian a "policy coordination group" (*zhengce xietiao xiaozu*) has been established by the mayor's office, headed by the vice-mayor in charge of industry, to foster the prompt resolution of all of these questions; its members include the heads of the

22. I suspect that Party bodies in each of these units play an important role in decision-making processes, but in my interviews I was unable to uncover their role. It is manifestly unclear, however, whether there is a meaningful distinction to be drawn between the leadership of a bank or a government agency and the Party committee of that unit, since Party committees and groups invariably include members of the top administrative leadership. I would suspect that especially in important and controversial decisions much of the influence exerted in these matters is actually brought to bear through this "shadow" network of committees. Some research on Hungary, for example, has documented the fact that a factory manager's membership in higher-level Party bodies, controlling for the size of the enterprise, is positively correlated with preferential credit and investment decisions (Maria Csánadi, "On the Structure of Political Decision-making," in *The Hungarian Economy: Theoretical and Empirical Analyses*, ed. M. Tardos, et al., London: Routledge and Kegan Paul, 1989). While this gives us additional detail about bargaining positions and influence processes, Party bodies still must operate within the institutional frameworks described here, because it is through these institutions, and not Party organs, that finances flow.

23. In Shenyang, the planning and economic commission does not have the rank and power of its counterparts in Beijing. There the mayor's office still makes almost all of the decisions through a recently established economic-adjustment office (*jingji tiaoji bangongshi*). It apparently uses the planning commission primarily as a planning bureau (interview 110, July 1986).

finance, taxation, price, and labor bureaus. When the mayor's office has spoken on such a matter, that is the end of the issue, at least for the current year.

MUNICIPAL BUDGETARY AND FISCAL PROCESSES

The most distinctive feature of China's local budgetary and fiscal process is how closely, and routinely, investment and taxation decisions are intertwined. What economists have called the "soft budget constraint" does not mean simply that enterprises can expect to be bailed out if they run into financial difficulty. It means that the decision to invest in industry is paired with a decision about changes in the division of revenues between enterprise and government, such that conditions for repayment will be created. Each decision about an investment loan is accompanied by a decision about the flow of revenues.

China's tax-for-profit reform (*li gai shui*) and its budgetary reform (*caizheng baogan*) have reinforced the tendency of local government to monitor closely the division of revenues between enterprise and government. The revenue share for the central or provincial budget, for local roads, hospitals, housing, and much of the funds for expansion of local industry (and thereby the further expansion of the local revenue base), all must come from locally collected taxes.

Since these reforms took effect in the early 1980s, local actors have had much more latitude in initiating industrial projects and have allocated greatly increased proportions of national investment.[24] Through the new tax system they have also become involved for the first time in continuous negotiation over the revenue flows between the city and industrial enterprises. This involves the development and evaluation of project proposals (*xiangmu jianyi shu*) and feasibility studies (*kexingxing baogao*); it requires successive rounds of meetings and approvals on each proposal; and it requires local actors to put together the funding from central, provincial, or local budgets, or from bank loans, to augment the funds provided by the enterprise.

In this short period of time a regular pattern of behavior and accompanying attitudes have already become evident. There is a marked tendency to appropriate and redistribute enterprise revenues when they are deemed inordinately high, to build consensus and thereby parcel responsibility among all local actors for specific investment decisions, and to reduce the risk of failed ventures beforehand by granting favorable terms to important projects. This behavior is accompanied by a clear set

24. The percentage of national investment made by local governments increased from 40 to 62 percent from 1977 to 1984. See Carl Riskin, *China's Political Economy: The Quest for Development Since 1949* (New York: Oxford University Press, 1987), 364.

of local attitudes toward the business environment and managerial responsibility, about welfare and employment, local development needs, and the legitimacy of claims to enterprise profit.

The Redistribution of Local Resources

Ironically, the same arguments that reformers use to argue for thorough price reform and greater enterprise autonomy are also used by local officials as the justification for their intervention in enterprise activities. Reformers argue that in today's half-reformed economy, unreformed prices do not yet send the proper signals to enterprises, and a number of objective conditions beyond the control of managers—transportation links, energy supply, state pricing decisions, existing state of capital stock—make the link between efficiency and profit tenuous and threaten to exacerbate existing distortions and imbalances. In the terminology of reform, these "objective conditions" (*keguan tiaojian*), beyond the control of enterprise managers, make it impossible for such "subjective factors" (*zhuguan yinsu*) as good management or hard work to be measured by factory profits. Local officials are highly conscious of this, and they take it as their right, indeed their duty, to protect enterprises under them from the consequences of unequal "objective conditions," ensure the balanced and stable growth of the local economy, and protect the welfare of local citizens.

The first consequence of this situation is a practice popularly referred to as "whipping the fast oxen" (*bianda kuai niu*)—in effect, tailoring effective taxation rates to rates of profit. As one factory director stated to me in a matter-of-fact fashion, "If our profits increase in future years, there will be supplementary taxes to adjust for changed performance."[25] This is often said, both in China and abroad, to reflect the desire of local officials to restrict enterprise autonomy and maintain their power. But even if local officials fully supported enterprise autonomy (and I encountered some very critical and outspoken advocates in various bureaus and banks), they would be compelled by circumstances to behave in this fashion.

Every city government will have a set of enterprises, typically producing raw or intermediate materials, whose products are in short supply and badly needed by other local enterprises, but whose price niche ensures that their profitability will be very low. These enterprises, typically producing steel or fabricated metal products, nonferrous metals, industrial chemicals, or simple components for engines or electrical equipment, will at best make profits that are quite small compared with their capitalization, and will frequently operate near the break-even point or below. They will be unable to cover more than a fraction of their badly

25. Interview 81, August 1984.

needed investments for plant renovation and expansion. Yet these are precisely the industries that need to develop most rapidly.[26]

At the same time, every local government will have a set of enterprises that are highly profitable and that succeed, not because their products are generally in short supply, but because the quality or specifications of their products are such that they find steady markets. These enterprises typically fabricate finished consumer or producer's goods; various kinds of machinery, electrical equipment, or consumer electronics are common examples. Their profit rates are much higher than those of older, inefficient plants and those producing raw or semifinished materials. Yet these high profits are arguably due to state pricing policies, which keep materials' prices relatively low and finished products' relatively high.

Unless it is to allow current bottleneck industries to stagnate, the city government has no choice but to favor the disadvantaged enterprises across a broad range of financial measures and administrative practices. The first measure it takes is to ration investment by setting its own priorities in local construction and renovation programs (guihua), allocating investment projects to those enterprises the city wishes to develop fastest, regardless of prevailing profit rates.[27] Every city and every industrial bureau has five-year investment plans that allocate investment quotas down to each enterprise. Every construction or renovation project must be approved by the industrial bureau, the planning commission, or higher authorities, depending on its size, and put into this plan, even if it is relatively small and funded entirely by the enterprise. Enterprises with the financial wherewithal to substantially fund investment projects are allowed to do so, but only up to the limits established in the plan. Those who have been allocated a place in the plan, but who cannot substantially cover their needed investment, will receive tax cuts or subsidized loans to allow them to complete the construction or renovation plans decided upon by their leading organs.

Effective taxation rates are tailored to the profit rates of each enterprise. The adjustment tax (tiaojie shui), designed to compensate for unequal competition due to price niches, different capital endowments,

26. A typical example was a large and important machine-building plant in Dalian, which was considered an excellent firm, based on the high quality and demand for its products, but which suffered from very low profitability. Despite the fact that it received tax breaks allowing it to keep 90 percent of its realized profits, it still could afford to contribute only 4–5 of the 77 million yuan earmarked for its investment in the Seventh Five-Year Plan (interview 125, August 1986).

27. Another reason for the investment quotas and tight controls over investment is the tendency for enterprises to overinvest, creating an "overheating" of the economy that feeds inflation, creates severe shortages of construction materials, and lowers the productivity of investment. It should be noted, however, that these controls were placed by the central government in order to restrain local governments and enterprises.

and other "objective factors," was instituted with the shift to enterprise taxation and is the best known of these leveling mechanisms.[28] But in practice it was found that this tax was too small and too inflexible to allow local officials to guide industry effectively (tax regulations specified that this tax rate remain unchanged for a certain number of years).[29] In fact, on paper the entire tax structure looks quite inflexible, since localities, as it was explained repeatedly to me, do not have the power to change centrally determined rates of taxation.

Localities do, however, have a free hand in deciding *how much* of a factory's profits shall be exempted from taxation during any given year, and for most products they also have the right to exempt any amount of sales revenues from taxes on products. The only limit on these tax breaks, other than central regulations forbidding sales tax breaks on such products as alcohol and tobacco, is the finance bureau's calculation of the effect they will have on local revenues.

Tax breaks are routinely considered in three kinds of situations. In the first, enterprises that have habitually operated at a loss, yet which continue to turn out badly needed materials or components for other local industries, will receive tax breaks to allow them to continue to operate. On occasion, such enterprises will receive even larger concessions to subsidize large investments if local officials deem it necessary to turn the situation around. In the second situation, a plant that normally operates with a profit may, because of "objective conditions," find itself in financial difficulties. The objective conditions may be any number of things: shortages of raw materials, energy blackouts, price rises for raw materials. A temporary tax break will be negotiated to permit the firm, which is in trouble through circumstances beyond its control, to keep operating. The third situation is when a sizable renovation or construction project is undertaken. Because nominal tax rates are so high, very few can afford to repay investment loans within the customary time period. Every such project has a variable tax subsidy in its "loan repayment contract" (*huankuan hetong*).

Although we have no data on the prevalence or magnitude of such tax

28. In an earlier article, based on the 1984 interviews, I described how the adjustment tax was set initially. One enterprise director (interview 84, August 1984) referred to five criteria, one of which was "how much profit the government thinks the factory should be making." See Andrew G. Walder, "The Informal Dimension of Enterprise Financial Reforms," in *The Chinese Economy Toward the Year 2000*, vol. 1, *The Four Modernizations*, Joint Economic Committee, Congress of the United States (Washington, D.C.: U.S. Government Printing Office, 1986), 630–45.

29. When that time period was up, which in some areas was three years and fell in the year of my 1986 interviews, the adjustment tax was readjusted only after a long process of "arguing, begging, and compromising" between the factory and the finance bureau (interview 90, May 1986).

breaks, one gains the impression from interviews—particularly in the detailed knowledge that people at all levels have of the subsidies and the conditions under which they may be secured—that favorable tax treatment is common. This means that the upper limit on taxation is the nominal tax rate, with widespread reductions in the effective tax rate through exemptions of varying magnitudes. The actual rate of profit retention appears to average between 20 and 25 percent.[30]

There is another important redistributive mechanism known as "the concentration of funds" (*jizhong zijin,* or *jizi*). These are administrative levies, usually by industrial bureaus but sometimes by planning commissions, on the retained profits of enterprises. One bureau official explained, "This is like an additional adjustment tax. We take more from those with more money, and less from those with less. All sixteen industrial corporations (bureaus) in Beijing do this."[31] The administrative agency simply takes away part of the factory's retained profits. At the industrial bureaus that described the practice to me, these levies ranged from 7 to 15 percent.[32] The bureau deposits the funds in a local bank or an investment and trust corporation and loans or grants them to needy enterprises under its supervision at preferential rates. In other cases, in a practice called "apportionment" (*tanpai*) in one city, the city government simply places a levy on the profits of a particularly large and profitable firm in its jurisdiction.[33] These practices were controversial in 1986, and since the press at that time carried articles critical of them, enterprise officials openly complained to me about such "arbitrary practices."[34]

30. A 1985 survey of 429 enterprises in 27 cities found these enterprises to retain an average of 22 percent of their gross profits. See Bruce L. Reynolds, ed., *Reform in China: Challenges and Choices* (Armonk, N.Y.: M. E. Sharpe, 1987), 89.

31. Interview 102, June 1986.

32. Interview 101, June 1986 (10%); interview 102, June 1986 (10–15%); interview 117, July 1986 (7.5%, but only for collectives, since the state firms successfully resisted). In Dalian, one bureau official explained, "We borrow without interest from our well-off plants to finance investment in others. The ones we take from don't like it but there's nothing they can do about it" (interview 122, August 1986).

33. One large factory claimed that the city put a special levy on its retained profits because the firm was by far the biggest in town and the city was revenue hungry (interview 128, August 1986). In Shenyang, various interviews revealed that in 1986 the city placed a 15 percent "construction" levy on retained profits of a number of enterprises that could bear it in 1986. It was to last for three years. In a large enterprise in a third city, the city kept 33 percent of the retained profits in 1985 and wanted to take 42 percent in 1986. "The proportion is different every year according to our profit level. We get to keep very little of the profits. This is because this is a very profitable line of production. This readjusts the profit earned between sectors. In effect, we are taxed three times" (interview 123, August 1986). Note that levies of this sort are not considered taxation and therefore are not divided with the Center.

34. "They shouldn't do this, but they do it anyway. There's no policy, they just have the power. They take more from the factories that make more money" (interview 101, June 1986).

Sharing Risk

One important consequence of the city government's mission to compensate for "objective conditions" is the provision of a kind of insurance against the risk of industrial undertakings. This is an ironic consequence of the new stress on having enterprises repay investment loans. The bank examines every feasibility study and loan application for the firm's ability to repay out of increased profits. Not uncommonly, an application will be flagged by the bank as having too much risk (*fengxian*) and as unacceptable, without awarding the firm favorable conditions.

At this point, industrial decision-makers are faced with a conflict between two principles, which they refer to as "economic efficiency" (*jingji xiaolu*) and "social utility" (*shehui xiaolu* or *shehui xuyao*). The prevailing attitude among those I interviewed is that the former is a rather narrow, blind, and calculating criterion, whereas the latter takes into account the greater public good. By the time a project application is rejected or flagged by a bank as unprofitable, it has already been approved by the industrial bureau involved, placed in the plan, and if it is large, already approved by the planning commission. In other words, the planning apparatus of the city has already pronounced upon its social utility.[35] There follows a protracted negotiation among industrial bureau, bank, tax bureau, finance bureau, and planning commission. The usual result is a set of "favorable conditions" (*youhui taiojian*) that will allow the venture to succeed.

The finance and tax bureaus have four mechanisms that, in combination, allow them to fashion "favorable conditions" of widely varying attractiveness. The first is to reduce or eliminate the interest rate on the loan. The financial system simply pays the interest directly to the bank, and the enterprise repays only the principal. This is an "interest free loan" (*wuxi daikuan*) or a "subsidized interest loan" (*tiexi daikuan*). The second mechanism allows the enterprise to deduct its annual debt repayment from the profit subject to taxation. But it is common practice on construction loans financed by budgetary funds ("special project loans," *texiang daikuan*) to allow up to a 100 percent income tax deduction on the debt repayment, or as the Chinese put it, to repay loans before taxes (*shuiqian huankuan*).[36] Since the various taxes on enterprises usually add up to a nominal tax rate of 70 to 85 percent, this can be a large subsidy,

---

35. Some cities routinely dispense with bank profitability studies if there is a pressing social need for the project (interview 110, July 1986).

36. For basic construction loans in Shenyang out of public finance funds, the standard treatment is for all projects to get 100 percent deductions (interview 113, July 1986). The treatment varies for different kinds of loans (it is different for technical-renovation loans), for the source of funds (it varies greatly for bank credit), and by local policy.

equal to the percentage the factory is allowed to repay before taxes times the tax rate.[37]

The third mechanism is to allow the enterprise an exception from the principle that it repay a loan out of new profits generated by the investment project. Enterprises whose projects are judged to be economically unprofitable but socially necessary will be granted the right to repay their loans out of their "old" profit, in addition to the new. The fourth mechanism, usually used only in projects with urgent social justification but poor financial prospects, is simply to treat loan repayments as taxes (*shitong shangjiao renwu*).[38] In this case, loan repayments are simply counted toward the factory's tax obligation, releasing them from their normal tax obligations until the loan is repaid. With so many mechanisms at their disposal, local officials can tailor tax breaks of any size. They can, and do, fine-tune loan and tax packages to create in advance the conditions for repayment.[39] One might reasonably ask, given this ability to fine-tune financial conditions, whether there is any criterion financial bureaus use to determine *how much* preferential treatment to give a firm, and if so, what.

The only clear standard that I was able to discover was evident in all the cities I visited: the factory's bonus and welfare funds shall not be allowed to fall below the level of the year reforms began (1983 or 1984). Even if, in extreme cases, the factory must use all of its reserve funds to repay loans or cover losses, wages and benefits must not be allowed to fall.[40] This standard was usually justified by the argument that "objective conditions" necessitate tax breaks in the first place, so the work force should not suffer from circumstances beyond their control. Others stated the point more baldly and said that workers' incomes should not be allowed to suffer in the course of reforms.

These practices reduce significantly the element of risk in enterprise operations. Enterprises can depend on leading organs and other agencies to devise an investment package designed to secure success. If the enterprise still runs into difficulties repaying because the feasibility study

37. The amount that a factory repays before taxes can, it is reported, be readjusted annually, at least in one enterprise's experience (interview 97, June 1986).

38. One factory I visited had 50 percent of its loan repayments counted toward its tax quota, in addition to being allowed to repay entirely before taxes, "because we are a high-priority development sector" (interview 101, Beijing, June 1986). Some cities have done the reverse: allowed tax payments to count as loan repayments, called *yishui huandai*, but this probably is limited to loans from government funds (interview 130, August 1986).

39. One city is reported to have spent 13.7 percent of its annual budget on subsidies for investment projects in 1985. It subsidized just under 30 percent of all debt obligations for construction projects that year.

40. In Beijing the common procedure is to exclude a factory's bonus and benefit funds from realized profit before the tax base is determined (interview 106, July 1986).

was too optimistic, or because of objective conditions, a firm can apply for a "hardship tax break" (kunnan jianmian). The plea of "objective conditions" is ruled out in only three cases: if labor costs go up; if materials use rises; or if sales go down because of poor quality of product. The loan repayment contract is viewed as legitimately open to renegotiation. After confirming this, one enterprise manager said, "Usually this is no problem if you are a well-run factory and aren't a chronic money loser."[41]

If poor financial performance can be traced to "subjective factors," this is a blight on the manager's record. But tax breaks are still given, usually for one year but sometimes longer, to help turn the situation around: "Whether it is due to bad management or not, we still reduce taxes if we want to save the enterprises in a certain line of production. We are after all a socialist country, and we don't want enterprises to go bankrupt."[42] If the problems persist, local authorities may eventually decide, if the plant is important, to give the firm a large renovation project to increase its technical productivity and start with a clean slate.

The Shared Responsibility of Collective Decisions

Just as much of the risk of investment projects is absorbed by local industrial circles, so is the responsibility for investment decisions. Since government agencies have taken it upon themselves to intervene actively and compensate for "objective conditions," they take up much of the responsibility for investment decisions.

An enterprise's initial project proposal (xiangmu jianyi shu) is submitted to its industrial bureau, but after that point various government agencies become involved. The industrial bureau commissions a feasibility study and may order revisions. Depending on its size, the project will then be taken to the planning commission, or to higher levels of government, for approval and to arrange a funding package. Finance bureaus and banks will examine the project proposal and arrange funding; when a tax break is required, the tax bureau must also be consulted. The loan repayment contract represents prolonged discussions by these agencies. Symbolically, it must be affixed with the seals of the enterprise itself, its industrial bureau, the finance bureau, bank, and tax bureau.[43]

41. Interview 87, August 1985. Another said, oversimplifying the matter but reflecting a common relaxed attitude on the subject, "If you have problems repaying your loans, you just talk it over with the finance bureau and they will lower your taxes" (interview 91, May 1986).

42. Tax bureau (interview 104, June 1986). Another tax bureau official said, when referring to the same practice, "We have to make sure that people can eat" (interview 112, July 1986). This official estimated that from fifteen to eighteen enterprises received this kind of treatment in his city annually.

43. Interview 133, August 1986.

In effect, the investment is not the enterprise's decision: it is a collective one of all of the local agencies that have discussed and approved it. "The responsibility is unclear, however, who it is that gives final approval, or who it is that has the right of final denial. If any one of these organs turns you down, you can't get it. So the responsibility is unclear. No one is entirely responsible."[44] In controversial cases, the decision follows from a long process of consensus building, which may in the end be settled by the planning commission or the mayor's office. The manager's plans have been scrutinized and approved by the entire local industrial circle. If something goes wrong that cannot be attributed directly to the manager's subsequent actions, all of the departments involved share responsibility for the initial decision to go ahead. This is one important reason, in addition to the more obvious economic ones, why local industrial circles are prone to save firms in financial difficulties. Not only can "objective conditions" be blamed, but they are themselves implicated, since they set the financial conditions under which firms operate.

REDISTRIBUTIVE POLITICS: BARGAINS AND STRATEGIES

Bargaining closely follows the design of local fiscal and planning processes. Since these processes are essentially ones of revenue redistribution, bargaining is designed to affect marginal changes in redistributive decisions. Managers have an identifiable set of strategies, but their effectiveness is limited by the enterprise's bargaining position—something that cannot be changed by the manager.

Bargaining Positions

The enterprise that enjoys the best bargaining position is the one on which the city depends substantially for the supply of scarce inputs for local industry. Steel foundries and rolling and stamping mills, for example, enjoy an excellent bargaining position if they are not located in a major steel center, and if the city has a substantial heavy-manufacturing base. Here the city will be highly dependent upon the firm for the completion of local production plans, and the factory's arguments for favorable treatment and complaints about "objective conditions" carry considerable weight.[45] When profit rates are low because of a firm's price niche, as for steel mills, such pleas are even harder to resist. In one of the cities I studied, one large metal-fabricating plant, with only a fraction of

44. Enterprise director (interview 97, June 1986).
45. One manager boasted, "The banks can't really refuse us. Our products are urgently needed for the development of the city's economy, so we never meet resistance from the bank. There's no problem borrowing more. If they give us a hard time, how can our economy develop?" (interview 94, June 1986).

its annual production, could supply all the needs of local industry. When the local bureau of material supply needed an urgent shipment of its product for a local enterprise, that firm could use its assistance as leverage in financial negotiations with the city.

Size, however, is not an unalloyed advantage. In another city, a large metal-fabricating plant, relatively profitable and the largest of its kind in the country, turned out a product urgently needed throughout the nation. However, local demand for that firm's products was not high: the city had a small industrial base. In fact, this firm was so large that its taxes contributed 25 percent of the city's annual budget. Its size and profitability, however, were too tempting for the city: not only did the firm pay a high adjustment tax, it was also required to turn over 40 percent of its *retained* profits. The city justified this by arguing that support costs for such a large plant were a great burden for the relatively poor city. Whether this was true, I could not tell, but the manager of the firm complained at length.[46]

These cases illustrate the vagaries of size and dependence as an advantage for the firm. If the firm is large, is relatively unprofitable, and is a crucial supplier for *local* industry, it will consistently obtain the most favorable of financial conditions. If, however, it is large, is relatively profitable, and supplies national rather than local industry, it can be preyed upon as a cash cow for the local budget. The only recourse a firm in this situation will have is to appeal to the relevant ministry, and perhaps even to the state planning commission, to bring pressures upon local officials. I suspect that in this last example the matter could only be resolved if pressure from central agencies was accompanied by a concession in the revenue-sharing agreement between the finance ministry and the city.[47]

National priorities also appear to affect bargaining positions of enterprises, although to what degree I cannot measure. While objective conditions are often difficult to separate from subjective ones, the price niches of most sectors are relatively well known. Reform plans at the national level specify certain sectors as suffering from distorted prices, and others as having an unfair advantage. If you plead "objective conditions" to gain favorable treatment, your task is made easier if you are in a sector that does suffer from the price system. If you are not in such a position, you may be in a sector—such as most machine-building industries—that is experiencing rising materials costs but steady product prices. Central policy mandates that these firms "absorb" (*xiaohua*) new costs through

46. Interview 128, August 1986.
47. In fact, I wonder in retrospect whether the city's blatant predation upon the ministry's firm was from the beginning part of a bargaining strategy to redraw the rules of *caizheng baogan.*

increased efficiency. Officials will be less immediately attentive to pleas from these firms, unless there are additional objective conditions that affect them.

Whether they are profitable or not, some sectors are designated in each city as "key points" for local development. Sometimes these are determined by long-standing local needs; in other cases, they may represent a response to the priorities of the national five-year plan. It was evident in some cities that certain sectors—especially electronics and the computer industry—were receiving preferential treatment as a matter of both local and national policy, relatively independently of their profitability. As new growing sectors, they were being given favorable conditions for rapid growth.

On the other hand, unneeded industries perennially operating in the red will be gradually phased out. In Beijing in 1986 such a sector comprised the small, antiquated, and unprofitable chemical-fertilizer plants that could not sell their poor-quality products. The city had for several years been phasing out this sector. Heavy-industry plants in the city center were receiving the same treatment that year because the city had a beautification plan that sought to relocate polluting firms in the suburbs.

Bargaining Strategies

When an enterprise manager seeks to improve his firm's position, his bargaining strategies are constrained by the objective bargaining position of the firm. An effective bargainer might be able to compensate somewhat for such disavantages, or might be able to capitalize on a firm's inherent advantages better than a poor bargainer. But the general odds of success are limited by one's objective position.

Nonetheless, every manager appears to follow a standard set of strategies. The first is not to let obvious indicators of poor management appear. Make sure that labor-productivity figures do not drop, or that costs of production do not rise. Keep the labor force happy by making sure that their bonus income does not fall, and show them that you are making sincere efforts to build housing and improve other factory benefits. If necessary, let the word out that you are bending state regulations to help out the workers.[48]

As insurance against the possibility that, despite your best efforts, indicators of "subjective factors" will appear, begin to lay the groundwork for the plea of objective conditions. If there are any delays in the deliveries of materials or components, or if there are any other problems that constitute an objective condition that might explain lower productivity or higher costs, be sure to complain early and repeatedly to your

48. See Walder, "Factory and Manager" (n. 10 above).

industrial bureau, the materials-management bureau, and even the economic commission, to make sure that it registers firmly that you are
besieged by myriad urgent problems beyond your control. If it turns out
that your costs stay down and your labor productivity goes up after all,
you may convince your superiors of your skill.

Another strategy is an adaptation of traditional "hoarding" behavior:
make sure that you do not do so well that you overfulfill your tax quota
by a substantial amount. That will provoke an upward revision of your
quota in the next period, making your life more difficult. Moreover,
under the principle of "whipping the fast oxen," city authorities will be
less amenable to your pleas for tax breaks or subsidized credit. Managers
commonly work operating surpluses back into costs by engaging in
small-scale renovation and construction, purchase materials, and "prepare for next year's production."[49] Managers commonly admit to this
practice and do not view it as illegitimate, and industrial bureaus fully
understand that this is going on and acquiesce in it. Tax and finance
bureaus view this as a violation of state regulations, but do not have the
capacity to monitor the bookkeeping techniques managers use to pad
costs. It is also not clear whether, as representatives of local interests,
they have a clear motivation to do so.[50] One tax official explained, "State
enterprises are usually guilty of tax evasion. They generally hide funds,
enter too many items into costs. We mainly use propaganda to control it,
make sure everyone knows the regulations. We can only do spot checks
of factory accounts, and rely on reports from the masses."[51]

Managers can also use the state plan to bargain for favorable financial
treatment. Getting into mandatory state plans or "guidance plans" (really

49. "If you surpass your tax quota by a lot this year, they will only raise it even more next
year. So you want to just meet the target, maybe overfulfill it a bit, and build up your
reserve productive capacity. . . . We do the same thing for our electricity and water allot-
ments" (interview 96, June 1986). An industrial bureau official concurred: "Naturally,
factories always will look at whether or not it is advantageous for them to overfulfill their
financial targets by much. Their target next year will go up if they do. They consider . . .
what's in it for me if I do? . . . They prevent themselves from overfulfilling by preparing
for next year's production" (interview 100, June 1986). "Factories don't greatly exceed it.
You just raise costs by engaging in plant repairs. You have to think of next year's production too, not just this year's, so you make preparations instead of pushing to overfulfill"
(interview 101, June 1986).
50. After 1986, as a direct response to this widespread strategy, many managers were
induced to sign "responsibility contracts" that bound them to turn over a fixed sum of
revenues as taxes over a period of three years. It is too early to tell whether this will prevent
managers from working profits back into costs, or whether local financial bureaus can
resist the temptation to renegotiate contracts when enterprises begin to reap "excessive"
profits.
51. Interview 112, July 1986.

mandatory plans imposed by local authorities) can be a real advantage.[52] If in the October planning work conference the planning commission wants you to increase your output of a certain product, or to produce a different one, a manager can use this request to bargain for a subsidized loan or a break on sales taxes for new products. One of the explicit rules of the game is that enterprise-government relations are in a state of moving equilibrium, or as one manager put it, "The standard is not what everyone else gets; its what you got last year. . . . If you must accept a higher target, try to get something in return. Ask for approval of a renovation project using imported equipment, and a loan in foreign exchange. Then the (industrial) bureau runs to the economic commission to argue for the loan."[53] If a request or a demand from the government upsets that equilibrium in one area, it is only fair that in compensation, negotiations proceed in other areas to allow the enterprise to meet that request.

Finally, if city authorities find that "subjective factors" have caused declining performance, try to turn defeat into victory. Are profits down because you cannot sell your poor-quality products? Argue that the root of the problem is poor and antiquated capital equipment; what you really need is a large loan to import advanced Western technology and build a modern new workshop capable of producing the best quality items. Are your costs of production rising in the absence of higher costs for raw materials? Argue that the problem is dilapidated equipment that continually breaks down, requiring expensive repairs and causing delays; what you really need is a large renovation loan to replace your outdated machinery. Managers in this position, if unwilling to accept defeat, can use their situation as an opportunity to display managerial talent. Aggressive advocacy of a project proposal to turn the situation around will often meet a receptive response from local officials, who are also interested in turning a liability into an asset.

No matter how skillfully managers bargain for favorable treatment, successful bargaining further undercuts managerial autonomy. For the notion that drives these bargaining strategies is that of "objective conditions"—a term that justifies the city's responsibility to intervene extensively in enterprise affairs and to redistribute resources among them. No matter how much managers complain that they retain too little profit and have insufficient business autonomy, as soon as they run into difficulty or seek investment they turn to their superiors as supplicants

---

52. We often wrongly assume that all enterprise managers will want to get out of state plans and gain the greater autonomy and profits to be enjoyed on the market. But this may undercut your bargaining position, and it should already be evident that much of your increased profits will be appropriated in some fashion.

53. Interview 93, June 1986.

seeking relief from objective conditions. In China's budgetary and fiscal processes, bargaining strategies reinforce the dependence of enterprises on their superiors.

CONCLUSION: BARGAINING IN PERSPECTIVE

If we view bargaining as a symptom of an institutional setting, it appears less consequential than if we focused exclusively on bargaining strategy and activity. For the rules of the game are given by a new system of revenue sharing that has given localities enhanced fiscal powers and a heightened incentive to regulate carefully the financial flows between the city budget and each enterprise. They are given by a system of unreformed prices and unequal capital endowments for which managers have no responsibility. They are also given, finally, by the city's quite legitimate task of managing local development, protecting fiscal stability, and safeguarding the income and employment of local citizens.

From this perspective, it makes little sense to account for soft budget constraints, or interminable delays in policy implementation, by invoking the phenomenon of bargaining. For bargaining is but a symptom of institutional realities that are themselves responsible for delays and soft budgets. The state's budgetary process and mechanisms for revenue generation are not premised on firm rules about property, responsibility, or entitlement. There are as yet no clear standards about what is legitimately the central government's or the city's or the enterprise's share of industrial profits. There are only customary practices and situational standards, which must be revised case by case. It is only out of the bargaining process that a "fair" determination of these matters can be reached.

The same is true of fiscal responsibility. Just as there are at best situational standards regarding shares of factory revenues, local industrial circles rarely assign final responsibility for investment decisions. Many agencies and officials are involved, and the responsibility is shared collectively. As a group they strive to create conditions that reduce risk, but they do not always succeed. Sometimes this failure can be laid to the manager's actions, but often it cannot. No matter how much managers may want autonomy in other areas of their jobs, in striving for these favorable conditions they willingly surrender their autonomy to city planners in return for insurance against financial risk and responsibility.

It is commonly said that China's industrial system, formerly a centralized bureaucracy, is becoming one in which autonomous firms face market situations. This is at best a half-truth, misleading because enterprises are not yet financially independent entities. They are more accurately seen, not as independent business entities, but as quasi-autonomous divisions within a corporate structure.[54] China's local industrial systems are becoming decentralized bureaucracies with expanded elements of market calculation. But they are still relatively coherent corporate structures. How these socialist corporations and socialist markets differ from their counterparts in market economies is beyond the scope of this chapter. Yet it is surely in the comparative study of corporate settings that we shall find answers to the most perplexing questions about China's industrial economy.

APPENDIX: CLASSIFIED LIST OF INTERVIEWS

Government Commissions
1. Beijing Economic Commission
2. Beijing Planning Commission
3. Chongqing Planning Commission
4. Dalian Economic Commission
5. Shenyang Planning and Economic Commission
6. Tianjin Economic Commission
7. Tianjin Planning Commission

Functional Bureaus
1. Beijing Taxation Bureau
2. Beijing Materials Management Bureau
3. Beijing Finance Bureau
4. Chongqing Finance Bureau
5. Chongqing Taxation Bureau
6. Shanghai Taxation Bureau
7. Shenyang Finance Bureau
8. Shenyang Taxation Bureau
9. Shenyang Price Bureau
10. Shenyang Materials Management Bureau
11. Sichuan Province Finance Bureau
12. Tianjin Material Supply Bureau
13. Tianjin Taxation Bureau
14. Tianjin Finance Bureau

Banks
1. Beijing Branch, Construction Bank
2. Chongqing Branch, People's Bank
3. Chongqing Branch, Industrial-Commercial Bank
4. Tianjin Branch, Construction Bank
5. Tianjin Branch, Industrial-Commercial Bank
6. Shenyang Branch, Construction Bank

54. I suspect that this statement holds for any system that administers industrial enterprises, whether it be ministry, province, city, county, township, or village.

Industrial Bureaus (Corporations) and Companies
1. Beijing Machine Building Corporation
2. Beijing Computer Corporation
3. Beijing Woolen Knitwear Company
4. (Beijing) Capital Iron and Steel Corporation
5. Chongqing Machine Building Bureau
6. Dalian Metallurgy Corporation
7. Dalian Machine Building Corporation
8. Shenyang Machine Building Bureau
9. Shenyang Second Light Industrial Bureau
10. Shenyang Auto Industry Company
11. Shenyang Materials Trading Center

Enterprises
1. Beijing Electric Motor
2. Beijing Internal Combustion Engine
3. Beijing No. 2 Chemical
4. Beijing No. 2 Textile
5. (Beijing) Yili Foodstuffs
6. (Beijing) Guanghua Wood Products
7. Beijing No. 3 Semiconductor
8. Chengdu Seamless Tubing
9. Chengdu Internal Combustion Engine Parts
10. Chengdu Scientific Instruments
11. (Chongqing) Jialing Machinery
12. Chongqing Woolen Textiles
13. Dalian Steel Rolling Mill
14. Dalian Heavy Machinery
15. Shanghai No. 7 Radio
16. Shanghai Machine Tools
17. Shanghai No. X Clothing (pseud.)
18. Shenyang Cable
19. Shenyang Signal
20. (Shenyang) Dongbei Pharmaceuticals
21. Shenyang Transformer (1985 and 1986)
22. Shenyang Metal Furniture
23. Zhejiang Machine Building (pseud.)

TWELVE

Urbanizing Rural China: Bureaucratic Authority and Local Autonomy

David Zweig

As with all major shifts in rural policy since 1949, the current Chinese reforms have altered the distribution of power, authority, and resources at the county and subcounty levels. Peasants have been freed from the dependent relations that bound them to their village leaders (Oi 1985); this change allows them greater leeway to determine their crops and their avocation. Some can now migrate into other rural or urban settlements. A booming rural industrial sector, legitimized by the central government in 1984, is generating new resources, strengthening the power of lower-level officials, who control and tax these new enterprises, vis-à-vis their administrative superiors.[1] And resurgent markets and market towns revitalize both the "natural economy" and the interregional trade that crosses administrative boundaries, further weakening the influence of administrators who previously had tightly controlled all rural marketing.

But the weakening of bureaucratic power through rural reforms does not hold true for all reform policies, as the bureaucracy continues to limit the effect of many reforms on the distribution of resources and authority in the rural areas. One such policy is rural urbanization. Since

Thanks to Yok-shiu Lee of the East-West Center, University of Hawaii, who shared much of his data and knowledge about small towns with me. Research assistance for this paper was supplied by Xu Ziwang at the Fletcher School of Law and Diplomacy. Nancy Hearst of the Fairbank Center Library, Harvard University, supplied bibliographic assistance. Funding for the field research in China in 1986 came from a grant from the Social Science and Humanities Research Council of Canada, Ottawa, and a one-week 1988 research trip was supported by the Sackler Foundation, Washington, D.C.

1. Under the retrenchment policy begun after the Third Plenum in September 1988, rural industries met hard times. Funds dried up. By early 1990 three million enterprises were closed and 13 million farmers returned to the land, found new jobs, or joined the 50–60 million migrant workers. *Foreign Broadcast Information Service* (*FBIS*), no. 245S (16 December 1989): 14. By late 1990 the situation had improved somewhat.

the early 1980s the state has called for increased urbanization, with the bulk of growth to occur in small cities, rural towns, and villages. Yet the process of rural urbanization shows that authority remains ensconced within the bureaucracy and distributed among the various levels within it, making bureaucratic authority, not the market, the best predictor of the outcome of decisions and the distribution of resources. County and town officials still possess important mechanisms of command and control over resources, production, migration, and economic opportunities. Although market forces are expanding, new pockets of local autonomy are developing, and county officials often must negotiate with subordinates, old patterns of authority have not decreased or changed as much as one might have predicted, given the sweeping nature of the reforms.

RURAL URBANIZATION AS AN ISSUE AREA

Like blind men studying the elephant, which aspect of the rural reforms one addresses determines one's perspective on the reforms' impact on the distribution of authority. A village-level focus may show a major transformation, as a new generation of rich peasants takes control from former production-team leaders (White 1987). The privatization of wholesale and long-distance trading would show a dramatic drop in state controls, depending on the location (Watson 1988). But studying "rural urbanization" demonstrates that a decreasing scope for the national plan need not lead to a total shift to a market economy.

This issue area is constrained for several reasons. First, unlike marketing reforms that cross administrative boundaries, these expanding settlements overlap with the existing administrative hierarchy, so prereform authority patterns persist within the reforming rural bureaucracy and community. Second, these settlements and towns remain the locus of Party and government committees and political authority at the county and subcounty levels. Towns are the site of income-enhancing opportunities, the end point of migration, and their governments own much of the expanding industrial base, allowing bureaucrats there to influence strongly the flow of people and resources.

Furthermore, the central government left responsibility for the rural urbanization process to county and county-town governments. (See the appendix to this chapter.) But limited resources for urban infrastructure lets the county influence resource allocations and maintain relations of dependency over lower levels in the hierarchy . This phenomenon mirrors that outlined in Chapter 11 in this volume.

To demonstrate how the rural bureaucracy influences the rural urbanization process I examine prereform rural settlements and administrative hierarchy and then describe administrative changes that have occurred under the reforms. Then I discuss how county officials control developments in the county. Through planning, imposing development labels, and "nesting" administrative offices and enterprises within the physical boundaries of the county-towns and townships, the county has maintained significant control over localities within its domain. A study of the struggle among the county, county-towns, and townships over funds for town development will help clarify this relationship. I also show how county-town and township officials control access to the towns. In conclusion I draw some generalizations about the relationship between resources, hierarchy, and political authority as they relate to rural urbanization.

THE PREREFORM STRUCTURE OF AUTHORITY AND SETTLEMENTS

In 1949 the Chinese Communist Party (CCP) inherited the Guomintang's local administrative hierarchy. Unlike the Qing dynasty, the Guomintang had established the district (*qu*) between the county (*xian*) and the administrative villages (*xiang*) or towns. The *qu* was a supervisory agent by which the *xian* government managed the *xiang*, which, with a fairly well developed governmental structure, constituted the most basic level of government administration (Barnett 1965, 318–38). Large *xiang*, whose location made them major marketing centers, were classified as market towns, or *zhen*.[2]

In their ceaseless efforts to control both the economy and the political administration, the CCP extended subcounty controls. With the *qu* as the administrative level for organizing land-reform teams, their number doubled by 1955 and became full-scale governments between the *xian* and the *xiang*. But as collectivization increased the size of each agricultural producer cooperative, the *xiang* expanded to ensure continued coherence between economic and administrative organizations. As the *xiang* grew they began to approximate the size of the *qu*, so in December 1955 the disbanding of the *qu* left the *xiang* as the major administrative level below the *xian* (Schurmann 1968, 453). Continuing state efforts throughout the 1950s and 1960s to control private marketing killed the market town (*jizhen*) as a commercial force and seat of autonomous authority.[3]

2. According to Schurmann (1968), settlements with urban character with 100–1,000 households became *zhen;* those with similar populations and rural character became *xiang*.

3. See "Jizhen fazhan de quzhe licheng," in *Dangdai Zhongguo xiangcun jianshi*, Editorial Board of Contemporary China Series (Beijing: Shehui kexue chuban she), 117–21. Songhe town in Hubei province, built in the Ming dynasty, had been a town of 65,000 before the 1946–49 civil war. The end of grain markets, collectivization, and the Great Leap forced 3,000 shops to close and the population to drop to 3,000 residents. In the Cultural Revolu-

When the 1958 Great Leap Forward amalgamated the agricultural co-operatives and the *xiang* government and placed the headquarters of the new People's Communes in former *jizhen* or *xiang* government centers,[4] the former bifurcation of the commercial system and administrative control was ended, leaving the commune seat as a powerful node in the rural bureaucratic hierarchy, which combined economic, political, and social control.[5]

The Great Leap's failure transferred ownership and control over land and most resources to the village or subvillage production team, leaving communes and brigades with weak economic bases. County-controlled market towns, which were not commune seats—by 1978 there were only 1,100 in all of China—disappeared from view, tiny islands afloat in a collectivized countryside with which they had little contact. With commune towns serving supervisory roles for county interests (Butler 1978)—county organizations, such as the Agricultural Bank, Supply and Marketing Co-ops, and the Grain Bureau, had commune-level branches that controlled production and investment decisions, migration, financial exchanges, and labor mobilization—infrastructure in commune seats did not expand, as most investment went into production.[6]

One common trend throughout this period saw county, commune, and even brigade officials expropriate bank funds, grain supplies, and peasant labor to establish rural enterprises, expand administrative capabilities, and build a semiautonomous political-economic base (Nee 1983, 236; Zweig 1989a). On the eve of reform the commune system defined not only a spatial distribution of rural settlements, smaller villages, and fields, but also a governmental and Party hierarchy from the county to the commune, through the brigade to the village, with each unit's location and rank or status within that hierarchy determining the economic

---

tion the town became a large village. In the 1930s there were about 45,000 market towns in China; by 1965 only 37,000 remained, and by 1978 there were only 33,000 (Chang and Kwok 1990, 101).

4. As the size of the Agricultural Producer Cooperatives increased, the number of *xiang* decreased from 220,000 in 1953 to 117,000 in 1956 and to only 80,000 by mid-1958. While the original number of communes, 24,000, may have been imposed on the standard marketing communities built around marketing towns (Skinner 1964), the shrinking of the communes in the early 1960s, leaving 74,000 communes, suggests that commune headquarters were established in the *xiang* that existed in mid-1958 (Barnett 1965).

5. Below the people's communes were production brigades, which in many parts of China were established either in large villages or in several villages that were linked together under one bureaucratic and economic authority. Below the brigade lay the production team, composed either of one village or of 20–30 families within the larger brigade.

6. A common characteristic of communist regimes is their refusal to invest in infrastructural development, such as roads, housing, et cetera. Ivan Szelenyi, personal communication.

resources under its political control, its relations to other organizations, and its economic and political power.

ADMINISTRATIVE STRUCTURES AND CHANGES SINCE 1983

Since the early 1950s the People's Republic of China (PRC) has maintained a sharp dichotomy, almost a "Second Great Wall," between urban and rural: for individuals it was their household registration; for settlements it was whether they were "designated towns" (*jianzhi zhen*).[7] For both, the critical question was whether the state would share with a larger population the benefits urbanites were receiving.[8] Thus the PRC has established a hierarchy of urban and rural towns that reinforces these differences and structures the distribution of these benefits.

There are four categories of small towns in China: county seats (*xian zhengfu suozaidi*), county-towns (*xianshu zhen*), township seats (*xiang zhengfu suozaidi*), and rural market towns (*nongcun jizhen*). Their characteristics are outlined in the appendix to this chapter. As part of the urban hierarchy of settlements, county seats and county-towns are "designated towns" in that their status within the urban hierarchy has been approved by the appropriate provincial authorities according to the guidelines of the State Council (Ma and Cui 1987: 376). Both are under the direct control of the county government. County seats, sites of the county government, are most directly controlled by that government, but before 1984 over 370 of the 2,074 county seats were not designated towns.[9] County-towns include market towns and former commune headquarters—now sites of township governments—whose population and employment structure meet the necessary criteria to become towns. These guidelines have varied over the years and today they vary regionally also.[10] Since 1984 the state has

7. For the best discussion of the discrimination toward peasants under state socialism, see Potter 1983. For a discussion of the changing nature of rural-urban relations under the reforms, see Zweig 1987 and Friedman 1990.

8. Whereas residents of designated towns were eligible for state-subsidized grain, nonagricultural residents in undesignated towns were counted as "rural population" and were ineligible for state grain (Ma and Cui 1986, 377–78). During the famine of the 1960s the state cut the number of designated towns and knocked millions of people out of the ranks of "state grain" eaters. Today, the introduction of the "households that are self-sufficient in grain" (*zili kouliang*) means that towns can become designated without increasing the demand for subsidized grain.

9. Larger county-seats may be cities (*shi*); also some administered towns in city suburbs are directly under the control of cities, not counties. These are not included here. See Cui and Ma 1987.

10. According to a 1955 State Council resolution, to be considered "urban" a settlement had to have a total population of over 2,000, of which half were not engaged in agricultural pursuits. Smaller places of between 1,000 and 2,000 people could be counted as urban if 75

raised the status of rural towns to brake the flow of peasants into larger cities, so the number of designated towns has expanded from 2,781 (1983) to 7,956 (1985) and by 1987 to 10,280 (*ZGTJNJ* 1988, 23). As part of the urban hierarchy, designated towns are eligible for more benefits than their poorer cousins, the township seat and small market town.

Township seats and market towns, which are under administrative control of the township government, are at the top of the rural hierarchy and are treated as part of the rural areas. Although their population is increasing as well, they receive little state assistance and must extract funds from their own industries and the surrounding countryside to expand their urban infrastructure.

But being "designated" has both advantages and disadvantages. Designation increases a county-town's authority vis-à-vis the county government, the township around it, and the county-town's "ability and authority to manage well enterprises and units established at the town over whose affairs they must have administrative authority and responsibility" (Zhang Yuelin 1986, 98). They can levy more taxes than undesignated towns.[11] Also, the county helps former commune headquarters that are designated as county-towns before it helps those that remain township government seats. As a result, some township officials seek ways, such as padding the number of "urban" residents, to shift into the urban hierarchy. Township leaders in Jiangpu county, Jiangsu province, argued successfully that because the residence permits of agricultural workers on the nearby state farm, who ate state-supplied grain, were kept in their town's police station, the town's "urban" population sufficed to qualify it as a county-town. Since then the county has helped build new roads, a drinking-water system, and a new school.

Yet after towns become part of the urban hierarchy, county penetration can increase. The current policy to expand the county's economic role could place more bureaucrats in the county-towns (T. White 1988, 29–31). Officials in a Guangdong township resisted designation because acquiring county-town status would subject their industries to demands from the state industrial sector and stricter tax supervision (Siu 1988). Also, after a town becomes designated, the county can determine its

---

percent of their inhabitants were registered as nonagricultural (Kirkby 1985, 74). In response to the great famine, the criteria became stricter in 1963: only settlements of 3,000 where nonagricultural laborers were 70 percent or over, or of 2,500–3,000 with 85 percent as nonagricultural population, could be designated as part of the urban sector.

11. This situation changed somewhat in 1986 with the establishment of the "township public finance system," which gave township governments the right to collect an above-quota tax, after the fixed tax quota had been paid to the county government, thereby increasing the township seats' financial resources and tax base.

"developmental nature" (*fazhan de xingzhi*) and make the town's economic plan.[12]
Other administrative changes have had only limited effect. Replacing
the commune administration with the township government only affected the size of the area they administered.[13] Efforts to separate township Party, government, and economic structures had little impact on the
real distribution of power; Party control still dominates. If these township seats do not meet the criteria of county-towns, they remain part of
the rural hierarchy with the same control over the countryside that they
exercised when they were the commune headquarters. Former brigades
have become administrative villages (*xingzheng cun*), but they are still run
by the Party branch, not the village management committee. Only their
size may have changed.[14]

AUTHORITY AND HIERARCHY UNDER RURAL URBANIZATION

We now turn to an analysis of how the distribution of power within the
local bureaucratic hierarchy affects rural urbanization. While numerous
indicators demonstrate the distribution of authority within the rural
political economy, I focus only on those related to the growth, development, and control of rural urbanization. Reform policies, by their very
nature, create possibilities for reallocating resources. Thus the extent to
which those resources are reallocated—compared with following the old
pattern—will be a good measure of the degree to which the rural reforms have affected the distribution of power within the Chinese bureaucracy and the extent to which that bureaucracy can still affect society at
large.[15]

---

12. According to Yok-shiu Lee, counties can make land-use plans for designated and
undesignated towns but can make economic plans for only the designated towns. Personal
communication.
13. As communes shifted to townships, many more townships were established, suggesting that on average, townships were about 65 percent the size of the former communes.
While the final number of communes we have was 56,331 in 1983, by 1984 there were
91,171 township and town governments (*ZGNYNJ* 1985, 94). Since the number of towns
was 7,320 (Ma and Cui 1987, 377), the number of townships must have been approximately 85,000, significantly more than the number of communes.
14. The size of these administrative villages increased, given that the number dropped
by 10 percent between 1985 and 1986. In 1985 the number of rural residence committees
(*cunmin weiyuanhui*), which are the local governmental committees for managing the "administrative villages," dropped from 940,617 to 847,894. See *ZGTJZY* 1987, 23.
15. A cautionary note: The situation on the ground is changing rapidly. Chinese articles
written in 1984 and published in 1986 or 1987 may reflect a reality that already has
changed. For a discussion of these problems, see chapter 1 in this volume.

The Special Case of Jiangsu Province

Writing about local changes in China is complicated by the vast regional discrepancies that have emerged. Although these were not insignificant under Mao, today less pressure for uniform policy implementation allows each locality's natural or historical characteristics to affect policy implementation. Therefore one must be cognizant of the uniqueness of Jiangsu province and the focal points of this discussion, Jiangpu county, outside Nanjing, where I did most of my interviewing, and southern Jiangsu (Sunan), where I also did some interviewing, but which is the primary locale referred to in many of the secondary sources used for this chapter. Jiangpu county, as a suburban county (*shiqu*), may be more tightly controlled than counties in China that are not directly under a city administration.[16] However, Nanjing has contributed little to its economic development, leaving it with only average per capita income for the nation as a whole. Jiangpu's county-towns and townships are poorer than Sunan's, and rural industries, though important, are less developed. Therefore Jiangpu reflects national trends more than Sunan. However, unlike those in Guangdong and Fujian provinces, private businesses in Jiangpu were quite restricted. As of 1986 there were few private entrepreneurs in the county-towns and townships, although in 1987–88 their numbers increased. Also, there has been little migration to this area from outside the county.

Conditions in Sunan, particularly in counties in Suzhou and Wuxi municipalities, do not reflect national trends. Sunan is more industrialized and urbanized, with a tradition of small towns. For example, Wujiang county, outside Suzhou, where I carried out some interviews in summer 1988, has seven county-towns that have historically been of significant size. As county-towns they had only two vegetable brigades under their authority. Since 1983, however, six of them have been combined with neighboring townships, thus increasing their control over the surrounding countryside. The extent to which this has occurred in other parts of China is unclear; moreover, it is unlikely that there were more than a thousand towns like these Wujiang towns in all of China in the early 1980s.

Towns in Sunan also have powerful industrial bases, and these local government-owned factories inhibit private industrial activity. Wujiang county's Supply and Marketing Co-op simply "swallows" private industrial firms before they become serious competitors.[17] Also, although rural migration is a major factor in parts of rural China (Vogel 1989, 404–

16. All counties in Jiangsu province are under the direct administration of some city. This policy was introduced throughout the province in March 1983. Some other provinces have followed suit.

17. Interview, Wujiang county, 12 July 1988.

5; Siu 1988), Wujiang and Wuxi factories employ outsiders mainly as construction workers. The townships treat the factories as community resources that should benefit local residents. Only one town in Wujiang county hires outside laborers. Another experimented with moving peasants into town; six hundred peasants moved in, but the policy was not introduced elsewhere in the county.

As owners of most enterprises in this area, Sunan township and county-town governments have more leverage with both peasants and the county government than governments elsewhere in China. Private enterprises may resist government demands for investment funds, but county-town governments can draw funds from factories they own far more easily. Also, county-towns in Wuxi county are wealthy, so the new "financial responsibility system" (caizheng baogan)—a new form of tax farming where each level of government has a fixed tax quota to pass up to the next level of government—makes them more independent, for with so many factories they still have enough funds for urban development.[18] On the other hand, towns in poorer areas in Jiangsu province, such as those in Jiangpu county, which rely on county assistance for urban development, remain vulnerable to county control. To this extent, Jiangpu is more representative of trends elsewhere in China, although the limited development of the private sector and the tighter constraints on migration there strengthen the town's authority vis-à-vis the peasants.

Indicators of the Persistence of County Control
As a formal level of government, the county has numerous measures for influencing local urbanization. It controls the taxation process, including the income tax for rural industries, a new value-added tax, as well as construction and commercial taxes available for infrastructural development; and since it can impose its own taxes, it can negotiate tax breaks in return for various concessions. Through its branch offices that are "nested" in the towns and townships—including the tax office, grain station, supply and marketing co-op, post office, market management committee, local police station, local branch of the Agricultural Bank of China or credit co-op, and middle school (Barnett 1965, 352–57)—it can directly and indirectly influence local development. Similarly, counties own factories, mines, forests, and other productive enterprises located within the spatial domain of county-towns or townships. Because of the

18. During a January 1989 visit to Wuxi county I was told by the director of Meicun town that the "financial responsibility system" made his town more independent; after it paid its taxes, the town could determine how to allocate the rest of its funds. Dongting town, also in Wuxi county, is undergoing a major urban expansion program, and when all current projects are completed the town will be more modern and bigger than Jiangpu county's county seat.

shortage of funds for town development and the major role taxes and profits from productive units play in local development, control over these enterprises gives the county significant leverage when dealing with town and township officials. Also, county investments in town development helps them control outcomes in their own favor. Other mechanisms include labeling designated towns, drawing up development plans, controlling land usage, making loans, and particularly in the case of the county seat, exercising direct administrative control.

Planning and Bureaucratic Control

Rural urbanization policy authorizes county governments to compose development plans for all county-towns, thereby increasing the county's control. In the case of the county seat, county governmental control is very tight. The plan for Zhujiang town, the seat of Jiangpu county, was composed by the county's Urban Planning Office, which reported that the town cannot evade the plan.[19] While officials from the county seat had to approve certain aspects of town construction, they had no decision-making authority: "We want total control of the town, but the county does not want to give it to us, so there is a conflict" (Jiangpu 1986). Mistrust of town planners and the large number of county governmental units in the county seat means that the county must ensure good conditions for its employees. Therefore town development is orchestrated to benefit the county, not the town, even though the county seat may benefit from better funding and urban planning.

Planning for the county seat of Wujiang county is "directly" under control of a fifteen-person County Urban Construction Leadership Small Group (*Xian cheng jianshe lingdao xiaozu*), whose sole task is to develop the county seat.[20] With fourteen members drawn from leaders of various county bureaus,[21] only one person represents the county-seat government.

A critical planning question concerns land use. Under China's Land Law of April 1987 the amount of land that can shift out of agriculture is fixed at the provincial level, with quotas passed down to counties and towns. Wujiang county can appropriate 144 *mou* each year,[22] whose distri-

19. Interview with officials from the Planning and Management Office, Department of Urban Development and Environmental Protection, Jiangpu county, Jiangsu province, 13 May 1986.

20. The following comments are based on an interview with the deputy mayor of Songling town and the deputy director of the county's Urban Construction Office (*Xiaocheng jianshi bangongwei*), 14 July 1988.

21. The units included the Materials Bureau, Public Security Bureau, Communications Bureau, Land Management Bureau, Environmental Protection Bureau, Industrial Electricity Bureau, Post Office, Labor Bureau, et cetera.

22. One *mou* is one-fifteenth of a hectare.

bution is determined by the county Land Management Bureau. Thus large projects using more than 3 *mou* of land need county authorization, further limiting county-town autonomy. County-towns have officials responsible to the county Urban Development Bureau who monitor land use and housing construction in the town and in the surrounding countryside as well. All peasants must now get permits from the town government before building new homes, even in distant villages.

But the extent of county control is unclear. If representatives of the Urban Development Bureau are indigenous to the locality, they will be enmeshed in local politics and will have difficulty denying their colleagues a chance to move onto land near the town.[23] Since towns can expropriate three *mou* of land without county approval, cadres can take land piece by piece for their homes, so long as the local official responsible for monitoring land usage is party to the scheme. In Tangquan town, between 1985 and 1987, all high-ranking township government officials, and many of their relatives and friends, moved into villages surrounding the town under the pretext of "town development." Inhabitants in these villages were furious, since each new home shrunk the allotment of land from which peasants made their living, but they could only send letters and photos to the provincial, city, and county governments. In response, county officials asked town officials to investigate. Thus, although the county may control large projects, town officials can ignore some county directives and expropriate land on the basis of small-town development.

Labeling County Towns

The county controls the "developmental label" a county-town receives; this in turn affects its position in the county's overall development strategy, its own budget priorities, and the type of outside assistance it receives.[24] While labels are not part of the formal planning scheme, Fei Xiaotong saw this classification process as "conducive to deciding the direction of future development of small towns" (Fei 1986, 26).

The five county-towns in Jiangpu county were labeled industrial, port, political, cultural, and tourist towns and received a development plan based on these designations. While county officials in the Urban Planning Bureau claim that the "basic direction" of development comes from the towns, the county looks at the issue from both the county's overall perspective and the needs of Nanjing city, whose Urban Planning Office has the ultimate decision-making authority. Tangquan town, a Nanjing test point for small-town planning since 1984, which had been earmarked for tourism (they had a beautiful reservoir), medicinal devel-

23. Chinese analysts recognize that the main desire of many rural cadres is to move into town (Zhao and Zhang 1986, 326).
24. The county cannot do this for undesignated towns.

opment (because of their hot spring), and tree nurseries, could not get county permission to develop potentially polluting factories.[25]

But local perceptions do not mesh with the county's view.[26] Some Tangquan officials felt that their label restricted their entrepreneurial efforts; they could only seek funds for hotels, while other towns were developing industry. The county's assistance had been limited, and its plan undermined their development. The higher authorities want to bring in foreign tourism, but local officials feel that their lack of funds, equipment, and a decent road from the county seat make plans to bring in foreign tourists unrealistic.

> Their plan is empty talk. We can't do it. We have our own plan which fits our reality. We put that plan forward, but the upper levels didn't agree. We want to proceed from the real situation, but they want to do it in a big way, to build a big hotel near the State Tree Farm. We have a contradiction with them, but they want to earn foreign currency. So the province, city, and county all helped draw the plan but it didn't work. There hasn't been any development.

Given that no foreign company appears willing to invest in this project, the local view appears justified. Moreover, the county planning commission is reconsidering its plan. Nevertheless, concern that the hospital and the public school were in the same building, making it easy to pass on diseases, led the county to donate over 300,000 yuan for a new school.

The degree of control incorporated in planning and labeling varies across counties. In Wujiang county, outside Suzhou, the wealth generated by township enterprises gave county-towns more autonomy (Wujiang 1987). However, in Jiangpu county, where the county-towns' weak industrial bases strengthen the county's role in the local political economy, labeling and planning were effective forces for county control, especially over county-towns needing development assistance. So long as towns depend on state budgets for construction funds and do not develop their own resources by promoting rural industries, they remain hostage to the decisions of the county government.

Nesting and Bureaucratic Authority

A widespread network of offices and enterprises owned and operated by the county government, but "nested" within the county-towns or township seats, increases the county's influence. These subbureaus or enterprises—

25. Restrictions on Tongli town, Wujiang county, Suzhou district, "one of the best preserved old water county-towns in existence," may limit the town's development, but according to Fei Xiaotong it is necessary to ensure that the concept of "destruction for construction does not destroy the town" (Fei 1986, 340).

26. The following discussion is based on conversations with local officials in Tangquan in summer 1986. Because the criticism is aimed at the county, I protect my sources.

such as mines, forests, factories, or shops—support county-government interests when they conflict with those of the town. County-owned enterprises resist the county-towns' request for "contributions" to development funds in ways factories owned by county-towns cannot. In the cases to follow, local development efforts were undermined by the nested county bureaucracy.

In Tongli town, a county-town in Wujiang county, the county grain bureau wanted to construct two residential buildings for its staff in an area not designated as residential in the town's plan. After several months of wrangling, the town had to concede to county administrators, and the housing construction was allowed (Fei 1986, 338). Similarly, a running-water and drainage pipeline, built by Dongliu town, Dongzhi county, Anhui province, "crossed the doorway of the dormitory for the county's transportation station workers; the workers did not agree, so there was no choice but to halt the project" (Bai, Song, and Tang 1987, 57). We do not know the content of the negotiations process, but in both cases the issue was not one of political equality or negotiations among equals; rather, decisions were made in favor of the more powerful county administration.

County domination harmed development in the pre-1984 county-towns, which have been the clearest losers in the hierarchy of towns. Factories in those towns were often owned by the county government; yet, while they used local facilities and resources, the county invested little in the towns. Jobs in them were allocated by the County Labor Bureau, so county-town youths did not necessarily receive first access. County businesses such as supply and marketing co-ops in these towns were nominally led by both the county-government departments and the county-town administrators, but "they accept only the leadership of departments and ignore town leadership"; thus in 1986 county-towns that are not county seats experience the sharpest conflicts within the current administrative system (Fei 1986, 85). As county employees these nested county administrators respond to the hierarchical system (*tiao-tiao*) rather than local (*kuai-kuai*) leaders.

In Jiangpu county these county-towns developed poorly before 1979 (Jiangpu 1982, 139). Of the proportion of people living in all towns in the county, the proportion living in the county-towns, compared with the county seat and commune or market towns, decreased from 24.9 to 10.5 percent from 1953 to 1979, while the increase in these towns' actual population over twenty-six years was almost minimal (table 12.1). Unlike commune towns, which became the sites for commune or township enterprises, as well as of centers of political administration, these county-towns developed little industry and few administrative jobs, hence their limited population growth. Data from other parts of Jiangsu from 1984

TABLE 12.1. Urban Population Growth by Town Type, Jiangpu County,
Jiangsu Province, 1953 and 1979

Type	1953	%	1979	%	Rate of Increase
County seat	4,643	28.4	16,927	37.4	2.65
County-run towns	4,061	24.9	4,266	10.5	0.05
Market towns	7,641	46.7	19,480	52.1	1.77
Total	16,345	100.0	40,673	100.0	1.49

SOURCE: "A County Directly Under the Administration of Nanjing City—A Preliminary
Investigation of Small Town Construction and Development in Jiangpu County," *Economic Geography*, no. 2 (1982):139.

show why these towns declined. Within the older county-towns, the indigenous government owns the smallest percentage of enterprises (in
output value terms) at 12.91 percent, almost 8 percent less than governments from surrounding townships and 33 percent less than the county
government (see table 12.2). With little outside investment, such county-
town governments have a weak tax base and little income for investment,
making the county's authority dominant.

To resolve the nesting problem, county-run factories outside the
county seat are expected to shift to the control of county-town governments (Zhao and Zhang 1986, 324). And nested officials in some towns
and townships are to come under greater horizontal administrative (*kuai-
kuai*) control, as county-town governments are empowered to hire, fire,
transfer, reward, and penalize them (*ZGNCJJ* 1987a). But the nesting
problem will persist. First, directors of these nested organizations will
remain outside county-town and township control. Second, not only are
county factories in some locations not shifting to county-town control,
but some county officials are taking over lucrative former township factories after these newly designated towns come under their control.[27] Finally, because county seats have many county-government offices within
them, county-government control over town development is imperative.
County-level organizations in the county seat will not obey the county-
seat government, which has no authority over them. Only a development
committee of the county government has the authority to compel these
county organizations to contribute to development projects in the county
seat.

County officials have long been the most powerful institutional actors
directing local development. And although market forces are decreasing
the county's control over some aspects of the rural political economy,

27. Personal communication, Yok-shiu Lee, 21 March 1988. In Zhujiang town, Jiangpu
county, county officials in 1986 took over a lucrative factory owned by the county seat, but
Jiangpu officials say this type of expropriation, common in the 1960s, is rare today. Recent
press reports suggest that this remains a problem.

TABLE 12.2. Ownership Composition of Industrial Enterprises in 190
Small Towns in Jiangsu Province, 1984
(by Industrial Output)

| | Location of Industrial Enterprises (%) | | |
Level of Ownership	County Seats	County-Towns	Township Seats
County government	50.58	45.15	7.52
County-collective	24.87	19.73	4.60
County-town government	11.38	12.91	0
Township government	8.60	20.74	76.77
Village	3.91	1.15	8.84
Subvillage entity	0.51	0.16	1.40
Individual	0.05	0.11	0.30
Others	1.16	0.04	0.58
Total	100.00	100.00	100.00

SOURCE: The Research Group on Small Towns in Jiangsu Province, "The Objectives and
the Experience of Small Town Construction in Jiangsu Province," Shehuixue yanjiu (Research in Sociology), 1986, no. 4, p. 16.
NOTE: Percentages may not add up because of rounding.

patterns of authority established through forty years of economic planning continue to play a major role. In fact, as townships become county-
towns, the county's formal right to dictate their development pattern
increases. No doubt wealthy towns are more independent, and their
ability to invest in their own future may expand under the "finance
responsibility system." But for county-towns seeking to improve their
urban infrastructure, county controls embodied in the labeling, nesting,
and planning processes remain significant factors in their day-to-day
existence.

CONTROL OF RESOURCES FOR TOWN DEVELOPMENT

Small-town growth is critical for successful rural modernization (Rondinelli 1984). The almost 100 million rural laborers liberated by the rural
reforms need to find work outside large urban centers. The commercialization of agriculture also increased the need for marketing centers
(Tang and Ye 1986, 340).[28] Expanding rural enterprises need public
services and infrastructural development, such as electricity, water, housing, and entertainment facilities. Thus the decision to expand rural
towns has created a public-policy environment within which county and
subcounty governments can allocate funds for expanding urban infra-

28. In Xingdian town, Jiangpu county, they had built one market in 1983, but it was
already too small, so the county was helping them build a new one.

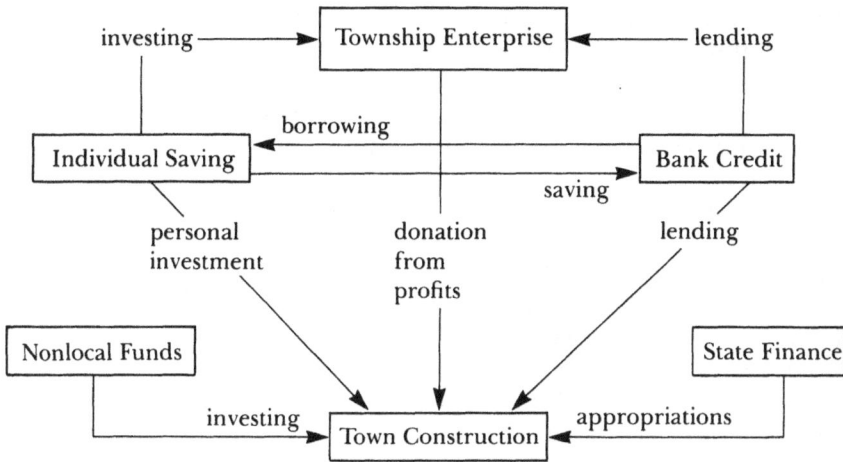

Fig. 12.1. Sources of Funding for Town Construction
SOURCE: "Reflections on the sources of capital for town construction," Tang and Ye (1986), 339.

structure and industry. Figure 12.1 shows the sources of that investment. But does the county, the county-town, or the township seat control the new funds? Does the county use its influence over funds to its own benefit? What does the allocation of funds tell us about the distribution of authority in the countryside?

County-towns now receive development assistance from the county. In two county-towns in Jiangpu county the county helped build roads, drinking-water pipes, a new school, a new market, and a new housing project. Similar investments are occurring all over Jiangsu province (Tang and Ye 1986, 341). Some of these funds, such as those for schools or hospitals, originate from government ministries, such as education and public health, whose investments in the rural areas improve town life.

Yet funds for town construction are limited. A vice-minister of construction in Beijing stressed that "people's towns should be built by the people themselves."[29] Others have referred to "using the town to develop the town" (*yi zhen yang zhen*) (Tang and Ye 1986, 343). But although local taxes and state budget assistance allow simply for "subsistence" governmental work (Byrd and Gelb 1988), the search for funding has

29. The slogan was *renmin de chengzhen, renmin jian.* Speech made to the National Meeting to Exchange Experiences Among Test Points in Town Construction (*Quanguo jizhen jianshe shidian gongzuo jingyan jiaoliu hui*), 16–21 February 1987, Guangzhou, cited in *Chengxiang jianshi* (City and Town Construction), no. 4 (1987).

been decentralized, making the struggle over local taxes and funding a meaningful reflection of the distribution of authority in the countryside.

Taxes and Small-town Development

The county receives a variety of taxes, which it can use for rural urbanization. Although these taxes change constantly, in 1987 they included public-facility fees (*gong yong shiye fei*), peasant income taxes, and local real estate or land use taxes. The income tax, paid by all rural enterprises, could take as much as 55 percent of their industrial income. Five percent of these funds are earmarked for urban construction. Recent findings show that a sales tax (or value-added tax applied to all goods produced in rural enterprises) supplies county governments with much of their funds (Walder 1989). However, it is not known for certain how this tax affects factories owned by county-towns or townships.

Still, because these funds are usually distributed to county authorities for investment in town construction, the county can invest the great majority of these funds in the county seat, not in county-towns. Although central and provincial governments stipulated that local industrial and commercial surtaxes, public utilities surtaxes, and real estate surtaxes should be used for small-town construction, "the funds they provide are too small to be of any help" (Fei 1986, 83–84). In Suzhou municipality, the sum from these three sources amounted to two million yuan, which was divided among eighteen county-towns. "But the greater part of the sum is spent on construction in county seats, while other towns get only a few tens of thousand yuan each. Many leaders of county-towns say their share is not enough even for repairing unsafe buildings in the town" (Fei 1986, 83–84). In other cases the county government keeps most of the funds for its own administrative costs. Factories in Qingyang town, a county seat, paid the county 13 million yuan in 1984 taxes, but between 1981 and 1984 county appropriations totaled only 380,000 yuan, less than 100,000 yuan a year. Although the county was expected to give the town the "three types of appropriations (*san xiang bokuan*), for many years this has been empty talk" (Zhao and Zhang 1986, 325). Moreover, because the county wanted its taxes first, some of the town's projects could not get off the ground. In one instance, county officials refused to let two enterprises—which, as beneficiaries of a town-run bridge-building project, had to contribute to it—draw their 10,000 yuan contribution out of their pretax profits. State taxes had to be paid first, even though their after-tax profits were insufficient for completing the project. After three years of wrangling, the money had still not been appropriated nor had the bridge been completed (Zhao and Zhang 1986, 325). The county is extremely judicious in distributing this most popular of tax breaks.

Similarly, all enterprises owned by the county-seat government in Wujiang county pay the county government an urban-construction protection fee (*chengshi jianshi weihu fei*) which is 7 percent of their pretax income. Before 1987 the county reinvested only 70 percent of these funds in the county seat, using the remaining 30 percent in other towns or projects. Thus the county used taxes and urban development to redistribute funds within the county. However, since 1987, when the county began a major project to expand the county seat, the county stopped investing in the building up of the other towns. Even in Jiangpu county, where the county government supplied the county seat with funds for administering the town—in 1985 the county gave 120,000 yuan and in 1986 it gave 260,000 yuan—much of this money came from taxes imposed on the county seat's own factories.

Yet the new "finance responsibility system," which is intended to make county-towns and townships collect taxes more aggressively and be fiscally more responsible and autonomous (*ZGNCJJ* 1987b), may increase county-town independence, particularly for wealthy towns that can meet their quotas. But in the case of Tangquan town, Jiangpu county officials appear to be holding onto 5 percent more funds than they should be. In summer 1988 a Tangquan official complained to a county cadre that the county had only returned 10 and not 15 percent of the expected funds. Even when the county official reminded him that the county had helped build the drinking-water system, the county-town manager argued that development assistance was separate from a policy that gave county-towns more funds for their own use. As we can see, the county was willing to invest in the town, but it tried to keep surplus funds in its own hands and thereby determine the locus of investment, rather than give the funds directly to the town. This way it could insure that most funds went to develop the county seat, where its bureaucrats live and work. Clearly the system of financial responsibility should put more taxes directly in the county-town governments' hands and help them invest in their own urban infrastructure. Yet one can feel confident that the county will use its authority to keep in its own hands as much as possible of the surplus taxes collected by the town.

Profits from Rural Industry and Small-town Development

Since township and village enterprises (TVEs) are the major source of new capital in the rural areas,[30] rural governments constantly try to control their fiscal activities (Oi 1987).[31] Poorly defined collective prop-

---

30. World Bank estimates for four counties in Jiangsu, Anhui, Jiangxi, and Guangdong provinces show that 1986 profits handed over by township-owned enterprises to township governments made up 38 percent of township revenues (Song and Du 1990, 349).

31. Byrd and Gelb call this "fiscal predation" (Byrd and Gelb 1990), 377–80.

erty rights facilitate government interference. Although township governments, reestablished in 1984, were to separate economic and political power, they still control TVEs under their jurisdiction, making them both levels of government administration responsible for a community's development *and* owners of community-run enterprises (Song and Du 1990).

A major debate ensues on how much after-tax profits of TVEs should go to county-town and township governments for urban development and how much should be left in the factory. Under a 2:2:5:1 system, 20 percent of after-tax profits of TVEs goes to town development, with another 20 percent supplementing agriculture (*yi gong bu nong*) (Tang and Ye 1986, 345).[32] A potentially inflated figure posits that 20–30 percent of the profits of locally controlled rural enterprises are going to develop educational and health services in small towns (Jin 1987, 34). Jiangpu county officials in the Rural Industry Bureau argued in 1986 that while 10 percent of the profits of TVEs went directly to the government that owned them, 30 percent went to these governments' industrial company (*gongye gongsi*) for investment in agriculture, for building new factories, or for saving bankrupt ones. Forty percent of the funds are turned over to the local government (Jiangpu 1986).[33] According to Yok-shiu Lee's data, the percentage of after-tax profits of TVEs going to "collective welfare"—monies for rural highways, schools, theaters, and market-town infrastructure—tripled from 1978 to 1984, rising from 5.9 percent to 15.7 percent (see table 12.3).

Before 1985, when county-towns in Wujiang county did not control the surrounding rural areas, county-town leaders had difficulty in attaching the profits of township-owned enterprises that existed within their geographic domain, even though they had previously used these funds for repairing streets, roads, and bridges. Unlike the county government's superior status vis-à-vis the county seat, the legal status of county-towns

32. Fifty percent was to go for reinvestment and 10 percent for workers' welfare.

33. Two different townships, one in Wuxi county, Jiangsu province, and the second in Shangrao county, Jiangxi province, made dramatically different contributions to rural urbanization. The Wuxi township spent 10.7 percent, or 1 million yuan, of its total income on "public and social services"; the Shangrao township spent 68.9 percent, or 285,700 yuan, of its total income on "public and social services." Ninety-five percent of the income available to the Wuxi township came from enterprise profits; in Shangrao the township got only 3.2 percent of its income from enterprise profits. Moreover, because Shangrao had so little rural industry it depended on a massive budget allocation from the county, which comprised over 50 percent of its income and over 73 percent of the funds utilized for "public and social services." (Byrd and Gelb 1990, table 17–5.) Because of the weak industrial base in Shangrao county, the county took funds for governmental administration from the township enterprises even before these enterprises could get off the ground; as a result most rural enterprises failed to expand.

TABLE 12.3. Percentage Distribution of After-Tax Profits of Township
and Village Enterprises, 1978–1984

	1978	1979	1980	1981	1982	1983	1984
Reinvest in TVEs	45.3	50.4	49.7	43.0	46.0	48.4	61.2
Assist agriculture	38.5	33.3	23.9	17.0	13.8	13.0	6.6
Purchase farm machinery	16.9	14.0	9.6	7.0	5.1	3.9	n.a.
Farmland infrastructure	17.1	14.5	9.9	8.0	6.9	6.9	n.a.
Aid to poor teams	4.5	4.8	4.4	2.0	1.8	2.2	n.a.
Distribute to team members[a]	—	—	n.a.	n.a.	21.7	16.3	6.4
Collective welfare[b]	5.9	6.1	7.2	7.0	9.1	10.9	15.7
Others	10.0	10.1	n.a.	n.a.	9.4	11.4	10.0

SOURCES: 1978–1979: *ZGNYNJ 1980*, 366.
1980–1981: *ZGNCTJNJ 1985*, 190.
1982: *ZGNYNJ 1983*, 83.
1983: *ZGNYNJ 1984*, 124.
1984: *ZGNYNJ 1985*, 181–82.

NOTE: This table was compiled by Yok-shiu Lee and appeared in a draft chapter of his dissertation, Department of Urban Studies and Planning, MIT.
[a]Team members here refer to those who have remained in farming jobs and not to the peasant workers.
[b]Collective welfare includes rural highways, schools, theaters, and market town infrastructure.

and township governments was formally the same, so leaders of township-owned enterprises simply refused funding requests from the county-town, accusing county-town officials of "levying contributions at random" (Fei 1986, 84). In fact, poorer towns in northern Jiangsu that took too much money from TVE profits for town development undermined industrial development (Tang and Ye 1986, 339–47). But the 1985 merger of county-towns and townships in Wujiang county has probably helped county-town officials raid factory profits for development projects. As a result, profits from TVEs are a critical source of funding for infrastructural development in county-towns and township seats, although the precise level of after-tax profits allocated for this investment remains unclear.

Banking and Small-town Development

While banking flexibility increased in some localities in the 1980s,[34] Jiangsu banks remained strongly influenced by county officials and were unlikely to invest in projects not approved by the county government.

34. In Nanhai county, Guangdong, where banks were deregulated and acted independently, they played a major role in developing private, as well as collective, enterprises. Luo 1990, 160. Many of the statements here about banking reflect policies before the Fifth Plenum of September 1988, after which local bank lending declined dramatically, while Rural Credit Cooperative loans to township industries increased.

Banks also became more responsible for their own profits and losses and became more independent of township or county-town officials than they had been of prereform commune officials, who took funds without authorization. So, without county guarantees or government prodding, they are unlikely to invest in such nonproductive projects as expanding urban infrastructure. Not surprisingly, banks are far more interested in investing in rural industries than in urban construction.[35]

In 1988, whether a settlement was a county seat, a county-town, or a township center affected its access to funds by determining the bank it could approach. Township governments and newly designated county-towns were to rely primarily on Agricultural Bank funds, but if the project called for capital construction, they could approach the Construction Bank for help. If the Agricultural Bank was short of funds, they could go elsewhere too, even though funds were constrained by the county's overall plan. But the county government had much more influence with the Construction Bank, which funds all large construction projects, than county-towns have, so county projects were more likely to find funding than were those of other towns.[36] In Jiangsu province, then, in the battle for bank loans, the county was likely to come out on top. County-towns that needed large funds for development projects must have their own funding or rely on the county to promote their case with the bank.

Migration Policy and Access to Towns
Town growth creates new opportunities, making access to town a scarce and valuable resource. As a result, some officials charge fees for access to town or for work permits, while others try to limit migration. In towns, peasants increase their wealth and improve their quality of life and their status. For many, work in town is more lucrative than work in the countryside. According to data from Yueyang district, Hunan province, the incomes of thirty specialized households still in their villages averaged 415 yuan per capita and 811 yuan per laborer, while incomes of specialized households who had moved to the town averaged 592 yuan per capita and 1,224 yuan per laborer (He and Zhang 1985, 31–35).

Since rural-urban migration is a contentious issue, social and legal limitations exist on peasant access to towns. Important social groups pressure

35. In Cheqiao town, northern Jiangsu, from 1980 to 1984, banks lent township enterprises 4,455,700 yuan, but lent only 220,000 yuan for town building, most of which went to private shops, department stores, and theaters that had some profits (Tang and Ye 1986, 342).
36. Interview with the Party secretary of a county seat, July 1988. In this county seat the construction bank was funding a major housing project.

cadres to restrict peasant migration.[37] State laws allow cadres to redirect rural migrants away from the county seat and into lower-status market towns and county-towns (*GWYGB* 1984b, 919). Migrants must have (1) a permanent place to live in the town; (2) management skills or longtime jobs in a town enterprise or unit; (3) a license from the local Industrial and Commercial Bureau; (4) a sublease on their contracted farmland to another peasant (so land is not abandoned); and (5) an independent source of food.[38] To ensure that migrants meet these criteria, local officials in larger towns lacking public security offices (*paichusuo*) were to set up "registration offices" (*huqi dengji bangongshi*) (*GWYGB* 1984, 920) to control population flows. After migrants get to town, Industrial and Commercial Bureau officials still control the permits needed for access to marketing opportunities.[39] And in smaller towns illegal migrants probably find even fewer opportunities for illegal businesses or places to hide.

Many peasants who applied for permission to move were turned down. In Taishan county, Guangdong province, over a four-month period in late 1984, 15,000 peasants applied for permission to move to the county seat; 9,000 (60 percent) were not allowed to move (Lee 1985). In the first half of 1985, out of 4,000 prospective migrants to Longgang town, Jiangsu, only 515 (13 percent) were permitted to move (Lee 1988b). When 580 households applied to leave their villages in Changsanqiao county, Sichuan province, 369 (64 percent) failed to get permits (*ZGNYNJ* 1985, 101). In the town Helen Siu studied, only rural residents with immediate family members in town could register, and only as *zili liang hu* (households who supply their own grain).[40] In Jiangpu, as of May 1986, only 268 peasants had moved into Zhujiang town and none had changed their residence status, receiving only "residence permits"

---

37. Town cadres fear that too many private businesses would change the social structure; financial cadres fear that migrants will hurt the Supply and Marketing Co-ops and the town's financial income; public security cadres and those responsible for monitoring the markets fear the disruption of social order; local businessmen fear that the competition would break their "rice bowls"; and village cadres are afraid that with migration, their control of the whole situation would collapse (He and Zhang 1985, 35).

38. Yok-shiu Lee found similar requirements in Taishan county, Guangdong.

39. In the early 1980s officials from supply and marketing cooperatives and other government-owned businesses in rural towns tried to persuade Industrial and Commercial Bureau officials to close private enterprises (Zweig 1989b). But the increased legitimacy of the private sector has made this type of harassment more difficult.

40. In Guangdong province, town officials kept peasants from the surrounding countryside out of county-town-owned enterprises, which paid higher wages, pressuring them instead to work in township-owned factories. The numbers of outsiders in county-town-owned factories was under 3 percent, and peasants had internalized the idea that county-town enterprises were part of a system that was beyond their reach (Siu 1990).

(*chang zhu hukou*).[41] Thus county-town officials still maintain serious controls over migration into town, although restraints on migration are breaking down year by year.[42]

Yet peasant migration can make county-town governments less dependent on county financial assistance. Migrants are a major funding source for new housing and buildings, particularly where rural industry is less developed. In Yueyang district, Hunan province, migrants built 62.2 percent of the floor space for new housing and shops (He and Zhang 1985, 34). In Chenggu county, Shaanxi province, peasants in 1984 contributed 5.02 million yuan toward town construction (*People's Daily*, 30 April 1985). And in Anhui province, average investment by each migrant household in the towns ranged from 4,700 to 15,500 yuan in 1984 (*Almanac of Anhui's Economy* 1985, 269–70; An Jian 1986, 25). They also pay taxes and fees for licenses, market management, land use, and construction (Tang and Ye 1986, 346).

Moreover, cadres can charge peasants fees or "rents" for access to income-increasing opportunities in these towns. Township and county-town governments charge aspiring factory workers an entrance fee, ranging from 1,000 to 7,500 yuan, calling them "workers bringing capital to factories" (*gongren dai zi ru chang*). Tangquan's government, hungry for funds for industry but unable to secure bank loans, pressured peasants and village leaders to give the factory a loan. Although some villagers resisted, brigade officials persuaded them to agree (Jiangpu 1986).

A main reason for small-town development is to channel rural laborers away from big cities. But small towns have limited resources and economic opportunities, so local officials often restrict access to these towns. In the parts of Jiangsu province covered by this study, they continue to control the number of peasants moving to town. The resulting floating population in cities such as Shanghai has passed one million, making it uncertain if the small-town strategy will alleviate demands for rural-urban migration.

CONCLUSION: THE POLITICS OF RURAL URBANIZATION

Freedom at the lowest levels of rural society has expanded as both state and collective cadres have withdrawn from the daily management of

41. Nevertheless, by 1987 the major restriction on rural-urban migration in Jiangpu county was economic. "Most people who want to come in, get in. We turn them down only if they want to work in some field that is already quite full. Anyway, if it's very full, they'll go back on their own" (Jiangpu 1988). For example, between 1983 and 1986, fifty to sixty migrant families ran sewing businesses; now there are only twenty families.

42. In Xingdian town, west of Tangquan in Jiangpu county, where only 110 peasant families had moved to town in 1983–85, the local government began a housing project in 1986 to move 200 peasant households into town.

village life. But at the middle reaches of the rural hierarchy, the relationship between the county government and expanding rural settlements demonstrates the continuing role of bureaucratic authority as a determinant of resource allocations. Although one might assume that increased rural urbanization would weaken the county's control over the local political economy, I suggest that the distribution of authority has not changed as dramatically as one might have expected. County officials, through their bureaucratic positions, still control resources that either flow into these towns or are created within them. No doubt, modernization's demands for bureaucratic specialization has fragmented power within the county leadership. But findings here appear to confirm the control image offered by Lieberthal and Oksenberg and the argument that "vertical" (tiao-tiao) authority remains more powerful than "horizontal" (kuai-kuai) ties even under the reforms (Lieberthal and Oksenberg 1988).

Two factors affect the relationship between hierarchy and power. First, disparities in resource bases can increase or decrease the impact of hierarchy. If resource distribution is highly asymmetrical, relations between bureaucratic superiors and inferiors are even more likely to be based on a command model, leaving the inferior actor in the interaction with only obedient or supplicant behavior as his major options (unless he threatens bankruptcy, which his superior cannot accept). In the current policy environment, where expanding a town's social and economic infrastructure becomes a town official's major responsibility, officials in poorer towns could become more dependent on county officials for development assistance. And although counties also have political obligations to help towns grow, making county officials reliant on cooperation from town managers, planning, labeling, and investments have kept the county firmly in control of the development process. Even efforts to strengthen county-town and township financial bases may increase county-town officials' dependence on the county, particularly for poor towns. Under the "finance responsibility system," counties can lend funds to strengthen county-town and township governments, which the recipients must repay through judicious tax collection. While surpluses will benefit the county-town —especially wealthy county-towns with strong tax bases—shortages will be cumulative, making tax-poor county-towns, like state-owned firms, highly dependent on county government support. And even for wealthier county-towns, the county's control over the planning process allows them to set the county-town's development agenda. By financing only a part of the projects and pressuring the county-town to fund the remainder, the county may determine how the county-town invests its own funds. Such "conditional grants" are a powerful mechanism by which administrators can indirectly control lower-level governments.

The nesting process compounds the impact of hierarchy on the distribution of authority by giving county governments a core of allies who have directly penetrated these towns and who participate in county-town and township-seat government and Party meetings. County-affiliated firms and bureaus make profits and collect taxes and fees in the towns, which revert to the county government, all the while contributing little directly to the town's growth. And while new policies try to expand a town's control over county-level factories and offices within its physical domain, these units' county-level status may keep them beyond the town's political reach. As we have seen with the county seat, the new impetus for rural urbanization ensures even tighter control by the county government and undermines any devolution of authority over these nested units to the county-seat governments.

On the other hand, towns with strong industrial bases can undo some of the power disparity inherent in hierarchy. County-town and township governments that can draw on the profits of their own rural enterprises to strengthen their economic base are better able to negotiate with county officials. As in Wujiang county, unifying county-towns with neighboring townships, particularly if the latter have strong industrial bases, should weaken the county's influence. How different relations must be between county and town officials in poor counties—such as Shangrao county, Jiangxi province, where the county finances all township-level administration—and wealthy counties, such as Wuxi, where county-towns fund themselves and have a surplus that the county can tax. Though county-towns or townships in Wuxi are hierarchically subordinate to the county government, their wealth should make them stronger adversaries in the negotiations process.

Power relations among peasants and bureaucrats are affected in a similar way. Farmers who plant their land and market only small surpluses remain relatively free of state intrusions. Unlike lower-level bureaucrats who have no "exit" option, these peasants can withdraw in the face of abusive or unjust cadre demands. Clearly, independence is relative, since many resources needed for farming—such as seeds, fertilizer, pesticides, and land—remain locally controlled, making farmers dependent on local cadres (Oi 1987). But the asymmetry of power expands dramatically as common peasants, seeking access to new sources of wealth developing in and around the town, become subject to bureaucratic authority vested in town officials. As gatekeepers to the boundaries of income-enhancing opportunities—such as small shops, factories, or factory jobs—cadres are extremely powerful vis-à-vis China's common man. They can take peasant land to build their own homes, and there is little peasants can do. No doubt, wealthier peasants or those with strong family alliances possess resources to confront cadre authority. But atomized individuals, stripped of their collective protection, remain in a highly vulnerable and inferior status in their confrontation with formidable bureaucratic forces.[43]

As of 1988, central control over local investment and development had decreased. Yet this devolution of central authority has not weakened bureaucratic control at the local level; in some ways it may have increased it. While forces unleashed by the commercialization of the rural economy—particularly the production and marketing of agricultural produce—no longer are monopolized by local officials, the county's control over development assistance and investment for expanding urban infrastructure at the county-town and township levels has ensured a continuing—in some locations an expanding—role for the local bureaucracy.

No doubt, rural urbanization is in its incipient stage, and the final distribution of authority derived from this process remains unclear. Efforts to reform both the financial relations between the county and the county-towns or townships and the authority relations between county-level nested units and the towns where they reside may weaken the county's authority. New resources, developing at all levels of rural society, create opportunities for redistributing authority. The prudent scholar must recognize that leaders in the emerging county-towns and townships, like their forebears in the communes, will use their political and economic authority over the countryside and their towns' critical point at the nexus between the rural and the urban economy to expand their financial and political resources. Yet a careful reading of past and current trends—tightening local finances in 1989 under the current retrenchment probably increased the county's influence—suggests that county officials through a multiplicity of channels will significantly influence the pattern of growth in the county-towns and townships and will remain the dominant force in the rural political economy in much of rural China.

APPENDIX

Types and Characteristics of Small Towns in China[44]

A. *Designated Towns (jianzhi zhen)*

Administered by county governments, all designated towns are part of the hierarchy of *urban* settlements. There are two types of designated towns:

  1. County seats (*xian zhengfu suozaidi*)

  These towns are directly controlled by the county government. Larger county seats are sometimes designated as cities and are directly under the control of the nearby urban administration. Their main function is administrative, although many have become industrial centers since the late 1970s.

43. For a forceful, but perhaps overstated, expression of this viewpoint, see Shue 1988.
44. Adapted from table 5-2 in Lee 1988b, 111.

2. County-towns (*xianshu zhen*)
This type of town decreased in the prereform era, but now many township seats have been designated as county-towns and have moved up into the hierarchy of urban settlements. Former township seats still control most of the countryside they administered as township seats, while some county-towns that were not formerly township seats control only a few villages, which supply food for town residents. In some instances, county-towns have been unified with the township government and now control much of the rural area administered by the township.

B. *Undesignated Towns (fei jianzhi zhen)*
These towns are administered by the township governments or may exist autonomously of higher-level governments. All undesignated towns are part of the hierarchy of *rural* settlements and are part of the countryside. There are two types of undesignated towns:

1. Township seats (*xiang zhengfu suozaidi*)
Linked with economic cooperatives in the late 1950s, these settlements served as commune headquarters from the 1960s into the 1970s. In the 1980s they changed names to townships. They have urban administrative functions as well as economic ones, given that many township governments own rural enterprises. They are often regional marketing centers. Leading officials may be state cadres who receive state-subsidized grain.

2. Rural Market Towns (*nongcun jizhen*)
Major marketing centers, these rural settlements declined under CCP rule and were resurrected under the reforms. They are often centers for service industries linked to marketing. In more advanced areas of the countryside they are likely to be run by the former brigade committee, now called "administrative villages."

BIBLIOGRAPHY

An Jian. 1986. "Longgang zhen de jizhen jianshi" (Town development in Longgang town), *Chengxiang jianshe* (Town Construction), no. 6.

Bai Yihua, Song Zhiqiang, and Tang Pusu. 1987. "Jinyibu wanshan xiangzhen zhengfu zhineng gaige de tiaokuai fenge xingzheng guanli" (Go a step further in perfecting the functions of town and township governments, reform the system of vertical and horizontal division of administrative management), *Zhengzhixue yanjiu* (Political Science Studies), no. 6.

Barnett, A. Doak, with Ezra Vogel. 1965. *Cadres, Bureaucracy and Political Power.* New York: Columbia University Press.

Butler, Steven B. 1980. "Conflict and Decision-Making in China's Rural Administration, 1969–1976." Ph.D. diss., Columbia University.

Byrd, William A., and Alan Gelb. 1990. "Why Industrialize? The Incentives for Rural Community Governments." In *China's Rural Industry: Structure, Development and Reform,* edited by William A. Byrd and Lin Qinsong, 358–88. New York: Oxford University Press.

Chen Guanyuan. 1986. *Shehui kexue* (Shanghai), no. 1.

Chang, Sen-dou, and R. Yin-wang Kwok. 1990. "The Urbanization of Rural China." In *Chinese Urban Reform: What Model Now?* edited by R. Yin-wang Kwok et al. Armonk, N.Y.: M. E. Sharpe.

Fei Hsiao Tung et al., eds. 1986. *Small Towns in China: Functions, Problems and Prospects.* Beijing: New World Press.

Friedman, Edward. 1990. "Deng versus the Peasantry." *Problems of Communism,* September–October, 30–43.

GWYGB. 1984. See State Council 1984b.

He Peijin and Zhang Pingyong. 1985. "Fazhan xiaochengzhen jingji de zhongyao buzhu" (An Important Phase in Small Town Development). *Zhongguo nongcun jingji* (Chinese Agricultural Economics), no. 4:31–35.

Jiangpu. 1982. Zhang Fubao, "Nanjingshi xia xian—Jiangpu xian xiao chengzhen de jianshi fazhan chubu yanjiu" (A county under Nanjing municipality— preliminary research on the development of small-town construction in Jiangpu county). *Jingji dili* (Economic Geography), no. 2:138–46.

Jiangpu. 1986 and 1988. Interviews by David Zweig in Jiangpu county, Jiangsu province, May–June 1986 and July 1988.

Jin. 1987. "Jizhen jianshe yao liangli er xing" (Small-town construction work should proceed cautiously). *Chengxiang jianshe* (Town Construction), no. 1.

Kirkby, R. J. R. 1985. *Urbanization in China: Town and Country in a Developing Economy, 1949–2000A.D.* New York: Columbia University Press.

Lampton, David M. 1987. "Chinese Politics: The Bargaining Treadmill." *Issues and Studies* 23, no. 3 (March):11–41.

Lee, Yok-shiu. 1985. Field notes from Yok-shiu Lee's trip to Guangdong.

———. 1988a. "Rural Nonfarm Activities in China: Growth and Effects of Township Enterprises, 1978–1987." Ph.D. diss., M.I.T.

———. 1988b. Chapter 5 of an earlier draft of Yok-Shiu Lee's Ph.D. dissertation that was not included in the final dissertation.

Lieberthal, Kenneth, and Michel Oksenberg. 1988. *Policy Making in China: Leaders, Structures, and Processes.* Princeton: Princeton University Press.

Luo Xiaopeng. 1990. "Ownership and Status Stratification." In *China's Rural Industry: Structure, Development and Reform,* edited by William A. Byrd and Lin Qinsong, 134–71. New York: Oxford University Press.

Ma, Lawrence J. C., and Gonghao Cui. 1987. "Administrative Changes and Urban Population in China." *Annals of the Association of American Geographers* 77, no. 3: 373–95.

Nee, Victor. 1983. "Between Center and Locality: State, Militia and Village." In *State and Society in Contemporary China,* edited by Victor Nee and David Mozingo, 223–43. Ithaca: Cornell University Press.

Oi, Jean C. 1985. "Communism and Clientelism: Rural Politics in China." *World Politics* 37, no. 2 (January): 238–66.

———. 1987. "Peasant Households Between Plan and Market." *Modern China* 12, no. 2 (April): 230–51.

———. 1990. "The Fate of the Collective After the Commune." In *Chinese Society on the Eve of Tiananmen: The Impact of Reform,* edited by Deborah Davis and Ezra Vogel, 15–36. Cambridge: Council on East Asian Studies, Harvard University Press.

Potter, Sulamith Heins. 1983. "The Position of Peasants in Modern China's Social Order." *Modern China* 9, no. 9 (October): 465–89.

Rondinelli, Dennis A. 1984. "Small Towns in Developing Countries: Potential Centers of Growth, Transformation and Integration." In *Equity with Growth? Planning Perspectives for Small Towns in Developing Countries*, edited by H. Detlef Kammeier and Peter J. Swan, 10–48. Bangkok: Asian Institute of Technology.

Schurmann, Franz. 1968. *Ideology and Organization in Communist China.* Berkeley and Los Angeles: University of California Press.

Shue, Vivienne. 1988. *The Reach of the State.* Stanford: Stanford University Press.

Siu, Helen F. 1990. "The Politics of Migration in a Market Town." In *Chinese Society on the Eve of Tiananmen: The Impact of Reform*, edited by Deborah Davis and Ezra Vogel, 61–82. Cambridge: Council on East Asian Studies, Harvard University Press.

Skinner, G. William. 1964. "Marketing and Social Structure in Rural China, Part III." *Journal of Asian Studies* 24, no. 3 (1964): 363–99.

———. 1977. "Cities and Hierarchy of Local Places." In *The City in Late Imperial China*, edited by G. William Skinner, 275–352. Stanford: Stanford Unversity Press.

Song Lina and Du He. 1990. "The Role of Township Governments in Rural Industrialization." In *China's Rural Industry: Structure, Development and Reform*, edited by William A. Byrd and Lin Qinsong, 342–57. New York: Oxford University Press.

State Council. 1984a. "Guowuyuan pizhun minzhengbu guanyu tiaozheng jianzhen biaozhun de baogao de tongzhi" (Circular of the State Council Concerning Approval of the Ministry of Civil Affair's Report on Revision of the Criteria for the Establishment of Towns). *Zhonghua Renmin Gongheguo guowuyuan gongbao* (PRC State Council Bulletin), no. 30 (20 December): 1012–14.

State Council. 1984b. "Guowuyuan guanyu nongmin jinru jizhen luohu wenti de tongzhi" (State Council Directive on the Question of Peasants Entering and Settling in Towns). *Zhonghua Renmin Gongheguo guowuyuan gongbao* (PRC State Council Bulletin), no. 26 (10 November): 919–20.

Tang Zhongxun and Ye Nanke. 1986. "Jizhen jianshe zijin laiyuan tansuo" (Reflections on the sources of capital for town construction). *Xiao chengzhen, xin kai tuo* (Small Towns, A New Beginning) (Huaiyang: Jiangsu renmin chubanshe), 339–47.

Vogel, Ezra. 1989. *One Step Ahead in China: Guangdong Under Reform.* Cambridge: Harvard University Press.

Walder, Andrew. 1989. Lecture presented at the Fairbank Center, Harvard University, 10 February 1989.

Watson, Andrew. 1988. "The Reform of Agricultural Marketing in China since 1978." *China Quarterly*, no. 113 (March): 1–28.

White, Gordon. 1987. "The Impact of Economic Reforms in the Chinese Countryside: Towards the Politics of Social Capitalism." *Modern China* 13, no. 4 (October): 411–40.

White, Tyrene. 1988. "Political Reform and Rural Government." In *Chinese Soci-*

ety on the Eve of Tiananmen: The Impact of Reform, 37–60. Cambridge: Council on East Asian Studies, Harvard University Press.

Wujiang. 1987 and 1988. Interviews by David Zweig in Wujiang County, Jiangsu Province, September 1987 and July 1988.

Xia Rushan. 1986. "Fazhan jianzhizhen, jiaqiang xiao chengzhen zhengquan jianshe" (Develop Designated Towns, Strengthen the Development of Political Power in the Small Towns). *Xiao cheng zhen, xin kai tuo* (Small Towns, A New Beginning), pp. 305–14. Huaiyang: Jiangsu Chubanshe.

Xiaochengzhen. 1987. Jiangsu Provincial Research Group on the Topic of Small Towns and Jiangsu Provincial Statistics Bureau, eds., *Xiaochengzhen quyu fenxi* (An Analysis of Small Town Regions): N.p.: Chinese Statistical Publishing House.

Zhang Yuelin. 1986. "Cheng-zhen-xiang wanglo he xiaochengzhen de zhengti buzhu" (City-Town-Township Network and Small Towns' Overall Distribution). *Xiao chengzhen, xin kai tuo*, 85–98.

Zhao Pengxing and Zhang Shouzheng. 1986. "Chengxiang gaige dai xiaochengzhen fazhan de yingxiang" (Urban-Rural Reforms' Influence on Small Town Development), *Xiao chengzhen, xin kai tuo*, 315–29.

ZGNCJJ. 1987a. Zhou Fuyuan, "Lishun tiaokuai guanxi, shixing fenji guanli" (Smooth vertical and horizontal relations, carry out administration according to levels). *Zhongguo nongcun jingji* (Chinese Agricultural Economics), no. 8:48–51.

ZGNCJJ. 1987b. "Dingzhou shi jian zheng fang chuan jiaqiang xiang (zhen) zheng chuan jianshi de diaocha" (Research Report on Dingzhou City Strengthening Xiang (Zhen) Administration by Simplifying and Decentralizing Its Administrative Powers), *Zhongguo nongcun jingji* (Chinese Agricultural Economics), no. 8:44–46, 54.

ZGNCTJNJ. 1985. *Zhongguo nongcun tongji nianjian* (Chinese Agricultural Statistical Yearbook). Beijing: Chinese Statistical Publishing House.

ZGNYNJ. 1980, 1983, 1984, 1985. *Zhongguo nongye nianjian* (Chinese Agricultural Yearbook). Beijing: Chinese Agricultural Publishing House.

ZGTJNJ. 1988. *Zhongguo tongji nianjian* (Chinese Statistical Yearbook). Beijing: Chinese Statistical Publishing House.

ZGTJZY. 1987. *Zhongguo tongji zhaiyao* (Chinese Statistical Abstract). Beijing: Chinese Statistical Publishing House.

Zweig, David. 1987. "From Village to City: Reforming Urban-Rural Relations in China." *International Regional Science Review* 11, no. 1:43–58.

———. 1989a. *Agrarian Radicalism in China, 1968–1981*. Cambridge: Harvard University Press, 1989.

———. 1989b. "Dilemmas Under Partial Reform: Collective and State Firms in Competition with the Rural Private Sector." In *China in a New Era: Economics*, edited by Bruce Reynolds. New York: Paragon Press, 1989.

CONTRIBUTORS

Nina P. Halpern is assistant professor of political science at Stanford University. She is the author of many articles on Chinese economic reform and on the role of specialists in Chinese policy making. She is currently working on a study of administrative reform in post-Mao China.

Carol Lee Hamrin is a research specialist for China for the U.S. Department of State and a lecturer and board member of the Reischauer Center for East Asian Studies in the School of Advanced International Studies, Johns Hopkins University. She recently published a study of the Deng Xiaoping reform era, *China and the Challenge of the Future,* and has written extensively on Chinese intellectuals and the foreign policy of the People's Republic of China.

David M. Lampton is president of the National Committee on United States–China Relations. Prior to assuming that post in 1988 he was associate professor of political science at Ohio State University and director of China Policy Studies at the American Enterprise Institute in Washington, D.C. One of his books, *Paths to Power: Elite Mobility in Contemporary China,* was issued in its second edition in 1989. Lampton's other publications have dealt with the politics of medicine in China, river basin planning, Sino-American relations, and Chinese foreign and domestic politics. He is the editor of *Policy Implementation in Post-Mao China* (University of California Press, 1987).

Kenneth G. Lieberthal is professor of political science and associate of the Center for Chinese Studies at the University of Michigan. A graduate of Dartmouth College, with his Ph.D. from Columbia University, Professor Lieberthal taught at Swarthmore College before moving to the University of Michigan in 1983. His most recent books are *Policy Making in China: Leaders, Structures and Processes* (with Michel Oksenberg) and *A Research Guide to Central Party and Government Meetings in China, 1949–1986* (with Bruce Dickson).

Melanie Manion is assistant professor of political science at the University of Rochester. She is the author of articles on cadre management and policy in the *China Quarterly* and the *Journal of Asian Studies*. She is currently working on a study of political corruption.

Barry Naughton is assistant professor at the Graduate School of International Relations and Pacific Studies at the University of California at San Diego. His current research focuses on macroeconomic policy and economic reform in China, and he is completing a book on Chinese economic reform.

Lynn Paine teaches educational sociology and comparative education at Michigan State University. Her research interests center around the connections between education and social change and the intersections of national policy and local experience in the process of reform. Her publications on China include chapters and articles on the organization and reform of teacher education, the culture of teaching, and patterns of authority and control in secondary education. She is currently engaged in an examination of patterns of socialization and stratification in rural education.

Jonathan D. Pollack is corporate research manager for international policy at RAND, Santa Monica, California. His recent publications include *U.S. Strategic Alternatives in a Changing Pacific* (1990) and *Into the Vortex: China, the Sino-Soviet Alliance, and the Korean War* (1991).

Paul E. Schroeder serves as program associate for economic development, management, and law at the National Committee on U.S.–China Relations, Inc. Previously he was senior trade representative for the State of Ohio, based in Wuhan, China, where he lived for three years. In that capacity he focused on provincial and municipal economic development policies, especially as they pertained to international trade. He negotiated the 1988 *Cooperative Agreement on Science and Technology Between the State of Ohio and Hubei Province,* the first such agreement between subnational governments in the United States and China. A former newspaper reporter, Dr. Schroeder holds degrees in zoology and journalism. He received his doctorate in political science from Ohio State University, where he specialized in Chinese and Third World economic development.

Susan L. Shirk is a professor in the Department of Political Science and Graduate School of International Relations and Pacific Studies at the

University of California, San Diego. She is the author of *The Political Failure of Economic Reform in China* (University of California Press, forthcoming) and *Competitive Comrades: Career Incentives and Student Strategies in China* (University of California Press, 1982).

Andrew G. Walder is professor of sociology at Harvard University. He is the author of *Chang Ch'un-ch'iao and Shanghai's January Revolution* (1978) and *Communist Neo-Traditionalism: Work and Authority in Chinese Industry* (1986). His current research interests are economic organization and inequality in urban China, and the Cultural Revolution social movements of 1966–69.

David Zweig is associate professor of international politics at the Fletcher School of Law and Diplomacy, Tufts University. His book *Agrarian Radicalism in China, 1968–1981* (Harvard University Press) was published in 1989. He is editor, with Christine Wong and William Joseph, of *New Perspectives on the Cultural Revolution* (Harvard University Press, 1991). He has published numerous articles on China's rural reforms. His current research focuses on the domestic impact of China's Open Policy.

INDEX

Academy of Military Science, 165, 166
Adjustment Office, 73
Administrative system, 19; decentralization of, 16
Agricultural Bank of China, 337, 342, 354
Agricultural Producer Cooperatives, 337 n.4
Allison, Graham, 10
Anhui province, 288, 351 n.30, 356
Armaments Department of the General Staff, 174, 175
Arms trade, 175–76
Authoritarian systems, 61 n.3
Authority: structure of, 34

Bachman, David, 42
Backbone teachers, 202, 204
Balance of power, 284
Bank of China, 302
Banking system, 258
Banks, 314–16; independence of, 315 n.20; loans by, 315 n.19
Bao Tong, 122, 123
Baoshan, 251
Baoshan steel mill, 257
Bargaining, 12, 19 n.36, 34–35, 51, 308–9, 331; arenas of, 51; and budgetary process, 40–41; and bureaucratic system, 9, 12, 245; causes of, 38–40; and decision making, 245; environment of, 246; and fragmentation of authority, 126; implications of, 57–58; importance of,

245; issues, 40–44; limits of, 284; participants in, 50–51; in policy formation, 51; process of, 44–50; as reciprocal accommodation, 37; and redistributive politics, 326–31; and reform, 35; relationships, 18, 309; in socialist states, 308; strategies for, 54–57, 328–31
Barnett, A. Doak, 102, 121, 222
Beijing, 239, 289, 291, 293, 304, 317 n.23, 322, 328, 349; Haidian district, 123; and revenues, 83; taxation in, 324; teachers in, 202 n.24, 205, 208
Beijing Jeep, 265
Beijing Military Region, 165
Beijing Municipal People's Government, 179
Beijing Normal University, 193, 198
Beijing Review, 50
Beijing University, 220
Bengbu, 288
Bengbu City's Chemical Industry Corporation, 288, 305
Bengbu City's Economic Commission, 288
Bilateral monopoly, 19 n.36, 271, 273, 274
Bo Yibo, 44, 66, 108 nn.16,17, 115, 116 n.30, 122, 123
Bourgeois liberalization, 169
Brigades, 337, 340
Budget, central, 8
Budgetary investment, 255–56
Budgetary process: and bargaining, 40–41
Bureau of Education, 187

People's Liberation Army, 3, 17, 151, 168,
172; access of to resources, 153, 170;
and Chinese Communist Party, 82, 151,
152, 163, 178; and defense-technology
planning, 177–78; and Deng Xiaoping,
178; General Logistics Department, 3,
161, 166; General Political Department,
161, 163, 166; General Staff Department, 161, 166, 168; leadership of, 152,
153–54, 170; manpower of, 157, 170;
ranks in, 76–77; and retirement, 159;
social control by, 154, 172; Soviet influence on, 152; technical cadres in, 159.
See also Military system
Personnel system, 222; and cadre retirement, 15; in local government, 223
Pingdu County Education Commission,
195 n.16
Planning commissions, 316–17, 320. *See
also* State Planning Commission
Policy coordination, 126–28; and information flow, 125; institutions of, 129; lack
of, 127; problems for, 128
Policy decisions, 76
Policy implementation: and authority relations, 242; at local levels, 217–18; and
middlemen, 218–19; and policy targets,
243
Politburo, 13, 40, 65, 97, 98, 114; and bar-
gaining, 51; decision making in, 53,
101, 102; leadership arrangements in,
111–21; and People's Liberation Army,
170; Standing Committee of, 60, 68
Political and Legal Affairs Commission,
101, 113, 119, 121–22
Political and Legal Affairs Leading Group,
119
Political organizations: grouping of, 2
Political Reform Study Group, 107
Political system, 21, 304; reform of, 305
Pollack, Jonathan, 76; on military system,
17–18, 30
Polytechnologies, 175
Price, Don K., 144
Price Research Center, 131, 132 n.18, 135,
137
Prices, 266, 327; control of, 266–67; re-
form of, 79, 81, 319
Priority projects, 256–57
Production brigade, 337 n.5
Production team, 337 n.5

"Professional guidance," 221
Propaganda and education bureaucracies,
2
Propaganda and Ideology Leading Group,
113, 122
Propaganda Department, 104, 113
Provinces: export revenues of, 296; and
foreign trade, 84; representation of,
72; and State Council, 72. *See also* Provincial governments; *names of provinces*
Provincial Bureau of Education, 201, 205
Provincial Education Commission, 187 n.5
Provincial governments, 18, 286; and
central-cities policy, 290; and central
government, 284, 305; and decentralization, 288; decision-making power of,
284, 305 n.75; and economic reforms,
85; and interprovincial competition,
285; resources of, 284, 296; and rural
urbanization, 350. *See also* Provinces;
names of provinces
Public supervision, 110–11

Qian Jiaju, 54
Qiao Shi, 40, 108
Qin dynasty, 284
Qin Jiwei, 108, 162, 163, 164, 169
Qing dynasty, 336
Qingdao, 292
Qingyang, 350

Rao Shushi, 97
Rationality model, 10
Redistributional bargaining, 268–70
Reforms, 26, 55; and bargaining, 39, 245;
and bureaucratic practice, 25, 36; and
consensus decision making, 80–81; and
corruption, 24; and ideology, 25; local
experimentation with, 270; and military
system, 18; objectives of, 23–24; policy
of, 16, 20, 84; strategy of, 263–64
"Relation of leadership," 221
Renmun Jiaoyu, 195
Research centers, 130–34, 131, 132, 146–
47; authority of, 138–43, 147; and
commissions, 133, 139; and competitive persuasion, 147; and coordination,
134–46; incentives for, 143–46; influence of, 147–48; and ministries, 139,
144–45; purpose of, 131; and State
Council, 139. *See also* National Re-

Compositor: Huron Valley Graphics, Inc.
Text: 10/12 Baskerville
Display: Baskerville

www.ingramcontent.com/pod-product-compliance
Lightning Source LLC
Chambersburg PA
CBHW030901270326
41929CB00008B/515